LANGUAGE CHANGE

CONTRIBUTORS

Barbara D. Greim	University of Wisconsin
Wayne Harbert	Cornell University
Henry and Renée Kahane	University of Illinois
Ilse Lehiste	The Ohio State University
Winfred P. Lehmann	University of Texas
David Lightfoot	Rijksuniversiteit, Utrecht
Raven I. McDavid, Jr.	University of Chicago
Yakov Malkiel	University of California, Berkeley
Els Oksaar	Universität Hamburg
Edgar C. Polomé	University of Texas
Irmengard Rauch	University of California, Berkeley
Frans van Coetsem	Cornell University

LANGUAGE CHANGE

Edited by

Irmengard Rauch

and

Gerald F. Carr

INDIANA UNIVERSITY PRESS
Bloomington

*This book has been produced from camera-ready copy
provided by the author.*

"Low-back Vowels in Providence: A Note in Structural
Dialectology" originally appeared in *Journal of English
Linguistics* (1981), © by Journal of English
Linguistics. "Paideia, A Linguistic Subcode"
originally appeared in *Wege zur Universalienforschung*,
edited by Gunter Brettschneider and Christian Lehmann,
© 1980 by Gunter Naar Verlag. "On Reconstructing
a Proto-Syntax" is a slightly revised version of an
article which appeared in *Linguistic Reconstruction and
Indo-European Syntax*, edited by Paolo Ramat, © 1980 by
John Benjamins, and in a French version in *Langages* 60
(Syntaxe générative et syntaxe comparée), edited by
Alain Rouveret, © 1980 by Didier Erudition.

Manufactured in the United States of America

Library of Congress Cataloging in Publication Data
Main entry under title:

Language change.

Includes index.
1. Linguistic change—Addresses, essays, lectures.
I. Rauch, Irmengard. II. Carr, Gerald F.
P142.L25   412   82-48626
ISBN 0-253-33196-X   1 2 3 4 5 87 86 85 84 83

CONTENTS

PREFACE

One of the most fundamental truisms in the story of
language is that a language changes. This certainly im-
presses as a blatantly simplistic statement; at the same
time, however, it conveys an ultimately impenetrable concept. It is for good reason, then, that the Modern Language Association of America regularly includes in its
annual meetings two sessions of an established Division
on Language Change. At the 1980 Houston MLA Convention,
seven of the contributions contained herein provided the
seminal idea for this volume. These papers were so well
received and stimulated such interest that the editors
realized the articles should be made available to the
wide audience which the timeless field of language change
attracts. Accordingly, plans were initiated to supplement
the work of an already exceptional panel of contributors
with an additional five contributions, drawn again from
among the world's leading experts on the subject of language change.

What is involved in the vast and elusive study of language change? Its attraction lies in the fact that it
deals with discernible realia, such as sounds or structured groups of sounds, or words and their intra- and
interrelationships. Experience has shown, however, that
in the very instant in which the researcher is prepared
to derive a conclusion from his empirical language data,
he finds that the data may be incomplete, i.e., they have
already mutated from one linguistic moment to the next,
or new linguistic circumstances influencing the interpretation of the data have come into play. Whether these
circumstances have in point of fact just arisen, or whether the observation of the linguist was remiss is of little
importance; at issue is the fact that in either case the
linguist must content himself with the knowledge that his
efforts necessarily remain incomplete.

On the one hand, description of language change has
the advantage of hard evidence. Where contemporary language is concerned, the linguist has the added advantage
of being an eyewitness. Historical evidence may be
plentiful or meager, but in both instances it presupposes
at least a degree of probability in comparison to the
relative certainty of present-day facts. Not only do documents and artifacts need to be datable and identifiable,
but at best the linguist can only surmise what a piece of
evidence represents. Extrapolation of linguistic fact is,
of course, the sine qua non in reconstructing prehistoric
data. Regardless of the time of a language change, however, data of some sort are available, and they are invi-
olable, i.e., no amount of manipulation on the part of
the researcher can alter the evidence. Linguistic evidence is what it is, and thus it provides a basis of

security for the linguist in monitoring the developments of a language.

On the other hand, the uncovering of the reasons behind the existence of a set of language data is not at all a secure task. Here the language change specialist meets his most difficult challenge. In both the description of the evidence and the subsequent explanation of the data, today's linguist has the benefit of a rich tradition of methods. Nevertheless, from philosophical and philological approaches through the various schools of modern structuralism, whether Neogrammarian, Bloomfieldian, Chomskyan or Post-Chomskyan, to psycho- and sociolinguistic as well as semiotic and again philosophical methods, the elusive WHY for the occurrence or non-occurrence of a given change remains unanswered. This is, of course, because language is integral to the human condition and, accordingly, reasons for its being what it is become of teleological interest, as does any characteristic behavior of man. To study a language change exhaustively, then, requires realistically the study of the many facets involved in a given human mental and physical act.

An analogical microcosm of the two polar areas in investigating language change is found in the levels of language: Phonology, with its immediate alliance to physiology and physics is ascertainable through laboratory techniques, offering the linguist a high degree of predictability in his results; semantics, with its penetration into the meaning of the world at large, transversed by pragmatics and the understanding of general action theory, affords at best a very diffused degree of certainty.

It is customary in a collection of the kind offered here to group the papers according to levels of language, i.e. phonology, morphology, syntax, lexicon, or according to schools of thought, i.e. Classical Phonemic, Generative Transformational, Relational, Semiotic. Although these designations are insightful parameters, we have chosen neither of the arrangements in the book itself, in an effort to shift the foci of attention of the reader, for the purpose of motivating innovative attitudes toward a very venerable and, to an extent, unexploited field of study. Writing on language change typically concentrates on past or historical changes, since these are viewable as historical events with a traceable beginning and end. The editors, accordingly, were solicitous to include research on changes occurring in our own time; almost half of the articles offer contemporary data. Part One includes three of these. We are indeed fortunate in publishing here Ilse Lehiste's 1980 Presidential Address to the Linguistic Society of America. She presents to the reader not only PHONOLOGICAL evidence which is difficult to capture and conceptualize, namely suprasegmental data, but data outside of Indo-European, i.e. from the Ural-Altaic Estonian. So certain is Lehiste of her approach, which is characteristically acoustically oriented, that

she is able to predict the change of Estonian into a pitch
language. She underscores an intent in her contribution,
writing: "... this analysis was to show that it is indeed
possible to study prosodic change in progress" ( ).
Raven McDavid, Jr. (Part Three), in a paper originally
presented in the Language Change section at the Houston
1980 meetings and first published in *Journal of English
Linguistics*, 15:21-9, deals as well with PHONOLOGICAL data
from Modern American English. He is intent on opposing
his findings concerning the production and perception of
low-back vowels in Providence, RI to the findings of other
established scholars on the same topic.

    Background literature is at issue in the entire array
of articles; it is, however, central in the contributions
of Part Three. Winfred P. Lehmann highlights the arduous
road of several key linguists from the nineteenth century
onward in penetrating the function of SYNTACTIC change.
Quite rightly he observes that "Disregard of syntactic
features in change has taken its toll ..." ( ). It is
all the more gratifying then that this volume offers the
reader an exhaustive display of regard for SYNTACTIC
change in the refined generative study by Wayne Harbert
(Part Two) of the reflexive in Germanic. David Lightfoot
(Part Two), in an article initially published in *Linguistic Reconstruction and Indo-European Syntax*, ed. by P.
Ramat, Amsterdam: John Benjamin, 1980, concentrates as
well on explicating SYNTACTIC change by demonstrating that
syntax may be restructured via LEXICAL change. His paradigm example is change in the meaning of Middle English
like 'to cause pleasure for;, to Modern English *like* 'to
derive pleasure from', thus the transformation from *the
king like pears* to *the king likes pears*. The development
of a currently evolving LEXICAL set is uncovered by
Irmengard Rauch (Part One) in her attempt to disambiguate
three intertwining technically popular terms in both linguistic and literary analyses. By applying principles of
SEMIOTICS to her data she derives fundamental distinguishing features for the terms *text*, *discourse*, *narrative*.
SEMIOTIC method is also employed by Barbara D. Greim (Part
One) in showing the reader that an idiom, contrary to
widespread belief, is not a staid, frozen expression, but
rather one that is subject at least in part to the muta-
tions of quotidian language. In Greim's article we observe the interplay of the lexicon with syntax and their
phonological/morphological reflexes, all of which are
pragmatically influenced.

    In the fifth article using contemporary evidence, Els
Oksaar (Part Four) expresses her conviction that the investigation of pragmatics leads the way to understanding
causality in language change. She writes: "One can hypothesize that the conditions and motives controlling language use also cause language shift" ( ). By examples,
principally from German, she shows how language interaction between varying STRATA in society, i.e. between and
among different and the same professions, regions, ethnic

origins, friends, strangers, listeners and hearers, results in reinterpretations and often in innovations. The
Kahanes (Part Four), in this Houston 1980 MLA talk published in *Wege zur Universalienforschung*, ed. by G.
Brettschneider and C. Lehmann, Tübingen: Narr, 1980, view
the admixture of forces in the evolution of Vulgar Latin
as the interaction of nature with nurture, viz., of an
indigenous Latin STRATUM with a Greek subcode, which is
non-inherited and learned—a paideia. The ample article
of Yakov Malkiel completes the group of articles under the
rubric Strata and Language Change in this volume. Malkiel
challenges the embodiments of linguistic STRATA concepts
which serve as disputable hypotheses rather than as reliable working frameworks, namely family-tree and wave
theories. He concludes that with some imagination and a
great deal of hard linguistic and cultural evidence, the
Iberian "branch" of Romance can be found to defy a family-
tree model and to evince two layers or waves of language
change influences.

     The classical domain of investigation of language
change, namely, the Historical Change of Part Two, includes the detailed MORPHOLOGICAL study of Frans van
Coetsem on the prehistoric composition of the reduplicating verbs in Germanic. Van Coetsem wrestles with this
long-considered-moot question of linguistics, and concludes that the so-called ablaut in the North-West Germanic reduplicating class represents, by assimilation of
the fixed reduplicating morpheme vowel *e* into the preterite root, a mirror image of the common Indo-European
and Germanic *e/o* present/past verb ablaut. The regularity
of MORPHOLOGICAL vowel alternation—ablaut—a hundred
years before it was thus named by Jakob Grimm, was observed by the grammarian Lambert ten Kate in the eight-
eenth century. Edgar C. Polomé (Part Three) traces the
perceptions and discoveries of ten Kate and other early
Netherlandic grammarians on language change. The time-
frame in which linguistic breakthroughs such as these
occurred prompts humbling thoughts indeed for today's
linguist, since, as Polomé reminds us "... only the discovery of Sanskrit and the reconstruction of Indo-European
[would] provide a better background to revise and improve
ten Kate's insight into Germanic morphology" (   ).

     By purposefully interlacing the four designated foci
of the collection, the discussion in this Preface means
to preview the multidimensional nature of these twelve
articles, which necessarily reflect the kaleidoscopic
essence of language change itself. The linguist, the
historian, the sociologist, the philosopher, the anthro-
pologist, the semiotist, whether student or seasoned
scholar, in grappling with a given language change, holds
in his hands, so to speak, a singularly elegant crystal,
the perception of whose full refinement ever eludes him.

LANGUAGE CHANGE

Part I

CONTEMPORARY

CHANGE

THE ELLIPTICAL IDIOM: CHANGE FROM
ICON AND INDEX TO SYMBOL

Barbara D. Greim

"You know what they say: Spare the rod ... !" And
indeed you do know what "they" say—or at least what
"they" mean—even though the speaker does not deign to repeat the condition's conclusion. Despite the fact that
this proverbial idiom is spoken in elliptical form, the
listener understands the intended admonition: an undis-
ciplined child is a spoiled and undesirable child. Ellipsis occurs with some frequency and predictability in idioms, and this paper proposes to offer an analysis of that
language change phenomenon. Ellipsis parallels other such
language change phenomena at various levels of language
and may be said to involve a three-stage process. First,
the reduction of lexical elements in the idiom string
causes a loss of semantic transparency. This loss of
transparency, in turn, leads to an encoding of the lost
semantic material in the remaining constituents of the idiom string. Finally, the idiom, thus shortened and bereft
of elements necessary to the correct decoding of its figurative meaning, becomes more fixed syntactically.
     Modern idiom researchers have not addressed themselves
specifically to ellipsis, except to mention in passing
that some idioms are shorter versions of others. Nevertheless, what they have said or implied about the syntactic behavior of the idiom is of import to this discussion.
To suggest that idioms become more fixed syntactically as
a result of ellipsis presupposes syntactic activity, or
the possibility of it, prior to the change to elliptical
form. Linguists are of two minds in regard to this syntactic activity. One group considers that idioms are, by
nature, anomalous, and should they ever occur in varied
form, they do so only very rarely and not according to any
discernible set of rules. The second group considers that
idioms are not so irregular in their behavior as previously supposed, and their observations are a compelling
challenge to the premise of the first group.
     Among those belonging to the first group is Adam
Makkai (1972) who presents, along with an involved and
studied typology of the idiom, stratificational analyses

of individual idioms. His treatment recognizes no universality in idiom behavior. He maintains further that tournure (A tournure is a lexemic idiom consisting of at least
three lexons and optionally containing the definite article *the* or the indefinite article *a* which occur in envi-
ronmentally conditioned compulsory morphotactic grids
without, however, realizing additional sememes on the se-
memic stratum subject to erroneous decoding or lack of
understanding.) idioms have only morphological freedoms,
no syntactic freedoms. Individual words within the idiom
string may become singular or plural, present or past, or
masculine or feminine, but the idiom remains syntactically
frozen. Terminology used to identify and discuss idiomatic material is also telling of this anomaly concept of
idiom behavior. Harald Thun (1978) uses the phrase *fi-
xiertes Wortgefüge* 'fixed word-construction' to describe
idiomatic phrases and suggests that in becoming idiomatic,
phrases undergo *Fixierung* 'fixing, becoming fixed'. Lack
of *Fixiertheit* 'fixedness' means that the phrase in question is not truly idiomatic. Harald Burger (1973) includes in his discussion of what is idiomatic the concept
of semantic incongruence, as in *kalter Krieg* 'cold war',
where two or more words not normally juxtaposed, are
brought together for the purpose of producing a special
and striking expression. Likewise, Linda Brannon (1975),
in her experiments with idioms, found that those idioms
which were semantically and/or syntactically ill-formed
(e.g. *to eat one's words*) were the most easily recognized
and understood as to their figurative meanings. Alan
Healy (1968) proposes that idioms themselves serve specific syntactic functions and types them accordingly: *at
close quarters* is an adverb of place, while *to play second
fiddle to* functions like a transitive verb. In the examples cited above semantic and syntactic peculiarities
are used to describe and define what is idiomatic. That
idioms should have characteristics which distinguish them
from other constructs in the grammar is not surprising.
Nor is it surprising that those characteristics which so
distinguish such a collocation of words are semantic and
syntactic in nature. Whether these idioms, so defined,
may be able to undergo syntactic variation in accordance
with rules already present in the grammar is the question
taken up by the second group of researchers.
    Wallace Chafe (1970) points out that idioms, such as
to fly off the handle, which is considered to be a verb
in Healy's analysis, do not function as single units. The
past tense of the idiom is *flew off the handle* and not
*fly off the handled. Idioms, as Makkai also asserts, are
not irregular as to their morphology. Chafe, as well as
Katz and Postal, directs attention to the fact that certain idioms cannot be passivized, whereas others can be.
According to Chafe the reason that the idiom *to kick the
bucket* cannot undergo passivization, for instance, lies
in the fact that its figurative meaning *to die* is intransitive. Both the formation of the past tense in idioms

and the inability of intransitive verbs to be passivized
are in complete accordance with rules that govern corresponding non-idiomatic constructs in the grammar.

Frederick Newmeyer in his 1974 article "The Regularity
of Idiom Behavior" proposes an analytical model which accounts for the failure of some idioms to undergo certain
transformations and for the ability of other idioms to
undergo those same transformations successfully. He maintains that "an idiom's behavior with respect to transformational rules is, in fact, predictable from constructs
required elsewhere in the grammar" (1974:328-9). He applies his analysis according to transformation type: (1)
those transformations which are semantically governed,
i.e. PASSIVIZATION, UNSPECIFIED OBJECT DELETION, CONJUNCT
MOVEMENT, SUBJECT RAISING, TOUGH MOVEMENT, and THERE IN-
SERTION, and (2) those transformations which are not semantically governed, i.e. TOPICALIZATION, QUESTION FOR-
MATION, RIGHT DISLOCATION, ADVERB INSERTION, PRONOMINAL-
IZATION, and PARTICLE MOVEMENT. His analysis of idioms
undergoing transformations which are semantically governed
recalls Chafe's explanation of the failure of *to kick the
bucket* to passivize. In Newmeyer's analysis, the verb in
each idiom to be examined is assigned two meanings: M_1
is the figurative meaning the idiom is intended to convey
and M_2 is the literal meaning of the verb which appears
in the idiom string. Both the M_1 and M_2 determine whether
a semantically governed transformational rule operates on
a given idiom or not. If either one fails to allow such
a rule to operate, then the idiom cannot undergo that
transformation. Therefore, the idiom *to pop the question*
(M_1 *propose* and M_2 *pop*) can be expected to undergo passivization successfully, since both the M_1 and M_2 are transitive verbs, while *to make the scene* (M_1 *arrive* and M_2
make) cannot be passivized since its M_1 *arrive* is intransitive. In like manner the model can be applied to idioms
undergoing the several other semantically governed transformations named above. As for those transformations
which are not semantically governed, Newmeyer concludes
that idioms uniformly cannot undergo them and cites several pertinent examples of such ungrammatically transformed idioms (1974:335), one of which is *Mary kicked the
bucket and Slim kicked it (one) too* (PRONOMINALIZATION).

My theoretical model for the syntactic behavior of
idioms introduces two dominant features: COMPATIBILITY
and semantic transparency, designated by the concepts
ICON, INDEX, and SYMBOL, borrowed from Charles S. Peirce's
semiotic theory. The compatibility feature extends the
Newmeyer model to include syntactic (S_1 and S_2), as well
as semantic (M_1 and M_2 factors). Idioms, therefore, are
not uniformly excluded from undergoing so-called non-
semantically governed transformations, as maintained by
Newmeyer. The idiom *to kick the bucket* is analyzed accordingly:

M_2 *to kick the bucket* M_1 *to die*
S_2 VERB + OBJ S_1 VERB

The idiom fails to undergo successful pronominalization,
not because the transformation is not semantically governed, but primarily because the S_1 of the idiom does not
contain an OBJ to correspond to S_2 OBJ. The idiom loses
its figurative meaning, therefore, as a result of this
transformation. The transparency feature designates the
degree of ease with which the figurative meaning is discernible from the literal constituents of the idiom
string. The more transparent or iconic an idiom is, the
more readily it can undergo successful transformation.

The term ICON is applied to those idioms whose literal
and figurative meanings show a relationship of FACTUAL
SIMILARITY. An iconic idiom gives a pictorial representation of its figurative meaning. The clock, an instrument used for telling time, is an obvious icon for time,
present, past, and future, and accordingly, the idiom *to
turn back the clock*, which means *to refer to an earlier
time*, can be considered to be iconic. The term INDEX is
applied to those idioms whose literal and figurative
meanings show a relationship of FACTUAL CONTIGUITY. In
indexical idioms, an element or elements in the idiom
string suggest or point to the figurative meaning. A semantic link between the two meanings leads to the correct
decoding of the idiom. In the case of the idiom *to take
the bull by the horns*, the semantic link of "danger, difficulty" leads to the figurative meaning *to confront a
problem*. In the case of the German idiom *sich ins warme
Nest setzen* 'to sit down in the warm nest', the semantic
link "comfort, security" suggests the figurative meaning
in eine wohlhabende Familie einheiraten 'to marry into a
well-to-do family'. Finally, the term SYMBOL is applied
to those idioms whose literal and figurative meanings show
a relationship of IMPUTED CONTIGUITY. The individual constituents of the idiom string give no hint as to the figurative meaning which that same string is supposed to convey. The idiom string has simply been endowed with an
additional meaning not based upon the semantic content of
its constituents. The constituents of the idiom *to kick
the bucket* do not suggest its figurative meaning *to die*.
Table 1 offers a pictorial, or in semiotic terminology,
an iconic representation of the relationship between the
two meanings in the three types of idioms. Iconic idioms
are located at the apex of the angle in the diagram by
way of demonstrating the similarity of the literal and
figurative meanings. The two meanings of the indexical
idioms appear at a greater distance from each other, with
DIFFICULTY or COMFORT acting as the semantic link between
them. Lastly, the literal and figurative meanings of the
symbolic idioms are the farthest apart of the three semiotic types. They are completely dissimilar and noncon-
tiguous factually by way of demonstrating that the two
meanings are related only through imputation. A short
note as to how the degree of semantic transparency is determined and represented by a suitable semiotic term is
appropriate here. It is nearly impossible to separate

I. The Semiotic Concepts: ICON, INDEX, and SYMBOL

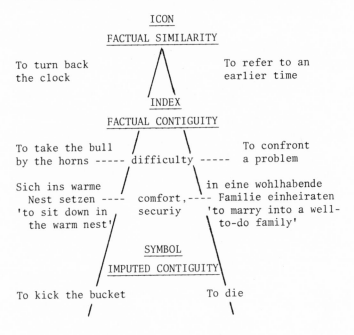

ICON

FACTUAL SIMILARITY

To turn back   To refer to an
the clock   earlier time

INDEX

FACTUAL CONTIGUITY

To take the bull   To confront
by the horns ----- difficulty ----- a problem

Sich ins warme   in eine wohlhabende
Nest setzen ----   comfort, ---- Familie einheiraten
'to sit down in   securiy   'to marry into a well-
the warm nest'   to-do family'

SYMBOL

IMPUTED CONTIGUITY

To kick the bucket   To die

II. Elliptical Idioms

    1. Du kannst mir mal (den Buckel
       herunterrutschen)
       'You can go to blazes!'
    2. To get the lead out (of one's pants)
    3. To be up a creek (without a paddle)
    4. To let the chips fall (where they may)
    5. To throw someone off (the scent)
    6. einen Vogel (im Kopf) haben 'To be crazy'
    7. bei jemandem piept's (im Kopf) 'To be crazy'
    8. If the shoe fits, (wear it)
    9. There's many a slip (between the cup and
       the lip)
   10. Ein gebranntes Kind (scheut das Feuer)
       'A burned child is wary of the fire'
   11. Ein blindes Huhn (findet auch einmal ein Korn)
       'A blind chicken also finds a kernel once
       in a while'
   12. Wer im Glashaus sitzt, (soll nicht mit
       Steinen werfen)
       'He who sits in a glass house shouldn't
       throw stones'

TABLE 1.

the three concepts completely. Any idiom may contain elements that are iconic, indexical, and symbolic. For the
purposes of this analysis an idiom will be judged to be
predominantly iconic, indexical, or symbolic.

Idioms which undergo ellipsis are originally pictorial
or suggestive representations of their figurative meanings, i.e. ICONS or INDICES. Loss of constituents in the
idiom string through ellipsis necessarily results in a
decrease in semantic transparency which can be graphically
described as a descent from ICON and INDEX near the apex
of the semiotic angle as pictured on the chart toward
SYMBOL. This loss of elements, which comprises the first
stage in the ellipsis process, occurs with the greatest
success and frequency in vulgar, insulting, or blasphemous
expressions where a conscious effort is made to avoid ut-
tering offensive words. An example is the German expression *Du kannst mir mal* for *Du kannst mir mal den Buckel
herunterrutschen* which freely translated is 'you can go
to blazes!' Two examples taken from English are *to get
the lead out* for *to get the lead out of one's pants* and
to be up a creek for *to be up a creek without a paddle.*
All three idioms boast a more pictorially vulgar history.
Of the complete idioms given above two sport substitutions, and one a further omission. *Den Buckel herunterrutschen* 'to slide down the hump' is a euphemism for the
much more graphic *den A---- lecken* 'to lick the a--'.
Naturally a person of good breeding does not speak such
words and seeks instead a more polite way of conveying
the same message. The idiom *to get the lead out of one's
pants* is described in idiom dictionaries as being a "rude"
expression. The reason is that the constituent *lead*,
like *den Buckel herunterrutschen*, is a euphemism substituted some time ago in the idiom's history for a socially
unacceptable and unpleasant, though likewise weighty substance, found under unfortunate circumstances in that lo-
cation. Finally the third idiom cited here as an example,
to be up a creek without a paddle, is the cleaned-up version of *to be up sh t creek without a paddle*, where the
difficulties of propelling one's boat or canoe are more
than apparent.

Through language change the three idioms lose their
picturesqueness. The once colorful and suggestive expressions become less indexical or even symbolic. The
elliptical German idiom *Du kannst mir mal* has certainly
lost its most semantically important elements and must be
described here as symbolic. The shortened English idiom
to get the lead out loses a significant portion, though
not all, of its most semantically important elements.
Out of one's pants leaves, but *lead* remains, though sev-
ering all ties with the original iconic idiom. The word
lead might still serve as an index to the figurative meaning to some degree, but through the loss of those elements
which formerly served to define *lead* and its particular
function in this expression, the elliptical idiom must be

considered to be now largely symbolic. Likewise *to be up a creek* has lost those elements which made the idiom a pictorial representation of a most distressing predicament. The remaining elliptical idiom is only a sketchy indication of the former icon.

In addition to the indelicate sort of expression, a second type of idiom which commonly undergoes ellipsis is the idiom which is in very frequent use. Examples of such idioms are: *to let the chips fall (where they may)*, *to throw someone off (the scent)*, and the two similar German expressions *einen Vogel (im Kopf) haben* 'to have a bird in the head' and *bei jemandem piept's (im Kopf)* 'There's peeping in someone's head', both of which have the figurative meaning 'to be crazy'. Like the idioms in the first group, all of the above examples have become less indicative of their figurative meanings through the loss of elements having pertinent semantic content. The first English idiom *to let the chips fall* loses elements expressing nonchalance about the consequences of an action, and, as a result, it becomes more symbolic. Likewise the second English idiom *to throw someone off* certainly becomes symbolic in that it loses the one really major contributing element to a correct decoding of its figurative meaning: the word *scent*. In the case of the two German idioms the element *im Kopf* 'in the head', which would suggest mental capacity iconically, can be presumed to have been lost. The lost element leaves a vestige of its former presence in the elliptical idiom *Er hat einen Vogel* paralinguistically in a gesture which often accompanies the spoken idiom: the speaker points at his head. The elliptical idiom by itself, however, is less than iconic.

Proverbial idioms comprise a third group of expressions that often undergo ellipsis. The fact that such idioms are frequently used in common parlance and the fact that they are usually longer than other types of idioms make them ready candidates for ellipsis. Examples of proverbial idioms are the following: *If the shoe fits, (wear it)*, *There's many a slip (between the cup and the lip)*, *Ein gebranntes Kind (scheut das Feuer)* 'A burned child is wary of the fire', *Ein blindes Huhn (findet auch einmal ein Korn)*, 'A blind chicken also finds a kernel once in a while', and *Wer im Glashaus sitzt, (soll nicht mit Steinen werfen)* 'He who sits in a glass house shouldn't throw stones'. All of the complete proverbial idioms in the above examples are pictorially suggestive expressions of folk wisdom. The loss of substantial segments of the idiom string reduces the expressions to symbols. The remaining constituents do not offer images of footwear in an appropriate size being worn, possible dribbling while drinking, wariness of the fire, a successful search, or a glass house shattered by stones. The elliptical idioms do, however, still convey the full figurative meaning of the whole idiom, which brings the discussion to stage two of the change process.

In stage two the entire figurative meaning of the complete idiom is encoded into its elliptical form. It must be noted here that, although this part of the change process is designated stage two, it must take place concurrently with stage one. That the encoding does indeed take place is evidenced in the fact that the elliptical idiom is understood as if the full idiom had been uttered. The person who is told *Du kannst mir mal* is insulted or annoyed. The individual who is ordered *to get the lead out*, though possibly offended at this historically rude remark, will begin to work harder and faster if he is obedient. And if the empty bottle of digitalis *threw him off*, we know that the detective was diverted from finding what he was looking for. While the change from full idiom to elliptical idiom is in progress, the shortened form may be said to call forth the full idiom in the mind of the listener, but eventually the elliptical idiom comes to exist as a separate and complete entity in itself, preserved finally through stage three of the change process.

In order to retain the encoded figurative meanings, elliptical idioms become more fixed syntactically. Full idioms are capable of syntactic variation in accordance with the rules of their grammar, as discussed above. One component of that grammar, semantic transparency, is of special consequence in this final stage of ellipsis. Iconic idioms undergo transformations more readily than indexical or symbolic idioms by virtue of the fact that their literal and figurative meanings are so close. The figurative meaning is always readily apparent in the constituents of the literal string. Indexical idioms undergo transformations less readily than iconic idioms since the figurative meaning is only indicated in the literal string. The figurative meaning is more likely to become hidden or lost as a result of transformations interrupting or otherwise rearranging the idiom string. Of the three semiotic types, symbolic idioms are the most resistant to transformations. Their figurative meanings, which are only imputed to them, easily become lost through transformational interruption and rearrangement of the literal strings. Thus, for instance, the passive transformation applied to the iconic idiom *to turn back the clock* results in an acceptable, if uncommon, construct: *the clock is turned back*. But the passivized symbolic idiom *the beans were spilled* can be understood only literally. The figurative meaning is lost as a result of the transformation. Thus the indexical full idiom *to throw someone off the scent* may be passivized without loss of figurative meaning: *he was thrown off the scent*. Its symbolic elliptical counterpart, however, cannot be passivized. *He was thrown off* can be understood only literally, and one envisions the separation of horse and rider. As previously discussed, not all idioms are capable of undergoing passivization or other transformations even in their full forms, but those that are capable of doing so, undergo those transformations much less successfully or not at

all as elliptical idioms, because in becoming elliptical,
they change from ICONS or INDICES to SYMBOLS
    Ellipsis, as analyzed here, has been presented as an
identifiable and predictable process within a framework
of regularity in idiom behavior. The behavior of idioms
conforms to rules governing other constructs in the grammar. In like manner ellipsis in the idiom parallels other
language change phenomena. Foremost among them, perhaps,
is the loss of inflectional endings that has occurred
throughout the history of the English language. The resulting fixedness of word order serves to preserve syntactic relationships, just as fixed syntax in the elliptical idiom serves to preserve a figurative meaning. On
the phonological level, ellipsis can be compared with the
loss of the nasal /n/ before Germanic ƕ, as in the preterite of certain weak -*jan* stem verbs. The original presence of the nasal is recalled in the compensatory lengthening of the preceding vowel. Ellipsis is thus shown to
be a language change phenomenon, reflected elsewhere in
the language, which affects idiom syntax and semantics
through a process consisting of: (1) a loss of semantic
transparency, followed by (2) encoding of the lost semantic material in the remaining constituents of the
idiom string, and (3) resulting in a more fixed syntax.

REFERENCES

Brannon, Linda L. 1975. On the understanding of idiomatic ex-
    pressions. Dissertation, University of Texas at Austin.
Burger, Harald. 1973. *Idiomatik des Deutschen*. Germanische
    Arbeitshefte. Tübingen: Max Niemeyer Verlag.
Chafe, Wallace. 1970. *Meaning and the structure of language*.
    Chicago: University of Chicago Press.
Greim, Barbara. 1979. A grammar of the idiom: Theory develop-
    ment and its application to Old French and Old West Germanic.
    Dissertation, University of Illinois at Urbana-Champaign.
Hartshorne, Charles, and Paul Weiss. (eds.) 1932. *Collected papers
    of Charles Sanders Peirce*. Cambridge: Harvard University
    Press.
Healey, Alan. 1968. English idioms. *Kivung* 1:71-108.
Katz, Jerrold J., and Paul M. Postal. 1963. Semantic interpretation
    of idioms and sentences containing them. MIT Research Laboratory
    of Electronics *Quarterly Progress Report* 70:275-82.
Makkai, Adam. 1972. *Idiom structure in English*. The Hague:
    Mouton.
Newmeyer, Frederick J. 1974. The regularity of idiom behavior.
    Lingua 34:327-42.
Thun, Harald. 1978. *Probleme der Phraseologie*. Tübingen: Max
    Niemeyer Verlag.

PROSODIC CHANGE IN PROGRESS:
EVIDENCE FROM ESTONIAN*

Ilse Lehiste

The problem I want to address today is prosodic change
in progress. History is full of examples of prosodic
change, but as a rule, change is noted when it has already
taken place. I am fully aware of the controversy concerning gradualness vs. abruptness of linguistic change, and I
am more than ordinarily conscious of the problems involved
in trying to observe an ongoing process: more often than
not, Heisenberg's uncertainty principle applies, and the
very fact of observation changes the process that is being observed. Nevertheless, I am going to attempt to describe what I consider to be prosodic change in progress;
I hope to present a reasonable argument for the possibility of observing and documenting ongoing prosodic change.
My test case will be the prosodic system of Estonian.
Estonian has received a certain amount of attention
from linguists in the past twenty years, and I will not
have to go into excessive detail in giving an overview of
its prosodic structure. It is well known that Estonian
has three degrees of phonemic quantity in vowels, and that
it distinguishes between a single consonant and two kinds
of geminates in intervocalic position. Usually this is
referred to as three degrees of consonant quantity. This
three-way quantity system interacts with a two-way opposition between "strong" and "weak" forms of word stems.
There are numerous words in the language that maintain the
same quantity throughout their respective paradigms, and
they do not concern us at the moment. But a fairly large
proportion of Estonian vocabulary is subject to what is
called "gradation" or "grade alternation", and what I have
been calling "degree change". This term refers to the
phenomenon that a word stem may appear in two different
phonetic shapes within the paradigm, traditionally called
"weak" and "strong". The conditioning factors for the
occurrence of the two degrees were originally phonetic/

---

* Paper presented at the Winter meeting of the Linguistic
Society of America in San Antonio, Texas, on Dec. 29, 1980.

10

phonological, and they can still be fairly well identified
in Finnish; but in Estonian the conditioning factors have
largely become opaque due to various sound changes as well
as analogical restructuring, and the degree change has
been morphologized. The appearance of the weak or strong
degree in a particular form is now determined by inflectional class. For example, members of a large class of
nouns have the weak degree in the nominative singular and
partitive singular; the other twelve cases of the singular
are in the strong degree. In the plural, on the other
hand, nom. pl. and part. pl. are in the strong degree and
the other twelve cases are in the weak degree in this
class of nouns. There are other inflectional classes that
have a different distribution of weak and strong degrees;
the morphophonemics of Estonian is extremely complicated.
The *Dictionary of Correct Usage* (Kull and Raiet 1976)
gives 90 different inflectional classes for nouns/adjec-
tives and 25 for verbs.

Word stems in Estonian were originally disyllabic,
and the degree change affects the consonant on the border
between the first and second syllable. Originally only
plosive consonants were subject to degree change. The
change was qualitative, when the intervocalic plosive was
single, and quantitative, when the consonant was geminate.
By qualitative change, we mean change of the plosive into
a fricative or glide (or zero); by quantitative change,
we mean the change of a long geminate into a short one or
vice versa. Inflection of the word *mõte* 'thought' offers
an example of a quantitative change:

Nom. sg.	mõte	Nom pl.	mõtted
Gen. sg.	mõtte	Gen. pl.	mõtete
Part. sg.	mõtet	Part. pl.	mõtteid
Ill. sg.	mõttesse	Ill. pl.	mõtetesse
etc.		etc.	

An example of a qualitative change is provided by the
word *sõda* 'war':

Nom. sg.	sõda	Nom. pl.	sõjad
Gen. sg.	sõja	Gen. pl.	sõdade
Part. sg.	sõda	Part. pl.	sõdasid, sõdu
Ill. sg.	sõjasse, sõtta	Ill. pl.	sõdadesse
etc.		etc.	

The original conditioning factor was the open or
closed nature of the second syllable of the disyllabic
sequence. The consonant between the first and second syllable of the stem was in the weak degree when the second
syllable was closed, and in the strong degree when the
second syllable was open. The syllable is open when it
ends in a vowel, and closed when it ends in a consonant.
The developments in the words *ratas* 'wheel' and *rada*
'path' illustrate the process:

Nom. sg. ratas   rada
Gen. sg. *rattahan > ratta *raðan > raja

The placement of the syllable boundary is automatic:
the boundary occurs before a short intervocalic consonant,
or within a geminate (or consonant cluster). Thus in
rattahan, the boundary is before /h/, the second syllable
is open, and the stem appears in the strong degree. In
ratas, the second syllable is closed, and the stem appears
in the weak degree.

There have been some recent attempts (Prince 1980) to
describe the prosodic structure of Estonian with reference
to strong and weak syllables. I find this inadequate, for
reasons that are too numerous to be reviewed at this moment; in the present context, though, I should like to
point out that the process of degree change does not operate with syllables, but with disyllabic sequences. For
purposes of degree change, consonants are to be defined
as internal within a disyllabic sequence. It does not
matter whether these consonants are syllable-initial or
syllable-final; what does matter is that they are intervocalic within a disyllabic sequence. The placement of
the syllable boundary is automatic and irrelevant from the
point of view of the application of the process of degree
change. Syllable boundaries get reassigned according to
the general syllabication rule of Estonian, after the degree change has operated. For example, the word *sõda*
'war', nom. sg., is in the strong degree; the genitive sg.
of the word, *sõja*, is in the weak degree (because the
genitive originally ended in -*n* which has disappeared
through a general sound change). The syllable boundary
falls before the intervocalic consonant in both cases,
and the first syllable is in the short quantity in both
cases. In this type of word, it is the initial consonant
of the second syllable that is subject to degree change.
Prince (1980) claims that only the syllable rime matters
for establishing whether the syllable is strong or weak,
and that syllable-initial consonants are irrelevant; this
is clearly not the case for determining whether a word
stem appears in the weak or strong degree.

The two-way opposition between weak and strong degrees
is older than the three-way quantity opposition. The
three-way quantity opposition developed originally only
in positions in which degree change also can occur, that
is within a disyllabic sequence (but not at the boundary
of two disyllabic sequences). The system arose in Estonian in conjunction with syncope and apocope that took
place approximately 500 years ago. Kask (1972) puts apocope in the 13th century and syncope between the 14th and
16th centuries. Both processes affected short vowels of
an open succeeding syllable after a long preceding syllable. Actually the two processes are two aspects of the
same phenomenon, since both involved the loss of a short
vowel after a long preceding syllable; the process is
called apocope when the lost vowel occurred in word-final

position, and syncope, when the lost vowel was word-internal. Syncope has not spread into all dialects to the same extent: the coastal dialect of the north-east is least affected, and it is this dialect that has not developed a three-way quantity system. The north-eastern dialect retains the old two-way system that Estonian used to share with Finnish, and that is still present in practically unchanged form in most Finnish dialects.

Analogical developments have led to the appearance of Q2 and Q3 also in stems that do not contain consonants liable to degree change; for example, there are long and overlong diphthongs in Estonian disyllabic words, e.g. *laulu* (gen.) - *laulu* (part.), with a long diphthong in the genitive and an overlong diphthong in the partitive.

This constitutes a bird's eye view of the Estonian prosodic system, described at a very abstract level and omitting practically all phonetic detail. The problem is that the system does not appear to be completely stable. For more than a hundred years, linguists have felt that the scheme I have just presented does not do justice to the prosodic system. Two proposals have to be considered: first, the claim that there are really four quantities rather than three, and second, that the distinction between Q2 and Q3 is not a distinction of quantity, but rather a distinction of tone.

The question of the fourth quantity has been around for more than a century. Mihkel Veske, the first Estonian to receive a doctorate in linguistics (from the University of Leipzig in 1872), claimed to hear a distinctive difference in overlong intervocalic /k/'s in words of different morphological structure. There is an emphatic particle in Estonian, *-ki*, which can be added to any form of a noun or verb. Let us take an i-stem noun ending in /k/, e.g. *tukk* 'firebrand'. Adding the emphatic particle to the nom. sg. of *tukk*, we get *tukk + ki* 'even the firebrand'; the part. sing. of this word would be *tukki*. Veske said that he could hear a difference between the first *tukki* and the second *tukki*, and he called the first *tukki* the fourth degree of quantity.

Later scholars have likewise claimed that they can hear a difference between morphologically different words that would be homophonous if there were no fourth quantity. In particular, these forms involve pairs of partitive vs. short illative, and abessive vs. da-infinitive. The regular illative is formed with the suffix *-sse*, but there are some words—actually quite a large number—that also permit the formation of a short illative simply by providing the first syllable with overlength. For example, the word *linn* 'town, city' forms a regular illative, *linnasse*, and a short illative, *linna*. Originally it was just the intervocalic consonant that could be geminated, but at the present time the short illative can be formed from many other kinds of words. Take another example, a loanword *kool* 'school', with a long illative *koolisse*, and a short illative *kooli*. The words of which the short

illative can be formed in addition to the morphologically
regular illative have to be marked in the dictionary;
there is no general rule as to whether the short illative
is permitted or not. In case the short illative is used,
the use of the long form can be restricted in various ways
that are not relevant at the moment.

If speakers do indeed distinguish between the short
illative and partitive in words like *linna* and *kooli*, the
illative would be, according to Polivanov (1928) and some
younger scholars who have rediscovered him, in the fourth
quantity, and the partitive would have regular third quantity. The other potential contrast between Q3 and quantity 4 is in sequences like *võita* abessive sg. 'without
butter', and *võita* 'to win', da-infinitive of the verb
võitma. (The abessive is presumably in Q4.)

> võit + ta > võita 'to win'
> võit + ma > võitma 'to win'
> või + ta > võita 'without butter', abessive sg.

I will return to the question of the fourth quantity
after reviewing some of the claims that Estonian is really
a tone language. There are two different problems involved here. One is the claim that the difference between Q2 and Q3 is really a tonal difference, so that Estonian has two degrees of contrastive quantity and that
there are two different tonal patterns that provide a
further distinction within the long degree of quantity.
A variant of this is the theory of Harms (1978), according
to which the differences between Q2 and Q3 are due to differences in stress accent rather than quantity. The other
claim is that there are really four oppositions, and that
the tonal distinction serves to separate the two kinds of
overlength. This latter theory is a variation of the
theory of four degrees of quantity: there are four oppositions, but the opposition between what some call Q3 and
Q4 is tonal and not quantitative.

I have already referred to Polivanov, who made the
first systematic attempt to treat Estonian as a tone language (1928). This treatment was popularized by
Trubetzkoy. Polivanov claimed that different pitch contours distinguish between different cases in Estonian, to
wit, between nominative, genitive, partitive, and illative.
Here are some of Polivanov's examples:

Word and case		Pitch on first syllable	Pitch on second syllable
pime	'blind', nom. sg.	high	falling
piima	'milk', gen. sg.	high + falling	low
piima	'milk', part. sg.	high + high + falling	low
piima	'milk', ill. sg.	falling-rising	low

Unfortunately many of Polivanov's examples are full
of errors, not only in the phonetic descriptions of different word types, but also errors in morphology. For
example, he forms the partitive of *tuul* 'wind' as *tuule*,
and the partitive is really *tuult*. There is no free variation here; all words of this class take a dental suffix
in the partitive. Polivanov, however, uses such nonexistent forms as members of his tonal minimal pairs.

The latest proponent of the tone theory is Helimski
(1977), who claims to have found lexical tone in Estonian.
Helimski's claims are based on about a hundred words produced by one informant, without any attempt to make a recording of the pronunciations, not to mention any acoustic
analysis or listening tests. I have not been able to dis-
cern any system in Helimski's observations. He claims to
have found tonal minimal pairs in the language, e.g., that
the word *maks* 'liver' and *maks* 'payment' constitute a
minimal pair, 'liver' having high tone and 'payment' having low tone. Helimski says that the informant agreed
that there really is a certain distinction between the two
words, but it remains unclear what the informant may have
had in mind. Other minimal pairs offered by Helimski include *koor* 'bark of a tree' with low pitch and *koor*
'choir' with high pitch, and a few others. I am afraid
that Helimski's claims cannot be taken seriously.

Leaving the question of lexical tone aside for the
moment, what most of these analyses have in common is a
feeling, not always clearly articulated, that the three-
quantity framework does not account for the way the language really functions. In my own opinion, the system is
out of balance because there is a morphologically determined two-way opposition between weak and strong degrees
and a phonological opposition between word-level durational patterns that sometimes parallels the morphological
pattern, but more often does not. There are frequent contradictions, e.g., when the strong degree is in Q1, and
the weak degree is in Q3. (The word *nuga* is an example,
cf. below.) There are also many words that are not subject to degree change, even though their phonetic shape
is not significantly different from those words that are
(e.g., *nuga* alternates with a weak form, but *vaga* does
not). And there are large numbers of homophonous forms
of different morphological makeup (e.g., the nominative,
genitive, and partitive of *vaga* all have the same form).
Partial paradigms of the words *lõpp* 'end', *hapu* 'sour',
nuga 'knife', and *vaga* 'pious' illustrate these points.

Nom. sg.	lõpp	hapu	nuga	vaga
Gen. sg.	lõpu	hapu	noa	vaga
Part. sg.	lõppu	haput	nuga	vaga
Abess. sg.	lõputa	haputa	noata	vagata

Different linguists see different ways in which the
system might readjust itself, either through the development of an additional quantity opposition or the emergence

of tone as a distinctive feature. There is a third theory
that I will add at this point, the theory of Mati Hint
that the language is in the process of changing from a
mora-counting prosodic structure to a syllable-counting
structure. My own theory is that the prosodic system of
Estonian is changing from primarily quantitative to basically accentual. By accentual I mean a phonological system in which stress, quantity, and tone all play a part.
The way people—even linguists—feel about a language constitutes part of the data; if it is felt by a number of
speakers, particularly by those who have a relatively
highly developed consciousness about language, that the
system is changing, one might just as well start looking
for the cause of their intuition.

The system got out of balance some five hundred years
ago with the development of the third quantity. At an
earlier stage, there were just short and long syllables,
no overlong ones; this earlier stage is reflected in folk
songs, the meter of which operates with just short and
long syllables. There are eight syllables in the folk
song line; since the meter is syllable-counting, the folk
song lines tend to preserve earlier forms—before the
occurrence of syncope and apocope. It is necessary to
take a closer look at overlength to understand some of the
changes that have been taking place and are still in
progress.

The phonetic characteristics of overlength include
extra length on the overlong syllable itself, and a falling Fo contour on the overlong syllable. Both features
can be explained as the result of a general tendency to
"preserve the integrity of the word." I have established—
in other contexts, working mainly with English—that there
exists a tendency to keep the duration of words approximately constant; thus a derived disyllabic word in English
has approximately the same duration as the monosyllabic
word that constitutes the base (e.g., *speed* is of the same
duration as *speedy*; cf. Lehiste 1971). In Estonian syncope and apocope, the loss of a vowel after a long syllable appears to have been compensated for at the word level
by the addition of extra length to that long syllable.
All monosyllabic words in Estonian are overlong, since all
monosyllabic words have resulted from the loss of a final
vowel after a long first syllable; the first syllable of
disyllabic words is overlong when the word was originally
trisyllabic, with a short open second syllable, etc. I
have proposed an explanation for the falling pitch contour
found on overlong syllables (Lehiste 1978): the pitch
contour is the result of transferring the pitch contour
of the whole disyllabic word onto the overlong first syllable.

The tendency to maintain the durational integrity of
the word has brought about another phonetic characteristic
of Estonian disyllabic words, namely the inverse relationship between the durations of the first and the second
syllable: a short first syllable is followed by a half-

long second syllable, long first syllables are followed
by somewhat shorter second syllables, and overlong first
syllables are followed by the shortest second syllables.
    Disyllabic words thus have three phonetic character-
istics: length of the first syllable (which can be due
to the length of the vowel of the first syllable, or to a
combination of vowel and intervocalic consonant duration);
Fo pattern applied to the word; and the ratio between the
durations of the first and second syllable. I ran an experiment ten years ago (Lehiste 1975) with synthesized
disyllabic Estonian words. In this set I used two minimal
triples, *taba-tapa-tappa* and *sada-saada!-saada*. In *taba-
tapa-tappa*, I changed the duration of the intervocalic
consonant in systematic steps, and provided each synthesized word with a second syllable of three possible durations, characterizing the three quantities. The words
were synthesized on a monotone. In *sada-saada!-saada*, I
changed the duration of the first vowel in seven 20-msec
steps and provided each word with three second syllable
durations and three pitch patterns: monotone, step-down
on the two syllables, and falling on the first syllable,
with low second syllable. The total number of test items
was 252. Listening tests were given in Tallinn to 26
reasonably monolingual subjects. Each listener gave four
responses; thus there were 104 responses per stimulus for
a total of 6552 responses for each set.
    Tables 1 and 2 summarize the results. It is obvious
that the pitch contour does not affect the perception of
Q1 very much, but that it has a rather dramatic effect on
the perception of Q2 and Q3. The step-down pattern favors
recognition of Q2, while the falling contour favors perception of Q3. The duration of the second syllable also
has an effect. Here the perception of Q2 is not very
strongly affected, but the shortest V2 favors judgments
of Q3, and the longest V2 favors judgments of Q1.

Fo contour	Q_1	Q_2	Q_3	Total
Monotone	669	1096	419	2184
Step-down	605	1326	253	2184
Falling on V_1	608	688	888	2184
Total	1882	3110	1560	6552

TABLE 1.
Saada responses with different Fo contours (all V_1
durations combined). V_2 duration = 90 msec.

V_2 duration, msec	Q_1	Q_2	Q_3	Total
180	717	1114	353	2184
120	596	1054	534	2184
90	569	942	673	2184
Total	1882	3110	1560	6552

TABLE 2.
Saada responses with different V_2 durations (all V_1
durations and Fo contours combined).

On the basis of a statistical analysis of these results (Lehiste and Danforth 1977), I concluded that the
distinction between Q1 and the other two quantities could
be made on the basis of the first syllable duration alone;
the distinction between Q2 and Q3 was strongly influenced
by the pitch contour, and relatively less strongly determined by the duration of the second syllable.

These results leave no doubt of the perceptual significance of Fo. I find it also illuminating (and logical)
that Fo should play a crucial role in distinguishing between the two "new" quantities. Duration separates short
from long; this is the inherited opposition. Pitch con-
tributes to the separation of long and overlong; this is
the new Estonian development. It is important to recall
here that there were some durations which could be changed
from Q2 to Q3 by the pitch contour alone. In these intermediate durations, then, it was the pitch contour that the
listeners used for making the distinction between the
words. But pitch is not the only distinction; overlong
Q3 is normally longer than long Q2 (recall the origin of
Q3 as a case of compensatory lengthening).

The phonetic characteristics of overlength have been
recently investigated by several Estonian linguists and
phoneticians in connection with an apparent rediscovery
of Polivanov's ideas (Remmel 1975, Lippus and Remmel 1976,
Eek 1977 and 1979). Particularly interesting in this connection is Remmel (1975). In analyzing 26 words produced
by 14 subjects, Remmel found that overlong short illatives
(as compared to overlong partitives) had a two-peaked
pitch contour and that some test words showed a decrease
in intensity in the middle of the overlong syllable, which
Remmel equated with the Danish and Livonian stød. The
stød-like effects were primarily found in diphthongs.

In a later experiment reported in Lippus and Remmel
(1976), Remmel used a research technique in which listeners were interacting with a computer. Ten subjects were
used who had been speakers in the previous study. Five
of them had employed somewhat different pitch contours
with the illative (as compared to the partitive); four had
the stød. The reaction to computer-synthesized stimuli
was obtained from three keys corresponding to the genitive, partitive, and illative cases, each key having ten
positions. The duration of the test words was the same;
what was changed was the pitch contour and the intensity
of the signal during a 60-msec period containing the pitch
peak. The results concerning the pitch contour were inconclusive, but an interesting correlation was found with
regard to the stød-like feature. Auditors were asked to
set the key for the proper value for the genitive, partitive, and illative for the word *kaevu* 'well'. Genitive
is in Q2, partitive is in Q3, and if there are four degrees of quantity, then the illative would be in Q4. The
auditors set the value of an intensity drop at the peak
of the pitch contour. For the genitive, the average setting was -3.6 db, for the partitive, the average was -8.2

db, and for the illative, the average was -6.8 db. Note
that the drop for the illative was smaller than the drop
for the partitive, while the opposite might have been expected. Remmel does not make any statement about whether
the difference between a drop of 8.2 db and 6.8 db is significant or not. The results show nevertheless that a
stød-like feature may be associated with overlength: the
genitive, in Q2, had an average intensity drop of 3.6 db,
while the two overlong cases had drops that were twice as
large. However, this experiment provides no evidence for
a possible distinction between Q3 and Q4.

Eek (1977) ran a perception experiment in order to
determine whether the supposed phonetic differences between overlong partitives and illatives—such as difference in length, difference in pitch contour, and presence
of something like stød—have perceptual significance.
There were seven speakers, who read 23 sentences five
times in succession. Thus there were 35 productions of
each test item. The test words were embedded in sentences, and consisted of three words in the genitive,
partitive, and short illative (*pütt, tünn, kool*), two
words in the partitive and illative (*maak, piim*), and one
pair of words for the distinction between an abessive and
a *da*-infinitive (*võita-võita*). Four perception tests were
run, consisting of different sets of the test items. I
will review only the first test, in which 46 listeners
were presented isolated words taken from the sentences and
asked to identify the case of the word. There were 350
test words in all. Eek reports that 215 of them, amount-
ing to 61%, were placed in the correct case category by
more than half the auditors. This "more than half" sounds
more impressive than it really is: the average identification for the partitive was 54%, and for the illative
46%. Eek did not report any significance calculations,
but I am not ready to believe that either 54% or 46% are
significantly different from 50%, i.e. from chance. A
certain amount of error is always present in listening
tests with human subjects; the correct score for the
genitive was 93%, where 100% would have been expected if
the listeners' attention had not wandered during the listening task. This difference between 100% and 93% is just
about comparable to the fluctuations around 50% (54% and
46%).

The 215 words (out of 350) that were placed in the
correct case category by more than half of the listeners
included all the words read in the genitive (94 items).
That leaves 128 partitives and 128 illatives to be accounted for. Only 70 out of 128 partitives, and only 51
out of 128 illatives, were placed in the correct category
by more than half of the listeners. It must be remembered
that the listeners were faced with a forced-choice decision in each case. I interpret Eek's results to mean that
the listeners identified the genitive correctly and were
simply guessing when they had to make a judgment regarding
an overlong word. However, in 1977 Eek was unwilling to

accept these results as conclusive counterevidence to the
existence of four degrees of quantity, and assumed that
the results reflected lack of accuracy in reading rather
than absence of any distinction between partitive and
illative.

By 1979 Eek seems to have changed his mind. In another paper published in 1979, he says that considering
the so-called fourth quantity degree possible is the result of an overestimation of the phonetic data. Eek admits now that the majority of listeners do not distinguish
Q3 and Q4; those who had tried to distinguish the partitive and illative had indicated as Q4 both the partitives
and the illatives that had been read with the longest
first syllable. These longer manifestations had generally
been produced in sentence-final position; listeners called
a sentence-initial illative partitive, and a sentence-
final partitive illative. Eek now realizes that it was
methodologically improper to ask listeners to compare
words that had not been produced under identical conditions, and accepts the fact that listeners can hear phonologically irrelevant differences within a category.

Not everyone who likes the fourth quantity is ready
to give it up, as Eek seems to have done. Viitso (1979),
for example, takes the four quantities as proven and uses
them to build a phonological system in which stress is
eliminated as a phonological unit.

While the existence of an opposition between Q3 and
Q4 can be dismissed on the basis of Eek's listening tests,
the studies just quoted have presented new information
about the phonetic manifestation of overlength. The phonological status of overlength has received a new interpretation in some recent research by Mati Hint (1978,
1979, 1980).

Hint recalls that apocope occurred in Estonian in two
word types: the final vowel was lost in disyllabic words
like *jalka, which became jalg, and in trisyllabic words
like *matala, which became madal. Hint reasons that this
was really one and the same process: a short syllable had
the value of one mora, while a long syllable had the value
of two morae. He reformulates the rule, as it applied
when apocope took place, to read that apocope happened
when the final open syllable was preceded by at least two
morae. Apocope did not apply when the final open syllable
was preceded by only one mora, for example in words like
kala. During the time of apocope, Estonian was a mora-
counting language. The most important change between that
time and the very recent past is the shift in the interpretation of what is considered long: now it is the overlong syllable that is considered equivalent to two morae,
and the short and long degrees are counted as consisting
of a single mora. Hint argues that contemporary standard
Estonian grammar is based on opposing Q1 and Q2 on the one
hand to Q3 on the other hand. Take, for example, the
placement of secondary stress. According to the standard
grammar, in polysyllabic words with Q1 and Q2, secondary

stress falls on the third syllable, but in words with Q3,
it falls on the second syllable. Hint formulates the rule
for the standard language as follows: secondary stress
must be preceded by at least two morae. (It is possible
to establish the position of secondary stress in a word
by objective measurements of duration.)

Standard grammar assigns words to inflectional classes
on the basis of quantity. Stems in Q1 and Q2 pattern in
ways that differ from the patterns of stems in Q3. The
types Hint concentrated on are trisyllabic in the genitive. The form of the partitive plural depends on the
quantity of the first syllable: words in Q3 form their
partitive plural with *-i*, while words in Q1 and Q2 form
the partitive plural with a diphthong and a dental suffix.
Thus a word like *endine* forms a partitive plural *endisi*,
while words like *punane* have a partitive plural *punaseid*.
Note that *endine* patterns in the same way as the four-
syllable word *inimene*, which has a partitive plural
inimesi: the overlong first syllable equals two short
syllables.

In these words, secondary stress should be falling on
the second syllable after an overlong first syllable:
éndìsi, *tȍȍlìsi* (this becomes even clearer in the comita-
tive: *éndìsega*, *tȍȍlìsega*). Hint observes that current
colloquial usage differs from that of the standard: he
claims that such words are currently being stressed on
the basis of syllable-counting rather than mora-counting,
namely that the stress falls on the third syllable in
words of four syllables, regardless of the quantity of
the first syllable. The innovating pronunciation, according to Hint, is *éndisèga* rather than *éndisega*. Thus
there is a tendency to structure words into disyllabic
sequences on the basis of a syllable count, rather than
using the principle that an overlong syllable counts for
two short syllables. The special nature of overlength is
in the process of being eroded, and the new principle,
which is taking over, does not consider overlength as a
basis for the assignment of a word to a morphological
class.

Hint's specific examples were taken from the merger
of the two types of words ending in *-ne* or *-s* which are
trisyllabic in the genitive. The earlier pattern, codi-
fied in the standard grammar, required a distinction between them on the basis of the quantity of the first syllable: short and long yield a diphthong and a dental
suffix in the part. pl.; overlong yields an *-i* without
the dental suffix. Standard forms would be *endisi*,
tȍȍlisi vs. *punaseid*, *näljaseid*; what has happened is the
generalization of the form of *punaseid* to produce words
like *endiseid*, *tȍȍliseid*.

Hint's arguments are based on a very extensive study
of the realization of morphological patterns by Estonian
schoolchildren. His tests consisted of 101 words, presented in various ways (e.g. in sentences where the blanks
had to be filled with appropriate forms) to pupils in nine

schools in different parts of the country. Public schools
have eleven grades in Estonia; the tests were taken by
pupils of the fifth, eighth, and eleventh grades. Over
800 pupils participated in the tests, and the number of
forms produced by them was 20,700. The results show that
the form with the diphthong is spreading at the expense
of the form with -*i*. The spread is gradual in every respect: the innovation spreads gradually through the lexicon, the change is most extensive in the youngest group,
and the change is spreading from the north to the south.
Hint describes the change as a simplification of the rule
for the formation of the partitive. The traditional rule
requires specification of the number of syllables AND the
quantity of the first syllable, whereas the new, expanding rule eliminates the specification of the quantity of
the first syllable and requires only the specification of
the number of syllables.

     This is a highly simplified presentation of Hint's
monumental study. (Another aspect of his study involved
presenting similar tests to large groups of Estonian
teachers.) Hint considers a fair number of other morphological types and sees the same tendency in all of them.
The pattern of morphological change constitutes evidence
for ongoing phonological change; the increasing percentage
of innovative forms in the usage of the youngest subjects
makes it possible to predict the direction of the change.

     This does not mean that Hint has abandoned the three-
way quantity system for the description of present-day
Estonian. It should be remembered that three quantities
are needed to describe words that are not subject to degree alternations within a paradigm. Hint's current point
of view is in fact very similar to mine. Hint (personal
communication, Sept. 1, 1980) believes that there are
three contrastive quantities in stressed syllables. The
first quantity is established on the basis of duration.
The distinction between Q2 and Q3 may depend on tone in
voiced syllables, and on duration in cases in which the
contrastive segment is voiceless. Both Q2 and Q3 are
long. In unstressed syllables, there are only two quantities: short and long. The unstressed long is neither
Q2 nor Q3, but a neutralized long degree.

     I would now like to put the development of tone as a
distinctive prosodic feature in a larger framework. In
1978, I published a paper entitled "Polytonicity in the
area surrounding the Baltic Sea." In this paper, I re-
considered the situation around the Baltic Sea which
Jakobson (1931) had used as an example for a Sprachbund
based on features of tone. In general, Germanic and
Baltic languages spoken around the Baltic Sea either have
preserved Indo-European tone in some form (Lithuanian,
Latvian) or have created new tonal systems (Swedish, Danish). The relationship between Latvian and Livonian is
of particular interest in the present context. The prosodic system of Latvian differs from that of Lithuanian
in two basic respects: accent in Latvian is fixed on the

first syllable in contrast to the free accent of Lithuanian, and Latvian has developed a third tone in addition
to the two inherited Indo-European tones which it shares
with Lithuanian. It is generally accepted that these two
differences from Lithuanian are due to contact with Livonian, a Finno-Ugric language with stress on the first
syllable.

The Latvian third tone, manifested as a glottal modification, is phonetically very similar to the Danish stød.
It arose in Latvian in connection with the retraction of
word stress to a first syllable that carried an original
acute. (I am using the term acute to refer to the pitch
pattern that appears in Lithuanian as a long falling tone
and in Latvian as a long even tone.) In words that were
already accented on the first syllable, the acute continued in Latvian as the long even tone. In words in
which the word stress was retracted to an originally unstressed first syllable with the acute, the first syllable
now carried the third tone, often referred to as broken
tone, phonetically similar to the Danish stød. In classical three-accent areas, the sole historical source of
the third tone is this reflex of Baltic and Slavic acute.
In a number of other dialects, the broken tone goes back
to both one of the reflexes of Baltic and Slavic acute
and to all reflexes of Baltic and Slavic circumflex; thus
the third tone may also appear in unaccented syllables
such as affixes and endings.

Evidence for the claim that the development of the
third tone is due to language contact is to be found in
a closer study of Latvian dialects. The so-called Tamian
(or Livonian) dialects of Latvian are spoken in areas for
which there is historical and archeological evidence that
they were formerly inhabited by Livonians. Most of the
Livonians have gradually shifted to Latvian over the past
700 years. In some of the areas Livonian became extinct
by the middle of the 19th century; it survives in Kurzeme,
on the coast, in the speech of a few hundred Latvian-
Livonian bilinguals. The Tamian dialects exhibit a considerable number of characteristics that are clearly
Finno-Ugric in origin, and it is possible to trace the
spread of many such characteristics into the standard
Latvian language.

Although most Livonians have shifted to Latvian (and
Livonian thus constitutes a substratum of Latvian, at
least for the Tamian dialects), the language survives in
Kurzeme and thus is available for investigation. It can
be shown that during the centuries of adstratum relationship, Livonian has, in turn, been influenced by Latvian.
The most dramatic parallel between Latvian and Livonian
is the presence of tonal oppositions in Livonian. No
other Finno-Ugric language has full-fledged phonemic tone.
Livonian has been variously described as having three
tones that are identical with those of Latvian (Posti
1942); as having a phonemic opposition between presence
and absence of stød (Zeps 1962); and as having an

accentual system involving five types of stressed syllables (Viitso 1974). Although Posti (1942) argued that
the rise of stød in Livonian is due to internal factors,
I consider the theory of borrowing from Latvian (Décsy
1965) to be the more plausible one, especially in the
light of extensive borrowing of many other features, both
phonological and grammatical, from Latvian into Livonian.
Taking all factors into consideration, it appears reasonable to assume that the development of tonal oppositions
in Livonian is due to language contact, and thus can be
attributed to the incorporation of Livonian into what
Jakobson (1931) described as a Sprachbund of polytonicity
around the Baltic Sea.

Jakobson included Estonian in the polytonicity-
Sprachbund on the basis of Polivanov's work. Even though
I consider Polivanov's descriptions inaccurate, I do not
doubt that Estonian prosody includes a tonal component.
At this point I should like to recall that Remmel found a
reduction in intensity in overlong quantity which he identified with the Danish stød and the Livonian broken tone.
I have suggested that the pitch contour characteristic of
overlong quantity is due to the transfer of the pitch contour of a whole disyllabic sequence to the first syllable
which became overlong in connection with apocope and syncope; this would support spontaneous tonogenesis in Estonian, without any necessary influence from neighboring
languages. Nevertheless some areal factors may be noted
that could conceivably argue for linguistic convergence.
These include the presence of tone in Lithuanian and Latvian and its documented spread northward into Livonian—
in the direction toward Estonia; the development of the
long-overlong opposition in Estonian, with its associated
pitch differences; and the most recent findings of stød-
like phonetic features in overlong syllable nuclei. The
presence of stød in Latvian and Livonian and its embryonic
emergence in Estonian are at least suggestive of linguistic convergence, even if they cannot be taken as conclusive proof.

Especially interesting in this connection is the recent evidence that some dialects of Finnish may likewise
be in the process of developing contrastive tone. Niemi
and Niemi (1980) carried out an experimental investigation
of southwestern dialects of Finnish in which words of the
type CVCV are developing a half-long vowel in the second
syllable. Their subjects, too, were schoolchildren—14-
year olds, 57 in all. As you may remember, the half-long
vowel in such words is a well-established feature in Estonian. The appearance of a half-long vowel in the second
syllable reduces the phonetic differences between words of
the types CVCV and CVCVV (e.g. *sata* 'hundred' - *sataa* 'it
rains'). One way to keep these words from becoming homophonous is gemination of the intervocalic consonant, and
this is indeed observed in many instances. In the southwestern dialects, however, a difference in the Fo contour
is likewise found on the second syllable: in CVCV, the Fo

contour on the second syllable starts at a higher value
than in CVCVV, so that the subjective impression is of a
rising tone in words like *sata*, even though the rise on
the first syllable in *sata* is no different from that in
sataa. In cases in which the difference in duration of
the second syllable vowels has been neutralized and gemination of the intervocalic consonant does not develop,
pitch may indeed acquire a distinctive function. It is
not claimed by Niemi and Niemi that this development is
due to language contact; it is nevertheless interesting
to note that these dialects of Finnish are spoken in territories adjacent to the Baltic Sea.

Additional evidence for the existence of a
polytonicity-Sprachbund is accumulating. For example,
Ellen Niit (1980) studied the intonation of twelve sentences in the coastal districts of Estonia. There were
173 different subjects and a total of 2076 productions.
The sentence intonation patterns recorded from these subjects were analyzed by means of a computer, and a number
of parameters of the acoustical signal were correlated
with each other. Niit found that the sentence intonation
in Western Estonia, and especially on the islands, was
characterized by a tonal contour in which the syllable
following the stressed syllable had higher pitch than the
stressed syllable. This feature is also found in Scandinavian accents. Niit appeared surprised that the Baltic
Sea did not seem to function as a natural barrier. Of
course there is abundant evidence that for seafaring
people, seas facilitate communication rather than inhib-
iting it. An additional example is provided by a recent
study by Vaba (1979) which documents extensive overlap in
vocabulary between two peninsulas, one belonging to Lat-
via, the other to Estonia, facing each other across the
Irben Strait within the Baltic Sea. The overlap in vocabulary is such that often it cannot be determined which
language borrowed from the other. The only possible explanation is intensive contact across the sea.

The prosodic system of Estonian is changing within the
larger framework of the Sprachbund of which it is a part.
I doubt whether it is going to develop a fourth quantity;
from a phonetician's point of view, it appears more reasonable that if a distinction is needed, it will be based
on a phonetic dimension that can be independently controlled. The most probable direction for development appears to be the emergence of an accentual system, in which
stress, quantity, and tone all play a part.

I would also like to put the ongoing morphological
changes that Hint has so extensively documented into a
larger framework. The phonetic developments that resulted
in the emergence of overlength also eliminated the phonetic features that conditioned the occurrence of weak and
strong degrees of the same stem within a paradigm. This
has led to the morphologization of the formerly phonetic
alternations. Hint's results show that the relative importance of the phonetic shape of the stem is gradually

diminishing: the distinction between inflectional classes
that was formerly based on the quantity of the first syllable of the stem is on the way out. I consider this to
be a further step in the lessening of the role of phonetic
factors in determining the shape of a paradigm; in other
words, a step toward strengthening the relative autonomy
of the paradigm as an element of linguistic structure.

The very special nature of the overlong quantity ultimately derives from the fact that it originally represented a disyllabic sequence. What we are observing at
the moment is the accumulation of evidence that overlong
syllables are losing the characteristics of disyllabicity.
Metaphorically speaking, it seems as if the language is
beginning to forget that overlong syllables were originally disyllabic sequences, and is readjusting itself to
the original system: overlong syllables are beginning to
be treated as if they were just single syllables, and
polysyllabic words are again being structured into disyllabic sequences on the basis of syllable count. This is
particularly clear in the readjustments in the placement
of secondary stress, but becomes evident also from the
changes in the assignment of paradigms to inflectional
types.

Thus there are two changes at work at the same time:
the change directed at eliminating the special status of
overlength, and the change directed at reinterpreting the
significance of the phonetic features accompanying overlength—from a manifestation primarily by quantity to a
manifestation involving contrastive pitch.

One of my purposes in presenting this analysis was to
show that it is indeed possible to study prosodic change
in progress. If prosodic change could be studied only
after it has already taken place, it would not be possible to make predictions. I am predicting now that Estonian will indeed develop into an accentual language. I
hope that there will be a future generation of linguists
interested in Estonian who will submit my prediction to
a conclusive test, and I hope likewise that the language
itself will survive long enough to make this test possible.

REFERENCES

Décsy, G. 1965. *Einführung in die finnisch-ugrische Sprachwis-
      senschaft.* Wiesbaden: Harrassowitz.
Eek, A. 1977. Experiments on the perception of some word series
      in Estonian. *Estonian Papers in Phonetics 1977*:7-33.
———. 1979. Further information on the perception of Estonian
      quantity. *Estonian Papers in Phonetics 1979*:31-57.
Harms, R. 1978. Some observations and hunches concerning Estonian
      prosody. *Estonian Papers in Phonetics 1978*:31-4.
Helimski, E. 1977. Some preliminary data on lexical and tonal
      oppositions in Estonian. *Estonian Papers in Phonetics 1977*:35-8.
Hint, M. 1978. Changes in the prosodical system of contemporary
      Estonian. *Estonian Papers in Phonetics 1978*:39-43.

———. 1979. Minevikuline ja tulevikuline aines keelesüsteemis.
Nõrgaastmeline i-mitmus. *Keel ja Kirjandus* 22:142-49, 200-8.
———. 1980. Minevikuline ja tulevikuline aines keelsüsteemis.
Prosoodiatüübi nihked ja selle tagajärjed. *Keel ja Kirjandus*
23:215-23, 270-8, 349-55.
Jakobson, R. 1931. Über die phonologischen Sprachbünde. *TCLP* 4.
[Reprinted in his *Selected Writings I: Phonological Studies*,
137-43. 's-Gravenhage: Mouton (1962).]
Kask, A. 1972. *Eesti keele ajalooline grammatika I*. 2nd ed.
Tartu: Tartu Riiklik Ülikool.
Kull, R., and E. Raiet. (eds.) 1976. *Õigekeelsus-sõnaraamat*.
Tallinn: Valgus.
Lehiste, I. 1971. Temporal organization of spoken language. *Form
and substance: Phonetic and linguistic papers presented to Eli
Fischer-Jørgensen*, ed. by L. L. Hammerich et al., 155-169.
Copenhagen: Akademisk Forlag.
———. 1975. Experiments with synthetic speech concerning quantity
in Estonian. *Congressus tertius internationalis Fenno-Ugris-
tarum*, 254-69. Tallinn: Valgus.
———. 1978. Polytonicity in the area surrounding the Baltic Sea.
Nordic Prosody, 237-47. Travaux de l'Institut de Linguistique
de Lund 13. Lund.
———, and D. G. Danforth. 1977. Foneettisten vihjeiden hierarkia
viron kvantiteetin havaitsemisessa. *Virittäjä* 4/1977:404-11.
Lippus, U., and M. Remmel. 1976. Some contributions to the study
of Estonian word intonation. *Estonian Papers in Phonetics 1976*:
37-65.
Niemi, J., and S. Niemi. 1980. Finnish half-long vowels, gemination
and word-tone. Manuscript submitted for publication in *Working
Papers in Language and Language Use 1*, Department of Languages,
University of Joensuu.
Niit, E. 1980. The structure of the Baltic prosodic area and the
place of Estonian dialects in it. Preprint KKI-17, Academy of
Sciences of the Estonian SSR. Tallinn.
Polivanov, E. D. 1928. *Vvedenie v jazykoznanie dlja vostokovednyx
vuzov*. Leningrad.
Prince, A. S. 1980. A metrical theory for Estonian quantity.
Linguistic Inquiry 11:511-62.
Posti, L. 1942. *Grundzüge der livischen Lautgeschichte*. Mémoires
de la Société Finno-Ougrienne LXXXV. Helsinki.
Remmel, M. 1975. The phonetic scope of Estonian: Some specifica-
tions. Preprint KKI-5, Academy of Sciences of the Estonian SSR.
Tallinn.
Vaba, L. 1979. Ob estonsko-latyšskix jazykovyx kontaktax. *Soviet
Finno-Ugric Studies* 15:71-5.
Viitso, T.-R. 1974. On the phonological role of stress, quantity,
and stød in Livonian. *Soviet Finno-Ugric Studies* 10:159-70.
———. 1979. Problemy količestva v estonskom jazyke. *Soviet
Finno-Ugric Studies* 15:1-17.
Zeps, V. J. 1962. *Latvian and Finnic linguistic convergences*.
Uralic and Altaic Series, vol. 9. Bloomington: Indiana
University Press.

EVOLUTION OF A SEMANTIC SET: TEXT, DISCOURSE, NARRATIVE

Irmengard Rauch

I

Wittgenstein writes in a letter to Ludwig von Ficker (von Wright 1969:35): "My work consists of two parts: the one presented here plus all that I have not written. And it is precisely the second part that is the important one." Could this quotation be used successfully in the application of the words TEXT, DISCOURSE, and NARRATIVE, which are current in the research of several disciplines including semiotics, linguistics, and literature? Confronted by this question we immediately appeal to *Webster's Third* (1964) for possible clues in the disambiguation of these concepts:

> DISCOURSE n 1 *archaic* a: the act, power, or faculty of thinking consecutively and logically: the process of proceeding from one judgment to another in logical sequence: the reasoning faculty: RATIONALITY b: the capacity of proceeding in an orderly and necessary sequence 2 *obs*: progression of course esp. of events: course of arms: COMBAT 3a: verbal interchange of ideas; often: CONVERSATION b: an instance of such exchange 4a: the expression of ideas; esp: formal and orderly expression in speech and writing b: a talk or piece of writing in which a subject is treated at some length usu. in an orderly fashion 5 *obs* a: power of conversing: conversational ability b: ACCOUNT, NARRATIVE, TALE c: social familiarity; also: familiarity with a subject 6 *linguistics*: connected speech or writing consisting of more than one sentence (647)

> NARRATIVE n 1 *Scots law*: the part of a document containing the recitals; *specif*: the part of a deed immediately following the name and designation of the grantor reciting the inducement for making

28

it   2:   something that is narrated (as the account
of a series of events):   STORY, NARRATION   3:   the
art or study of narrating   4:   the representation
in painting of an event or story or an example of
such a representation (1503)

TEXT   n   1a(1):   the original written or printed
words and form of a literary work   (2):   an edited
or emended copy of the wording of an original work
b: a work containing such text   2a: the main
body of printed or written matter on a page exclusive of headings, running title, footnotes, illustrations, or margins   b: the principal part of
a book exclusive of the front and back matter
c: the printed score of a musical composition
3a(1):   a verse or passage of scripture chosen
esp. for the subject of a sermon or for authoritative support   (2):   a passage from an unauthoritative source providing an introduction or basis (as
for an essay, speech, or lecture)   b: something
providing a chief source of information or authority   c: TEXTBOOK   4a: TEXT HAND   b: a type
considered suitable for printing running text
5a: a subject on which one writes or speaks:
THEME, TOPIC   b: the form and substance of something written or spoken   6:   the words of something (as a poem, libretto, scriptural passage,
folktale) set to music (2365-6)

We may conclude, but not with much conviction, that
perhaps Wittgenstein's written words are primarily text,
his unwritten words primarily discourse, and his letter a
type of narrative. The immediate effect of this conclusion, however, is a mental jolt into the reality of the
terminological pollution in which we find ourselves in the
burgeoning field of an act of verbal behavior, regardless
of our particular research discipline. In particular,
text is interchanged with discourse, and discourse is confused with narrative. The problem of their distinction is
not trivial, if it concerns relevant conceptual differences. The purpose of this paper is to ascertain whether,
in fact, there exist cogent reasons for maintaining these
three terms as independent concepts; if there are such
cogent reasons we are witnessing the rapid evolution of a
semantic set.

II

It appears undeniable that at least at some time in
the history of two of these terms they reflect European
versus State-side wording. Certainly the use of text in
the "*text* linguistics" of Wolfgang Dressler (1973) rings
with greater familiarity to the European ear, while the

use of discourse in Zellig Harris' "*discourse* analysis"
(1952) possibly accounts for the currency of the latter
term in the United States. In brief, there may exist a
layer of purely English versus, in particular, German labeling of this discipline called variously text or discourse linguistics or grammar. With that disclaimer, we
can turn to the definition of the first of these terms,
text. Our working hypothesis is then that there is indeed a terminological distinction to be found in the set
text, discourse, narrative.

Isenberg (1970:1) defines text as "eine kohärente
Folge von Sätzen, wie sie in der sprachlichen Kommunika-
tion Verwendung finden." Petöfi (1973:205) writes: "The
term next will refer ... to a sequence of spoken or written verbal elements functioning as a single whole, which
is qualified according to some (mostly extralinguistic)
criterion as being a 'text.' " These two definitions rest
on underlying coherence conditions in determining text.
Alternately, Gülich/Raible and Hartmann understand text
as a supersign. Gülich/Raible (1977:40-1) write: "Ein
Text, allgemein gesagt, ein sprachliches Zeichen, und zwar
das primäre (bzw. originäre) sprachliche Zeichen ...
Dieses primäre sprachliche Zeichen ist seinerseits aus
weniger umfangreichen, hierarchisch niedrigeren sprachlichen Zeichen aufgebaut ... Texte [werden] nicht in der
Art einer 'linguistique de la parole' betrachtet ... ,
weil sowohl ihre konstitutiven Elemente als auch ihre
konstitutiven Regeln auf der Ebene der Langue erfaßt werden." Hartmann's (1971:10) definition reads: "Der Text,
verstanden als die grundsätzliche Möglichkeit des Vorkom-
mens von Sprache in manifestierter Erscheinungsform, und
folglich jeweils ein bestimmter Text als manifestierte
Einzelerscheinung funktionsfähiger Sprache, bildet das
originäre sprachliche Zeichen."

The above definitions underscore two widely held parameters of text: coherence and supersign; however, they
make no mention of discourse. In these definitions it is
nonexistent as a separate entity. In fact Dressler (1973:
12) defines text as "die höchste sprachliche Einheit" e-
qual to English *discourse*, French *discours*, Italian *dis-
corso*, Russian *tekst*. We need then to turn to those discussions that utilize both words. Halliday (1978:108-9)
defines text as "the instances of linguistic interaction
in which people actually engage: whatever is said or
written, in an operational context, as distinct from a
citational context like that of words listed in a dictionary." Halliday's use of discourse appears synonymous with
that of text. The text is realized in the context of a
theoretical sociolinguistic construct called "situation,"
which is identified in three parts: (a) what is actually
taking place, (b) who is taking part, (c) what part the
language is playing (109-10). In his 1964 *The Linguistic
Sciences and Language Teaching* Halliday, along with Mc-
Intosh and Strevens, calls the three components of the
situation "field of discourse," "style of discourse," and

"mode of discourse," respectively. In his 1978 book
Halliday does not insist on the use of field, style (now
tenor), and mode in a collocation with discourse. Instead
he emphasizes how they are determinants of the text (122,
110). Aside from the above collocations Halliday has two
instances in his 1978 book in which discourse is used in
a rather general concrete sense: to explain that text is
not a supersentence (109) and to attribute genre to each
text (134). Consequently, the most we can perceive in
Halliday's two unqualified uses of the term discourse, is
that discourse is the raw material of text.

Van Dijk in his 1977 *Text and Context: Explorations
in the Semantics and Pragmatics of Discourse* quite clearly
recognizes two separate entities in text and discourse.
He writes (3): "utterances should be reconstructed in
terms of a larger unit, viz. that of TEXT [which] de-
note[s] the abstract theoretical construct underlying
what is usually called a DISCOURSE." Discourse, on the
other hand, van Dijk considers (5) "as a sequence of lin-
early ordered n-tuple of sentences" constrained by semantic and pragmatic rules which differentiate it from com-
posite sentences. For van Dijk then, text is a theoretical unit, while discourse has linguistic flesh and blood—
an attitude which somewhat supports the supersign or
LANGUE concept of Gülich/Raible and Hartmann above. Instead of text linguistics, Gülich (1970) speaks of macro-
syntax in dealing with the text, whereas Halliday (1978:
135) insists that text is a semantic concept, not merely
a supersentence.

Evidence from psycholinguists points to no distinction
in text and discourse, but to a division between syntax
and semantics. Frederiksen in an article entitled "Semantic Processing Units in Understanding Text" (1977:66)
distinguishes "between semantic units (such as events)
and textual units (such as sentences)". Frederiksen seems
to equate text production with discourse production.
Frederiksen, who holds that text structure reflects knowledge structure (57), postulates three decision levels for
what he labels alternately the process of text generation
or discourse production. From the propositional network
or the "message domain" a textual message is chosen. This
message or propositional knowledge is selected through
memory search and pragmatic decisions; it results in level
one, the "message base." To the message base the speaker
or writer applies decisions about sequence, topicalization, reference, and correspondence between semantic and
textual units, yielding level two, the "text base." To
the text base the speaker applies decisions of sentence
structure to yield "a sequence of grammatical sentences
(text)" (67).

Similarly, Hurtig in "Toward a Functional Theory of
Discourse" (1977:101) holds unequivocally that "the sentence is the largest linguistic unit whose structure is
syntactic." Hurtig uses the word text only in the equivalence "text or discourse" (99); he strongly favors the

view that sentence grammars deal primarily with syntactic
constituents, while discourse grammars are concerned mainly with semantic, logical, or cognitive constituents
(102). The text or discourse itself is "a string of successive sentences ... [which] can be monologues, dialogues, or multiperson interchanges ... [and have] topical
or logical structure" (90).

To summarize thus far, the two psycholinguistic studies employ text or discourse interchangeably to designate
a physical set of related sentences which comprise a linguistic message. They hold that the explanation of text
or discourse requires the so-called interactionist theory
of linguistic behavior, which is based on the interaction
of formal linguistic grammar with the principles of perception and production outside the grammatical system.
This position is supported also by linguists such as
Bever, Katz, and Labov in opposition to the so-called in-
clusive theory, which holds that the separation of grammatical facts from linguistic but nongrammatical facts is
arbitrary and intuitively unmotivated. Halliday would
support the psycholinguistic conventions. Van Dijk's notion of discourse approximates the psycholinguistic /
Halliday attitude toward discourse or text, while his notion of text appears closer to that of Gülich/Raible and
Hartmann's supersign.

The viewpoint of the litterateur opens yet other win-
dows on our discussion of text. In particular our hori-
zons are broadened by theories such as those of the Soviet
School (e.g. Lotman, Uspensky), which consider texts as
comprising a system of many and varied interconnected modalities that is tantamount to culture (cf. Shukman 1976,
Baran 1976). However, within literature narrowing trends
exist, for example, that of Marie-Laure Ryan (1979), who
prefers to study a literary system in terms of rules instead of in terms of signs, maintaining that the linguistic sign is limited to the lexicon. Ryan is intent, as
are most literary theorists, on determining the dichotomy
between literary and non-literary texts. She is convinced
that the opposition between literature and non-literature
should be studied with a focus on typology, which includes
genre theory. Her premises are that genre applies only to
a text and a text is a self-sufficient linguistic utterance. She illustrates her thesis by maintaining that conversation, for example, is a type of discourse but not a
type of text. Thus for Ryan text must be governed by
"global requirements and conditions of coherence" (311;
cf. Isenberg, Petöfi above). Such coherence is lacking
in the case of conversation since, she claims, "real-life
dialogues" are comprised merely of "a loose linear ...
concatenation of sentences ... not preventing speakers
from changing topics and interrupting each other" (1979:
311). The distinction here, then, between text and discourse is that the former always falls within genre theory. Observe, however, that Ryan's view of conversation
is in stark contrast with that of Halliday; recall that

in one of the two uses of discourse (above) Halliday
states (1978:134): "there is generic structure in all
discourse, including the most informal spontaneous conversation." For Halliday conversation can qualify indis-
criminately as text or discourse; for Ryan it can only be
discourse, not text. In some anthropological circles the
term text appears to be shunned altogether. Thus, for
example, Butterworth (1978:321) simply speaks of "a piece
of conversational behavior" and Mathiot (1978:203, 217)
refers to language as but one possible ingredient of "communicative episodes." In another article, "The Theoretical Status of Discourse" (1979), Mathiot says outright
that "Discourse is not a part of language."
    Nevertheless, Halliday does consider the possibility
of NON-TEXT. He postulates three factors to designate
text in opposition to non-text. Besides generic structure
and the commonly held cohesion principle, Halliday speaks
of textual structure, that is, thematic and informational
patterns which contribute to the well-formedness of the
texture. He demonstrates (1978:134) that the thematic
structure is scrambled in the following, and consequently
it is a non-text:

> Now comes the President here. It's the window he's
> stepping through to wave to the crowd. On his vic-
> tory his opponent congratulates him. What they are
> shaking now is hands. A speech is going to be made
> by him. 'Gentlemen and ladies. That you are con-
> fident in me honours me. I shall, hereby pledge I,
> turn this country into a place, in which what peo-
> ple do safely will be live, and the ones who grow
> up happily will be able to be their children.'

    Ryan (1979), in turn, identifies two sorts of texts
in literature which do NOT have coherent logico-semantic
representations; the one is nonsense poetry, the second
is what litterateurs have come to label simply as "text,"
which refers to avant-garde literature well formed at the
sentence level, but ill-formed at the sentence concatenation level. If nonsense poetry and avant-garde "text" can
qualify as text, then it would seem reasonable that sentence sequence sets of schizophrenics, seniles, or small
children should likewise qualify as text. Van Dijk (1972:
308) would exclude these on the basis of lack of semantic
coherence. Consider, for example, the following "representative of 'schizophrenic language' " as cited by
Lorenz (1961:604):

> Contentment? Well uh, contentment, well the word
> contentment, having a book perhaps, perhaps your
> having a subject, perhaps you have a chapter of
> reading, but when you come to the word "men" you
> wonder if you should be content with men in your
> life and then you get to the letter T and you
> wonder if you should be content having tea by

> yourself or be content with having it with a
> group or so forth.

The passage appears less grammatically scrambled than
Halliday's "non-text" citation above. Whether we would
judge it as necessarily schizophrenic, had we seen it in
isolation, is an open question. Lorenz would answer the
question with a qualified affirmative; she writes (603):
"We are faced with the paradox that while we recognize
schizophrenic language when we see it, we cannot define
it." But Brown (1973:400) tells us "that only some of
the linguistic productions of schizophrenics appear dis-
organized or deluded; very many do not." In view of the
qualifying of nonsense poetry and avant-garde literature
as text and in view of the inability of linguistics to
define satisfactorily pathological language, it appears
that the coherence condition requires revision to embrace
texts which do not pass the standard coherence test.

Returning to Lotman, non-text occurs "the moment when
a simple fact of linguistic expression ceases to be perceived as sufficient for a linguistic message to become a
text" (cited in Rewar 1976:362-3); in its stead the cultural "text" emerges. Barthes (1971, 1968) prefers to
speak of more or less text in which text represents the
new. By text he means not so much a positive object with
well-marked boundaries, but more a methodological field,
a syntagm, a chain of meaning. Again text becomes a very
broad concept in the hands not so much of the litterateurs
Lotman and Barthes, but of the semiotists Lotman and
Barthes.

III

Let us now shift the focus to the association of discourse with narrative as part of this evolving terminological set. In narratology proper, discourse is the second arm of a complex sign function, the first being STORY
according to Barthes (1966) and Todorov (1966). Here discourse refers to Hjelmslev's "expression plane," Saussure's
"significant." Thus Greimas considers discourse to be the
primary datum in every sentence concatenation; he speaks
of scientific discourse, interpretive discourse such as
art criticism, persuasive discourse such as advertising
(Greimas/Courtés 1976).

However, Greimas is convinced that "every discourse
entails a narrative dimension" (Nef 1977:19). He introduces (1977:29) a propositional formula for a minimal narrative utterance, "NU = F(A)," which is reminiscent of
van Dijk's (1972:307) "deep structures ... similar to the
internal structure of the propositions in a modal predi-
cate logic." Not only do Greimas and van Dijk overlap in
their propositional base (function:actant, relation:argu-
ment, predicate:subject), both are engaged in identifying
global modalities. Thus van Dijk (1977) works with the
mental structures of action such as wants, desires,

intentions, purposes, while Greimas (Greimas and Courtés
1976:443) postulates three *"modalities* of doing": *"voli-
tion-to-do,"* *"cognition-to-do,"* and *"power-to-do."*   To
these fundamental features we may add still another global
category which we call "inferential structure" (cf. Rauch
forthcoming), structure which emulates the way we think,
our basic tripartite thought process consisting of a general proposition, a specific proposition, and a conclusion.   Thus the Aristotelian concept of narrative action
composed, in essence, of an orientation, complication, and
resolution, parallels the basic inference.   Van Dijk
(1977:245-6) extends the "conventional organization of
discourse [to those] ... of the corresponding speech acts,
and of action in general," while Greimas (1971:793)
states: "Narrative structures are distinct from linguistic structures because they can be revealed by languages
other than the natural languages   (in   cinema,   dreams,
etc.)."

It must be amply clear from the immediately preceding
discussion that narrative is not bound to literary language, written language, or even to language in its ordinary sense (cf. further Rauch forthcoming).   Less important is the observation, which is a terminological matter,
that van Dijk's use of discourse approximates Greimas' use
of narrative (for van Dijk narrative is a genre type,
1977:243).   However, the extension of narrative beyond
verbal language to nonverbal communication certainly be-
speaks a conceptual breakthrough.   It makes quite palata-
ble Mathiot's rather provocative statement (quoted above)
that "Discourse is not a part of language."   Indeed, one
does not have to look far for concrete applications of
this concept: consider, for example, Bouissac's (1977:
149-50) description of a circus act as a "primarily visual
meta-discourse ... a micro-narrative."

IV

We return now to our experimental data, the Wittgenstein quotation and the definitions in *Webster's Third* of
text, discourse, narrative.   Faced with having to pit the
Wittgenstein quotation against the three dictionary entries our initial intuitions yielded no strong prejudices
in assigning Wittgenstein's written words, unwritten
words, and letter.   In fact, the original task appeared
unfruitful since the dictionary senses of the three terms
do not strike individually discriminating tones.   As the
dictionary compilers warn of their definitions (*Webster's
Third* 1964:19a):   "The system of separating [the sense] by
numbers and letters ... is only a lexical convenience.   It
does not evaluate senses or establish an enduring hierarchy of importance among them.   The best sense is the one
that most aptly fits the context of an actual genuine
utterance."   Yet the dictionary glosses of "ideas" for
discourse may have influenced its assignment to unwritten
words, namely, the whole world of Wittgenstein's thoughts,

while text and narrative fell then to the more concrete written words and letter, the former having appeared more general and accordingly more appropriate to the seemingly wider latitude offered by the many dictionary glossings of text.

Such floundering in terminological uncertainty, however, is entirely absent in the evolving usage which we document in the crossdisciplinary applications of text, discourse, narrative for acts of verbal and verbal-like behavior. Albeit the parameters we are seeking are similar, the terms shift considerably. At its simplest the following distinctions hold to bind the emerging semantic set:

	text	discourse	narrative
physical	+	+	
abstract	+		+
	(letter)	(written words)	(unwritten words)

Compelling arguments for this evolving triad come from Peircean semiotics. Here all phenomena, including language, action, and thought, are signs; indeed man himself is a sign, to quote Sebeok (1977:181): "man is ... a process of communication ... , or, in short, a TEXT" (emphasis mine). Beyond this, however, the glue for cementing this semantic set resides in Peirce's phenomenological categories of Firstness, Secondness, and Thirdness, into which we can set text as a First, discourse as a Second, and narrative as a Third. Alternately, text is the sign proper, discourse is the object, and narrative is the interpretant within Peirce's classic definition (1931:§339): "A sign [text] stands FOR something [discourse], TO the idea [narrative] which it produces or modifies." The qualities of the categories serve to reinforce the assignment of the terms. Thus, a letter is mere possibility and belongs to the past, written words exist in fact and are part of the present, while unwritten words have imputed existence and belong to the future thought. That these qualities interlace is to be expected, since that factor is inherent in all phenomena; nonetheless, their PRIMARY qualities serve to identify them distinctively. What remains of the features reviewed above such as syntax:semantics, sign:rule, genre:non-genre; coherence:incoherence, text:non-text, more text:less text, normal language: pathological, child, and senile language is relegated to connotative senses in the evolving set of definitions within a study which is then most graphically (iconically) termed TEXT GRAMMAR.

REFERENCES

Baran, Henryk. (ed.) 1976. *Semiotics and structuralism: Readings from the Soviet Union.* White Plains, NY: International Arts and Sciences Press.

Barthes, Roland. 1966. Introduction à l'analyse structurale des récits. *Communications* 8:1-27.

———. 1968. *Elements of semiology*. Trans. by A. Lavers and C. Smith. New York: Hill and Wang.

———. 1971. De l'oeuvre au texte. *Revue d'Esthétique* 24:225-32.

Bouissac, Paul. 1977. Semiotics and spectacles: The circus institution and representations. *A perfusion of signs*, ed. by T. A. Sebeok, 143-52. Bloomington: Indiana University Press.

Brown, Roger. 1973. Schizophrenia, language, and reality. *American Psychologist* 28:395-403.

Butterworth, Brian. 1978. Maxims for studying conversations. *Semiotica* 24:317-39.

Dressler, Wolfgang. 1973. *Einführung in die Textlinguistik*. 2nd ed. Tübingen: Niemeyer.

Frederiksen, Carl H. 1977. Semantic processing units in understanding text. *Discourse production and comprehension*, ed. by R. O. Freedle, 57-87. Norwood, NJ: Ablex.

Greimas, A. J. 1971. Narrative grammar: Units and levels. *Modern Language Notes* 86:793-806.

———, and Joseph Courtés. 1976. The cognitive dimension of narrative discourse. *New Literary History* 7:433-47.

Gülich, Elisabeth. 1970. *Gliederungssignale in der Makrosyntax des gesprochenen Französisch*. Munich: Fink.

———, and Wolfgang Raible. 1977. *Linguistische Textmodelle. Grundlagen und Möglichkeiten*. Munich: Wilhelm Fink.

Halliday, Michael Alexander Kirkwood. 1978. *Language as a social semiotic: The social interpretation of language and meaning*. Baltimore: University Park Press.

———; Angus McIntosh; and Peter Strevens. 1964. *The linguistic sciences and language teaching*. London: Longman.

Harris, Zellig S. 1952. Discourse analysis. *Language* 28:1-30.

Hartmann, Peter. 1971. Texte als linguistisches Objekt. *Beiträge zur Textlinguistik*, ed. by W.-D. Stempel, 9-29. Munich: Wilhelm Fink.

Hurtig, Richard. 1977. Toward a functional theory of discourse. *Discourse production and comprehension*, ed. by R. O. Freedle, 89-106. Norwood, NJ: Ablex.

Isenberg, Horst. 1970. Der Begriff "Text" in der Sprachtheorie. *Arbeitsstelle Strukturelle Grammatik*, Berlin: Deutsche Akademie der Wissenschaften zu Berlin, Bericht 8.

Lorenz, Maria. 1961. Problems posed by schizophrenic language. *Archives of General Psychiatry* 5:406-10.

Mathiot, Madeleine. 1978. Toward a frame of reference for the analysis of face to face interaction. *Semiotica* 24:199-220.

———. 1979. The theoretical status of discourse. Paper presented at the Fourth Annual Meeting of the Semiotic Society of America.

Nef, Frederic. 1977. Introduction to the reading of Greimas: Toward a discursive linguistics. *Diacritics* March 1977:18-22.

Peirce, Charles Sanders. 1931. *Collected papers of Charles Sanders Peirce*, ed. by. I. C. Hartshorne and P. Weiss. Cambridge, MA: Harvard University Press.

Petöfi, János. S. 1973. Towards an empirically motivated grammatical theory of verbal texts. *Studies in text grammar*, ed. by J. S. Petöfi and H. Rieser, 205-75. Dordrecht: D. Reidel.

Rauch, Irmengard. Forthcoming. Semiotics in search of method. *Semiotica*.

Rewar, Walter. 1976. Notes for a typology of culture. *Semiotica* 18:361-78.

Ryan, Marie-Laure. 1979. Toward a competence theory of genre. *Poetics* 8:307-37.

Sebeok, Thomas A. 1977. Ecumenicalism in semiotics. *A perfusion of signs*, ed. by T. A. Sebeok, 180-206. Bloomington: Indiana University Press.

Shukman, Ann. 1976. *Literature and semiotics: A study of the writings of Yuri Lotman*. Amsterdam: North Holland.

Todorov, Tzvetan. 1966. Les catégories du récit littéraire. *Communications* 8:125-51.

Webster's Third New International Dictionary of the English Language Unabridged. 1964. Springfield, MA.

Van Dijk, Teun. 1972. Foundations for typologies of texts. *Semiotica* 6:297-323.

———. 1977. *Text and context: Explorations in the semantics and pragmatics of discourse*. London: Longman.

Von Wright, Georg Henrik, and Walter Methlagl. (eds.) *Briefe an Ludwig von Ficker I*. Salzburg: Otto Müller.

Part II

HISTORICAL CHANGE

THE DEVELOPMENT OF THE GERMANIC REDUPLICATING CLASS:
REANALYSIS AND COMPETITION IN MORPHOLOGICAL CHANGE

Frans van Coetsem

1. INTRODUCTION

1.1. The replacement of one morphological pattern by another in historical development often follows an indirect route and as such is a provocative problem in the study of language change. A primary example of this is found in the Germanic language family. In the Germanic parent language there was a class of reduplicating verbs, i.e. verbs using REDUPLICATION for indicating the preterite: present = root ᴧ preterite = reduplicative element + root. This principle was preserved in Gothic. In North and West Germanic, however, it was replaced by different new formations, especially one applying the well-known ablaut principle. The modalities of the development from reduplication to ablaut have been, since Grimm, a subject of hot debate, with none of the numerous attempts to solve the problem receiving general acceptance.

Although we now concur with Bech (1969) in explaining the development from reduplication to ablaut as a result of morphological REANALYSIS of the reduplicated form, we crucially disagree with him about the form of this reanalysis. Unlike Bech we consider the full implications of the Germanic accent shift for this reanalysis. Furthermore, while he views the different new formations resulting from the reanalysis mainly as successive stages in the development from reduplication to ablaut, we see them as parallel and competing with one another, with the structurally most adequate formation, one based on ablaut, being ultimately the only one to survive. The development of the Germanic reduplicating class offers then a prototypical case of reanalysis and competition in morphological change.

1.2. Germanic had a relatively small class of mainly nonablauting verbs that used the reduplication principle for indicating the preterite, e.g. present-infinitive *Xait- ᴧ preterite *Xexait-, *laik- ᴧ *lelaik-.[1]

1.2.1. This principle was preserved in East Germanic,
namely Gothic, e.g. present-infinitive *haitan* ∿ preterite
haihait, aukan ∿ *aiauk, fallan* ∿ *faifall, slepan* ∿ *saislep,*
flokan ∿ *faiflok*; in some cases the verb was also ablauting, *letan* ∿ *lailot*.

1.2.2. In the earliest documented stages of the North
and West Germanic languages, however, the reduplication
principle appears to have deteriorated, and to have been
replaced by different mechanisms.

(i) A so-called *r* preterite formation, a formation
with internal *r*, is documented clearly in Old Norse (ON),
Old High German (OHG), and hypothetically in Old English
(OE).

(α) In ON it occurred exclusively in verba pura, i.e.
in verbs with vowel final roots, e.g. *rōa* ∿ *rera, sā* ∿
sera, grōa ∿ *grera, snūa* ∿ *snera*. Such verbs were limited
in number. In a case like *sā* ∿ *sera*, when compared to
Gothic *saian* ∿ *saiso*, the original reduplication principle
is easily recognizable. Considering its productivity
-(*e*)*ra* was in such forms obviously felt as a suffixal
formation, in which the conjugation endings, *a*, etc., were
those of the weak preterite (singular). As a suffixation
the formation is somewhat comparable with the dental preterite of the weak conjugation. Yet it was unusual, and
as such must have been subject to shift and analogy; cf.,
e.g. the fact that *sā* was weak in Old Swedish (Noreen 1904:
449).

(β) In other Germanic languages the verba pura were
treated differently and were often weak. They could develop or generalize glides *y,w* between the verbal root and
the inflectional endings, and thus acquire a more regular
consonant final root type (Van Coetsem 1956:66-9, Rauch
1972). In OHG the *r* preterite formation is found in one
original verbum purum; this, however, developed a glide
and became a verb with consonant final root. It is documented only in *biruuuis/biruuis* ∿ *būwan/būan* (South-
Rhenish Franconian, Otfrid). We should note that the regular preterite form was *būta*. Otherwise in OHG the verba
pura (*bluoen, gruoen, sāen*) were generally weak (Braune-
Mitzka 1959:284).

Besides *biruuuis, biruun*, and outside the limited group
of verba pura, there were some other OHG *r* preterites,
which are documented only in *pleruzzun, capleruzzi* ∿
bluozan (normally weak, *plōzta*, past participle strong,
kaplōzan; pl- Alemannic for *bl-*), *kiscrerot* (documented
only once) ∿ *scrōtan; steroz/sterozun* ∿ *stōzan* (cf. also
Kögel 1892:500-1, Schatz 1907:152). These forms were
Upper German, mainly Alemannic. Since South-Rhenish
Franconian (*biruuuis, biruun*) constitutes a transition
area to Alemannic, the OHG *r* preterites were by and large

found in Upper German. The formation is very scantily
documented and clearly residual, disappearing in the later
development of German. The verbs *scrōtan* and *stōzan* regularly had the new ablaut pattern as a preterite formation
[see (iii) below], while *bluozan* was   normally   weak
(Braune-Mitzka 1959:284).

(ii) OE had some forms in which the reduction of the
second, nonprominent syllable resulted in the disappearance of that syllable. These forms generally appear to be
the outcome of CONTRACTION of the original reduplicative
element and the verbal root. They were Anglian [cf.,
however, *heht* under (α) below] and of restricted usage
(e.g. poetic). Co-occurring with this formation were
forms showing a new ablaut formation [see (iii) below],
the latter being the regular formation in West Saxon, and
also weak forms (cf., e.g. Sievers-Brunner 1951:335-40).
The shift to the weak conjugation became more pronounced
in the subsequent development of English. By the time of
Middle English the contracted forms had disappeared.

(α) Some cases are fairly obvious examples of contraction: *heht* (occurring also in West Saxon texts, beside *hēt*) ∿ *hātan*, *leolc* ∿ *lācan*, *beoftun* ∿ *bēatan* and
speoft/speaft, *speoftun*, probably belonging to *spātan*.

(β) Similar cases have generally, though not always,
been viewed as contracted forms as well: *reord/hreordun*
(the latter as mentioned in Sievers-Brunner 1951:336, beside *rēdon* and some weak forms) ∿ *rēdan*, West Saxon *rǣdan/*
ondreord/ondreard (in West Saxon also weak, *ondrǣdde*) ∿
ondrēdan, West Saxon *ondrǣdan*, and *leort/forleortun* (beside *lēt*) ∿ *lētan*, West Saxon *lǣtan*. The form *leort* is
ordinarily assumed to result from **leolt* with dissimilation. If *leort* is considered an analogical formation
after, e.g. *reord*, though, we could regard these forms
as *r* preterites in Old English (Anglian). Actually, Bech
(1969:23) considers such forms *r* preterites, but he does
so in a perspective quite different from ours.

(iii) There is also a formation showing a new ablaut
pattern, whose origin remains unexplained. It became the
dominant usage throughout the North and West Germanic language area, and is the so-called NORMAL TYPE (Bech 1969:
e.g. 15). The original, basic form of the new ablaut pattern has been generally reconstructed as follows (cf.,
e.g. Hirt 1932:144):

$$\text{present } ai/\bar{e}^1 \sim \text{ preterite } \bar{e}^2$$
$$au/\bar{o} \sim \qquad\qquad eo \ (e\underset{.}{u})$$
$$a \qquad \sim \qquad\qquad e \ (\bar{e}^2)$$

The following examples from OHG, ON, and OE reflect
the ORIGINAL, BASIC ablaut pattern: OHG *heizan* ∿ *hiez*,
lāzan ∿ *liez*, *(h)loufan* ∿ *liof*, *(h)ruofan* ∿ *riof*, *fallan* ∿

fiel, ON *heita* ∿ *hēt*, *lāta* ∿ *lēt*, *hlaupa* ∿ *hljōp*, *falla* ∿
fell, OE *hātan* ∿ *hēt*, *lētan/lǣtan* ∿ *lēt*, *hlēapan* ∿ *hlēop*,
hrōpan ∿ *hrēop*, *feallan* ∿ *fēoll/feoll*.

The above-mentioned pattern is called BASIC because
certain phonic variants and forms of a more incidental
nature may have been present alongside it from the start.
It is also called ORIGINAL because it was subsequently affected by changes, shifts, or analogical extensions (for
more details, cf., e.g. Van Coetsem 1956:56-69 and 1963).
Since minor aspects of these distinctions are subject to
discussion, the reconstruction of the original basic form
of the new ablaut formation itself may be to a certain degree debatable. In general a combination of criteria
(time, degree of expansion, and nature of the occurrence
of the form) allows us to establish what is original and
what is not.

(iv) An example of a much more sporadic formation is
seen in cases where the forms of the present and the preterite were completely identical (no reduplication, ablaut,
or other differentiating factor), e.g. ON *heita* ∿ *heit*,
sveipa ∿ *sveip*, OE *gangan* ∿ *gang*.

1.3. Thus, the three most important new preterite
formations in the North and West Germanic reduplicating
class were the *r* preterites, the OE contracted forms (including possible examples of the *r* preterite formation),
and the new ablaut formation. In areas where they coexisted, they were in competition. Yet the *r* preterites
and the OE contracted forms were moribund phenomena. They
appear to be peripheral in the North and West Germanic
area,[2] and to exhibit only residual and restricted usages
next to the prevalent new ablaut formation, which was used
virtually throughout the whole area. Outside the reduplicated class, the weak conjugation appears to be the fourth
competitor. In later development it became more and more
influential, and in certain cases it totally supplanted
the new ablaut formation.

1.4. In the present study we hope to provide at least
an acceptable basis for explaining the development, occurrence, and interrelationship of these new preterite formations, especially the new ablaut formation. For this
we will follow the general language evolution step by
step, considering the chronological order of the changes
involved and their respective impact on the development
of the reduplicating class. In conjunction with this we
will carefully examine the different formations, paying
equal attention to each of them; in this we basically follow an approach advocated by Bech (1969: e.g. 15, 54).
These formations constitute precisely the main focus of
our study, not the changes, shifts, or analogical extensions which reduplicating verbs have undergone in the
subsequent development of the separate Germanic languages.

1.5. We will view and discuss in greater detail in
our further treatment the development of the Germanic reduplicating class. The following, however, may serve as
a general outline.

As a result of changes, of which the accent shift was
the most determinant, the reduplication principle became
increasingly weakened and obscured. In Gothic the development was REVERSED, that is, the reduplication principle
was preserved or reinstated. In North and West Germanic,
speakers may occasionally have resorted to the same procedure, but in general, REANALYSIS WAS APPLIED to the reduplicated form. In this reanalysis the reduplicative
element, e.g. *le- in *lelaik-, was reinterpreted as the
initial part of the verbal root, while the initial part
of the verbal root, as -la- in *lelaik-, was felt not to
belong to the root any more, although it did not necessarily or immediately acquire affixal (morphemic) status.
To indicate this, we will use the term SPECIFIC NONROOT
MATERIAL; it is specific insofar as it is differentiated
from other nonroot elements such as affixes.[3] Bech (1969:
9) does not make such a distinction and considers the reanalysis in question a direct change from a reduplicated
or prefixed form to an infixed form (the latter becoming
suffixed in the case of the ON verba pura).[4]

In spite of certain lexical and distributional readjustments that seem to have affected the reanalyzed preterite form over the whole of the North and West Germanic
area, this form remained structurally inadequate due to
the combination of two mutually supportive factors. These
were its generally BISYLLABIC ROOT STRUCTURE   and   the
SPECIFIC NONROOT MATERIAL. They were extremely unusual
features within the paradigm of the strong verb; their
deviant character is readily apparent when the reanalyzed
preterite form is compared with the unmarked present (or
nonpast), whose monosyllabic root structure was representative of the general root type of the strong verb.[5] Yet,
through the reanalysis the constant e of the original reduplicated form (i.e. e as in *lelaik-) was brought within
the bounds of the verbal root, yielding a new ablaut pattern, present (a in *laik-) ∿ preterite (e in *lelaik-).
Ablaut was precisely the dominant principle for differentiating principal parts within the paradigm of the
strong verb. Through further corrective or "remedial"
changes (Malkiel 1969:26), PARALLELING and COMPETING formations developed. In this way the r preterites, the OE
contracted forms, and the formation showing the new ablaut
pattern arose. While the r preterites analogically generalized one form of the specific nonroot material, namely
r, the OE contracted forms, preserving the specific nonroot material in its different forms, reduced the original
bisyllabic preterite to a monosyllabic structure. On the
other hand, the new ablaut formation resulted from a consistent structural re-formation of the reanalyzed preterite form based on the model of the present; the new

preterite form evolving this way was monosyllabic and did
not contain the specific nonroot material.

1.6.   The three formations reflect to different degrees a well-known basic principle of language development
aiming at structural generalization and adequacy.   This
principle promotes generalization, the PRESERVATION of
what is structurally relevant or motivated, and the LOSS
or REJECTION of what is structurally irrelevant or unmotivated.   The operation of this principle is, however,
relativized by the indeterminate and gradual nature of
such notions as RELEVANCE or MOTIVATEDNESS.   It may also
be counteracted by a number of things, such as the high
frequency of the lexical items or patterns involved.   It
goes without saying that the degree of, e.g. relevance or
motivatedness of a given element may vary from one developmental stage to another.

Preservation and rejection reveal themselves in certain circumstances as "defense mechanisms" of the language.   They are directed at maintaining, as much as possible, the existing structural properties of the language,
in particular its distributional characteristics and root
structure.   It is well known that when a language is (suddenly) confronted with deviations from its structural
properties, as may be the case with borrowing or reanalysis, it will tend to eliminate or adapt these deviations
(the notion of DEVIATION being again a relative and gradual one).   Uhlenbeck's work (1966[1949]) on the Javanese
morpheme is in this respect illustrative.

In the reanalyzed preterite form the generally bisyllabic root structure and the specific nonroot material
were both structurally deviant and deficient in structural
relevance or motivatedness, ablaut being the primarily
relevant principle for differentiating, e.g. the preterite
from the present within the paradigm of the strong verb.
This made the bisyllabic root structure and the specific
nonroot material susceptible to loss.   It is a significant
fact that the above-mentioned basic principle was only
partly effected in the r preterites and the OE contracted
forms (the bisyllabic root structure and/or the specific
nonroot material being preserved), but was consistently
carried through in the new ablaut formation (the bisyllabic root structure and the specific nonroot material being
lost).   This difference underscores the fact that the r
preterites and the OE contracted forms were, at the time
of documentation, residual and peripheral, while the new
ablaut formation became the dominant usage, being precisely THE MOST COMPATIBLE WITH THE STRUCTURE AND DEVELOPMENT
OF THE LANGUAGE.

1.7.   The development of the reduplicating class in
North and West Germanic thus offers a highly illustrative
case of competition in the realm of morphological change,
with the structurally most adequate formation being ultimately the only one preserved.   In such a perspective one

cannot but compare with a TRIAL AND ERROR procedure. The
notion of COMPETITION has long been recognized in various
forms of language change. With reference to sound change,
the term was coined by Wang (1969) together with a theoretical discussion of the notion; illustrations with a
discussion of the phenomenon are found earlier, e.g. in
Van Wijk (1936:70), Van Coetsem (1956:38).

1.8. The above also shows that we have modified our
earlier stand on the topic (a stand that employed the
notion of inverted analogy), as first set forth in our
study of 1956. We will discuss this further in Appendix
I. In that earlier work we reviewed rather extensively
previous research. In the present treatment (especially
Appendix II) we take particular note of more recent work,
primarily Bech's (1969), which, although unsatisfactory
as a whole, may be credited with some useful ideas.

2.   THE WEAKENING OF THE REDUPLICATION PRINCIPLE

2.1. The reduplication principle in the Germanic reduplicating class is of Indo-European origin. Like ablaut
in other verbs it distinguished verbal morphological categories. Three changes in the development of the Germanic
parent language, each acting in a different way and with
different impact, weakened the reduplication principle.
These were the $\breve{a}$-$\breve{o}$ merger, the accent shift, and Verner's
Law. The last two changes were closely related, in that
Verner's Law may be considered a segmental reflex of the
accent shift.

2.2. The $\breve{a}$-$\breve{o}$ merger appears to have chronologically
preceded the accent shift, or at least the latter's completion. The following can support this assumption.

2.2.1. First, there may be system-internal evidence.
Raising and lowering changes (umlaut- and consonant-
conditioned changes) seem to have operated with or directly after the accent shift (Van Coetsem 1956: e.g. 38).
The $\breve{a}$-$\breve{o}$ merger counterfed one of these changes; specifically, the $\breve{a}$-$\breve{o}$ merger (short vowels) preceded $u > o$. We
have then the following diachronic order:

(1) a-$o > a$ (originally $\overset{\circ}{a}$)
       $u > o$

If the changes had occurred in the reverse order, namely,

(2) $u > o$
       a-$o > a$

the resulting a would show reflexes of Indo-European u,
which is not the case. Of course, such argumentation is
not completely watertight, because the o's involved in the
two changes may have been of different quality and status.

2.2.2. Second, there is system-external evidence, which, although not compelling, has confirming power. It concerns the areal-linguistic fact that the ă-ŏ merger shows a wider spread within the Indo-European language family (Germanic, Slavic, Baltic, etc.) than the accent shift, the latter being a shift of both the nature and the place of the accent (Germanic and Old Irish). Thus we can assume that the ă-ŏ merger preceded both the accent shift and Verner's Law.

2.3. We will now discuss the effects of the three changes on the reduplication class.

2.3.1. The ă-ŏ merger introduced a paradigmatic re-arrangement of verbs into a so-called *a* group, based on the vocalism of the present. Aside from the reduplicating class (*Xait-, *Xlaup-, *fall-; cf. OHG *heizan*, (*h*)*loufan*, *fallan*) this *a* group then contained the traditional 6th ablaut series (*far-, *grab-;[6] cf. OHG *faran*, *graban*). Al-though its constituents are clearly of Indo-European ori-gin, the *a* group is a Germanic formation. It tended to organize itself along the lines of the older *e* group, which had *e* as vocalism of the present. It contained the traditional ablaut series 1 to 5 (*reid-, *leug-, *Xelp-, *stel-, *geb-; cf. OHG *rītan*, *liogan*, *helfan*, *stelan*, *geban*). Each of the two groups had specific structural properties. In addition to the *e* and *a* groups, there were a number of ē and ō (originally ā̊) verbs (*slēp-, *lēt-, *Xwōp-/*Xwāp-; cf. OHG *slāfan*, *lāzan*, Gothic *hwopan*), with some of the ē verbs being not only reduplicating, but also ablauting (ē ∿ ō) (for more details, see Van Coetsem 1980). Within this overall, cohesive system of the so-called strong verbs, reduplication would clearly consti-tute a minority principle and be therefore strongly sub-ject to pressure from ablaut.

2.3.2. The accent shift contributed more directly, and with far more impact than the ă-ŏ merger, to the weakening process of the reduplication principle. It led to the obscuring and even disruption of that principle. The accent shift involved two changes, one of NATURE and one of PLACE. The change of nature concerns a change from a NONDOMINATING to a DOMINATING PROMINENCE (Van Coetsem-Hendricks-McCormick 1981), which is traditionally but im-properly called a change from a PITCH to a STRESS ACCENT. The change of place refers to a change from a FREE to a FIXED PROMINENCE, namely an initial or root syllable prominence.

(i) The sound change referred to as Verner's Law, i.e. the voicing of the Germanic fricatives *f*, *þ*, *X*, *s* to *b*, *d*, *g*, *z* [ƀ, đ, ǥ, z], under accent conditioning, presupposes only a change of nature and not a change of place, since Verner's Law is conditioned by an

Indo-European accent placement. For example, the alternation *þ* ᴧ *ð* [-đ-] for Indo-European *t*, under accent conditioning, is shown by Gothic *broþar* [-þ-] ᴧ *fadar* [-đ-]
as compared to Greek φράτηρ, Sanskrit *bhrātar-* vs. Greek
πατήρ, Sanskrit *pitár-*.

It is worth noting that Verner himself had already
come to that conclusion concerning the order   of the
changes of nature and place. This is clearly apparent in
his own words: "Erst nachdem sich das germanische von
seinem nächsten verwandten, dem slavo-litauischen geschie-
den und sein sonderleben angefangen hatte, treffen wir den
accent in seinem wesen etwas verändert: er war expirato-
risch geworden oder vielleicht, da er wohl noch seinem
chromatischen character behielt, chromatisch-expiratorisch.
Aber die zweite characteristische eigenschaft, die frei-
heit, hatte die urgermanische accentuation in wunderbarer
vollständigkeit behauptet. Der dann folgende übergang zur
gebundenen accentuation (wurzelbetonung) ist eine gründ-
lich durchgeführte analogiebildung." (Rooth 1974:28).

While the present form of a reduplicating verb has one
anlaut, the corresponding reduplicated form of the preterite may be analyzed as having two. Here we will follow
Bech (1969:4) in calling the anlaut of the reduplicated
form the ABSOLUTE ANLAUT and the anlaut of the verbal
root, as also found in the present, the THEMATIC ANLAUT.
For example, in the preterite **XeXlaup-*, the absolute
anlaut is *X* while the thematic anlaut is *Xl*, also found
in the present **Xlaup-*.

The reduplication principle derives the absolute anlaut from the thematic anlaut by specifying that: (1) Before vowels the reduplicative element consists of the vowel *e* (Gothic *ai*, e.g. **auk-* ᴧ **eauk-*; cf. Gothic *aukan* ᴧ
aiauk). (2) Before one or more consonants of the thematic
anlaut the reduplicative element consists of one consonant
(the first) + *e* (e.g. **Xait-* ᴧ **XeXait-*,   **frais-* ᴧ
*fefrais; cf. Gothic *haitan* ᴧ *haihait, fraisan* ᴧ *faifrais*).
However, when the thematic anlaut is *st* or *sk* (*sp* not being documented) the reduplicative element consists of this
cluster + *e* (e.g. **staut-* ᴧ **stestaut-*; cf. Gothic *stauten*
ᴧ *staistaut*). In Gothic, *hw* (<ƕ>) is treated as one consonant (monophonematic) (e.g. *hwopan* ᴧ *hwaihwop*). It is
important to note that the vowel *e* is the ONLY CONSTANT
in the reduplicative element.

As we have seen, Verner's Law emerged with or after
the change of nature of the accent. That it also was applied to the thematic anlaut of the reduplicated forms can
hardly be doubted and has long been recognized (cf. e.g.
Streitberg 1896:328). This implies that the accent was
on the root and not on the reduplicative element. (Perhaps we cannot exclude the possibility that the application of Verner's Law was already in the reduplicated forms
of the Germanic parent language somehow restricted or even
levelled at a later stage.) Witnesses to the application
of Verner's Law are the various *r* preterites (e.g. ON *sā*
ᴧ *sera*) and possibly Gothic *saizlep* of *slepan*. The form

with *-zl-* does not occur consistently in the Gothic corpus, which has *gasaizlep, gasaizlepun,* but also *saislep,*
anasaislep, anasaislepun, each of them documented once;
Gothic also does not show **saizo,* comparable to ON *sera,*
but only *saiso, saisost* (Streitberg 1965:lexicon, De
Tollenaere-Jones 1976). This is not so surprising in
light of the overall restricted representation of Verner's
Law in Gothic, a fact which is usually ascribed to levelling (Van Coetsem-Hendricks-Siegel 1981:172-3).

Insofar as Verner's Law was applied, the thematic anlaut became differentiated from the absolute anlaut, e.g.
*Xait- ∿ **Xegait-* [-g-] (X ∿ X/g for earlier X ∿ X/X),
*Xlaup- ∿ **Xeglaup-* [-gl-] (X ∿ X/g for earlier X ∿ X/Xl),
*fall- ∿ **feball-* [-ƀ-] (f ∿ f/b for earlier f ∿ f/f).
However, at this point, the voicing alternation was purely
phonologically (suprasegmentally) conditioned and, as
such, automatic. In other words, the underlying representation for X ∿ g, Xl ∿ gl and f ∿ b must originally
have been X, Xl, and f, respectively (e.g. **Xegait-* was
thus a phonetic realization of **XeXait-*).

Assuming that Verner's Law was consistently carried
through in the reduplicated forms of the Germanic parent
language, Bech (1969:6) submits the following   (here
slightly adapted) diagram (Table 1). It shows the verb
types that were subject to the alternations of Verner's
Law (B.I-II) and those that were not (A.I-II). The diagram also illustrates how in the four verb types, the absolute anlaut and the thematic anlaut differed from one
another. The rather rare verb type with a vowel initial
root (cf. Gothic *aikan* ∿ *aiaik, aukan* ∿ *aiauk*) has not
been included in the diagram; if necessary, it could be
listed in A.I.

	I		II	
A	*laikan ∿ *lelaik-		*blandan ∿ *bebland-	
	*rēdan ∿ *rerōd-		*blōtan ∿ *beblōt-	
	*bannan ∿ *bebann-		*grētan ∿ *gegrōt-	
	*waldan ∿ *wewald-		*grōan ∿ *gegrō-	
B	*saltan ∿ *sezalt-		*slēpan ∿ *sezlēp-	
	*fallan ∿ *feball-	[-ƀ-]	*flokan ∿ *feblok-	[-ƀ-]
	*Xaitan ∿ *Xegait-	[-g-]	*Xlaupan ∿ *Xeglaup-	[-ƀ-]
	*Xaldan ∿ *Xegald-	[-g-]	*Xropan ∿ *Xegrop-	[-g-]

TABLE 1.

The application of Verner's Law to the reduplicated
forms suggests that their thematic anlaut was not felt as
a word anlaut.[7] This is further supported by the fact
that in the verbal pattern 'reduplicative element + verbal
root' the link between the two constituents was definitely
stronger than in the general pattern 'prefix + verbal
root'. For this we can refer to, e.g. Gothic *afaiaik* ∿
afaikan, gastaistald ∿ *gastaldan,* in which *af-* and *ga-*

did not separate the reduplicative element from the verbal root.

(ii)   The change in accent placement, particularly the concentration of the accent on the reduplicative element, is clearly evidenced by such cases as OE *heht* of *hātan*, *leolc* of *lācan*, and ON *sera* of *sā*.   It has two further consequences:

(α)   The alternations produced by Verner's Law were no longer phonologically (suprasegmentally) conditioned. This caused a change in underlying representation.

(β)   In general, the verbal compound 'prefix + root' had the prominence on the root (cf. Gothic *fra'letan*), while the corresponding compound had the prominence on the prefix (cf. Gothic *'fralets*).   The best interpretation of this is that in verbs the prefix was still unbound, while in nominalization it was really compounded.   We can then consistently speak of an initial accentuation, with the implication, however, that in verbs the initial accentuation was also a root accentuation.   In other words, the verb was always root-accented.   A deviation from this principle arose as a result of the concentration of the prominence on the reduplicative element.   This accentuation was related to the closeness in composition of the pattern 'reduplicative element + verbal root', as stated above.   In this blending process the status of thematic anlaut became obscured.   Such a situation was subject to regularization, and was in fact regularized through reanalysis, as we will discuss in Section 3.   Regarding this we agree fully with the strong emphasis that Meid (1971: 97) places on the determining nature of the accent shift, namely a shift "vom beweglichen zum festen, an die Anfangssilbe des Wortes gebundenen Akzent."[8]

(iii)   In conclusion, the change in accent placement was the primary determinant in the blending process of the reduplicative element and the verbal root.   After the change in accent placement, the results of the earlier operation of Verner's Law became contributing factors to this process.

3.   COUNTERDEVELOPMENTS TO THE WEAKENING OF THE RE-
DUPLICATION PRINCIPLE, ESPECIALLY THE REANALYSIS
OF THE REDUPLICATED FORM WITH THE EMERGENCE OF A
NEW ABLAUT PATTERN

3.1.   After the *ā-ō* merger, the accent shift and the alternations produced by Verner's Law were in their cumulative effect particularly efficient in weakening, obscuring, and even disrupting the reduplication principle. There appear to have been two counterdevelopments to this weakening process, developments which were complementary and which operated in opposite directions.   They were

ultimately realized in two different areas of the Germanic
language community. The two developments have been recognized by Bech (1969:9 ff.).

3.2.   In Gothic, the alternations produced by Verner's
Law were systematically levelled, but the reduplication
principle was preserved or reinstated. In other words,
by ruling out factors that contributed to the weakening
of the reduplication principle, a REVERSAL occurred in
Gothic. For example, for *Xegait- and *feball- we find
accordingly in Gothic haihait and faifall.[9]

3.3.   On the other hand, in North and West Germanic
the alternations produced by Verner's Law were generally
maintained, but the reduplication principle was given up.
It is, however, quite possible that a reversal procedure
similar to that in Gothic had occasionally been utilized.
Yet, REANALYSIS seems to have been the more general procedure. We realize that the different possibilities regarding Verner's Law may have resulted in co-occurring
forms like *XeXait-/*Xegait-, where the first might be considered not as good a candidate for reanalysis as the
second. It is crucial to keep in mind, however, that the
concentration of the accent on the reduplicative element
was the overriding factor in reanalysis, in which case
both forms were good candidates. In view of this, rather
than referring always to, e.g. *XeXait-/*Xegait-, the form
reflecting Verner's Law, e.g. *Xegait-, will be used to
refer generally to both possibilities.

3.3.1.   While the Germanic verb was root-accented, the
reduplicative element in North and West Germanic was ac-
centually prominent. The pattern 'reduplicative element
+ verbal root', then, could be reinterpreted or reanalyzed
in such a way that the reduplicative element became the
initial part of the verbal root; the unusual nature of reduplication in the Germanic verb was undoubtedly a contributing factor. It is in any case not uncommon for a
reduplicative element to be reinterpreted as a root (cf.
German beben, zittern and see also Henzen 1957:258-60
[173]). This reanalysis brought the original reduplicated
form in line with the general accentuation pattern of the
verb. However, with the reanalysis, the preterite form
generally acquired a BISYLLABIC ROOT STRUCTURE, e.g.
*Xegait- (∿ present *Xait-), and along with this, the so-
called SPECIFIC NONROOT MATERIAL, which continued the
initial part of the verbal root of the earlier reduplicated form, e.g. -ga-. In addition, in a number of cases
a lexical anlaut discrepancy between the present and the
preterite form resulted, e.g. *Xl ∿ *X in *Xlaup- ∿
*Xeglaup-.
The yardstick for establishing what belonged to the
root and what was the specific nonroot material, was the
root of the present. Not only was the present the unmarked tense (the nonpast), but its monosyllabic root

structure was compatible with the general root type of the
strong verb in Germanic. Therefore, there can be no doubt
about the deviant character of the generally bisyllabic
root structure of the reanalyzed preterite form, and about
the nonroot status of the specific nonroot material. Also,
the form of the present must have served as the standard
in the case of lexical anlaut discrepancy.

The prominent part of the reanalyzed preterite form,
e.g. *Xe- in *Xegait- was, then, quite normally identified
or equated with the initial part of the root; *Xe- of the
reanalyzed preterite form corresponded to *Xa- of the
present *Xait-, yielding a new ablaut pattern, present *a*
∿ preterite *e*, and thus bringing the form in line with the
dominant principle for differentiating principal parts
within the paradigm of the strong verb.

The second, nonprominent part of the reanalyzed preterite form comprised the specific nonroot material and the
final part of the root. The distinction between the root
and the specific nonroot material was determined by the
root structure of the present, so that, e.g. -gait- in
*Xegait- must ideally have been reanalyzed as -ga-, spe-
cific nonroot material, and -it-, final part of the root;
-it- of the reanalyzed form corresponded then to -it- of
the present form *Xait-.[10] However, the vocalism of the
second, nonprominent part of the root must have been directly subject to reduction, as we will discuss in Section
4.4.

The difference in morphological analysis between the
reduplication and the subsequent reanalysis can be schematically illustrated by the following examples (Table 2),
which also show the different aspects of the emerging new
ablaut pattern.

3.3.2. In the reanalysis verba pura came to be analyzed as suffixed. In, e.g. *sezō-, *se- was then the
initial part of the verbal root with *e* as an ablaut alternant, *z* a suffix, while *ō* became identified with a conjugation ending, e.g. ON *sā* ∿ *sera* [cf. 1.2.2 (i) (α)].

3.3.3. Bech (1969:9 ff.) identifies the pattern 'reduplicative element + verbal root', e.g. *Xe + gait-,
with the pattern 'prefix + verbal root'. He does not see
the reanalysis as *Xe + ga + it-, like we do, but as *X
+ eg + ait- (his notation being *h + eg + ait-), i.e.
*X-ait-, verbal root, and -eg-, infix. In his view the
change is basically one of prefixation to infixation (or
suffixation).

Bech's conception of the reanalysis ignores the full
implications of the accent shift, and is therefore insufficiently founded and unsatisfactory. Indeed, in his
view, the prominence continues to be on the affix and not
on the verbal root, and his analysis does not take into
consideration the discrepancy or differentiation within
the verbal accentuation pattern. Our conception of the
reanalysis, however, does take into consideration the full

implications of the accent shift. At the same time it
accounts for the introduction of the constant *e* of the
original reduplicative element into the bounds of the
verbal root. The divergent conceptions of the reanalysis
are the source for crucial differences between Bech's view
and ours.

(1)   Reduplication

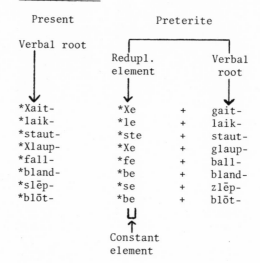

(2)   Reanalysis

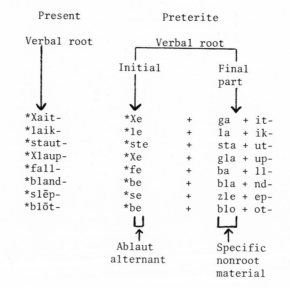

TABLE 2.

4. STRUCTURAL AND DEVELOPMENTAL IMPLICATIONS OF THE REANALYSIS

4.1. As stated, the general bisyllabic root structure and the specific nonroot material as combined character- istics of the reanalyzed preterite form were structurally deviant; in the presence of ablaut they could not be the primarily relevant markers of the preterite. The lexical anlaut discrepancy between the present and the preterite that resulted from the reanalysis also yielded an unstable situation in a number of cases. Following the general principle of structural generalization and adequacy (Sec- tion 1.6), these deviations brought on readjustments or changes, which we will now discuss further.

In coping with these deviations, the reanalyzed pret- erite form must have undergone certain lexical and dis- tributional readjustments over the whole of the North and West Germanic area. These adjustments, which for the sake of convenience we will call PRIMARY READJUSTMENTS, are found in or presupposed by all the formations described in Section 1. Further readjustments or changes from which these formations emerged seem to have had a more specific character.

In our treatment of these deviations, that is of the structural and developmental implications of the reanaly- sis, we will consider three points which bear on both the primary readjustments and the further readjustments or changes of the reanalyzed preterite form. Together with these general considerations we will discuss in this sec- tion the primary readjustments, while the further read- justments or changes will be studied in Section 5. The three points in question are: (1) the principles availa- ble for distinguishing between the present and the pret- erite, (2) the relation between the absolute and thematic anlauts, and (3) the bisyllabic root structure of the re- analyzed preterite form.

4.2. Our first point concerns the principles availa- ble for distinguishing between the present and the pret- erite.

4.2.1. Prior to the reanalysis there was in general one principle available for distinguishing the preterite from the present, namely reduplication (e.g. preterite *Xegait- ~ present *Xait-).[11] This was true of the *a* verbs which constituted the greater part of the redupli- cating class. Only a few *ē* verbs of that class exhibited both reduplication and ablaut (e.g. present *lēt- ~ pret- erite *lelōt-, Gothic *letan* ~ *lailot*). It is important to note that the reduplicative element contained with its constant *e* a potential ablaut alternant, i.e., the poten- tial ablaut alternant *e* and the reduplication constituted an amalgam.

4.2.2. On the other hand, the reanalysis of, e.g.
*Xe + gait- to *Xe + ga + it- produced a preterite *Xe-it-
vs. a present *Xait-, i.e. an ablaut alternation present
a ∿ preterite e (which was only one aspect of the new
ablaut pattern), with the specific nonroot material ga.
In other words, the reanalyzed preterite form contained
both the ablaut alternant e and the specific nonroot material ga (the latter in combination with a bisyllabic
root structure to be discussed in Section 4.4), which differentiated it from the present; the ablaut alternant e
and the specific nonroot material ga were, however, separate entities. How then did ablaut relate to the specific nonroot material in the reanalyzed preterite form, and
what were their respective statuses?

Ablaut was, within the paradigm of the strong verb,
the formal principle for the differentiation of principal
parts. In other words, given that paradigm it was the
principle necessary for the maintenance of the differentiation between, e.g. the present and the preterite, and
as such it was structurally primarily relevant and fully
motivated. On the other hand, the specific nonroot material was within the same paradigm associated with the
preterite only in a minority group of verbs. It was quite
susceptible to loss, being at best a concomitant signal of
the preterite; at the same time it was in the majority of
cases directly instrumental in preserving another deviant
characteristic of the reanalyzed preterite form, namely
the bisyllabic root structure. Considering this, the potential for loss is understandable. Furthermore, the
specific nonroot material exhibited a structurally unmotivated variety of lexical forms (cf. ga/la/sta, etc., in
Table 2), which made it lack structural relevance or motivatedness not only in its occurrence but also in its
form; this is precisely the original impetus for the emergence of the r preterite formation. Through its productivity the latter formation also illustrates the potential
affix status of the specific nonroot material.

4.2.3. We can schematize the above differences between the present and the preterite in the reduplication
and in the reanalysis as follows:

1. Reduplication

    preterite (*Xe + Xait->) *Xe + gait- ∿ present *Xait-
               ‿‿‿   ‿‿‿
               (I)   (I)

    *Xe-: potential ablaut alternant e and reduplicative
    element constituted an amalgam
2. Reanalysis

    preterite *Xe + ga + it- ∿ present *Xait-
              ‿‿‿ ‿‿‿
              (I)   (II)

Xe + *ga-*: ablaut alternant *e* (I) primarily relevant and fully motivated, and specific nonroot material *ga* (II) structurally deviant and deficient in structural relevance or motivatedness, were separate entities

4.3. Our second point examines the relation between the absolute and thematic anlauts in the reduplicated form, and between the absolute anlaut and the specific nonroot material in the reanalyzed preterite form.

4.3.1. In the reduplicated form, e.g. (*XeXait-*->) *Xegait-* and (*XeXlaup-*->) *Xeglaup-*, there was a lexical (phonological) relationship of dependence of the absolute anlaut on the thematic anlaut. In other words, a form such as *feXait-* (∿ *Xait-*) would have violated the reduplication principle.

4.3.2. With the reanalysis, however, the thematic anlaut of the reduplicated form lost its status as anlaut and became the specific nonroot material. Concomitantly, the absolute anlaut and the specific nonroot material were no longer in a lexical (phonological) relationship to one another. As a result, they were free to change and develop independent of one another. Yet, the absolute anlaut remained lexically (phonologically) dependent on the thematic anlaut as found in the present, and this triggered lexical readjustment of the anlaut of the preterite to that of the present whenever necessary. Compare OHG present *bluozan* ∿ preterite *pleruzzun*, that is *blōt-* ∿ *blerot-*, the latter with analogical spread of the *r* infix (Section 5.2) and lexical readjustment of the anlaut from *beblōt-* to *bleblōt-*.

4.3.3. The described anlaut relations, in particular the lexical anlaut readjustment, can be schematically illustrated as follows:

1. Reduplication

     preterite *Xe* + *glaup-*   present *Xlaup-*

2. Reanalysis

     preterite *Xe* + *gla* + *up-*   present *Xlaup-*
               Xl

4.4. Our third point concerns the fact that the reanalysis produced a generally bisyllabic root structure (cf. OHG *bluozan*, *stōzan* ∿ *pleruzzun*, *steroz*). Such a bisyllabicity was extremely unusual within the paradigm of the strong verb, and lacked structural relevance or motivatedness in the differentiation between the present and the preterite; it was therefore not only developmentally but also structurally subject to reduction.

4.4.1. Given the prevailing accent type (dominating prominence) and the structural (distributional) require- ments of the language, reduction of the second, nonpromi- nent syllable of the reanalyzed preterite form, that is reduction of the vocalism involved, was a quite normal reaction.

Taking the examples *Xegait- (*Xe + ga + it-) and *Xeglaup- (*Xe + gla + up-), the prominence being in each case on the first syllable, the sequences ai and au of the second, nonprominent part of the reanalyzed preterite form were directly subject to reduction on purely distribu- tional grounds (cf. OHG stōzan ∿ steroz). It is, however, not certain in what way the reduction could have been im- plemented in the case of a diphthong. It may have been achieved by assimilative contraction of the two components (ai > e, au > o: *Xeget-, *Xleglop-, the latter with lex- ical anlaut readjustment as described in Section 4.3). It may also have been realized by total reduction of one of the components, presumably the first (ai > i, au > u: *Xegit-, *Xleglup-). The resulting reduced vocalism i/e, u/o in the reanalyzed preterite form was then short and nonlow, and at the time regularly subject to umlaut and/or consonant conditioning. It was also comparable to the second component of a diphthong, which in Germanic could behave like a vowel under umlaut and/or consonant condi- tioning, and is then to be characterized as "vocalic" but "nonsyllabic" (Van Coetsem 1979): *Xait-/*Xaet- ∿ *Xegit-/ *Xeget-, *staut-/*staot- ∿ *stestut-/*stestot-. While umlaut and/or consonant conditioning of the second com- ponent of a diphthong is clearly evidenced by eu/eo/iu (cf. OHG beotan ∿ biutu/biutis), it is less well or only indirectly attested in the case of ai/ae and au/ao (Van Coetsem 1968, especially 521 ff., and compare Van Coetsem 1975a).

It does not appear valid to view such reduced vocal- ism, i/e, u/o, as possible reflexes of an originally Indo- European zero grade of the preterite plural, as has been done in earlier research (e.g. Boer 1924:110). Such an idea depends on cases like ON sveip ∿ svipom, which are, however, clearly analogical extensions from the e verbs (cf. Noreen 1904:444 and see Van Coetsem 1956:56, 60-1 with further references). We should also keep in mind that the absence of vocalic alternation opposing singular and plural in the root of the preterite was an important structural property of the a verbs, as opposed to the e verbs, where such a vocalic alternation was the rule (Van Coetsem 1980:290-1, 327).

Not only in a diphthong (e.g. *Xait-), but also in the case of a long vocalism (e.g. *slēp-), the reduction seems to have been of one mora, that is, of one minimal unit of length (cf. OHG bluozan ∿ pleruzzun); in the case of a long vocalism (X̄) as well as in the case of a diphthong (X̆X̆) the reduction would thus again have produced a short and nonlow vocalism (*X̌*), comparable to what may have happened in a diphthong.

In the case of a short vocalism (e.g. **fall-*), the reduction of one mora may have been carried through, producing zero vocalism (**fall-* ∿ **fe + b + ll-*). However, on general distributional grounds the short vocalism could have been maintained as well (**fall-* ∿ **fe + b + all-*).12

4.4.2. There was an obvious difference between the OHG *r* preterites and the OE contracted forms insofar as the former show partial reduction and the latter total reduction. The partial reduction in OHG would reflect the primary readjustment described in Section 4.4.1.

(i)   The OHG forms maintained their bisyllabic root structure: *bluozan* ∿ *pleruzzun, capleruzzi*, i.e. *uo* ∿ *u* (the latter possibly reflecting umlaut of *o* before *u, i* of the following syllable), *stōzan* ∿ *steroz*, i.e. *ō* ∿ *o*, *būwan* ∿ *biruuuis*, i.e. *ū* ∿ *u*. Because of the similarity, it would seem that the reduced vocalism of the second, nonprominent syllable of such forms was felt as (part of the) root vocalism and not as the specific nonroot material. (This would imply that the reduced vocalism could be readapted depending on change in the root vocalism of the present.) We should also note that the total vocalism of the preterite in each of the examples under consideration was: *e-u* in *pleruzzun*, *e-o* in *steroz* and *i-u* in *biruuuis*; these remind us of the familiar realizations of the Germanic *eu* diphthong in OHG, namely *eu/eo/iu*.

(ii)   The OE contracted forms displayed total reduction of the vocalism of the second, nonprominent syllable of the original bisyllabic form. The resulting form was monosyllabic (although still containing the specific nonroot material): *hātan* ∿ *heht, lācan* ∿ *leolc, bēatan* ∿ *beoftun*. This is very possibly a secondary development as compared to the partial reduction in OHG discussed in (i) (further on this and related questions in Section 5.3).

(iii)   The documented OHG *r* preterites show back vocalism, Germanic *au, ō, ū* (**staut-, *blōt-, *bū(w)-*; OHG *ō* (before dental), *uo, ū, stōzan, bluozan, būwan, būan*). There are no examples with Germanic *ai, ē* vocalism (OHG *ei/ē, ā*). This is probably coincidental. If it is not, it could suggest that the lack of a sharp distinction between the *e* vocalism in the initial part of the root of the preterite and the reduced vocalism *i/e* (from *ai, ē*) in its final part did not favor the preservation of *r*.13 Furthermore, the OE contracted form *beoftun* ∿ *bēatan* reflects a case of a Germanic *au* vocalism (**baut-*). It does not, therefore, appear valid to assume with Bech (1969: 32) an earlier differentiating development between front and back vocalism, the front vocalism being completely reduced, the back vocalism, however, only partially.

(iv)   In the case of a short vocalism, e.g. *fall-
(Section 4.4.1), if there was reduction at all, it was
total by the very nature of things, *fe + b + ll-.   A
distinction between partial and total reduction is then
not applicable.   In such cases unusual (unacceptable) or
unstable distributions or clusters might also have developed, which were subject to change and/or structural readjustment.

4.4.3.   As we have observed (Section 3.3.2), verba
pura came to be reanalyzed as suffixed, e.g. ON sā ∿ sera.
In this case the verbal root was again monosyllabic.

4.5.   In conclusion, given the general structural and
developmental implications of the reanalysis, there were,
we may assume, two primary readjustments of the reanalyzed
preterite form, namely the lexical anlaut readjustment
applied whenever necessary, and the partial reduction of
the second, nonprominent syllable.   In spite of these readjustments the reanalyzed preterite form remained deviant
insofar as it had a bisyllabic root structure and/or the
specific nonroot material.   Three different strategies
were applied to the (readjusted) reanalyzed preterite
form.   This produced the three different preterite formations of North and West Germanic.

5.   THE SPECIFIC STRATEGIES OF NORTH AND WEST
     GERMANIC, IN PARTICULAR THE EMERGENCE OF A
     NEW ABLAUT FORMATION

5.1.   Let us now return to the formations themselves.
As stated (Section 3.3), in North and West Germanic a reversal procedure similar to that in Gothic may have occasionally been utilized; it might even be considered the
basis for the OE contracted forms.   A preserved or restored reduplication could also account for some sporadic
forms which appeared without reduplicative element, e.g.
ON heita ∿ heit, sveipa ∿ sveip, OE gangan ∿ gang.[14]   However, at least some of these preterites can also be considered analogical forms modelled after the e verbs, cf.
ON bīđa beiđ (preterite singular) biđom (preterite plural),
sveipa ∿ sveip ∿ svipom, in which case the plural svipom
is the best evidence for analogy (Van Coetsem 1956:56-6,
65).   ON sveip ∿ svipom are analyzed by Bech (1969:46) as
suppletive forms of a Germanic verb continued in Middle
High German swīfan.   Old Frisian hēta ∿ hēt [discussed in
Appendix II. 4.2 (ii) (β)] is clearly the result of change
and analogy and has nothing to do with a loss of the reduplicative element.
     In general, the reanalysis serves as a starting point
for a description of the North and West Germanic development of the reduplicating class.   The (readjusted) reanalyzed preterite form gave rise to three corrective strategies from which PARALLELING and COMPETING preterite

formations originated. On the basis of the principle of
generalization and adequacy (Section 1.6), we have found
the generally bisyllabic root structure along with the
specific nonroot material to be structurally deviant and
deficient in structural relevance or motivatedness; this
made the reanalyzed preterite form susceptible to further
readjustments or changes.

Taking into consideration the development of suffixation with the verba pura, and the analysis of the OE contracted forms as possibly resulting from preserved or restored reduplication, we can schematically distinguish
and characterize the three strategies as follows:

1. Analogical generalization of one form of the specific
   nonroot material (infix or suffix), as found in the *r*
   preterite formation.
2. Preservation of the specific nonroot material (or of
   the thematic anlaut in case of a reduplicated form)
   with reduction to a monosyllabic structure, as found
   in the OE contracted forms.
3. Consistent structural re-formation of the reanalyzed
   preterite form on the model of the present, resulting
   in a preterite form which was monosyllabic and did
   not contain the specific nonroot material. This preserved the new ablaut pattern which had emerged with
   the reanalysis.

Keeping in mind that the weak conjugation was also a possible recourse for the reduplicating verbs, we will now
examine points 1-3 in greater detail.

5.2. The first strategy discussed is the analogical
generalization of one form of the specific nonroot material (infix or suffix), as found in the *r* preterites. As
pointed out (Section 4.2.2), the specific nonroot material
appeared in a structurally unmotivated variety of lexical
forms. A reaction to this was the spread of one of these
forms by analogical extension outside of its original lexical domain; with this, other forms of the specific nonroot material were levelled. This produced the so-called
r preterite formation.

5.2.1. The analogical spread is nicely illustrated
by the ON verba pura. Besides *rōa* ~ *rera* and *sā* ~ *sera*
we find, e.g. *grōa* ~ *grera*, *snūa* ~ *snera*, in which the *r*
was a suffix. With the suffixation and the reinterpretation of the endings, a monosyllabic root structure evolved.
The analogical spread is also exemplified by the OHG *r*
preterites, e.g. *būwan* ~ *biruuuis*, *stōzan* ~ *steroz*, in
which the *r* was an infix;[15] in this case the bisyllabic
root structure was preserved. Thus, this formation contained forms in which the *r* infix or suffix occurred analogically, and in the broader sense also forms from which
the analogical extension started.

5.2.2.   Another question here concerns the origin of
the *r* in the *r* preterites.

(i)   For the ON verba pura some have assumed (e.g.
Boer 1920:190) that the analogical spread originated in a
verb with *r* anlaut.   Here the thematic anlaut of the original reduplicated form was *r*, *rōa* ∿ *rera* (**rerō-*).   A similar origin, that is an analogical extension from a verb
with *r* anlaut (verbum purum or not), may be posited for
the OHG *r* preterites.

(ii)   It has been more generally assumed that the *r*
developed from a verb with *s* anlaut (verbum purum or not),
in which the thematic anlaut of the original reduplicated
form was voiced to *z* (Verner's Law) and subsequently rhotacized to *r*.   We can again refer to an ON verbum purum,
namely *sā* (Gothic *saian*) ∿ *sera* (**sezō-*, Gothic *saiso*).[16]
Actually, this second assumption has a better foundation;
an analogical spread was better motivated in a case where
the anlaut and the specific nonroot material were different.
Based on the requirements of his theory, Bech (1969)
assumes the analogical spread to have started from a verb
with *s* anlaut.   He considers an *ez* infix in accordance
with his conception of the reanalysis (cf. our Section
3.3.2).   He posits an analogical extension of *ez* to all
the verb types of the reduplicated class, and views the
new ablaut pattern as a development from this *ez* infix as
well.   There are several serious shortcomings in his
theory, which we will discuss in greater detail in Appendix II. 3.

5.2.3.   A question related to the previous discussion
of the origin of *r* in the *r* preterites concerns the choice
of *z* (> *r*) as a model for analogical extension, rather
than another consonantism, such as *l* (cf. Gothic *lailaik*),
m, or even a consonant cluster.   In trying to answer this
question we can only speculate.   Verb types with single
initial consonants were probably more plausible candidates for the analogical spread in question than those
with initial consonant clusters.   Following Bech (1969:
20-1), we may perhaps assume that of the verb types with
single initial consonants, those occurring in both the
verba pura and impura were the most probable candidates,
and these were then precisely the verb type with *s* anlaut
(**sē-*, e.g. ON *sā*, **salt-*, e.g. OHG *salzan*) and the one
with *r* anlaut (**rō-*, e.g. OE *rowan*, **red-*, e.g. ON *rāđa*).
As we have noted, of these two verb types the former would
have offered a better motivation for analogical extension
of its specific nonroot material.

5.3.   Preservation of the specific nonroot material
(or of the thematic anlaut in case of a reduplicated form)
in its original different forms is found in OE (Anglian)

heht of *hātan*, *leolc* of *lācan*, etc.; these were evidently
the result of contraction.

5.3.1. We could hardly talk of a "corrective strategy"
here, if it were not that the second, nonprominent syllable of the reanalyzed preterite form had in the OE contracted forms CONSISTENTLY disappeared [for this reduction
cf. Sections 4.4.2 (ii) and (iii)]. In OE bisyllabic
roots with a short vocalism in the first, prominent syllable (that is, in trisyllabic words when inflectional
endings are involved), the second, nonprominent syllable
was either not so consistently dropped or it remained altogether (Sievers-Brunner 1951:141 [159,c]). The OE contracted forms seem, therefore, to reflect primarily a readjustment mechanism, eliminating the structurally deviant and unmotivated bisyllabicity of the root, i.e. producing a monosyllabic root structure in accordance with
the root structure of the present and the general root
type of the strong verb. Yet, with the preservation of
the specific nonroot material a structurally deviant and
unmotivated factor remained.

In comparison with the OHG *r* preterites, which show
partial reduction of the vocalism of the second, nonprominent syllable, the OE readjustment mechanism resulted in
total reduction of that vocalism. It seems reasonable to
assume that this total reduction (as opposed to partial
reduction) represents a second step diachronically, and
is accordingly not a primary readjustment. Perhaps there
is, then, a relationship of developmental complementarity
between OE on the one hand and OHG on the other; in its
contracted monosyllabic forms OE preserved the specific
nonroot material in its different forms, while the OHG *r*
preterites maintained the bisyllabic root structure with
analogical extension of the *r* infix.[17]

5.3.2. Some further remarks are necessary.

(i) In assuming a virtually generalized spread of
the *ez* infix after reanalysis, Bech (1969:23) can explain
such cases as *heht* only as the direct continuation of a
reduplicated form. This may be possible. The question
is, however, whether reduplication is compatible with the
occurrence of the strong reduction in the OE contracted
forms. We should also note that in a case like *heht*, the
second *h* may have developed from *g* as well as from *X*.

(ii) Through regular development and/or structural
readjustment in the case of unusual (unacceptable) or unstable distributions or clusters, the contraction process
may have occasionally produced forms with modified specific nonroot material or forms showing the new ablaut pattern in a way similar to those discussed in Section 5.4.

(α) If some verbs with *s* anlaut (*s* cluster) met the
conditions, an occasional form with *ez* + voiced consonant

could have resulted in the pattern '$\bar{e}$ + voiced consonant'
[cf. Appendix II. 3.3 (iv) (ε)].

Similarly, in a case like OE *hwōpan* [assuming that
the alternation produced by Verner's Law had been erased;
cf., however, OE *wōpian* (weak) and *wēpan* (red)], a preterite like **hwe(h)wp-* could have developed (proposed by
Sacks 1977:17). Whether this actually happened cannot be
stated with any certainty. The assumption of such a development is also plausible for, e.g. OHG *wiof* $\sim$ *wuofan*,
if Pre-OHG knew the formation with total reduction of the
second, nonprominent syllable.

(β) Structural readjustment in the case of an unusual
(unacceptable) or unstable distribution or cluster may be
evidenced by OE *speoft/seoftun*, with *ft* from *pt* adapted
from *spt* in **spespt-*, probably belonging to *spātan*.

(γ) We have noted [Section 4.4.2 (iv)] that in the
case of a short vocalism total reduction of the vocalism
of the second, nonprominent syllable, e.g. **fe + b + ll-*
$\sim$ **fall-*, could have occurred over the whole of the North
and West Germanic area, with, perhaps in certain cases,
change and/or structural readjustment of unusual (unacceptable) or unstable distributions or clusters.

(iii) The form *hēt* of *hātan*, which will be discussed
further (Section 5.4), cannot have developed from *heht*,
as Prokosch (1939:176) quite correctly points out: "If
heht was the regular phonetic development of **hehāt* = Go.
haihait, it seems improbable that at a comparatively late
period it should have gone through the altogether irregular development to *hēt*; if the form had been preserved at
all, it would have remained *heht* in Anglian, as in *reht*,
cneht, or become **heoht* in West Saxon,   as in *reoht*,
cneoht."

(iv) Aside from *lācan*, the roots of the OE contracted
forms ended in *t* or *d*. Considering the scarcity of the
examples, this is probably coincidental; it could also
reflect some form of phonetic preference.

(v) Finally, if *leort* of *lētan* actually had an analogical *r* after the model of, e.g. *rēdan* (verb with *r* anlaut), the latter represents the prototype in which the
analogical extension must have originated. In virtue of
our earlier discussion (Section 5.2.1), we can then consider all of them *r* preterites. Bech (1969:23) does this
as well, but within the bounds of his own analysis. Since,
however, all of the involved OE (Anglian) forms, e.g.
heht, *leolc*, *reord*, can uniformly and plausibly be accounted for by simple contraction (with *leort* being considered a dissimilation from **leolt*), there are no unambiguous examples of *r* preterites in OE. There is then
little evidence for assuming that OE ever had an *r* preterite formation.

5.4. In spite of the applied readjustments or
changes, the r preterites and the OE contracted forms
continued to show structural inadequacies, i.e., characteristics which were structurally deviant and deficient
in structural relevance or motivatedness, namely the bisyllabic root structure and/or the specific nonroot material (affix). These formations were unfavored ones compared to the new ablaut pattern (and the weak conjugation).
The formations showing this new ablaut pattern resulted
from a third corrective strategy applied to the reanalyzed
preterite form. We will examine this strategy now.

5.4.1. In order to properly approach the problem, we
must first consider how FORMAL DIFFERENCES comparable to
that between the present and the reanalyzed preterite form
generally manifest themselves, and how they develop further. We thus focus on the occurrence and development of
such differences between, e.g. the present and the preterite (and the past participle) within the paradigm of the
strong verb.

(i) What types of differences (which do not include
phonologically conditioned variations) can we isolate?

(α) Our primary concern being the reanalyzed preterite form, we have seen until now one type. Here one or
more segments (S) alternates with zero (∅), i.e. $∅ \sim S$,
e.g. $∅ \sim ga$: Present *$Xa + ∅ + it-$ $\sim$ Preterite *$Xe + ga$
$+ it-$. Such an alternation or difference between the present and the preterite is found in e.g. $∅ \sim n$: OHG *fāhan*
$\sim$ *fieng*, and in reverse order $S \sim ∅$, or in e.g. $n \sim ∅$:
Gothic *standan* $\sim$ *stoþ*, English *stand* $\sim$ *stood*.

(β) In another type none of the alternants is ∅,
i.e., $S \sim S'$, e.g. $z \sim r$: Dutch *verliezen* $\sim$ *verloor*. More
recent developmental stages of ablaut show the type $S \sim S'$
$(\sim S'')$ [e.g. $i \sim a (\sim u)$, German *trinken* $\sim$ *trank* $\sim$ *ge-
trunken*, English *drink* $\sim$ *drank* $\sim$ *drunk*]. Ablaut was also
an $S \sim ∅$ type, namely in Proto-Germanic (Van Coetsem 1980:
e.g. 290-1).

(γ) The distinction between (α) and (β) presupposes
PARTIAL difference (and partial identity) between the present and the preterite forms. This distinction is neutralized in cases of TOTAL difference, that is in cases of
suppletion (e.g. Gothic *gaggan* $\sim$ *iddja*, English *go* $\sim$
went). In relation to our problem, the reanalyzed preterite form, partial difference is the pertinent one.

(ii) How do such differences relate to the notion of
DEVIATION (as described in Section 1.6)?
Such differences correspond to degrees of deviation
from the structural properties of the language. When the
difference falls completely within the bounds of structural

properties of the language, its structural deviation is
zero. As S ∿ Ø or S ∿ S', ablaut represents a zero deviation. In the Germanic languages in general the type S ∿
Ø (cf. Gothic *standan* ∿ *stoþ*) appears structurally more
deviant than the type S ∿ S' (e.g. alternations of Verner's Law).

(iii)   How do such differences relate to the question
of RELEVANCE or MOTIVATEDNESS?

(α)   In principle, the types, Ø ∿ S (S ∿ Ø) and S ∿
S', may be primarily relevant or fully motivated, secondarily relevant or less motivated, and even irrelevant or
unmotivated. Both types may occur together within the
same lexical item (e.g. English *stand* ∿ *stood*, i.e. *a* ∿
oo, S ∿ S', *n* ∿ Ø, S ∿ Ø) or the same type may occur more
than once in the same lexical item (e.g. Dutch *verliezen*
∿ *verloor*, i.e. *ie* ∿ *oo* and *z* ∿ *r*, S ∿ S').
Of these differences we can now clearly single out
one, namely ablaut, which, as pointed out in Section 4.2.2,
was the necessary and dominant marker of the differentiation between, e.g. the present and the preterite within
the paradigm of the strong verb. As such, the difference
(alternation) brought about by ablaut was primarily relevant or fully motivated and structurally nondeviant; it
was thus quite distinct from the formal difference between
the present and the reanalyzed preterite form.

(β)   From the above examples we can see that a difference between the present and preterite forms may emerge in
a variety of ways. For example, in Gothic *standan* ∿ *stoþ*
it resulted from the occurrence of a presential *n* infix.
In OHG *fahan* ∿ *fieng* there was a phonological change in
the present form. Such differences are, in the development of a language, likely to change in relation to their
degree of relevance or motivatedness and deviation.

(iv)   What can happen to such differences?

(α)   Independent of the fact that the two types, Ø ∿
S (S ∿ Ø) and S ∿ S', may replace one another in language
development, such differences are often ruled out by re-
modelling the preterite form on the basis of the present.
For example, OHG *stantan* ∿ *stuot* (cf. Gothic *standan* ∿
stoþ) developed to *stantan* ∿ *stuont* (Braune-Mitzka 1959:
280). That in such a case *n* was integrated into the preterite form and became part of the root indicates that the
original presential *n* infix had lost its status and had
become irrelevant to the differentiation between the present and the preterite. The other example, OHG *fahan* ∿
fieng, developed more occasionally to *fahan* ∿ *fieg* [Braune-
Mitzka 1959:283 and cf. (β) below]. The fact that in
such a case *n* was dropped from the preterite form indicates again that it was irrelevant to the differentiation

between the present and the preterite; actually it probably never had affix status.

There are more such examples. E.g., while OHG had
lāzan ∿ *liez*, Middle High German developed a contracted
form *lān*(root *lā-*; cf. present *lān*, *lāst/laest*, *lāt/laet*,
lān, *lāt*, *lānt*); the preterite *lie* was formed on this model. Similar readjustments of the preterite form to the
present in Middle High German were *gān* ∿ *gie*, *vān* ∿ *vie*,
hān ∿ *hie*(Weinhold-Ehrismann-Moser 1965:118); such cases
apparently did not involve any form of affixation. Middle High German offers a further example of this in the
preterite forms *kom/kōmen* (Bavarian, since 11 C.), *kam/*
kāmen (e.g. Alemannic), and Modern German *kam/kamen*, which
had *kw* anlaut in OHG *quam/quāmen* (cf. also Gothic *qiman/*
qam/qemum/qumans, OHG *queman*, etc.), but acquired *k* anlaut as a readjustment to the present *komen* in Middle
High German (Braune-Mitzke 1959:277, Weinhold-Ehrismann-
Moser 1965:94 and cf. Modern English *come* ∿ *came*, but also
komen ∿ *kwam* in Modern Dutch). This can also be considered a repetition of the primary lexical anlaut readjustment discussed in Section 4.3. In previous work we have
emphasized as well the dominant role of the present in
similar and related cases (Van Coetsem 1980: e.g. 325,
329-30).

The above are examples of the type difference ∅ ∿ S
(S ∿ ∅). These are nearest to the difference between the
present and the reanalyzed preterite form. Levelling of
differences of the type S ∿ S' is also well documented.
The levelling of the alternations of Verner's Law in the
Gothic strong verb (mainly on the basis of the alternant
of the present) is a famous case in point (Van Coetsem-
Hendricks-Siegel 1981:172-3). Another well-known example
is the preterite form *brang-* ∿ *brung-/brong-* (for *braht-/*
bracht-, cf. German *bringen* ∿ *brachte*, *gebracht*, English
bring ∿ *brought/brought*, Dutch *brengen* ∿ *bracht/gebracht*),
formed after the present *bring-/breng-*, and following the
appropriate ablaut pattern. It is a repeatedly introduced
and suppressed innovation found in old and new Germanic
languages or dialects (for further discussion see Van
Coetsem 1975b:280-1).

One might like to speak of INSERTION in the case of
OHG *stuont*, and of DELETION in the case of OHG *fieg*. A-
side from the fact that this represents an unnecessary restriction to the type ∅ ∿ S (S ∿ ∅), the forms *stuont* and
fieg did not result either from a direct insertion process, *stuot* > *stuont* or a direct deletion process, *fieng* >
fieg. The insertion or deletion of *n* in these examples
was not determined by the forms *stuot* and *fieng* themselves, but resulted from a readjustment of the preterite
to the present. If, nonetheless, we speak of insertion
or deletion in such cases, we do so on the basis of a comparison of the competing preterite forms, namely *stuot* vs.
stuont and *fieng* vs. *fieg*.

(β) Less usual but certainly not uncommon is the levelling or readjustment of the present form on the basis of
the preterite (and past participle). For example, it is
generally assumed that the present-infinitive *fangen* in
German (cf. OHG *fāhan*) and *vangen* in Dutch (cf. Middle
Dutch *vaen*) owe their forms with *ng* to the preterite and
past participle, *fingen, gefangen* in German and *vingen,
gevangen* in Dutch. Also, there are a number of well-known
cases with alternations where the alternant of the preterite (plural) and the past participle has been introduced
into the present. In addition to the example of *ng* in
German *fangen*, Dutch *vangen*, compare, e.g. *r* in German
verlieren, verlor, verloren with *z* ᴨ *r* in Dutch *verliezen*
ᴨ *verloor, verloren*, the latter representing an earlier
situation.

(γ) In some instances the difference remains. For
example, *n* ᴨ ∅ in Gothic *standan* ᴨ *stoþ* is still present
in Modern English *stand* ᴨ *stood*. In such cases several
preserving factors may be at work, such as the high text
frequency of the lexical items involved. Occasionally a
difference along these lines is not only maintained, but
may even become relatively productive. In Middle Dutch
staen developed *sting(stong)* for regular *stont* on the a-
nalogy of *gaen* ᴨ *ging(gong)*, *vaen* ᴨ *ving(vong)* (Schönfeld-
Van Loey 1964:180).
   OHG *fāhan* ᴨ *fieng* is interesting in that, next to the
dominant ablaut alternation *ā* ᴨ *ie*, the differences ∅ ᴨ
n (∅ ᴨ S) and *h* ᴨ *g* (S ᴨ S') occurred between the present
and the preterite. In the development of *fāhan* ᴨ *fieng*
to *fāhan* ᴨ *fieg*, the difference ∅ ᴨ *n* was ruled out while
h ᴨ *g* remained intact. This illustrates possible distinctions in the degree of relevance or motivatedness and the
degree of deviation. Differences of frequency should not
be discounted either.

(δ) We can schematize the interrelationships of such
differences in the following way:

		OHG *stantan* ᴨ *stuot*
1.	Primarily relevant, fully motivated (ablaut)	*a* ᴨ *uo*
2.	Concomitant, less mo- tivated or unmotivated, more deviant	*n* ᴨ ∅
3.	Preservation of 1 and loss of 2	*stantan* ᴨ *stuont*

		OHG *lāzan* ᴨ *liez*
		MHG *lān* ᴨ —
1.	Primarily relevant (ablaut)	*ā* ᴨ *ie*
2.	Concomitant, more deviant	∅ ᴨ *z*
3.	Preservation of 1 and loss of 2	*lān* ᴨ *lie*

However, preserving factors may be at work:

                              English *stand* ∿ *stood*
1. Primarily relevant (ablaut)   *a* ∿ *oo*
2. Concomitant, more deviant   *n* ∿ *Ø*
3. Preservation of 1 and 2   *stand* ∿ *stood*

                              OHG *fāhan* ∿ *fieng*
1. Primarily relevant (ablaut)   *a* ∿ *ie*
2. Concomitant (α) less deviant   *h* ∿ *g*
         (β) more deviant   *Ø* ∿ *n*
3. Preservation of 1 and 2 (α)
   and loss of 2 (β)   *fāhan* ∿ *fieg*

5.4.2. We now return to the (readjusted) reanalyzed preterite form. Referring to Section 4.4.1 (i), where the treatment of the second component of a diphthong is discussed, we can posit, e.g. present **Xait-/*Xaet-* ∿ preterite **Xegit-/*Xeget-* (for earlier **Xegait-*).

(i) The formation showing the new ablaut pattern resulted from a consistent structural re-formation of the reanalyzed preterite form on the model of the present. As this strategy was applied, a form without the specific nonroot material and with a monosyllabic root structure evolved. Because the formation was based on ablaut, it was in accordance with the fundamental principle governing the distinction of principal parts within the strong verbs. It was thus completely compatible with the structure and development of the language. As such, it is not surprising that it became the dominant usage and supplanted the two other competing formations.

In comparison with the examples discussed in Section 5.4.1, the need for structural re-formation was all the more urgent in the reanalyzed preterite form, since the latter involved characteristics that without any doubt were structurally deviant and deficient in structural relevance or motivatedness. Furthermore, that the re-formation occurred on the basis of the present and not on that of the preterite is all the more understandable with the reanalyzed preterite form, since the preterite was in this case different from both the present and the past participle, unlike the examples discussed in Section 5.4.1 (iv) (β).

The structural re-formation of the reanalyzed preterite form can be illustrated as follows:

                    *Xait-/*Xaet- ∿ **Xegit-/*Xeget-*

1. Primarily relevant
   (ablaut)   *a* ∿ *e*
2. Concomitant,
   deviant   *Ø* ∿ *g*
3. Preservation of 1
   and loss of 2   **Xait-/*Xaet-* ∿ **Xeit-/*Xeet-* ($\bar{e}^2$)

                                        *Xlaup-/*Xlaop- ∿ *Xleglup-/*Xleglop-
1. Primarily relevant
    (ablaut)   a ∿ e
2. Concomitant,
    deviant   ∅ ∿ gl
3. Preservation of 1
    and loss of 2   *Xlaup-/*Xlaop- ∿ *Xleup-/*Xleop-

[Compare here the realizations *e-u/e-o/i-u* in the OHG *-r-* preterites *pleruzzun, steroz, biruuuis*, Section 4.4.2 (i).]

                                        *fall- ∿ *febll-
1. Primarily relevant (ablaut)   a ∿ e
2. Concomitant, deviant   ∅ ∿ b
3. Preservation of 1 and
    loss of 2   *fall- ∿ *fell-

[In the latter example there may also have been a development *-bll-* to *-ll-*, Sections 4.4.2 (iv) and 5.3.2 (ii).]

                                        *slē¹p- ∿ *slezlep-
1. Primarily relevant (ablaut) $\bar{e}^1$ ∿ e
2. Concomitant, deviant   ∅ ∿ zl
3. Preservation of 1 and
    loss of 2   *slē¹p- ∿ *sleep- ($\bar{e}^2$)

The new ablaut formation thus clearly contained the constant *e* of the original reduplicative element. Although he does not account for the development itself, Hirt (1932:145), for one, has recognized the presence of that vowel in $\bar{e}^2$/*eo/e* of the new ablaut pattern. He states: "Mir scheint es vor allem auffallend, dass in dem Perfektum, mag es einer Reihe angehören, welcher es will, immer ein *e*-Vokal erscheint, as. *hēt, *hleop, feng*, und das legt doch die Vermutung nahe, dass es sich um reduplizierende Formen handelt."

We can conclude, then, that the new ablaut formation derived from the maintenance of a primarily relevant difference (ablaut). At the same time, less motivated, deviant differences were not preserved here. On the other hand, the *r* preterites and the OE contracted forms both maintained less motivated, deviant differences; this is comparable to cases like OHG *fāhan* ∿ *fieng* vs. *fāhan* ∿ *fieg*. With this analysis it is not surprising that the formation which was most compatible structurally with the language, that is, the new ablaut formation, was exactly the formation to become the dominant usage.

(ii) We will now consider some further questions that relate to the new ablaut formation.

(α) In comparison with the examples examined in Section 5.4.1, one specific aspect of the reanalyzed preterite form has not been discussed. This is the fact that

the specific nonroot material occurred in intervocalic
position, i.e. in so-called "interlude" or "ambisyllabic"
distribution. This is a highly uncommon position for nonroot elements in Germanic. As such, it made the specific
nonroot material structurally all the more deviant and
susceptible to loss. Yet this does not make it ESSENTIALLY
different from such examples as OHG *fāhan* ∿ *fieng* (> *fahan*
∿ *fieg*). As a matter of fact, the reanalysis caused the
unusual distribution, which is unambiguously reflected in
the OHG *r* preterite formation. The fact that in this formation the specific nonroot material developed to an *r*
infix shows how much the intervocalic position may be compared, in the question at hand, to other distributions in
the word. Moreover, as we will discuss under (β), the re-
formation could also have applied to a monosyllabic structure in which the specific nonroot material did not occur
in intervocalic position.

   (β) The re-formation proposed in Section 5.4.2 started from a bisyllabic root structure that had partial reduction of the second, nonprominent syllable, as reflected
in the OHG *r* preterites. This is, in our view, the most
probable analysis. However, the re-formation could also
have applied to a bisyllabic structure before any reduction of the second, nonprominent syllable took place. It
must also have applied in specific cases to a structure
exhibiting total reduction of the second, nonprominent
syllable [Section 4.4.2 (iv)]. If a more generalized total reduction of the second, nonprominent syllable of the
reanalyzed preterite form came about early [although this
was probably a second step in the reduction process; see
Section 5.3.1, but cf. also Sacks (1977) discussed in
Appendix II.4] the re-formation could even have applied
to contracted forms such as Old English *heht* [cf. 5.3.2
(ii)]. The re-formation would in such a case have depended even more on the form of the present. Cf. **Xait-/*
*Xaet- ∿ **XeXt-* with *i/e* ∿ *X* > *i/e* ∿ *i/e*, yielding **Xait-/*
*Xaet- > *Xeit-/*Xeet-*; preterites as *slē̥p-* (OHG *slief*)
would then be best explained as analogical.
   In any case we should be well aware of the fact that
a formation does not have to derive from one single form.
As Hirt (1932:156) has stated in a general perspective:
"Es ist ein Köhlerglaube, dass eine scheinbar einheitliche
Bildung immer auf eine einzige Grundform zurückgehen
muss." And as far as our specific problem is concerned,
we should also heed Fourquet's words (1962:67): "On a
plus de chances d'être dans le vrai, si l'on admet que la
systématisation westique et nordique de la VIIe classe a
pour base une multiplicité de formations."
   We should also remember that once the ablaut formation
was established, it must have been productive and expan-
sive. The forms of the other formations were then gradually supplanted. There is no need to assume that the
same re-formation was utilized again and again. In fact,
forms like OE *heht* and OHG *steroz* apparently went out

of style, rather than being eliminated through a repeated
re-formation process.

(γ) Umlaut and consonantal conditionings operated
with or after the accent shift, that is, at the time of
the evolution of the above forms. The role of umlaut
(Section 4.4.1) is not in all respects clear, but consonantal conditioning before checked nasal is unambiguously
attested, e.g. *feng- > *fing- (subtype of *fell-), although not in a consistent way. In West Germanic the
form with e is found most commonly, e.g. Old Saxon feng.
This has been called a "restoration of e-vocalism" (Kerns
1937:14) following the model of *fell-. Actually, this is
only one example of a clearly marked and more general
preference for the "mid" vocalism $\bar{e}^2$/eo/e (as compared to
$\bar{\imath}$/iu/i) in the preterite part of the new ablaut formation;
in other words, the prevailing distinctions or alternations between such "mid" and "high" vocalisms in the present are not found in the preterite. Likewise, the $j\bar{u}$/
$j\bar{o}$ split in ON, based on consonantal conditioning (in general $j\bar{u}$ before labials and velars, e.g. krjūpa, and $j\bar{o}$ before dentals, e.g. bjōđa) is not upheld in the preterite,
and $j\bar{o}$ (for earlier eo) is generalized (e.g. hljōp). For
further discussion and more examples see Van Coetsem
(1956:65-6).[18]

(δ) The original, basic form of the new ablaut formation was subsequently affected and to a certain extent
obscured by changes, shifts, or analogical extensions
(Van Coetsem 1956:56-69 and 1963).
     For example, $\bar{e}^2$ seems to have spread from the *Xait-
type to the *fall- type in OHG fiel. In the development
of Dutch we see a strong expansion of $\bar{e}^2$ (or its developments) even outside of the reduplicating class   (Van
Coetsem 1951 and 1980:336-7). Perhaps we should not rule
out the possibility that a form like OHG fiel goes back
to a variant of the reanalyzed preterite form in which the
vocalism of the second, nonprominent syllable had not been
reduced to zero (Section 4.4.1).
     The $\bar{e}^2$ of ON blēt of blōta is apparently a good ex-
ample of analogical extension as well. The verb blōta,
the only one of this type in the reduplicating class of
ON (the verba pura have to be considered separately), has
adopted the $\bar{e}^2$ of the preterite of the more frequent verb
types with ai, ON heita ∿ hēt, leika ∿ lek, and $\bar{e}^1$, ON
blāsa ∿ blēs, grāta ∿ grēt (cf., e.g. Karstien 1921:114);
the regularly expected vocalism eo is found in OE blēot.
     A third example is OE fallan ∿ fēoll/feoll. It may
be that the vocalism ēo (old eo) was analogically extended
to the *fall- type, paralleling the assumed analogical extension of $\bar{e}^2$ in OHG. Yet eo may be a direct development
of e as well; cf. ON, Old Saxon fell, and see Van Coetsem
(1956:65) with further references. An example of analogical extension in Old Frisian is discussed in Appendix
II. 4.2 (ii) (β).

(ε) The verba pura could develop or generalize glides
(*y*, *w*) between the verbal root and the inflectional endings, and thus acquire a regular consonant final root
type₊ In such a case, aside from a strong tendency to
switch to the weak conjugation, they could follow the general development of the reduplicating verbs. A form like
OE *sēow* can then be directly derived from **sezow-* (<
*sezō-); cf. Old Saxon *sāian* (with *y* glide) but preterite
oƀar-seu (otherwise regularly weak), Middle Dutch *saien* ∿
zieu (otherwise regularly weak), Modern Dutch *zaaien* ∿
zaaide (weak).

(ζ) The *ē*² in ON OE *lēt*, OHG *liez*, etc., can have
developed from **lelet-* < **lelēt-* (cf. Gothic *saislep* ∿
slepan) occurring beside **lelot-* < *lelōt-* (cf. Gothic
lailot ∿ *letan*); it may also be analogical [see (β) above].

(η) The verb with vowel initial root, a rare type
(cf. Gothic *aikan* ∿ *aiaik*, *aukan* ∿ *aiauk*), must have favored the emergence of the new ablaut formation (**e + aik-*
> **e + ek-*, **e + auk-* > **e + ok-*).

5.5. While the formal prehistory of the three formations may be in our perspective basically clarified,
their respective areal-linguistic expansion (with the possible social or stylistic connotations) previous to their
attestation remains more hypothetical. As we have seen
(Section 1), at the time of their documentation they exhibited not only areal-linguistic but also stylistic differences. We cannot, however, simply project that picture
into the past. Were the *r* preterites and the new ablaut
formation each originally confined to a specific area? Or
did they areally overlap, mutually and with the formation
from which the OE contracted forms derived; were they then
used with differences in social or stylistic connotation?
Although the *r* preterites and the OE contracted forms may
originally have known a larger lexical and areal expansion
than the materials reveal, the only thing we are really
certain of is that at the time of documentation they were
fighting a losing battle against the new ablaut formation.

APPENDICES

I. OUR OWN RESEARCH AND THE MIRROR IMAGE THEORY

I.1. First we will discuss the mirror image view as
presented in our earlier work (e.g. 1956, 1963). We assumed there that the new ablaut pattern in the reduplicated class had originated from a so-called INVERTED ANAL-
OGY between the present and the preterite of the *e* and *a*
groups of the strong verbs:

	e Group			*a* Group	
Present		Preterite	Present		Preterite
*greip-	∿	*graip-	*Xait-	∿	*Xeit-
*beud-	∿	*baud-	*Xlaup-	∿	*Xleup-
*Xelp-	∿	*Xalp-	*fall-	∿	*fell-

that is,

$$\frac{\text{Present } e}{\text{Preterite } a} = \frac{\text{Present } a}{\text{Preterite x} = e}$$

We interpret inverted analogy here strictly as a mechanism that effected or created the mirror image alternation in question, not as a possible lexical expansion of an already existing mirror image alternation (productivity).

I.1.1. The above analogy was based on the fact that reduplication in the *a* verbs (*Xait-*, etc.) was a minority principle within the paradigm of the strong verbs. As such, it was subject to replacement by the prevailing ablaut principle. The assumption of such an inverted analogy seemed warranted at the time, as clear examples of REGULAR analogy between the *e* and *a* groups had already been found (Van Coetsem:1956, e.g. 61). The question of the validity of inverted analogy, however, even in the presence of regular analogy, was not addressed. In order to distinguish this view from other theories on the origin of the new ablaut formation (contraction, Indo-European origin, etc.), this explanation has come to be known as the MIRROR IMAGE THEORY, *e* ∿ *a/a* ∿ *e*, especially by Dutch linguists.

I.1.2. In the MIRROR IMAGE ALTERNATION, *e* ∿ *a/a* ∿ *e*, that we posited for the new ablaut formation, there were two problems, namely a synchronic problem concerning functionality and a diachronic problem dealing with the origin of the alternation.

(i) As we have just pointed out, we did not address the latter question, i.e. the one concerning the validity of the mirror image alternation as a form of language change; we did not have empirical evidence for substantiating it. Consequently, the explanation of inverted analogy was merely a hypothesis which tried to account for the subsequent evolution in a coherent and simple way. This latter fact implies that the positing of *e* in the preterite of the reduplicating class can be motivated by reconstruction and must therefore be distinguished from the problem of origin of that *e*. [See the assumption of *e* in $\bar{e}^2/eo/e$ by Hirt (Section 5.4.2 (i) above.]

(ii) As to the synchronic problem of functionality, we made the following remark: "dieser Ablaut wurde zur Unterscheidung der Tempora angewandt, ohne dass dabei *e* und *a* charakteristisch zu sein brauchen für das Präsens

bzw. das Präteritum; nicht der Vokalismus an sich, sondern
der betreffende Unterschied und Ablaut war funktionell.
Das Nebeneinander von z.b. *ie/oo* in ndl. *ik schiet* 'ich
schiesse' und *ik schoot* 'ich schoss' (Präteritum) und *ik
loop* 'ich laufe' (Präsens) und *ik liep* 'ich lief' (Präteritum) dürfte eine beweisende Parallelle dafür bieten."
With the Dutch example *ie* ∿ *oo/oo* ∿ *ie* we merely meant to
illustrate the functional validity of a mirror image alternation, and not its origin, as Bech (1969:52) errone-
ously thinks. The fact that *ie* ∿ *oo/oo* ∿ *ie* belongs historically to the ablaut alternation *e* ∿ *a/a* ∿ *e* cannot
then be an objection.

I.2. Let us now turn to the question of the mirror
image alternation with the knowledge and the perspective
that more recent research has provided us.

I.2.1. In the SYNCHRONIC perspective, we find that
mirror image alternations are not at all uncommon (Chomsky-
Halle 1968:355-6), and that mirror image properties have
been attributed to natural languages (Langacker 1969:575-
98, 844-62 and see also Chomsky 1973:233).

Chomsky-Halle examine mirror image alternations and
mention that as early as 1912, Meinhof coined the term
POLARITY RULES for that kind of alternation. Chomsky-
Halle discuss these as a general phenomenon which can be
formulated in a simple rule: [α feature x] ⟶ [-α feature x], being itself an abbreviation of two rules that
apply disjunctively, namely [- feature x] ⟶ [+ feature
x] and the reverse [+ feature x] ⟶ [- feature x]. This
formulation shows the greater generality allowed by a mirror image alternation. Chomsky-Halle mention an example
of mirror image alternation (low ∿ nonlow) from Biblical
Hebrew, which exhibits certain features similar to our
Germanic example:

> perfect *a* ∿ imperfect *o*, lamad ∿ yilmod 'learn'
>   *o* ∿   *a*, qaton ∿ yiqtan 'be small'
>   *e* ∿   *o*, zaqen ∿ yizqan 'age'

There has been a discussion about the nature of polarity
rules and whether they are exclusively "morpho-lexical" or
also phonological (Stephen Anderson, Wayles Browne, James
McCawley, etc.; see Zonneveld 1976 also for a summary of
the discussion and further references), but it is not necessary to go into that here.

I.2.2. As to the DIACHRONIC aspect, i.e. the origin
of mirror image in language, there is no doubt that on
the phonic level (i.e. the one of "mere otherness") inversion directly producing a mirror image of an earlier
situation is not at all uncommon. There is, for example,
a well-known type of inversion represented in, e.g. *g* ∿
z > *z* ∿ *g*, in French *magazin* > popular French *mazaguin*
(Grammont 1939:348-52), but this is not a form of analogy.[19]

There are more complex forms of inversion based on analogical hypercorrection (with possible spelling influence) and involving stylistic (social) connotation or function (cf. Anttila 1972:90-1). Both phonological and lexical factors are involved. An example of this is the syncope of intervocalic *d* and its hypercorrect restoration in the history of Dutch (Zonneveld 1978).

However, when grammatical categories like present and preterite are involved, an inversion or inverted analogy would imply inversion of function, e.g. present *e* ∿ preterite *a*/present *a* ∿ preterite *e*. For the origin of such a mirror image alternation unambiguous proof in the way of clear examples of direct inversion has not been found, and therefore the notion of inverted analogy has not only been doubted, but also flatly rejected. Bech (1969:52) for one insists that analogy follows a direct proportion (ax:ay = bx:by), never an inverted one (ax:ay = by:bx). Yet proponents of the generative approach, although generally opposed to the notion of analogy, tend to regard an inversion that produces a mirror image alternation as possible. Chomsky-Halle (1968:356), in their discussion of mirror image alternations and polarity rules, state that "polarity rules may arise in a language in a great many ways IN ADDITION TO BEING ADDED DIRECTLY TO THE GRAMMAR" (our emphasis). The latter points to the fact that the authors believe in the possibility of a direct inversion. Earlier Kiparsky (1965:2-38) noted: "It is reasonable to suppose that changing fixed polarity values to variably specified polarity values in a rule should make it more general. If that initial assumption is right, then in view of the idea of analogy as a simplificatory process inverted analogy is just what we would expect to find."

Unfortunately it remains a fact that, as yet, we do not have a single, unambiguous example of such an inverted analogy.[20] Thus, the validity of the notion itself may, indeed, be rightfully questioned. This seems to be reason enough not to turn to it for an explanation of the origin of the new ablaut formation. This is especially the case since there may be a better evidenced basis for accounting for it, as we hope to have demonstrated in previous sections of this study.

I.3. In conclusion, while leaving the question of inverted analogy open, we can maintain here the concept of mirror image, as it characterizes an original property of the new ablaut formation. Yet we should adapt it to our current view. The new ablaut formation appears to have originated from the inclusion of the constant *e* of the original reduplicative element within the bounds of the verbal root. Keeping in mind that the original reduplicative element contained the potential ablaut alternant (Section 4.2), it is very important to note that BY SIMPLE APPLICATION OF THE REDUPLICATION PRINCIPLE THE MIRROR IMAGE ALTERNATION WAS POTENTIALLY PRESENT: *e* (**greip-*) ∿ *a* (**graip-*)/*a* (**Xait-*) ∿ *e* (**XeXait-*). In the reanalysis

the latter *e* became integrated into the verbal root, and
with the resulting new ablaut pattern, the mirror image
alternation was actualized. However, it soon became obscured in several parts (resulting from, e.g. the change
ei > *ī* in **greip-*). As a phenomenon that allowed for
greater generality, it may have helped the productivity
and expansion of the new ablaut formation.

II. OTHER RESEARCH

II.1. The development of the Germanic reduplicating
class, especially the origin of the new ablaut formation
in North and West Germanic, is one of the subjects in Germanic linguistics which have been endlessly researched,
discussed, and debated. As a consequence, virtually anything said here about the topic has already been stated in
some perspective or other. However, previous research has
not produced a generally accepted type of explanation of
the total development. Such an explanation is precisely
what we have been focusing on in the present study.

II.2. In our earlier work (1956:47-52; cf. also 1970:
89-91) we reviewed the different theories that have been
proposed, and thus we can restrict ourselves here to a
summary of that review.

II.2.1. The first general type of explanation is the
contraction theory, which goes back to Grimm and on which
subsequently several variants have been submitted. According to this theory the new ablaut formation evolved
through contraction of the reduplicative element with the
verbal root. Such developments as dissimilation and deletion of the initial consonantism of that root have been
assumed. Another suggested origin for the contraction has
been the vowel initial verbal roots (**auk-   *e + auk-*).
In the way it has been generally proposed, the contraction
theory is ill-founded and unconvincing.

II.2.2. While the contraction theory brings the North
and West Germanic formation together with the Gothic reduplicated forms, a second theory, which goes back to
Brugmann (Wood), explains the new ablaut formation as or-
iginating from different Indo-European ablaut alternants.
The North and West Germanic new preterite vocalism is then
derived from Indo-European *ē* + *y/w/l/r/m/n*; there is, however, no evidence whatsoever for such an assumption.
Moreover, it seems highly improbable that we would have a
Pre-Germanic ablaut here, since there is no reflex of it
in the derivational morphology (Van Coetsem 1956:50 with
further references).

II.2.3. Another theory, proposed by Karstien (1921),
has been generally abandoned (Van Coetsem 1956:50). However, we should note that it assumed the loss or dropping
of the reduplicative element, an idea which cannot be

completely left out of consideration (cf. our Section
5.1). Finally, our own earlier theory of inverted analogy has been discussed in Appendix I. In the following
review of the recent literature on the subject we will
focus only on those views (Bech 1969, Sacks 1977) that
are germane to our analysis.[21]

II.3. On several occasions we have referred to Bech
(1969), either in agreement or disagreement. Since a number of his ideas have been adopted here, we will now systematically examine Bech's argument, comparing it with the
explanation offered in our analysis.

II.3.1. A first point concerns the general approach
to the problem. It is to Bech's credit that he has recognized the importance of considering the different formations for explaining the development of the Germanic
reduplicating class, and the emergence of the new ablaut
formation, i.e. of the so-called NORMAL TYPE. As previous
research, including our own, paid little or no attention
to anything which was not that normal type, it missed precisely the basis for an overall explanation: "Man hat es
von jeher in viel zu hohem Grade versäumt, die gesamte
Prät.-Bildung der nwg. (*North and West Germanic*) 7. starken Konjugation als eine Einheit und die vorhandenen Va-
rianten derselben als verschiedene je nach der Zeit und
Ort variierende Produkte einer und derselben Entwicklungs-
kette anzuschauen und hat es schon deswegen zu keiner
überzeugende Lösung bringen können" (Bech 1969:54). However, Bech's view of the relation between the normal type
and the other formations is basically different from ours.

II.3.2. Bech's explanation provides a second positive
point which we have adopted. This is the assumption of a
systematic levelling in Gothic of the alternations produced by Verner's Law with the preservation of reinstatement of the reduplication principle and, conversely, the
preservation of such alternations with the abandoning of
the reduplication principle in North and West Germanic
(cf. Sections 3.1 - 3.3 above).

II.3.3. A third constructive point in Bech's treatment, which has become part of our own as well, is his assumption of a reanalysis of the original reduplicated form
in the North and West Germanic area. This reanalysis produced a nonroot element within the bounds of the verbal
root called SPECIFIC NONROOT MATERIAL by us and INFIX by
Bech; in reviewing his theory we use his term infix. The
reanalysis constitutes the point at which crucial differences between his view and ours arise.

(i) The basic differences between Bech's view and
ours can be traced back to our respective conception of
the reanalysis.

(α) We noted (Section 3.3.3) that Bech's conception
(namely *X + eg + ait- with *X-ait- being the verbal root
and -eg- the infix), ignores the full implications of the
accent shift, and is therefore insufficiently motivated
and unsatisfactory. In his view the constant e of the
reduplicative element became in the reanalysis part of the
infix, not of the verbal root as in our explanation. Since
his view, like ours, implies that this e became integrated
into the verbal root, he must account for this in the subsequent development of the reanalyzed form. How does Bech
see this subsequent development?

He takes into consideration the productivity of the r
preterites, but is limited by his own theory in his explanation of their origin [cf. our Section 5.2.3 above and
(iii) below]. He assumes r to have originated from z,
that is, from verbs with s anlaut (*sē-, *salt-) and suggests that the various forms of the infix were replaced by
ez in all the verb types of the North and West Germanic
reduplicating class (*X + eg + ait- > *X + ez + ait-, *X
+ egl + aup- > *Xl + ez + aup-, the latter with anlaut readjustment). The emergence of e in ez as a root vocalism
must then be seen in relation to the so-called syncope
[in our terminology (total) reduction] of the vocalism of
the second, nonprominent syllable of the reanalyzed form;
in Bech's opinion this reduction was a total one in the
case of ai, a, ē (ǣ), but a partial one, namely to w, in
the case of a back vocalism au, ō, ū (cf. *Xezait- >
*Xezt-, *Xlezaup- > *Xlezwp-). Subsequently ez developed
to ē through so-called Ersatzdehnung 'compensatory lengthening' (*Xezt- > *Xēt-, *Xlezwp- > *Xlewp-). Thus, for
Bech the basic development is a succession of four steps,
namely (1) reanalysis (with anlaut readjustment whenever
necessary), (2) generalization of ez, (3) syllable reduction, and (4) compensatory lengthening. This can be illustrated by the following examples:

$$(1)$$

*Xait-	∿ *X + eg + ait-		>
*Xlaup-	∿ *X + egl + aup-	(*Xe + egl + aup-)	>
*fall-	∿ *f + eb + all-		>
*slēp-	∿ *s + ezl + ēp-	(*sl + ezl + ēp-)	>
(*sloēp-)			
*Xrōp-	∿ *X + egr + ōp-	(*Xr + egr + ōp-)	>
*būw-	∿ *b + eb + ūw-		>

(2)		(3)		(4)	
*Xezait-	>	*Xēzt-	>	*Xēt-	$(\bar{e}^2)$
*Xlezaup-	>	*Xlezwp-	>	*Xlewp-	(eo)
*fezall-	>	*fezll-	>	*fēll-	$(\bar{e}^2)$
*slezēp-	>	*slezp-	>	*slēp-	$(\bar{e}^2)$
*Xrezōp-	>	*Xrezwp-	>	*Xrewp-	(eo)
*bezūw-	>	*bezww-	>	*bēww-	(eo)

(β) In our view, however, the constant *e* was, with
the reanalysis, directly integrated into the verbal root.
This allows for a simpler solution than Bech's, as we
have seen.

(ii) We have stated (Section II.3.1) that Bech's view
of the relation between the normal type and the other formations is basically different from ours.

(α) While Bech sees the formation from which the *r*
preterites evolved (*ez*) as a stage leading to the new ablaut, his view of the relationship between the *ez* formation, the *r* preterites, and the normal type is for the
most part not one of parallel formations. In our view,
on the other hand, the formations are in more of a relationship of simultaneity, with one of them, the new ablaut, becoming the dominant usage.

(iii) It is now apparent why Bech, in his explanation
of the origin of the *r* preterites and the normal type,
must assume an analogical spread starting from *ez* (verb
with *s* anlaut) and not from *er* (verb with *r* anlaut). A
form like **Xerait-* would have become **Xert-* (following
Bech's view of the reduction). No compensatory lengthening to *ē* could then take place. Cf. Bech 28: "Dass in
den ahd. (*OHG*), an. (*ON*) und angl. präteritalen *r*-Formen
kein germ. *r*, sondern germ. *z* steckt, indem in diesen
Präterita ein verallgemeinertes -*ez*- vorliegt, und kein
germ. -*er*-, haben wir ... einfach behauptet. Die ent-
scheidende Begründung dieser Behauptung wird erst mit dem
ē-Prät. erbracht, indem der Übergang von *ez* > *ē* es uns
erlaubt, dieses *ē*-haltige Prät. als Ergebnis einer wei-
teren Entwicklung synkopierter *ez*-Formen und somit das gesamte Material des nwg. Prät. der 7. starken Konjugation
als eine historische Einheit zu betrachten, was eine An-
nahme von Formen mit innerem germ. -*er*- nicht ermöglichen
würde. Denn aus germ. -*er*- vor Kons. entsteht jedenfalls
kein nwg. *ē*, sondern das vorkonsonantische *r* bleibt ja
überall als *r* erhalten, z.b. germ. **bergan* > got. *bairgan*,
an *bjarga*, ae. *beorgan*, as. ahd. *bergan*." In order to
strengthen his case, Bech continues: "Wenn man z.B. angl.
reordon direkt aus germ. **rerōdun* durch Verlust des *ō* ent-
stehen lässt, wie man ja dies im allgemeinen tut, so ist
ipso facto jede Möglichkeit vernichtet, diese Form den
entsprechenden *ē*-Formen der übrigen nwg. Dialekte, an.
rēþu, as. *rēdun* usw., etymologisch gleichzusetzen."
However, as we have shown, Bech's is not the only way
to account for such forms as ON *rēþu* within the total development of the reduplicating class in North and West
Germanic. Moreover, Bech's explanation, using *ez* as the
source of the new ablaut formation in North and West Germanic, contains a number of serious weaknesses, flaws,
and unnecessary complications.

(iv) Let us consider in some detail some of these shortcomings.

(α) First, Bech's assumption of an original distinction in the degree of reduction of the second, nonprominent syllable of the reanalyzed form (total or partial), depending on the nature of the involved vocalism, is very questionable. As we have pointed out [Section 4.4.2 (iii)], the OHG r preterites contained only a back vocalism (original au, $\bar{o}$, $\bar{u}$). In view of the strongly limited number of such r preterites, this may well be coincidental; it may also reflect a specific OHG situation. Furthermore, considering OE $beoftun$ ($\sim b\bar{e}atan/*baut-$), which was nicely in line with OE $heht$, $leolc$, etc., but counters Bech's assumption, it seems more plausible to view the distinction in question as an areal-linguistic one; it is then even conceivable that there was some form of complementarity between the development of the OHG r preterites and the OE contracted forms (Section 5.3.1).
Compounding the problem is another of Bech's hypotheses, namely that the partial reduction of the back vocalism au, $\bar{o}$, $\bar{u}$ resulted in the so-called "consonant" w; to make the view more acceptable he refers to cases like Gothic $skadwjan$, $balwjan$, $triggws$. This explanation is necessary to save the theory, since only before a consonant could ez become $\bar{e}$, and the only "consonant" that could result from a reduction of au, $\bar{o}$, $\bar{u}$ was the glide w. If the partial reduction had produced a vowel, u or o, the preceding z of ez would have been rhotacized to r, as the OHG r preterites $pleruzzun$, $steroz$, etc., prove. Still, the little evidence we have with the OHG r preterites favors the view of a partial reduction yielding not w, but a vowel, which was apparently felt as (part of the) root vocalism [Section 4.4.2 (i) and also Bech 1969:23]. While Bech concludes that ez must have been followed by w, we may as well dismiss the whole assumption of ezw as a pure construct to serve the theory.

(β) Another flaw in Bech's argumentation concerns the development of ez to $\bar{e}$ before t in $*lez\bar{e}t-$ [of $*l\bar{e}t-$ ($*l\bar{æ}t-$)] > $*lezt-$ > $*l\bar{e}t-$. By all known standards zt would have to develop to st, yielding $*lest-$ instead of $*l\bar{e}t-$. Yet Bech (1969:27-8) maintains that this ez became $\bar{e}$ before t. To account for this he makes again an ad hoc claim, namely that z of ez be regarded not as a "normal" z, but as a sound of the r type ("ein Laut vom r-Typus"), namely R. But then, why did this R not develop to r, as is normally the case? Bech assumes this for OE (Anglian) $leort$, but persists in believing that such an eR before t changed to $\bar{e}$ in the other Old Germanic languages. Clearly, the assumption of a development $*lezt-$ to $*l\bar{e}t-$ is again only necessary to maintain the theory.

(γ) Unnecessary complication is evident when Bech
(1969:33), consistent with his theory, considers the analogical extension of *ez* to have applied also to the verb
type with a vowel initial root, e.g. *eauk- of auk- developing to *ezauk- > *ezwk- > *ēwk-, and *eaik- of *aik-
developing to *ezaik- > *ezk- > *ēk-.

(δ) Similarly, Bech (1969:34 ff.) is consistent with
his general explanation when he compares the ON and OE
verba pura. Using ON sā ~ sera, OE sāwan ~ sēow, he posits a development *sezōwV- > *sezwV-, in which w occurred
before a vowel V. He assumes that in *sezwV-, w was
dropped in ON (before *ez could develop to ē), yielding
*sezV-, sera (he compares *sungwun > ON sungu, OE sungon,
OHG sungun), while *ez developed to ē before w in OE,
yielding *sēwV-, sēow.

The question whether *sezwV- can be validly compared
with *sungwun aside, there is the argument that the traditional derivation of ON sera directly from *sezō- is far
simpler and linguistically more realistic than Bech's theoretical constructions. Furthermore, because of the integrated character of his theory, Bech would also have to
account for the i in Old Saxon sāian (cf. preterite oᵬar-
seu) which he does not and cannot do; cf. Middle Dutch
saeien (preterite zieu), Modern Dutch zaaien (weak). For
similar examples with the y glide vs. w, see Van Coetsem
(1956:68), Rauch (1972), and especially the Middle Dutch
verba pura, Van Loey (1955:82-5). Such glides in hiatus
position either have developed from the preceding vocalism
or have been generalized; areal-linguistic differences
must be taken into consideration.

(ε) Finally, Bech (1969:26) lists a set of equations,
which would seem to support his theory and which we re-
produce here:

		mizdo	(rairoþ)		(lailot)
Gothic		mizdo	(rairoþ)		(lailot)
ON			rēþ		
OE	Anglian	meord	reord	ondreord	leort
	West Saxon	mēd	rēd	ondrēd	lēt
Old Saxon		mēda	rēd	andrēd	lēt
OHG		miata	riat	intriat	liaz

If one looks at this set more closely, the evidence
for Bech's view is no more than an "optical illusion."
The fact that Anglian meord and West Saxon mēd came from
*mezd- (Gothic mizdo) does by no means prove that Anglian
reord, ondreord, leort and West Saxon rēd, ondrēd, lēt
were derived from *rezd-, *lezt-. If Anglian reord came
from *rezd-, we would also expect a *Xezt- to produce an
Anglian *heort (as a preterite of hātan), but instead we
find the regularly contracted form heht. In other words,
it is very suspicious that *ez would have been analogically
extended only to verbs with r (or l anlaut). This

precisely justifies the traditional explanation of the
preterites *reord* and *leort* (< *leolt*) as contracted forms
paralleling *heht*. If, however, we prefer to account for
leort as an analogical form after the model of a form like
reord, we can also speak here of *r* preterites, but in
quite a different way from Bech's. A form such as West
Saxon *rēd* could be derived from *rezd-*, if we have proof
that there was such a form. And explaining *lēt* in West
Saxon, etc., as the outcome of *lezt-*, is, as we have seen
(β), merely a device to save the theory. In conclusion,
here again we can better dismiss Bech's *ez* hypothesis.

(ζ) As one can see, in spite of its valid foundations
Bech's argument is an accumulation of assumptions. The
shortcomings of his treatment ultimately result from his
unsatisfactory conception of the reanalysis, which, in
turn, is a consequence of his failure to recognize the
full implications of the accent shift.

II.4. As we do, Sacks (1977) follows Bech in taking
into consideration the various forms and not only the normal type. He suggests that "the confused situation of the
Gmc. seventh class seems best explained by a solution ultimately based upon the vocalism of the reduplicating
class followed by analogical — not phonological — developments" (1977:250).

II.4.1. His starting point is contraction as represented in the OE contracted forms, e.g. present *rēd-* ~
preterite *rerd-* (which he apparently considers the inherited preterite plural replacing *rerōd-* of the singular). A number of analogical developments would then
have followed. For example, after the model of the present *rēd-* ~ preterite *rerd-*, we would have (following
his notations): *hait* ~ *heht-*, *blōt-* ~ *blelt-* [*wōp-*
~ *weup-*; OE had *hwōp-*, *wōp-*, *wēp-*, cf. Section 5.3.2 (ii)
(α) above], *hlaup-* ~ *hlelp* (*baut-* ~ *beft-*). Similarly, *hald-* would have developed a preterite *hehld-*, the
latter becoming *held-*. The pattern *hald-* ~ *held-* would
have generated *rēd-* ~ *rē²d-* (~ *rerd-*), *hait-* ~ *hē²t-*
(~ *heht-*), *blōt-* ~ *blē²t-* (~ *blelt-*), *hlaup-* ~
hlē²p- (~ *hlelp-*).

II.4.2. There are some difficulties with Sacks' view.

(i) In cases like *rēd-* ~ *rē²d-* (~ *rerd-*), we would
have a kind of analogical lengthening or a sort of "compensatory lengthening," although Sacks admits that "the
idea of compensatory lengthening in an analogical process
is theoretically a difficult one" (1977:246). Instead of
a lengthening in the preterite we would expect the model
of *hald-* ~ *held-* to generate, e.g. *hlaup-* ~ *hleup-*
(instead of *hlē²p-*; Sacks assumes that *hlaup-* ~ *hleup-*
was made after the model of *wop-* ~ *weup-*).

(ii)   Another problem with the treatment of Sacks is
a lack of distinction in the time perspective.

(α)   In view of the OHG *r* preterites and the areal-
linguistic restriction of such forms as OE *heht* at the
time of documentation, one may wonder whether it is diachronically justified to use forms with (generalized) total reduction of the second, nonprominent syllable as a
general starting point for explaining the new ablaut formation [cf. Section 5.4.2 (ii) (β) above]. It seems haz-
ardous to make the emergence of the new ablaut formation
exclusively dependent on either one of the other formations, and that is what both Bech and Sacks do. While the
former accounts for the normal type by following the line
of the *r* preterites, the latter starts from the type represented in the OE contracted forms.

(β)   While Sacks does not clearly distinguish between
what is original and what is secondary in the development
of the new ablaut formation, he does not view the analogical processes within the system in which they are supposed
to have taken place. For example, when positing a preterite $*Xl\bar{e}^2p-$ for the $*Xlaup-$ type, he must have been primarily considering Old Frisian *hlāpa* ⌣ *hlēp* (*hlīp*) [for ON
blēt of *blōta* cf. Section 5.4.2 (ii) (δ) above]. However,
such a *hlēp* form cannot have belonged to the original ablaut formation. The Old Frisian generalization of *ē* in
both the $*Xait-$ and $*Xlaup-$ types is the result of both a
specific merger and analogical extension; it will have
occurred only after *ai* and *au* had merged, each regularly
becoming *ā* and *ē* (the latter with *i* umlaut). In the concrete case of *hlāpa* ($*Xlaup-$) the occurrence of the preterite *hlēp* can be readily explained as an analogical extension, for example, from the past participle *hlēpen* (<
-in, earlier *-en*). For more details see, e.g. Steller
(1928:63-4) and for a discussion of other forms, Van
Coetsem (1956:59-60) with further references.

II.4.3.   On the other hand, Sacks' view and ours are
conceived on comparable principles in spite of differences
in factual interpretation. First, like us, Sacks regards
the constant *e* of the original reduplicative element as
the basis for the new ablaut formation, which is an idea
already implied in earlier work, as we have seen [Section
5.4.2 (i)]. Second, in our two approaches the further
justification of the new ablaut formation is founded on
the principle of structural re-formation of the preterite.
In Sacks' view this re-formation is analogically carried
out on the model of patterns developed from contraction;
in our view it is implemented on the model of the root
structure as found primarily in the present, with preservation of the ablaut alternant developed in the reanalyzed preterite form.*

NOTES

1. The second components of the reconstructed diphthongs are transcribed as *i* (**Xait-*) and *u* (**auk-*), following a practice common in European Germanic tradition. For the period of the Germanic parent language *i* and *u* cover both the nonsyllabic and syllabic variants; of course, we could use *y* (*j*) and *w* as well. Cf. Van Coetsem (1972: 179 ff., 1979, and 1980:301-2).

2. The documented *r* preterites reflect an areal-linguistic pattern ON—Upper German (hypothetically OE). Whether this represents the original expansion of the *r* preterites is unclear. For such an areal-linguistic pattern, see Maurer (1952).

3. Such material as *-la-* in **lelaik-* is residual and has no clear-cut status; it cannot be considered a morpheme or affix, although it could develop to one. It is comparable, for example, to *w* in Dutch *kwam* 'came' of *komen* 'to come' (cf. German *kommen* ᴠ *kam* and English *come* ᴠ *came*, where *w* has been levelled out; further on this in Section 5.4.1). See in this connection Bolinger (1965). Furthermore, the distinction between SPECIFIC NONROOT MATERIAL and AFFIX complies with the traditional European differentiation between MORPHOPHONOLOGY and MORPHOLOGY proper [cf., e.g. Uhlenbeck 1966:258 (Uhlenbeck 1949)]; see also the view expressed in Van Coetsem-Hendricks-Siegel (1981:175).

4. Following Uhlenbeck (1962:especially 428-9), we also prefer not to use the term PREFIX with relation to the reduplicative element, since the involved process is root reduplication, i.e. repetition, and not affixation.

5. This was actually the root type of the Germanic verb in general.

6. In our reconstructed forms, *b, d, g* cover both the stop and fricative allophones [b, ƀ], [d, đ], [g, ǥ], respectively; [b] and [ƀ], etc., were in complementary distribution. The difference is only indicated when necessary.

7. Attempts to show that Verner's Law also operated in word-initial position have been unsuccessful. The standard example Latin *co-* (*communis*) vs. Gothic *ga-* (*gamains*) is now far more convincingly explained as a reflex of an Indo-European alternation *k* ᴠ *gh* (in traditional notation); other examples of such an alternation are Latin *capio* ᴠ *habeo*, *cis* ᴠ *hic*. For a further discussion, see Fourquet (1976).

8. His further treatment, however, differs from ours and follows partly Bech (1969).

9. We are badly informed about the place of the accent in the (Pre-)Gothic reduplicated form; the evidence seems contradictory. Cf., e.g. Bennett (1967), Hopper (1969), but also Schmierer (1977: 60 ff.).

10. It is conceivable that there were (individual) deviations from this ideal analysis. Yet there is no reason to assume that the totality of the second, nonprominent syllable was felt as specific nonroot material or as suffix. There appears to be consistency of identity between the final consonantism of the reanalyzed preterite form and that of the verbal root as found in the present, e.g. *t* in **XeXait-* ᴠ **Xait-* and *k* in **lelaik-* ᴠ **laik-*; therefore final

consonantism such as this must have been felt as part of the root.

11. Of course, we are not considering inflectional endings here.

12. Cf. as a possible example OHG *piheialt* 'held' (Rauch 1972: 776).

13. The following can perhaps serve as a parallel case. There are only a few unambiguous examples of development of VzC (short vocalism + z + consonant) to either $\bar{V}$C or VrC. Here again there seems to be more involved than merely differences in areal-linguistic distribution, at least if we may draw some conclusions from the a-vailable material. In OHG we find $\bar{V}$C in *miata* (Gothic *mizdo*), that is, contraction in the case of front vocalism + z + C; however, we find also VrC in *hort* (Gothic *huzd*) and *rarta* (Gothic *razda*), that is, rhotacism of z to r after back vocalism.

14. Cases in which the present and the preterite were formally the same were not necessarily confusing, as modern language situations show; cf., for example, English *burst* and *hit*.

15. Whether OHG *scrian* ∿ *screi* ∿ *scrirum* ∿ *giscriran* may be considered an r preterite is very questionable (Bech 1969:44). First, the verb did not belong to the reduplicating class. Second, the pattern of occurrence of r in the principal parts (preterite plural and past participle) was quite different from that of the r preter-ites, and rather reminds us of the alternations of Verner's Law. Third, the areal-linguistic area of *scrirum* ∿ *giscriran* was differ-ent from the area of the r preterites, at least at the time of docu-mentation (Braune-Mitzka 1959:271, Rauch 1972:775).

16. In the particular case of OHG *steroz*, one could consider r a development of s from the *st* anlaut. However, this seems less plausible in view of the general analogical expansion of r as at-tested in the ON and OHG r preterites.

17. A more or less comparable case of complementarity of devel-opment is discussed in Section 3. This concerns (1) Gothic pre-serving or reinstating the reduplication principle, but levelling the alternations produced by Verner's Law, and (2) North and West Germanic reanalyzing the reduplicated form, but preserving the al-ternations produced by Verner's Law.

18. Our present explanation does not at all imply a renunciation of our theory that $\bar{e}^2$ developed primarily and under certain condi-tions from *ei*. With "primarily" we refer to the way in which $\bar{e}^2$ emerged in the vocalic system of Germanic. For this we rely on such cases as OHG *stiaga* (*$st\bar{e}^2g$-), in which $\bar{e}^2$ represented a member of an earlier (morphophonemic) alternation, partly preserved in the verbal ablaut, Germanic *ei* ∿ *ai* ∿ *i* ∿ *i*, Gothic *steigan* ∿ *staig* ∿ *stigum* ∿ *stigans*. Other $\bar{e}^2$ attestations, which occurred in loan words and in, e.g. OE (West Saxon) *mēd* (Gothic *mizdo*), are clearly secondary. Bech (1969:49-54) rejects our explanation of $\bar{e}^2$. Al-though this is not the appropriate place for a discussion of this topic, we would like to point out that he refers only to our mono-graph of 1956 and ignores more recent studies of, e.g. 1962 and 1968, in which we reconsider the problem from very different angles, and address the arguments he uses against our explanation of $\bar{e}^2$. The notion of COMPETING CHANGE must also be taken into account in any future consideration of the problem.

19. Forms of dissimilation show mirror image as well; cf. Thurneysen's Law in Gothic, e.g. *d* ∿ *þ/þ* ∿ *d*, *mildiþa* ∿ *auþida*.

20. The case of Middle Dutch *werden* ∿ *word* developing to Modern
Dutch *worden* ∿ *werd*, mentioned by Weijnen (1966:30), probably does
not reflect inverted analogy. It is more plausible to assume here
that, while *e* in Middle Dutch *werden* became rounded after *w*, a preterite form was introduced with the *e* vocalism of the structurally
corresponding *a* verbs (of the reduplicated class), e.g. *vallen* ∿ *vel*
(also *viel*), *houden* ∿ *helt* (also *hielt*) [Schönfeld-Van Loey 1964:67
(57, b, Rem. 2)]. We should note that *worden* also had a preterite
with *ie* vocalism, Middle Dutch *wiert*, dialectal Modern Dutch *wier(d)*.
Cf. furthermore such *e* verbs as *werpen* ∿ *wierp* and *sterven* ∿ *stierf*
in Middle and Modern Dutch; the latter verb had equally *sterf* in
Middle Dutch (Van Loey 1955:73-6).

21. For other studies after 1956 cf. Lüdtke (1957), Höfler
(1970) (on Höfler's *Entfaltungstheorie*, Buyssens 1965:135-80), Meid
(1971:67-106), and see the survey of Durrell (1975).

Addendum. After completion of our study, the following article was
published: J. B. Voyles. 1980. Reduplicating verbs in North-West
Germanic. *Lingua* 52:89-123.

REFERENCES

*For useful comments on a preliminary version of this paper I would
like to thank L. Draye, P. Hopper, J. Jasanoff, O. Leys, I. Rauch,
E. M. Uhlenbeck, and L. Waugh. I am also very grateful to Susan
McCormick for discussions which helped clarify my views and for her
assistance in preparing the text for publication.

Anttila, R. 1972. *An introduction to historical and comparative
    linguistics*. New York: MacMillan.
Bech, G. 1969. *Das germanische reduplizierte Präteritum*. Det
    Kongelige Danske Videnskabernes Selskab. Historisk-filosofiske
    Meddelelser 44.1. København: Munksgaard.
Bennett, W. H. 1967. Some phonological effects of Pre-Gothic
    juncture. *Language* 43:661-5.
Boer, R. C. 1920. *Oudnoorsch Handboek*. Haarlem: H. D. Tjeenk
    Willink.
———. 1924. *Oergermaansch Handboek*. 2nd ed. Haarlem: H. D.
    Tjeenk Willink.
Bolinger, D. L. 1965. On defining the morpheme. *Forms of English*.
    Accent, morpheme, order, ed. by Iramu Abe and Tetsuya Kenekiyo,
    183-9. Cambridge, MA: Harvard University Press. [Reprinted
    from *Word* 4 (1948).]
Braune, W. (W. Mitzka, ed.) 1959. *Althochdeutsche Grammatik*.
    8th-9th ed. Tübingen: Niemeyer.
Buyssens, E. 1956. *Linguistique historique. Homonymie - stylis-
    tique - sémantique - changements phonétiques*. Université Libre
    de Bruxelles, Travaux de la Faculté de Philosophie et Lettres,
    Tome XXVIII. Bruxelles: Presses Universitaires de Bruxelles.
Chomsky, N. 1973. Conditions on transformations. *A Festschrift
    for Morris Halle*, ed. by S. R. Anderson and P. Kiparsky, 232-86.
    New York: Holt, Rinehart and Winston.
———, and M. Haale. 1968. *The sound pattern of English*. New York,
    Evanston, and London: Harper & Row.

De Tollenaere, F.; R. L. Jones; et al. 1976. *Word-indices and word-lists to the Gothic bible and minor fragments*. Leiden: Brill.

Durell, M. 1975. Reduplication and ablaut in the Germanic strong verb. *German Life and Letters* 29:48-59.

Fourquet, J. 1962. Germanique *skulum* et *munum* et la classification des prétérits forts. *Festgabe für L. L. Hammerich*, 61-67. Kopenhagen: Naturmetodens Sproginstitut.

———. 1976. Spuren eines vorindogermanischen Wechsels Tenuis/Aspirata. *Sprachwissenschaft* 1:108-14.

Grammont, M. 1939. *Traité de phonétique*. 2nd ed. Paris: Delagrave.

Henzen, W. 1957. *Deutsche Wortbildung*. 2nd ed. Tübingen: Niemeyer. [The third edition of 1965 has not been consulted.]

Hopper, P. J. 1969. An Indo-European "syntagm" in Germanic. *Linguistics* 54:39-43.

Hirt, H. 1932. *Handbuch des Urgermanischen. Teil II: Stambildungs- und Flexionslehre*. Heidelberg: Carl Winter.

Höfler, O. 1970. Die germanischen reduplizierenden Verba im Lichte der Entfaltungstheorie. *Folia Linguistica* 4:110-20.

Karstien, C. 1921. *Die reduplizierten Perfekta des Nord- und Westgermanischen*. Giessen: Wilhelm Schmitz Verlag. [Swets and Zeillinger 1968.]

Kerns, J. A. 1937. E^2 and EU in Germanic strong preterits of class VII. *Language* 13:11-7.

Kiparsky, P. 1965. Phonological change. Dissertation, M.I.T.

Kögel, R. 1892. Zu den reduplicierten Präterita. *Beiträge zur Geschichte der deutschen Sprache und Literatur* 16:500-2.

Langacker, R. W. 1969. Mirror image rules I: Syntax. *Language* 45:575-98. Mirror image rules II: Lexicon and phonology. *Language* 45:844-62.

Lüdtke, H. 1975. Der Ursprung des germanischen $\bar{e}^2$ und die Reduplikationspräterita. *Phonetica* 1:157-83.

Malkiel, Y. 1968. The inflectional paradigm as an occasional determinant of sound change. *Directions for historical linguistics. A symposium*, ed. by W. P. Lehmann and Y. Malkiel, 21-64. Austin and London: University of Texas Press.

Maurer, F. 1952. *Nordgermanen und Alemannen. Studien zur germanischen und frühdeutschen Sprachgeschichte. Stammes- und Volkskunde*. Bern: A. Francke Verlag, München: Leo Lehnen Verlag.

Meid, W. 1971. *Das germanische Praeteritum. Indogermanische Grundlagen und Ausbreitung im Germanischen*. Innsbrucker Beiträge zur Sprachwissenschaft. Band 3. Innsbruck: Institut für Vergleichende Sprachwissenschaft der Universität Innsbruck.

Noreen, A. 1904. *Altschwedische Grammatik mit Einschluss des Altgutnischen*. Halle: Niemeyer.

Prokosch, E. 1939. *A comparative Germanic grammar*. Philadelphia: Linguistic Society of America, University of Pennsylvania.

Rauch, I. 1972. Old High German vocalic clusters. *Issues in Linguistics. Papers in honor of Henry and Renée Kahane*, ed. by B. B. Kachru, et al., 774-9. Urbana: University of Illinois Press.

Rooth, E. 1974. Das Vernersche Gesetz in *Forschung und Lehre 1875-1975*. Acta Reg. Soc. Humaniorum Litterarum Lundensis, Skrifter

utgivna av Kungl. Humanistiska Vetenskapssamfundet i Lund LXXI.
Lund: C. W. K. Gleerup.

Sacks, R. 1977. Germanic seventh class strong verbs. *Indo-
European studies III*, ed. by C. Watkins, 227-55. Cambridge, MA:
Department of Linguistics, Harvard University.

Schatz, J. 1907. *Altbairische Grammatik*. Göttingen: Vandenhoeck
& Ruprecht.

Schmierer, R. J. 1977. Theoretical implications of Gothic and Old
English phonology. Dissertation, University of Massachusetts
Amherst.

Schönfeld, Moritz (A. van Loey, ed.) 1964. *Schönfeld's Historische Grammatica van het Nederlands*. 7th ed. Zutphen: N. W.
J. Thieme.

Sievers, E. (K. Brunner, ed.) 1951. *Altenglische Grammatik nach
der Angelsächsischen Grammatik von ----*. 2nd ed. Halle: Niemeyer.

Steller, W. 1928. *Abriss der Altfriesischen Grammatik*. Halle:
Niemeyer.

Streitberg, W. 1896. *Urgermanische Grammatik*. Heidelberg: Carl
Winter.

----. 1965. *Die Gotische Bibel. Erster Teil: Der Gotisch Text ...*
(5th ed.). *Zweiter Teil: Gotisch-Griechisch-Deutsches
Wörterbuch* (4th ed.). Heidelberg: Carl Winter.

Uhlenbeck, E. M. 1949. *De structuur van het Javaanse morpheem*.
Batavia: Koninklijk Bataviaasch Genootschap van Kunsten en
Wetenschappen.

----. 1962. Limitations of morphological processes. *Lingua* 11:
426-32.

----. 1966. The structure of the Javanese morpheme. *Readings in
linguistics II*, ed. by E. P. Hamp, F. W. Householder, and R.
Austerlitz, 248-70. Chicago and London: The University of
Chicago Press. [Reprinted from *Lingua* 2 (1959).]

Van Coetsem, F. 1951. De Oorsprong van het Ndl. Praeteritum *hief*.
Tijdschrift voor Nederlandse Taal- en Letterkunde 59:40-8.

----. 1956. *Das System der starken Verba und die Periodisierung
im älteren Germanischen*. Med. der Kon. Ned. Akademie van Wetenschappen, Afd. Letterk., N.R., Deel 19, No. 1. Amsterdam:
Noord-Hollandsche Uitgevers Maatschappij.

----. 1962. Zur Analogie im Germanischen. *Zeitschrift für
Mundartforschung* 29:216-27.

----. 1963. Zur Frage der internen Ordnung der Ablautsalternanzen
im voreinzeldialektischen Germanischen I. *Orbis* 12:264-83.
[Reprinted 1970 in *Vorschläge für eine strukturale Grammatik
des Deutschen*, ed. by H. Steger, 385-413. Wege der Forschung,
Band CXLVI. Darmstadt: Wissenschaftliche Buchgesellschaft.]

----. 1968. A syntagmatic structure in development. "Umlaut" and
"consonantal influence" in Germanic. *Lingua* 21:494-525.

----. 1970. Zur Entwicklung der germanischen Grundsprache. *Kurzer
Grundriss der germanischen Philologie bis 1500*, ed. by L. R.
Schmitt, 1-93. Berlin: Walter de Gruyter.

----. 1972. Proto-Germanic morphophonemics. *Toward a grammar of
Proto-Germanic*, ed. by F. van Coetsem and H. L. Kufner, 175-209.
Tübingen: Niemeyer.

----. 1975a. Generality in language change: The case of the Old
High German vowel shift. *Lingua* 35:1-34.

———. 1975b. Remarks concerning the generative model of language change. *Leuvense Bijdragen* 64:273-91.

———. 1979. The features "vocalic" and "syllabic." *Linguistic method. Essays in honor of Herbert Penzl*, ed. by I. Rauch and G. F. Carr, 547-56. The Hague: Mouton.

———. 1980. Germanic verbal ablaut and its development: A contribution to the theory of internal inflection. *Contributions to Historical Linguistics. Issues and Materials*, ed. by F. van Coetsem and L. R. Waugh, 281-339. Leiden: E. J. Brill.

———; R. Hendricks; and S. McCormick. 1981. Accent typology and sound change. *Lingua* 53:181-201.

———; ———; and P. Siegel. 1981. On the role of function in sound change. *Cornell Working Papers in Linguistics* 2:166-85.

Van Loey, A. 1955. *Middelnederlandse Spraakkunst*. 2nd ed. Groningen: J. B. Wolters.

Van Wijk, E. 1936. *De Klinkers der Oergermaanse Stamsyllaben in hun onderling Verband*. Bilthoven, Tegal: De Boer.

Wang, W. S-Y. 1969. Competing sound change as a cause of residue. *Language* 45:9-26.

Weinhold-Ehrismann-Moser. 1965. Weinhold, K. and G. Ehrismann (H. Moser, ed.) *Kleine Mittelhochdeutsche Grammatik*. 14th ed. Wien-Stuttgart: Wilhelm Braumüller.

Zonneveld, W. 1976. Fonologische Polariteit en de Vlaamse Brusselse Vokaalverschuiving. *Leuvense Bijdragen* 65:471-83.

———. 1978. *A formal theory of exceptions in generative phonology*. Dissertation, University of Utrecht. Lisse: The Peter de Ridder Press.

GERMANIC REFLEXIVES AND THE IMPLEMENTATION
OF BINDING CONDITIONS

Wayne Harbert

1.0. In this paper, I will be concerned with the
problem of explaining certain changes in the distribution
of reflexive and nonreflexive pronouns in the Germanic
languages. I will show that there are systematic tenden-
cies in evidence in those changes which suggest that aspects of the distribution reconstructable for the parent
language were inherently unstable, and I will argue this
instability in turn can be considered to follow from a
somewhat modified version of the Theory of Binding developed in Chomsky (1979). That theory characterizes as
marked precisely those aspects of Germanic pronominal syntax which prove to be liable to change, since they all
involve violations of a single condition on binding in
universal grammar. The changes in question may therefore
be regarded as individual manifestations of the implementation of that condition.
    It will be seen, however, that in many of the lan-
guages considered, the condition does not appear to have
been suddenly implemented in its entirety. Its effects,
rather than appearing abruptly across the board in all
environments where they are expected, appear first in some
subset of those environments, and only later in others.
Thus, the introduction of the condition seems in many
cases to have taken place gradually by way of the introduction of a series of less general conditions which it
entails.

2.0. We may begin by considering the distribution of
the two forms in Gothic—the earliest extensively documented of the Germanic languages. The bulk of the extant
corpus of Gothic consists of a translation of portions of
the Bible from New Testament Greek—a translation which
is on the whole rather literal, but which exhibits numerous instances of systematic failure to imitate the Greek
model, motivated apparently by the desire to avoid producing ungrammatical constructions.[1] Evidence from this
sort of systematic deviation allows us to arrive at a

fairly clear picture of conditions on anaphor binding in
Gothic.

New Testament Greek, like Gothic, distinguished between reflexives (e.g. ἑαυτον 'himself') and nonreflexive
pronouns (e.g. αὐτον 'him'), but the distribution of these
forms in the Greek text differs systematically from that
of the corresponding Gothic forms (*sik* 'self', *ina* 'him')
in a number of environments. In both languages, reflexives were used in simple clauses to corefer with the subjects of those clauses.[2] Nonreflexive pronouns were understood as disjoint in reference with tautoclausal subjects. These facts are illustrated in (1). [+R] designates a reflexive form, and [-R] designates a nonreflexive form.

(1) a.   *Iesus*$_i$ ... *gafalh* *sik*$_i$ (+R: = GK+Ø) *faura* *im*
         Jesus^i hid   self^i from them
         (-R: = GK-R)

         'Jesus hid himself from them.'   (Joh 12:36)

    b.   *guþ*$_i$ *hauheiþ* *ina*$_j$ (-R: = GK-R) *in* *sis*$_i$
         God^i glorifies him^j in self^i
         (+R: = GK+R)

         'God glorifies him in himself.'   (Joh 13:32)

As demonstrated by the glosses on these examples, this
distribution is shared by English as well.[3]

Example (2a) shows that in both Gothic and Greek (as
well as English), nonreflexive pronouns which are accusative subjects of infinitives were also understood as disjoint in reference with the subject of the higher clause.
Reflexives were used in that position to corefer with the
higher subject, as illustrated by (2b).[4]

(2) a.   (*ija*$_i$) *hugjandona* $_S$[*in* *gasinþjam* *ina*$_j$
         they^i thinking   in company   him^j
         (-R: = GK-R) *wisan*]
                      be

         'They thinking him to be in the company ...'
                                                   (Luk 2:44)

    b.   *jabai* *has*$_i$ *gatrauaiþ* $_S$[*sik* *silban*$_i$
         if   someone trusts   self ^{i}
         (+R: = GK+R) *Xristaus* *wisan*]
                      of Christ he

         'If someone trusts himself to be of
         Christ ...'   (Cor 10:7)

The distribution of reflexive and nonreflexive forms
in Gothic, however, differs from that found in Greek (and
English) in the following ways. First, in Gothic, but not

in Greek, reflexive pronouns in nonsubject positions in
infinitive complements could be bound to the subject of
higher clause.[5] This is illustrated by the examples in
(3). As demonstrated by the glosses, English patterns
with Greek in this respect.

(3) a. *þai$_i$ -ei   ni   wildedun* $_S$[*mik$_j$ þiudanon ufar*
       who^i Compl not wanted   me ^{j} to-rule over
           sis$_i$ (+R: = GK-R)]
           selves^i

       'Who did not want me to rule over them.'
                                        (Luk 19:27)

   b. *Jah (is$_i$) ni fralailot* $_S$[*ainohun$_j$ ize miþ*
      and he^i not permitted   any ^{j}of-them with
      sis$_i$ (+R: = GK-R) *afargaggan*]
      self^i to-follow

      'And he did not let any of them follow him.'
                                        (Mk 5:37)

   c. *jah [is$_i$] gawaurtha* $_S$[*twalif$_j$ du wisan miþ*
      and he^i caused   twelve^j to be   with
      sis$_i$ (+R: = GK-R)]
      self^i

      'And he caused twelve to be with him.'
                                        (Mk 3:14)

   d. *jah bedun ina$_i$ allai   gaujans$_j$* ... $_S$[PRO$_i$
      and asked him^i all   inhabitants^j 6
      galeiþan fairra   sis$_j$ (+R: = GK-R)]
      go [INF] from   selves^j

      'And all of the inhabitants asked him to
      go from them.'   (Luk 8:37)

The same difference between languages is found in participial relative clauses, as demonstrated by the examples
in (4).

(4) a. (*is$_i$) qaþuh   -þan* $_{NP}$[*þamma$_j$* $_{\bar{S}}$[PRO$_j$
       he^i said-and then   to the one
       haitandin sik$_i$ (+R: = GK-R)]]
       inviting self^i

       'And then he said to the one inviting him ...'
                                        (Luk 14:12)

   b. *jah (is$_i$) gaf* $_{NP}$[*þaim$_j$* $_{\bar{S}}$[PRO$_j$ *miþ   sis$_i$*
      and he^i gave   to-those   with self^i
      (+R: = GK-R) *wisandam*]]
                   being

'And he gave to the ones being with him.'
(Luk 5:4)

c. (is_i) qaþ du $_{NP}$[þaim atgaggandeim manageim
      he   said to   those coming   multitude
      $_S$[PRO$_j$ daupjan   fram sis_i (+R: = GK-R)]
             to be baptized by   self

'He said to the multitudes coming to be
baptized by him ...'   (Luk 3:7)

Second, the two languages differed with respect to their
treatment of possessive modifiers on NPs. In New Testament Greek, the genitive form of the nonreflexive pronoun
αὐτου was normally used to indicate both possession by the
subject and possession by some NP other than the subject.
The genitive of the reflexive ἑαυτου appears to have been
used as a possessive only emphatically. In Gothic, on the
other hand, nonreflexive possessives were used just where
possession by some NP other than the subject was intended
In order to indicate possession by the subject, the reflexive form sein- was used. The usual Gothic/Greek correspondences are illustrated in (5).[7]

(5) a.   sa auhumista gudja$_i$ frah   Iesu$_j$ bi ...
         the highest   priest   asked Jesus   about
         $_{NP}$[laisein is_j (-R: = GK-R)]
              teaching his

'The high priest asked Jesus about his
(Jesus') teaching.'   (Joh 18:19)

b.   qaþuh   þan Iesus$_i$ bi $_{NP}$[daupau is_j
     spoke-and then Jesus   about   death   his
     (-R: = GK-R)]

'And then Jesus spoke about his (Lazarus')
death.'   (Joh 11:13)

c.   jah (is_i) qaþ im_j in $_{NP}$[laiseinai
     and he   spoke-to them   in   teaching
     $seinai_i$ (+R: = GK-R)]
     self's

'And he spoke to them in his (own) teaching.'
(Mk 4:2)

d.   Herodis$_i$ $_{NP}$[mela $_{NP}$[gabaurþais
     Herod   on occasion   of birth
     $seinaizos_i$ (+R: = GK-R)]] nahtamat   waurhte
     self's   evening-meal prepare

'Herod prepared an evening meal on the
occasion of his birth.'   (Mk 6:21)

Example (5e) shows that subjects of NPs in Gothic could also serve as antecedents for reflexive possessives.

(5) e. *in* NP[*quma* NP[*fraujins*$_i$ *unsaris*] PP[*miþ*
        in   coming   lord's   our   with
        NP[*allaim þaim weiham   seinaim*$_i$ (+R: =
           all   the   holy-ones   self's
        GK-R)]]]

        'In the coming of our Lord with all of
        his holy ones.'   (I Thess 3:13)

As illustrated by the English glosses on these examples, English once again patterns with Greek. That is, in English, as in Greek, distinctly reflexive possessives are not used systematically in cases of possession by the subject. (The reflexive possessive *his own* is used only emphatically.) Correspondingly, as in Greek, nonreflexive pronouns occurring as possessives are not understood as necessarily disjoint in reference with the subject. Gothic differs from Greek and English in both respects.

Finally, Gothic differs from Greek in that, with certain prepositions, the nonreflexive pronoun is used in Greek in prepositional object position to refer back to the subject, while the reflexive is used in the corresponding Gothic constructions. This is demonstrated by the examples in (6):

(6) a. (*is*$_i$) *galausida af   sis*$_i$ (+R: = GK-R) *þos*
        he$_i$ tore   from self$_i$ the
        naudibandjos
        chains

        'He tore the chains from him.'   (Mk 5:4)

    b. *gasaihands þan   Iesus*$_i$ *managans hiuhmans*
        seeing   then Jesus$_i$ large   multitudes
        bi sik$_i$ (+R: = GK-R)
        by self$_i$

        'Jesus then seeing large multitudes by
        him ...'   (Mat 8:18)

Once again, as illustrated by the English glosses, English patterns like Greek.[8]

    2.1. We can summarize the similarities and differences discussed above by means of the following chart. [+] in a column means that, in the position in question, reflexives are used routinely to refer to the subject of the matrix clause and nonreflexive pronouns are interpreted as being disjoint in reference with the subject of the matrix clause. [-] means that, in the position in question, (nonemphatic) reflexives are not used to refer back to the matrix subject, and nonreflexive pronouns are

not understood as necessarily disjoint in reference with
the matrix subject.

			Gothic	Greek (and English)

(7) a. Simple S

$_S[NP \ldots _{VP}[\ldots X \ldots]]$ +   +

b. Subject of infinitive
   complement
   $_S[NP \ldots _S[X\text{-}acc \ldots]]$ +   +

c. Nonsubject of infinitive
   complement
   $_S[NP \ldots _S[\begin{Bmatrix} NP\text{-}acc \\ PRO \end{Bmatrix} \ldots$ +   -
   $X \ldots]]$

d. Within participial RCL
   $_S[NP \ldots _{NP}[NP _{\bar{S}}[PRO \ldots$ +   -
   $X \ldots]]]$

e. Possessor NP (subject
   of NP)
   $_S[NP \ldots _{NP}[X \bar{N}] \ldots]$ +   -

f. Object of certain
   prepositions
   $_S[NP \ldots _{PP}[PX] \ldots]$ +   - (but
                                                                 see note 8)

Thus, there are at least four different positions which
are normally inaccessible to binding in Greek and English,
but accessible to it in Gothic.[9] Of course, we would not
wish to propose that Gothic differs from Greek and English
with respect to four independent conditions, each specifying a separate construction. The simplest hypothesis
would hold rather that the four cases in which Gothic
differs from the other languages are actually just individual consequences of its failure to observe a single,
general condition which is observed in those languages.
In fact, most of the differences which we have noted between Gothic and Greek/English would follow directly from
the assumption that Gothic, but not the other languages
failed to observe the condition on anaphors and pronouns
attributed by Chomsky (1979) to Universal Grammar. This
condition is given in (8).

(8) a. An anaphor [e.g. a reflexive] cannot be free
       in its minimal governing category. [That is,
       it must be coindexed with a c-commanding ele-
       ment within its m.g.c.]

    b. A pronoun must be free in its minimal
       governing category.

The minimal governing category of an NP can be taken, for
the present purposes, to be the minimal NP or S within
which it is assigned case.[10] An object NP, for example,
is assigned its case by virtue of being governed by the
verb which is the head of VP. Its minimal governing category, therefore, is the S dominating VP. The subject of
a tensed clause received its nominative case by virtue of
being c-commanded by tense. Its minimal governing category is the S dominating it and tense. The minimal governing category for the accusative subject of an infinitive, on the other hand, is the higher S, since it receives its case from the verb of the higher S.[11] The
minimal governing category for a possessor NP is the NP
dominating it, since it receives its genitive case by
virtue of its membership in that NP.[12] Now, if we assume
that condition (8) is observed in Greek and English, but
not in Gothic, then the differences reflected in (7c),
(7d), and (7e) can be accounted for rather simply. In
each case, Gothic allows a reflexive to be bound outside
of its minimal governing category, while the other two
languages do not; and, in each case, Greek and English
allow nonreflexive pronouns to be interpreted as corefer-
ential with subject NPs outside their minimal governing
categories, while Gothic apparently does not.[13] We may
explain this by claiming that Gothic, Greek, and English
all share the unbracketed portion of condition (8'), but
that only the grammars of English and Greek incorporate
the bracketed portion.[14]

    (8') a.   An anaphor cannot be free [in its minimal
             governing category].

        b.   A pronoun must be free [in its minimal
             governing category].

    Still unexplained by this proposal would be the dif-
ference reflected in (7f), involving the position of
prepositional object. It has been seen that this position, at least with locative prepositions, is opaque for
the purpose of disjoint reference assignment or in Greek
and English, but apparently transparent to DR in Gothic.
This difference could be accounted for under the proposal
being considered if we added PP to the list of phrase
types which may constitute governing categories. (However, cf. note 8.)
    Now a grammar of Gothic containing the truncated ver-
sions of (8a) and (8b) as its only conditions on binding
and disjoint reference would, in fact, be insufficiently
constrained. In Gothic, as in Greek and English, nonreflexive pronouns in nonsubject positions in TENSED embedded clauses are not interpreted as necessarily disjoint in reference with the subject of the higher clause.
This is illustrated by (9).

(9) a. (eis_i) *bedun ina$_j$* $_S$[*ei*   (*is$_j$*) *uslaubidedi*
         they^i asked him^j Compl he^j allow
         im$_i$ (-R: = GK-R) ... *galeiþan*]
         them^i to go

'They asked him that he allow them to go.'
                                              (Luk 8:32)

b. (*eis$_i$*) *bedun* $_S$[*ei*   (*is$_j$*) *usliþi hindar*
    they^i asked   Compl he^j go   beyond
    markos   *ize$_i$* (-R: = GK-R)]
    borders their^i

'They asked him that he go beyond their
borders.'   (Mat 8:34)

c. (*is$_i$*) *bidjands ina$_j$* $_S$[*ei*   (*is$_j$*) *qimi jah*
    he^i asking   him^j Compl he^j come and
    ganasidedi þana skalk   *is$_i$* (-R: = GK-R)]
    save   the   servant his^i

'He asking him that he come and save his
servant.'   (Luk 7:3)

It appears moreover that, as in Greek and English, it was
not possible for a reflexive in such a position to be
bound to the higher clause subject. There are, at least,
no instances in the corpus where this occurs.[15]
     In English and Greek, the failure of the lower clause
pronoun and the higher clause subject to be assigned mandatory disjoint reference in such constructions would
follow from the fact that, by subcondition (8b), a pronoun
is required to be free only within its minimal governing
category. However, this cannot be the reason for the
failure of DR in the Gothic examples in (9) if, as we
have suggested, the Gothic version of (8b) did not refer
to minimal governing categories. In English and Greek,
the opacity of tensed clauses needs no special mention,
since it follows from the fact that any NP or S meeting
the definition of a minimal governing category is opaque,
but in Gothic there is an asymmetry between tensed clauses
on the one hand and untensed clauses and NPs on the other.
The former, but not the latter are opaque. It appears
therefore that the minimal set of binding conditions posited for Gothic will have to contain, in addition to the
truncated versions of (8a) and (8b), a principle which,
like the Propositional Island Condition proposed by
Chomsky in earlier work, singles out tensed clauses in
particular as opaque domains.[16]
     For the sake of orderly exposition, I will assume in
the following that the syntax of reflexive and nonreflexive forms in the Germanic parent language was essentially
like that found in Gothic. At the end of the paper, I
will return to show that this assumption is justified.

2.2. If, as Chomsky proposes, condition (8) has the status of a principle of Universal Grammar, then two predictions fall out concerning the patterns of distribution of reflexive and nonreflexive forms which we might expect to find crosslinguistically. First, languages like English and Greek, in which NPs, participial relative constructions, and infinitive complements are opaque, should be commonplace, while languages like Gothic, in which they are transparent, should be rare. Second, if a language observes (8), then we should expect to find its effects in all relevant constructions, and if a language does not observe it, we should not expect to find its effects anywhere. Thus, for example, if a language exhibits a systematic distinction between reflexive and nonreflexive possessives, we should expect to find that it also allows reflexive binding and DR to operate into nonsubject positions in infinitive complements, and conversely, if NPs are opaque to reflexive binding and DR in some language, then infinitive complements should be opaque in that language as well. (Of course, if this turned out generally not to be the case, then the claim that the opacity of NPs and the opacity of infinitive complements are to be accounted for by a single condition would be called into question.)

I have insufficient data to assess the validity of the first prediction. Languages like Gothic do not appear to be particularly rare within the Indo-European family, where they include at least Icelandic, Swedish, Danish, Latin, Russian, and Hindi,[17] but I have no idea about their relative frequency outside of Indo-European. The second prediction appears to be borne out by most of the available evidence. In Greek and English, where infinitive complements are opaque to reflexive binding, the original systematic reflexive/nonreflexive possessive distinction has been lost. On the other hand, languages in which infinitive complements are transparent generally distinguish systematically between reflexive and nonreflexive possessives. Compare the following examples from Russian and Latin.[18]

(10) a.   *mat'$_i$ poprosila   doč'$_j$ $_S$[PRO$_j$ nalit'*
             mother^i asked   daughter^j to-pour
             sebe$_i$ (+R) vodu]
             self^i water

             'The mother asked the daughter to pour
             her water.'   (Faltz 1977:158)

      b. *On$_i$ poexal v* $_{NP}$[*ego$_i$* (-R)/ *svoj$_i$* (+R)
          he^i went   to   *his^i /self's^i
          golovnoj otrad]
          front   lines

          'He went to his (own) front lines.'
                                        (Timberlake 1980:793)

(11) a. *illos qui*$_i$ *noluerunt* $_S$[*me regnare super*
         those who^i did-not-wish   me to-rule over
              se$_i$ (+R)]
         selves^i

         'Those who did not want me to rule over
         them.'   (Lat Vulgate Luk 7:9)

     b. [*is*$_i$] *dixit* $_{NP}$[*discipulis*   *suis*$_i$ (+R)] ...
         he^i said   to-disciples self's^i

         'He said to his disciples ...'
                                        (Lat Vulgate Mat 26:36)

As will be seen below, however, this correlation is not
always found.

2.3.   There are also some indirect diachronic predictions inherent in the claim that (8) is a universal principle. In particular, it follows from that claim that
binding in languages like Gothic, insofar as it does not
observe (8), is marked, and if we make the not unreason-
able assumption that marked grammars are unstable and
therefore liable to change over time, we may expect to
find that such languages will tend diachronically to come
into conformity with the pattern exhibited by languages
like English and Greek.[19] This is the diachronic counterpart of the first synchronic prediction. The second also
has a diachronic counterpart. We have hypothesized that
all of the observed differences between languages like
Gothic and those like Greek and English with respect to
binding and disjoint reference result from the fact that
the former fail to observe a single unmarked principle.
If that principle is subsequently incorporated into the
grammar, we should expect to see its effects in all relevant environments roughly simultaneously.
     In the following sections, I will present evidence
showing that at least the first of these predictions appears to be borne out in several Germanic languages. For
each of them, I will show that at an early stage the distribution of reflexive and nonreflexive pronouns resembled
that found in Biblical Gothic, but that later stages reflect the predicted development in the direction of a distribution more like that found in English. I will also
consider the relative chronology of changes in individual
environments, to see to what extent these conform with
the second prediction.

     3.0. First, let us consider some evidence for change
in the pronominal syntax of Gothic. For Gothic, unlike
most of the Germanic languages, we do not have documents
spanning a long period of development. Thus, evidence for
syntactic change in Gothic is sparse—but, I propose, not
altogether lacking. First of all, in the Gothic Bible
there are sporadic instances in which, contrary to the

pattern in evidence in the great majority of like constructions, a nonreflexive pronoun—rather than a reflexive—appearing in nonsubject position in an untensed
clause corefers with the subject of the matrix clause.
In (12) I have listed the five examples of this type appearing in the corpus.

(12) a. *is$_i$ silba sunus$_i$ gakann sik faura*
   he^i self son submits himself before
   $_{NP}$[*þamma$_j$* $_{\bar{S}}$[(PRO$_j$) *ufhnaiwjandin uf*
   the one subjecting beneath
   ina$_i$ (-R) *þo alla*]]
   him^i those all

   'The son himself submits himself before
   the one subjecting all to him.'(I Cor 15:28)

b. (*eis$_i$*) *riqizeinai gahugdai wisandans,*
   they^i of-dark understanding being
   framaþjai libainais gudis in unwitjis
   alienated from-life God's because of ignorance
   $_{NP}$[*þis$_j$* $_{\bar{S}}$[PRO$_j$ *wisandins in im$_i$* (-R)]]$_i$
   that being in them^i
   in daubiþos hairtane seinaize$_i$ (+R)
   because of deafness of-hearts their

   'They being of darkened understanding,
   alienated from the life of God because of
   the ignorance being in them, because of
   the deafness of their hearts ...' (Eph 4:18)

c. *jah allai þai gahausjandans$_i$ sildaleikidedun*
   and all those hearing marvelled
   bi $_{NP}$[*þo$_j$* $_{\bar{S}}$[PRO$_j$ *rodidona fram þaim hairdjam*
   at those said by the shepherds
   du im$_i$ (-R)]]
   to them^i

   'And all of those hearing marvelled at the
   things said by the shepherds to them.'
   (Luk 2:18)

d. (*is$_i$*) *gasaƕ usluknans himinans jah* $_{\bar{S}}$[*ahman$_j$*
   he^i saw unlocked heavens and spirit^j
   swe ahak atgaggandan ana ina$_i$ (-R)]
   like dove coming-down on him^i

   'He saw heaven unlocked and a spirit like
   a dove coming down on him.'   (Mk 1:10)

e. *ei* (*is$_i$*) *gebi unsis$_j$ unagein ...*
   that he^i might-give us^j fearlessly
   $_{\bar{S}}$[PRO$_j$ *skalkinon imma$_i$* (-R)]
   to-serve him^i

   'That he might allow us fearlessly to
   serve him.'   (Luk 1:73-74)

The prevailing pattern found in all constructions of this
type, except for these five instances, would lead us to
expect a reflexive form in the underlined positions [com-
pare examples (3) and (4)].

Similarly, in the three examples in (13), the translator used nonreflexive possessive pronouns where (under
the usual interpretation of the passages in question) coreference with the subject is intended. These examples
are once again rare exceptions to the overwhelmingly attested use of reflexive possessives where reference to the
subject is intended, and of nonreflexive possessives where
reference to some NP other than the subject is intended.

(13) a. sa_i-ei skal stojan qiwans jah daupans
          who^i Compl shall judge quick and dead
          bi $_{NP}$[qum $\underline{is}_i$ (-R) jah $piudinassu$
          at   coming his^i and kingdom
          $\underline{is}_i$ (-R)]
          his^i

          'Who shall judge the quick and the dead at
          his coming and his kingdom.'   (II Tim 4:1)

     b. $wairps$ sa $waurstwa_i$ $_{NP}$[$mizdons$ $\underline{is}_i$ (-R)]
          worthy the worker ^{i} of-reward his^i

          'The worker is worthy of his reward.'
                                           (I Tim 5:18)

     c. ip $Herodes_i$ sa $taitrarkes$ $gasakans$ $fram$
          but Herod ^{i} the tetrarch   reproved by
          $imma$ bi $Herodiadein$ $_{NP}$[qen $_{NP}$[$broprs$
          him   about Herodias   wife   of-brother
          $\underline{is}_i$ (-R)]]
          his^i

          'But Herod the tetrarch, reproved by him
          about Herodias his brother's wife ...'
                                           (Luk 3:19)

The failure of the translator to meet our expectations in
(12) and (13) admits of a few possible explanations. For
example, we may be dealing here with simple lapses, in
which, under the influence of the nonreflexive form in the
Greek model, he carelessly used a nonreflexive form where
he should have used a reflexive. (Note that in a number
of these examples a great deal of material intervenes between the higher subject and the underlined form.) Or it
may be that an exegetical error is involved. The Greek
text in all such instances, of course, would have used a
nonreflexive pronoun whether coreference with the higher
subject was intended or not, and the model constructions
would be ambiguous except for context. Finally, however,
a more principled explanation is available for the "errors" in question.   In all of these instances, a

nonreflexive form appears where the grammar seems to dic-
tate that a reflexive should appear (given that the translator shared our understanding of the passages), but where
the proposed universal principle (8) predicts that reflexives should be excluded. Thus, we might suggest that
examples (12) and (13) in fact reflect incipient syntactic
change in the direction of a less marked binding situation. This explanation, in addition to not invoking ac-
cident, finds support in the developments to be discussed
below.

3.1. Next, let us turn to the Gothic of the Commentary on the Gospel of John, or *Skeireins*,—the only major
Gothic document besides the Gospel translation. Since
the *Skeireins* quotes from the Bible translation extensively, it is to be regarded as a later composition.[20]
The commentary is a relatively short text, and therefore provides comparatively little basis for generalization about the language it represents. Significantly,
however, there are two participial relative constructions
in the corpus which contain pronominal forms coreferring
with the matrix subject, and in both, those forms are
nonreflexive pronouns—as in the exceptional Biblical
Gothic examples in (12)—rather than reflexives—as in
the normal Biblical Gothic examples in (4). The two examples in question are given in (14).

(14) a.   *(eis$_i$) andhofun auk* $_{NP}$[*jainaim$_j$* $_S$[PRO$_j$
            they^i answered for   those

            anahaitandam   im$_i$ (-R)]]
            rebuking   them^i

        'For they answered those rebuking them.'
                                      (Sk VIII b:5)

      b.   *(eis$_i$)   ni andsitandans jainaize* $_{NP}$[*unselein*
            they^i not fearing   of those   evil
            $_{NP}$[*þize$_j$* $_S$[PRO$_j$ *anahaitandane   im$_i$*
                of-the-ones   rebuking   them^i
            (-R)]]]

        'They not fearing the evil of the ones
        rebuking them ...'   (Sk VIII b:9)

These examples indicate that participial relative
constructions have become opaque to disjoint reference by
this stage in Gothic—a development whose beginnings, as
we have noted, may be reflected in the Biblical Gothic
examples in (12), and one which is consistent with the
predictions of our hypothesis concerning likely changes
in Gothic binding conditions. On the basis of these examples, it appears as if we could claim that the Gothic
of the Commentary has departed from Biblical Gothic by
instituting the full version of condition (8). Unfortunately, this claim is not borne out by the remainder of

the evidence provided by the *Skeireins*. First of all, as
illustrated by (15), *Skeireins* Gothic continued to maintain the systematic reflexive/nonreflexive possessive distinction.

(15) a.   *iþ nasjands$_i$* $_{NP}$[*þana anawairþan dom*
          but savior   the   future   distinction
          is$_j$ (-R)] *gasaihands* ...
          his   seeing

          'But the savior seeing his (Nicodemus')
          future distinction ...'   (Sk II c:8-10)

     b.   (*is$_i$*) *qaþ* $_{NP}$[*siponjam seinaim$_j$* (+R)] ...
          he   said   disciples self's

          'He said to his (own) disciples ...'
                                            (Sk VII d:13)

Moreover, nonsubject positions in untensed clauses other
than those involved in participial relative constructions
appear to have remained bindable to clause-external subjects, as illustrated by the absolute participial construction in (16):

(16)   (*Iohannes$_i$ qaþ*) "*so   nu   faheþs meina*
          John   said   the now joy   my
          usfullnoda.   jains   skal wahsjan, iþ
          is-fulfilled. That-one shall grow   but
          ik minznan," $_S$[*eiþan nu siponjam seinaim$_i$*
          I   lessen   since now disciples self's
          (+R) *þaim bi   swiknein   du Iudaium*
                those about cleansing to Jews
          sokjandam jah qiþandam   sis$_i$ (+R) ...]
          disputing and saying   to-self

          "John said, 'My joy is fulfilled; that one
          shall grow and I become smaller,' since now
          his disciples disputing with the Jews about
          cleansing and saying to him ..."
                                            (Sk IV a:1-10)

In this example, the two reflexives in the participial
phrase refer back to the (reconstructed) matrix subject
Iohannes.[21]
     Thus, while the scant data from the *Skeireins* in part
support our hypothesis, by showing that a change in distribution apparently did take place in one construction
in which it was expected to take place, they also pose
some problems for that hypothesis, since parallel changes
appear not be have occurred in other environments where
the hypothesis predicts that they should have.   If
Skeireins Gothic did in fact differ from Biblical Gothic
in that it had implemented the bracketed portion of the
conditions in (8), then we should expect that changes

would have taken place in all relevant environments, and
that reflexives should not be possible in (15b) and (16).
Rather than rejecting the hypothesis in favor of a weaker
one on the basis of the few *Skeireins* examples, however,
I will continue to regard it as a potentially useful one,
pending examination of data from the other dialects.   It
will be seen in the following discussion that similar
problems arise in the history of German.

    3.2.   The syntax of reflexive and nonreflexive pro-
nouns in German has, from the period of first attestation,
resembled that found in Biblical Gothic in the following
respects: first, in simple sentences, nonreflexive (accusative) pronouns are understood as disjoint in reference
with the subject.[22] In order to indicate coreference with
the subject in such instances, it has at all stages been
necessary to use a reflexive.   This is illustrated by the
following examples from the Old High German *Tatian*.[23]
(The *Tatian* is a translation from Latin.   I have indicated
in the examples taken from it the nature of the Latin pronouns which served as models for the underlined German
forms.)

(17) a.   *bithiu   erlosit her$_i$ inan$_j$* (-R = Lat-R) *nu*
          therefore free   he^i him^j now

          'Therefore let him free him now.'
                                          (Tat 205:3)

     b.   *uuanta her$_i$ sih$_i$* (+R = Lat+R) *gotes sun*
          because he^i self^i God's son
          teta
          made

          'Because he made himself the son of God.'
                                          (Tat 197:6)

Second, as in Gothic, nonreflexive forms in tensed
clauses, whether in subject or nonsubject position, are
not interpreted as disjoint in reference with the subject
of the higher clause.   Nor do reflexives occur in tensed
clauses with higher clause subjects as antecedents.   These
facts are illustrated by the examples in (18).   (The same
restrictions hold for Modern German as well.)

(18) a.   *brahtun sie$_i$ inan thô in   Hierusalem*
          brought they^i him then into Jerusalem
          $_{\bar{S}}$[*thaz   si$_i$* (-R: = Lat Ø) *inan gote*
            that they^i him to-God
          giantvvurtitin]
          might present

          'They brought him into Jerusalem, that they
          might present him to God.'   (Tat 7:2)

b. *Tho   quad her*$_i$ $_{NP}$[*themo*$_j$ $_{\bar{S}}$[*ther*$_j$ *inan*$_i$
    then said he   to-the-one   who   him
    (-R: = Lat+R) *ladota*]] ...[24]
                  invited

'Then he said to the one who invited
him ...'   (Tat 110:4)

c. *Inti* (*sie*$_i$) *batun   ín* $_{\bar{S}}$[*thaz her*$_j$ *sie*$_i$
    and they   asked him   that he   them
    (-R: = Lat-R) *ni   tribi uzan   thero*
                  not drive out-of the
    lantskefi]
    region

'And they asked him that he not drive them
out of the region.'   (Tat 53:8)

Third, in Old High German, as in Gothic, nonreflexive pro
nouns in the position of accusative subject of an untense
clause appear to have been interpreted as necessarily dis
joint in reference with the subject of the higher clause.
When coreference was intended, a reflexive was used. Thes
facts are illustrated in (19).

(19) a. (*sie*$_i$) *uuântun* $_S$[*in*$_j$ (-R: = Lat ∅) *uuesan*
         they   thought   him   to-be
         in thero samantferti]
         in the   company

'They thought him to be in the company.'
                                            (Tat 12:3)

b. *íogiuuelih*$_i$ ... *uuanit* $_S$[*sih*$_i$ (+R: = Lat ∅)
    each   thinks   self
    ambaht bringan gote]
    service to-bring to-God

'Each thinks himself to be rendering a
service to God.'   (Tat 71:3)

This is also true in Modern German for the small group of
verbs (e.g. *lassen* 'cause/permit', *sehen* 'see') which can
still take infinitive complements with lexical subjects.
      However, the distribution of forms in Old High German
(and Modern German) also differs in some ways from that
found in Gothic. First of all, as the examples in (20)
show, the reflexive/nonreflexive possessive distinction
has been wholly levelled. *Sîn* (Modern German *sein*), originally a strictly reflexive form (as evidenced by the fact
that its cognates in all other dialects are reflexive),
had lost its reflexive function by Old High German times.
It could be used either to indicate coreference with the
subject (e.g. in translation of the Latin *suus*) or to

indicate disjoint reference (e.g. in translation of the
Latin *eius*).

(20) a.   *tho   quad her*$_i$ *zi* $_{NP}[\overset{\wedge}{sinen}_i$ (= Lat+R)
           then said he   to   his
           iungiron] ...
           disciples

           'Then he said to his (own) disciples ...'
                                          (Tat 180:3)

      b.   *inti nemnis thû*$_i$ $_{NP}[\overset{\wedge}{sinan}_j$ (= Lat-R) *namon]*
           and name you   his   name
           Iohannem
           John

           'And name him John.'   (Tat 2:5)

We are justified in claiming, on the basis of the comparative evidence, that at some point in the prehistory of
Old High German the distinction was observed; that $\overset{\wedge}{sin}$
was exclusively reflexive, and that possession by nonsubjects was expressed by means of the genitive of the nonreflexive pronoun paradigm. The development between that
stage and the stage represented by attested Old High German, then, involved the generalization of the reflexive
form at the expense of the nonreflexive. Now, it is perhaps possible to view this development as the result of
an accidental syncretism local to German—of the type apparently represented by the loss of the dative reflexive
(cf. note 22). However, the hypothesis which we have developed allows for a more principled explanation of this
change. As reflexive binding became restricted to minimal
governing categories, we would expect that reflexive possessive forms should lose their obligatory anaphoric interpretation, therefore becoming subject to generalization into environments where disjoint reference was intended. An explanation based on such changes in binding
conditions has the considerable advantage of allowing us
to relate the loss of the reflexive/nonreflexive distinction in German to the remarkable instability of that seemingly quite useful distinction elsewhere in Germanic. We
have already observed some variation with respect to it
in Biblical Gothic, where nonreflexive possessives sometimes occurred in place of expected reflexive possessives.
Evidence of a similar sort from other dialects will be
introduced below. (Interestingly, the same development
is found in Romance as well, where the forms descended
from the reflexive possessive *suus* have become the general
third person possessive forms.) It should also be noted
that the feminine/plural possessive *ihr* 'her, their,' historically a nonreflexive, is now also used in German to
refer back to subject antecedents.
     German has also, from the earliest period of

attestation, differed from Biblical Gothic in that reflexive pronouns are blocked from appearing in participial
relative constructions when their antecedents are external
to those constructions. Correspondingly, nonreflexive
pronouns in such constructions admit an interpretation of
coreference with the higher subject. This is illustrated
by the Old High German example in (21a) and the Modern
German example in (21b).

(21) a. *íuuer fater*$_i$ ... *gibit guotu* $_{NP}[_{\bar{S}}[\underline{inan}_i$
         your   father^i gives good $\overline{him}$
         (-R = Lat+R) *bitentên*]]
                      asking
         'Your father gives good to those asking
         him.'   (Tat 40:7)

     b. *Er*$_i$ *sprach zu* $_{NP}[den_{\bar{S}}[\underline{ihm}_i$ (-R/*$\underline{sich}_i$ (+R)
         he^i spoke to   the$^{\bar{S}}$ $\overline{him}^i$ *self^i
         folgenden] Kindern]
         following children

         'He spoke to the children following him.'

On the basis of this restriction and the disappearance of
distinctly reflexive possessive forms, we could propose
that German, like English, differs from Biblical Gothic
in that at some point in its prehistory it incorporated
the minimal governing category condition into its grammar.
In fact, though, such a claim would lead to incorrect predictions about the treatment of nonsubject positions in
untensed clauses other than those found in participial
relative constructions. As illustrated by example (22a)
(Old High German) and examples (22b-d) (Middle High German), reflexives in such positions could in fact be bound
to the subject of the higher clause.

(22) a. *inti (her*$_i$) *gisah* $_S[gotes\ geist_j$ ...
         and   he^i saw   God's spirit
         quementan ubar $\underline{sih}_i$ (+R: = Lat+R)]^{25}
         coming   over self^i

         'And he saw God's spirit coming over him.'
                                                        (Tat 14:4)

     b. *er*$_i$ *lie* $_S[die\ clâren$ $\underline{sich}_i$ (+R) *verhern*]
         he^i let ^{S} the beauties self^i conquer

         'He let the beauties conquer him.'
                                         (Konrad, Troj. 14,777)

     c. *diu künegin*$_i$ *den*$_j$ $_S[PRO_j$ $\underline{sich}_i$ *küssen] bat*
         the queen that-one ^{S} $_j$ self^{i}to-kiss asked

         'The queen asked that one to kiss her.'
                                         (Wolfram, Parz 806:28)

d. *Uote$_i$ bat   dô   drâte   die boten$_j$*
    Ute asked then quickly the messengers
    $_{\bar{S}}$[PRO$_j$ *für   sich$_i$ gên*]
              before self to-go

'Ute then quickly asked the messengers to
precede her.'   (Nibelung 772:1)

We will return to these constructions shortly.

The similarities and differences between Gothic and
German discussed above are summarized in the following
chart:[26]

			Bib Goth	Sk Goth	OHG	Eng
(23)	a.	Simple S $_S$[NP ... $_{VP}$[... X ...]]	+	+	+	+
	b.	Subject of infinitive complement $_S$[NP ... $_S$[X-acc ...]]	+		+	+
	c.	Nonsubject of infinitive complement $_S$[NP ... $_S$[$\left\{\begin{array}{l}\text{NP-acc}\\\text{PRO}\end{array}\right\}$ ... X ...]]	+*		+	-
	d.	Within participial RCL $_S$[NP ... $_{NP}$[NP$_{\bar{S}}$[PRO ... X ...]]]	+*	-	-	-
	e.	Possessor NP (subject of NP) $_S$[NP ... $_{NP}$[X $\bar{N}$] ...]	+*	+	-	-
	f.	Nonsubject of tensed S $_S$[NP ... $_{\bar{S}}$[... tns ... X ...]	-	(see note 15)	-	-

(* = with sporadic exceptions)

Once again, our hypothesis is partially supported by these
results. The distribution of reflexive forms in early
German differs from Gothic and resembles Modern English
in some predicted ways. In particular, NPs and participial relative clauses have become opaque for binding and
DR. Again, however, the data are somewhat problematic
for the hypothesis. If the failure of such processes to
operate across the boundaries of these constructions were
due to the implementation of the minimal governing category condition, then we should find that infinitive complements had also become opaque for them. The examples
in (22) indicate that this is not the case.

There is evidence, though, that the grammar of German has in fact tended in historical times toward realization of the predicted state of affairs with respect to such constructions. Thus, for example, in Modern German, unlike Middle High German, a nonsubject reflexive in the complement of *bitten* 'ask' cannot have the subject of *bitten* as its antecedent. In (22e), the literal Modern German translation of the Middle High German example (22d), the reflexive pronoun is disallowed.

(22) e.   *Ute*$_i$ *bat*   *die*   *Boten*$_j$ [PRO$_j$ *vor*   *ihr*$_i$
          Ute asked the messengers   before her
          (-R)/*$sich_i$ (+R) *her zu gehen*]
          *self$_i$ to go

          'Ute asked the messengers to go before her.'

With certain verbs in Modern German (e.g. *lassen* 'cause, permit,' *sehen* 'see'), a nonsubject reflexive in the complement can still be bound to the matrix subject. This is possible, however, only when the reflexive is complement-initial or the object of a preposition.[27]

(24) a.   *Hans*$_i$ *lässt* $_S$[*Paul*$_j$ *für* $sich_i$/ihn_i *ein Bier*
          Hans lets   Paul   for self^i him^i a   beer
          bestellen]
          order

          'Hans lets Paul order a beer for him.'

     b.   *Er*$_i$ *lässt* $_S$[$sich_i$ *die Suppe schmecken*]
          he^i lets   to-self the soup   taste

          'He enjoys the soup.'

     c.   **Hans*$_i$ *lässt* $_S$[*den Diener*$_j$ $sich_i$ *ein Bier*
          Hans^i lets   the servant self^i a   beer
          bringen]
          bring

          'Hans lets the servant bring him a beer.'

A comparison of (24b) with (22b) demonstrates that this restriction did not exist in earlier stages of German. Thus, the accessibility of complements of verbs like *lassen* to reflexive binding is more limited in Modern German than it was at earlier stages of the language. Note also that the reflexive is not required in (24a). That is, matrix controlled DR does not have access to the underlined position.

Such changes are consistent with the predictions of our hypothesis, but we are still faced with the problem that they did not occur at the same time as the other changes considered. Should the hypothesis be abandoned in view of this lack of simultaneity? As an alternative,

we might propose that the parent language was marked with
respect to several less general conditions, rather than a
single condition of greater generality. Thus, for example, the fact that nonsubject positions in Gothic infinitive complements were bindable by the matrix subject could
be attributed to nonobservance of the Specified Subject
Condition of Chomsky (1980), while the obligatory disjoint
reference assigned to nonreflexive possessives in Gothic
but not Greek or English could be explained by claiming
that, in the unmarked case represented by the latter languages, assignment of disjoint reference is subject to the
A-over-A condition. According to this approach Gothic and
like languages will be marked with respect to both constructions and both may be expected to change over time,
but not necessarily simultaneously since two separate conditions are involved.

The disadvantage of this solution is that it characterizes as accidental the strikingly high degree of cooccurrence between the two marked binding situations.
There is, according to this view, no particular reason
why Gothic should differ from Greek and English with respect to both. We might equally well expect to find languages in which there is a systematic distinction between
the two types of possessives, but in which infinitive complements are opaque to reflexive binding and DR. Indeed,
there should be more such languages than languages like
Gothic, since the former are marked with respect to one
less universal condition. I know of no languages of this
type. Although pre-Old High German appears to have been
a language in which the opposite situation is represented,
it also appears atypical. Numerous other languages besides Gothic, including Icelandic, Danish, Swedish, Latin,
Russian, and Hindi, differ from English and Greek with
respect to both constructions.[28] Examples from Latin and
Russian were cited above. Examples from Icelandic, Danish,
and Swedish will be introduced below.

What is needed therefore, is an analysis which will
predict that if infinitive complements in a language are
transparent for binding, NPs are also likely to be transparent and the converse, but which will be compatible with
a diachronic situation in which one remains transparent
while the other becomes opaque. Perhaps the resolution
of this apparent paradox is to be found in the manner in
which the conditions are implemented. In particular, we
might assume that languages like Gothic are in fact marked
with respect to a single condition, resulting in the
transparency of a number of constructions which ought to
be opaque; the language learner, however, rather than cor-
recting this situation by wholly implementing the unmarked
condition, might attempt instead to effect local repairs,
singling out individual constructions and incorporating
into his or her grammar only as much of the condition as
pertains to those constructions—the particular constructions chosen perhaps having to do with their relative order of acquisition. Those constructions not singled out

in this way will remain marked, and therefore subject to
later change. Under this not implausible view of syntactic change, we can reconcile the generally parallel treatment of infinitive complements and NPs by binding processes with asymmetrical changes of the type observed in
the history of German.

  3.3. Let us turn next to the history of reflexive
binding in English, which is closely related to German
within the Germanic language family. The evidence for
the reconstruction of this history is sparse, since English and immediately related languages lack the reflexive
pronouns of the Germanic *sik paradigm. If those languages did in fact possess such forms at some point, their
loss must have occurred in prehistoric times, at least
prior to the exodus of the English tribes from the con-
tinent. Throughout the Old English period, historically
nonreflexive pronouns were used in both reflexive and nonreflexive roles. The new reflexive pronouns of the *self*
type became established as normal (nonemphatic) reflexive
pronouns only in Middle English. Significantly, though,
since the time of their systematic incorporation into the
grammar, they seem to have been subject to the same (presumably unmarked) conditions on distribution which prevail
in Modern English.
  Also significant is the fate of the one Germanic reflexive form which did survive into attested English—the
reflexive possessive adjective *sīn*. This form is cognate
with Gothic *sein* and Old High German *sîn*, and unlike the
latter it remained reflexive, occurring only where co-
referential with the matrix subject, as in (25a).

  (25) a. *and him Hrōdgar*$_i$ *gewat to hofe *sīnum*$_i$*
           and him Hrodgar^i went to house self's

           'And Hrothgar betook himself to his house.'
                                            (Beow. 1236)

Example (25b) shows, though, that even at this stage the
maintenance of the form was unnecessary, since nonreflexives in the position of possessive modifier were not interpreted as necessarily disjoint in reference with the
subject.

  (25) b. ... (*hē*$_i$) *sealde *his*$_i$ hyrsted sweord* ...
               he^i gave his^i decorated sword
           ombihtþegne
           servant

           'He gave his decorated sword to the
           servant.'   (Beow. 672)

The reflexive possessive was lost altogether by the classical Old English period. Its disappearance, not to be
connected with the apparent loss of the reflexive

pronominal forms, which must have taken place at least several centuries earlier, is consistent with our hypothesis. Thus, the hypothesis finds support in at least one bit of direct evidence from the history of reflexives in English.

3.4. Next, let us turn to the North Germanic languages. In Old Icelandic, the earliest extensively documented of these, the situation with respect to reflexive binding and disjoint reference is essentially like that found in Gothic. Within simple sentences, coreference with the subject had to be expressed by means of the reflexive. Nonreflexive pronouns were interpreted as disjoint in reference with the subject. This is illustrated by (26a) and (26b):

(26) a. $hann_i$ *nefndi* sik_i (+R) $\acute{O}laf$
      he   named self   Olaf

      'He called himself Olaf.'
                  (Hkr. 128:9; Nygaard 1905:338)

   b. *siðan veitti hann* $\underline{honum}_j$ (-R) *banasár*
      then gave he   him   death-wound

      'Then he mortally wounded him.' (Njal. V:15)

As shown by (26c) and (26d), the same was true of accusative subjects of infinitives:

(26) c. [$hann_i$] *kvað* $\underline{sik}_i$ (+R) *vera þann finninn*
      he   said self   to-be the Finn

      'He said that he was the Finn.'
                  (Hkr. 66:25; Nygaard 1905:223)

   d. *ok* [$hann_i$] *sagði* $\underline{þá}_j$ (-R) *vera litla*
      and he   said them   to-be little
      í skapi
      in spirit

      'And he said that they were mean-spirited.'
                       (Hrafn. 888)

Subject and nonsubject positions in tensed embedded clauses were opaque to these processes—or at least to DR—as illustrated by (27).[29]

(27) a. *þa sagði* $konungr_i$ $_S$[*at* $\underline{hann}_i$ (-R)
      then   said King   that he
      mun taka við honum]
      will receive him

      'Then the king said that he would receive him.' (Fráskemtun Islendings; Ranke 1967:80)

b. *ƀaƌ   konungr*ᵢ *ƀess* ₅[*at   ƀeir skyldu*
    asked King   that ˢ that they should
    *hann*ᵢ (-R) *vita láta*]
    him   know let

    'The king asked that they should let him
    know.'   (OH 189:3; Nygaard 1905:342)

On the other hand, as in Gothic, nonsubject positions in
TENSELESS complements were transparent (28a, b), as were
the positions of subject of NP (28c) and object of locative PP (28d):[30]

(28) a. *ƀá   baƌ   hann*ᵢ *Hǫskuld*ⱼ ₅[PROⱼ *fara   til*
         then asked   he   Hoskuld   ˢ   ⱼ to-go to
         *skips   meƌ   sér*ᵢ (+R)]
         ship with self

         'Then he asked Hoskuld to go to the ship
         with him.'   (Njal. II:13)

     b. [*hann*ᵢ] *gerdi frá sér   menn*ⱼ ... ₅[*at* PROⱼ
         he   sent from self men   ˢ to   ⱼ
         *fá   sér*ᵢ (+R) *liƌ   ok   skip*]
         get self   troop and ship

         'He sent men from him to get him a troop
         and a ship.'   (Hkr 783:13; Nygaard 1905:341)

     c. *Unnr*ᵢ *gekk til* ₙₚ[*búƌar* ₙₚ[*fǫƌur   síns*ᵢ
         Unnr went to   ᴺᴾ tent ᴺᴾ father's self's
         (+R)]]

         'Unnr went to his father's tent.'
                                          (Njal. VI:21)

     d. *ok* [*ƀeir*ᵢ] *fundu fyrir   sér*ᵢ (+R)
         and they   found before selves
         skála nǫkkurn
         hall some

         'And they found a hall before them.'
                         (SE 28:39; Nygaard 1905:338)

However, there are, as in Gothic, sporadic instances of
constructions of the first type in which nonreflexive
pronouns are used, rather than reflexives, to corefer with
the matrix subject. The following is such a case:

(29)   *ƀá   skal hann*ᵢ *beiƌa goƌa* ... ₅[*at fá*
         then shall he   ask   priest   ˢ to get
         *honum*ᵢ (-R) *ƀriƌjungsmann   sín*ᵢ]
         him   thridjungsman self's

         'Then he will ask the priest to get him
         his thridjungsman.'
              (Godernes Grág. I, 50:7; Nygaard 1905:341)

Again, it is possible to interpret this marginal variation as incipient syntactic change, in the direction predicted by our hypothesis.

The modern West Scandinavian languages, to which Old Icelandic is immediately ancestral, do not seem to differ from it substantially in terms of pronominal syntax. See Beito (1970:246) for examples from New Norwegian, Lockwood (1964:117 ff.) for examples from Faroese, and Thráinsson (1976b) for examples from Modern Icelandic. The value for the present study of the evidence provided by West Scandinavian lies in the fact that it supports the claim that the Gothic type of binding situation was the original one in Germanic. I will discuss this issue at greater length below.

3.4.1. Evidence from North Germanic supporting the main contention of this paper comes from languages of the eastern group of that branch: specifically, Danish and Dano-Norwegian. The references I have consulted on those languages present a relatively sketchy picture of developments in pronominal syntax, and a number of questions remain to be answered regarding dialect and relative chronology, but the distinction of reflexives and nonreflexive pronouns in both possessive modifier position and nonsubject position in untensed clauses has undergone changes consistent with the predictions of our hypothesis. First, let us consider possessive constructions. As illustrated by (30a) and (30b), Old Danish continued the Germanic distinction between reflexive and nonreflexive possessives.

(30) a. $th\bar{a}$ ... $tak\alpha e$ (han_i) $_{NP}[\underline{sit}_i$ (+R) $\bar{e}ghit]$
          then   take he^i $\overline{self's}^i$ property

'Then let him take his property.'
(Erik's Law 58; Ranke 1967:155)

b. $th\bar{a}$ $\bar{a}$ han_i at $giu\alpha e$ $bryt\alpha n_j$
    then has he^i to give administrator^j
    $tw\bar{a}$ $\emptyset rae$ for $_{NP}[\underline{hans}_j$ (-R) $umr\emptyset ct]$
    two Öre for his^j care

'Then he has to give the administrator two Ore for his care.'
(Erik's Law 58; Ranke 1967:155)

However, it is possible at a very early date to find instances in which the nonreflexive pronoun is used as a possessive where coreference with the subject is intended:

(31) a. han_i ... $mist\alpha e$ $_{NP}[alt$ $\underline{hans}_i$ (-R) $gooz]$
          he^i loses   all $\overline{his}^i$ goods

'He loses all of his goods.'
(Flensburg Law 89; Ranke 1967:159 circa 1316 A.D.)

According to Falk and Torp (1900:134) this became general
in later stages of the language:

(31) b. *oc takær nokær man han*_i *i*   NP[*hans*_i
         and takes   some   man he[i]   into   his[i]
         (-R) *korn*]
              corn

'And he takes some man into his corn.'
                                (Falk and Torp 1900:134)

c. *det er Disciplin . nock,   at   hand*_i *er*
    that is to-disciple enough that   he[i] is
    sem   NP[*hans*_i (-R) *mestere*]
    like   his[i]   master

'It is enough for a disciple that he is
like his master.'
                    (Bib. 1550; Falk and Torp 1900:134)

d. *effter   at bispen*_i *vaar gaaen ind paa*
    after   that bishop[i] was   gone   in   into
    NP[*hans*_i (-R) *kammer*]
       his[i]   chamber

'After the bishop had gone into his
chamber ...'
                    (J. Niels; Falk and Torp 1900:134)

e. *en kone,   som* S[[*e*_i] *er opsætsig   mod*
    a   woman that   is   disobedient against
    NP[*hendis*_i (-R) *Mand*]]
       her[i]   husband

'A woman who is disobedient against her
husband.' (Sneedorf; Falk and Torp 1900:134)

Falk and Torp give the impression that the replacement of
the reflexive by the nonreflexive possessive was normal
during the period in question, and it seems to have persisted for a considerable time. It is not, however, a
feature of Modern Standard Danish, as illustrated by
(32a).

(32) a. *han*_i *solgte* {**hans*_i (-R)/*sine*_i (+R)} *bøger*
         he[i] sold   **his*[i]   /self[i]s   books

'He sold his books.'

In Modern Danish, the effects of the replacement survive
only in the plural, where the originally nonreflexive
deres is used to express possession by both subjects and
nonsubjects.[31] (This is not true of Standard Dano-
Norwegian, where *sin* is still used in reflexive meaning
even in the plural.) In the Jutish dialect, on the other

hand, the distinction has been levelled in favor of the
nonreflexive pronoun in both singular and plural:

(32) b.   hvor   den rige mand$_i$ har $_{NP}$[hans$_i$ peng]$_i$
          where the rich man^i has   his money
          og   hvor   e   frow$_j$ har $_{NP}$[hende$_j$ klær]
          and where the woman^j has   her   clothes

'Where the rich man has his money and
where the woman has her clothes.'
(Falk and Torp 1900:135)

Thus, the neutralization of the opposition, which, as we
saw earlier, took place in English and German, has also
occurred in some varieties of Danish, providing further
support for our hypothesis. The apparent countertendency
in Standard Danish reflected in the reinstatement of *sin*
in the singular is of course problematic for the hypothesis, but it could possibly turn out to be an artifact of
dialect conflict.

Corresponding to this development in possessives in
Danish, we also find the expected change in nonsubject
position in tenseless complements. Falk and Torp (1900:
132) note this change, citing the example in (33a) from
the literature (mid-nineteenth century) and presenting
sentences like (33b) and (33c) as representative of contemporary usage in Danish and Dano-Norwegian.

(33) a.   han$_i$ saa langt borte $_S$[en Fodgjænger$_j$ kome
          he^i saw far   away   a pedestrian^j come
          ham$_i$ (-R) imode]
          him^i toward

'Far away he saw a pedestrian come toward
him.'   (Heiberg; Falk and Torp 1900:132)

     b.   hun$_i$ bad ham$_j$ $_S$[PRO$_j$ give hende$_i$ (-R) tid]
          she^i asked him^j to-give her^i time

'She asked him to give her time.'

     c.   hun$_i$ forstillede sig $_S$[ham$_j$ tænkende paa
          she^i imagined   him^j thinking about
          hende$_i$ (-R)]
          her^i

'She imagined him thinking about her.'

They also admit the reflexive in such constructions,
though, as in (33d) and (33e), so it appears that DR
only, not reflexive binding, was constrained from applying to the position in question.[32]

(33) d. *hun_i forstillede   sig _S[ham_j tænkende*
          she[i] imagined   to-self   him[j] thinking
          paa   sig_i (+R)]
          about self[i]

'She imagined him thinking about her.'

e. *han_i fik ham_j _S̄[til at PRO_j laane sig_i (+R)*
     he[i] got him[j]   to   loan self[i]
     penge]
     money

'He got him to loan him money.'

Spore (1965:162 ff.) still characterizes the use of the
nonreflexive pronoun in constructions like (33a)-(33c) as
normal in Danish where reference to the higher subject is
intended. However, my informant, a native of Copenhagen,
rejects the nonreflexive in similar sentences, which again
suggests the existence of dialect differences:

(33) f. *han_i bad   mig_j _S̄[PRO_j hialpa sig_i (+R)/*
          he[i] asked me[j]   to-help self[i]   /
          *ham_i (-R)]
          *him[i]

'He asked me to help him.'

Iversen (1918:33 ff.) reports for the Tromsø dialect of
Dano-Norwegian facts which are similar to those presented
by Falk and Torp. He states that around the turn of the
century it was not uncommon for the nonreflexive pronoun
to be used in nonsubject position in infinitive complements to corefer with the higher subject (although the
reflexive was also possible):

(34) a. *han_i bad   guten_j _S̄[om å PRO_j bære*
          he[i] asked boy-the[j]   to   carry
          kofferten   hjam for han_i (-R)]
          suitcase-the home for him[i]

'He asked the boy to carry the suitcase
home for him.'

b. *ho_i fikk   broren_j _S̄[te' å PRO_j låne*
     she[i] got   brother-the[j]   to   loan
     a ho_i (-R) nån penga]
        her[i]   some money

'She got her brother to loan her some money.'

c. *ho_i narra søstra_j _S̄[te å PRO_j klæ a ho_i (-R)*
     she[i] tricks sister[j]   to   undress her

'She tricks her sister into undressing her.'

Although the reflexive had been extensively reintroduced
in such constructions by the time of Iversen's study, at
the expense of the nonreflexive, the latter was still
generally used in at least some of them.

In summary, we have observed that in Danish nonreflexive pronouns coreferring with the matrix subject began
appearing in two environments where DR assignment had
previously prevented their occurrence—subject position
within NPs and nonsubject position within infinitive complements. These changes took place during overlapping,
though apparently not simultaneous periods, and they were
carried through to different degrees in different dialects. In Standard Danish, as spoken by my informant,
they are reflected only in the use of *deres* as the sole
possessive form in the plural.

While the details of these developments merit further
investigation, the facts outlined above are sufficient to
show that the predictions of our hypothesis are borne out
in North Germanic as they were in East Germanic (represented by Gothic) and West Germanic. In Danish, as in
the languages considered earlier, two positions which
should be opaque to binding processes according to (8)
have in fact tended to become opaque. Moreover, the
rough chronological correspondence between the two
changes provides some support for the claim that a single
general principle was responsible for both.

3.4.2. In Swedish, the other major language of the
Eastern North Germanic group, the distribution of the two
forms appears to be much the same as in Gothic and the
West North Germanic languages. As the following examples
from Edmondson and Lindau (1974) show, reflexives must be
used in the positions of subject of an NP (35a), subject
or nonsubject of a tenseless complement (35b,c), and object of a locative preposition (35d) when coreference with
the matrix subject is intended.

(35) a. $Kerstin_i$ *blev kysst i* $_{NP}[\underline{sitt}_i$ (+R) *kök*]
         $Kerstin^i$ was kissed in self's^i kitchen

         'Kerstin was kissed in her kitchen.'

     b. Jan_i *tror* $_S[\underline{sig}_i$ (+R) *vara en god*
         Jan^i believes self^i to-be a good
         lingvist]
         linguist

         'John believes himself to be a good
         linguist.'

     c. Jan_i *bad* Ali_j $_{\bar{S}}[PRO_j$ *gå*   *in i* $\underline{sitt}_i$
         Jan^i asked Ali^j to-go into self's^i
         (+R) *tält*]
              tent

         'Jan asked Ali to go into his tent.'

d. Jan_i sag en orm $_{pp}[bredvid$ $\underline{sig}_i$ $(+R)]$
   Jan^i saw a snake ^{pp} beside self^i

'Jan saw a snake beside him.'

4.0. We claimed earlier that the Germanic parent
language must have been essentially like Gothic in that
NPs and tenseless (but not tensed) clauses were transparent to disjoint reference and reflexive binding. The
comparative evidence introduced in the last several sections leaves little room to doubt the correctness of this
claim. The Gothic facts are duplicated in North Germanic
by Old Icelandic and its descendents, by Swedish, and by
some varieties of Danish. In West Germanic, the original
reflexive/nonreflexive possessive distinction is reflected
vestigially in Old English, and the transparency of infinitive complements is still found in earlier stages of
German.

4.1. We have also seen that various Germanic languages have tended to move away from this original situation. In Biblical Gothic, nonreflexive pronouns occasionally appear in place of expected reflexives in both
of the abovementioned positions, as well as nonsubject
positions within participial relative clauses. In
Skeireins Gothic, nonreflexive pronouns appear exclusively
in place of expected reflexives in the latter. In German
participial relative constructions have also become opaque
to reflexive binding and DR, and the reflexive/nonreflex-
ive distinction has been wholly neutralized in the case
of possessives. Moreover, during the history of German,
the ability of reflexives in nonsubject position in infinitive complements to corefer with the higher subject
has become increasingly restricted. In English, the reflexive possessive *sin*, the only surviving Germanic reflexive form, first became optional (indicating that NPs
were no longer transparent to DR) and then was lost from
the language. By the time the *-self* reflexives became
established, both NPs and tenseless clause were opaque to
reflexive binding. In Danish, too, reflexives have tended
to be replaced by nonreflexives in both NPs and tenseless
clauses where coreference with a subject external to those
constructions is intended.
   In some of the languages investigated, it appears
that NPs and tenseless clauses were not affected by the
observed changes at the same time; nonetheless, in those
languages in which one environment was affected, the other
was eventually affected as well. Unless we wish to dismiss this correspondence as accidental, we must assume
that the changes in both are to be assigned some common
cause, such as the implementation of principle (8).
   The correspondence also argues against traditional
accounts of the restriction on reflexives in infinitive
complements, which attribute it to the fact that it eliminates the potential for ambiguity existing when both the

higher subject and the lower subject are grammatically possible antecedents for a lower clause reflexive. No such explanation is available for the elimination of the reflexive possessive, since that change creates, rather than eliminates ambiguity.

It should also perhaps be mentioned that the changes discussed here do not seem to be connected with the general typological shift from SOV to SVO word order which has been claimed to be responsible for several other systematic changes in the syntax of the Germanic languages, since they have taken place in German, which preserves SOV order except in root clauses, but not in Icelandic, in which the word order shift has been entirely carried through.

4.2.   In Chomsky's Government Binding model, the class of anaphors is held to include not only phonologically realized forms such as reflexives, but certain phonologically null elements as well: specifically, the traces left by NP movement.   Bounding conditions on raising to subject, passive, and other movements whose targets are argument positions are claimed to derive from the anaphoric nature of these traces.   If this claim is true, then we should expect that the changes in conditions on anaphors in Germanic should also be reflected in radical changes in the operation of NP movement.   I know of no evidence suggesting that this is the case.   This apparent asymmetry raises interesting questions about the nature of the relationship between bounding conditions on movements and bounding conditions on binding of lexical anaphors.

NOTES

1.   Although the translation dates from the fourth century, it is represented only in sixth century manuscripts.   Citations in this paper are taken from the edition of Streitberg (1971), whose version of the Greek original I have also consulted.

2.   In Gothic, unlike Greek and English, distinct reflexives exist only in the third person.   In the first and second persons, the personal pronouns are used in both reflexive and nonreflexive functions.   Robertson (1914:687 ff.) claimed that personal pronouns in all persons could also be used reflexively in New Testament Greek. However, virtually all of his examples involve pronouns which are either the objects of locative prepositions or possessive modifiers of NPs.   My own examination of the distribution of personal pronouns and reflexive pronouns in the Greek text leads me to believe that he drew the wrong conclusion from these occurrences.   It appears that personal pronouns were in fact uniformly interpreted as disjoint in reference with a tautoclausal subject EXCEPT when they occurred in one of these positions.   An explanation of the opacity of these two constructions to disjoint reference assignments will be presented below.   In other cases of intended coreference with a clause-mate subject, overtly reflexive pronouns are used almost exclusively. The only two counterexamples of which I am aware are Mat 6:19 and

Joh 2:24. Robertson noted both of these, but proposed that the
pronoun in the latter could in fact be an abbreviated form of the
reflexive, indistinguishable from the corresponding personal pronoun
because the manuscripts did not indicate accents and breathings.
3. In Gothic and Greek, unlike English, only subjects could
serve as antecedents for reflexives. In these languages, therefore,
it will not suffice to define potential antecedents solely in terms
of c-command, as can be done in English.
4. In (2b), the Gothic version translates the Greek reflexive
with the emphatic reflexive *sik silban*, to be discussed at greater
length in note 7. The Gothic reflexive also appears in the position
in question independent of the Greek, however, as in (a):

(a) [*eis*$_i$] *munandans* $_S$[*sik*$_i$ (+R: = GK Ø) *aglons*   *urraisjan*]
     they^i thinking   themselves   tribulation to arouse

     'Supposing that they arouse tribulation.'   (Phil 1:17)

5. Correspondingly, nonreflexive pronouns in these positions
appear to have been interpreted consistently as disjoint in reference
with the matrix subject. The few exceptions will be discussed below.
It should be noted, incidentally, that the evidence for obligatory
disjoint reference assignment in Gothic—and all historical languages—is necessarily indirect. The only way to argue that a nonreflexive pronoun in some position HAD to be interpreted as disjoint
in reference with the subject is to show that reflexives were uniformly used in that position whenever coreference was intended.
6. The claim that the infinitive complements in such examples
do in fact have PRO subjects can be justified in the following way:
As observed in note 3, reflexives in Gothic required subject antecedents. In examples like (a), however, there is no overt subject
antecedent. The reflexive *seinamma* is understood to corefer with
the dative *qenai*.

(a) *anabiuda qenai*$_i$ $_S̄$[... PRO$_i$ *du abin seinamma*$_i$
     I-command woman-DAT   to husband self's
     (+R) *aftra gagawairþjan*]
          later to-reconcile

     'I command a woman ... later to be reconciled with
     her husband.'   (I Cor 7:10-11)

Unless we wish to abandon the well-established generalization about
subject control, we must posit a PRO subject, controlled by *qenai*,
as the real antecedent of the reflexive. Similar examples motivate
the PRO subjects posited for participial relative constructions, to
be discussed below.
7. Whenever the Greek uses αυτοῦ to corefer with the subject,
the Gothic translates it as *sein-*. This is also the usual translation for the emphatic reflexive ἴδιος 'one's own'. However, the
emphatic reflexive possessive ἑαυτοῦ is routinely translated as *seins
silbins* 'self's own', probably because it is bimorphemic as well as
emphatic.
8. Compare also Joh 17:13, Col 2:15, Eph 2:16. In Greek, the
reflexive is occasionally used in the position of object of a

locative preposition to refer back to the subject, indicating that
this position was accessible to reflexive binding. However, the
fact that nonreflexive pronouns could also be used indicates that it
was inaccessible to disjoint reference assignment (cf. also note 2).
The facts seem to be the same for English. Many speakers accept the
reflexive in (a), but for most, the nonreflexive is preferred.

(a)   He$_i$ put the glass beside [him$_i$/?himself$_i$]

Thus, while not opaque to reflexive binding, locative prepositional
phrases in English do appear to be opaque to DR. Note that only
locative PPs are so restricted: "case" PPs are not:

(b)   He$_i$ bought it for [himself$_i$/*him$_i$]

9. I assume that the linking of emphatic reflexive possessives
like *his own*, ἴδιος, ἑαυτοῦ to their antecedents is not effected by
core grammar binding processes, but by discourse-level processes.
Even if this is not accepted, it remains the case that Gothic differs
from English and Greek with respect to disjoint reference in all of
these environments. It should also be noted that all anaphors do not
behave alike in English. Thus, for example, unlike the reflexive,
the reciprocal *each other* occurs freely in possessive position.
10. For a more technical definition, see Chomsky (1979).
11. Chomsky proposes that infinitive complements with lexical
subjects have undergone S̄ deletion, allowing the higher verb to
govern the subject. When an untensed complement fails to undergo
S̄-deletion, its subject can only be PRO, since only PRO can occur in
an ungoverned position. The subject of an infinitive is not governed
by any element in its own clause, and S̄-boundaries are absolute
boundaries to governance from outside.
12. According to Chomsky, adnominal modifiers are not assigned
genitive case by the head noun, since nouns do not assign case.
Rather, case is inserted in these constructions by a special rule
$[_{NP} \ NP\text{-}\bar{X}] \rightarrow [_{NP} \ NP_{gen}\text{-}\bar{X}]$.
13. Except as noted in note 9; in Greek and English, emphatic
reflexive possessives (ἑαυτοῦ, ἴδιος, *his own*) can be bound outside
of their governing NPs. Another apparent exception is found in English constructions like (a), in which either a reflexive or a nonreflexive may be used to corefer with the matrix subject, across the
boundary of an NP.

(a)   He$_i$ gave me [$_{NP}$ a picture [$_{pp}$ of himself$_i$/him$_i$]]

The admissibility of this type of alternation, however, may be accounted for by assuming an optional rebracketing convention of the
form $[_{NP} \cdots [_{pp}]] \rightarrow [_{NP}] \ [_{pp}]$, whose application puts the reflexive
in an accessible position. Such a restructuring rule has already
been proposed to account for extractions involving constructions of
this type.
14. By contrast, under Chomsky's earlier models (e.g. Chomsky
1977, 1980), it would have to be assumed that Gothic differed from
English and Greek with respect to more than a single condition. In
those models, the differences in (7c) and (7d) could be attributed
to the fact that English and Greek, but not Gothic, observe the

Specified Subject Condition. However, this would not explain the
difference reflected in (7e), where the SSC is not applicable. Instead, it would probably be necessary to account for this difference
by claiming that reflexive binding and disjoint reference assignment
in Greek and English, but not Gothic, were sensitive to the A-over-A
condition. The single-condition account made available by the Government Binding model thus involves an empirical claim not made by
the two-condition account required in the earlier models. In particular, it predicts that in a given language either the position of
nonsubject of an infinitive complement and the position of subject
of an NP should both be inaccessible to binding processes, or, if
the condition is not observed, they should both be accessible. On
the other hand, if two separate conditions are involved, then re-
laxation of one should have no necessary effect on the other. We
will return to this question below.
     15. However, in the *Skeireins*, the other major Gothic text, we
find the following, in which a reflexive possessive modifier in the
subject of a tensed clause has the higher clause subject as its
antecedent:

(a) *akei* (*is$_i$*) *was kunnands* $_{\bar{S}}$[*þatei swaleikamma waldufnja*
     but   he^i was knowing   that   by-such   authority
     [$_{NP}$*mahteis seinaizos$_i$* (+R) *naups*] *ustaiknida   wesi*]
        of power   self's^i force revealed   would-be

     'But he knew that by such authority the force of his
     power would be revealed.'   (Sk I b:12)

The reflexive here admits of a few possible explanations. It will
be noted, for instance, that it is in a position prohibited according to principle (8a) but not prohibited by either the Nominative
Island or the Specified Subject Condition of the earlier binding
model presented in Chomsky (1980). Thus, the example could be construed as evidence in favor of the earlier model. Alternatively,
this may be taken as a logophoric use of the reflexive, of the type
discussed in note 29. In any case, since the example is unique, and
since it occurs in a text of uncertain provenance, it doesn't appear
possible to determine what significance is to be attached to it.
     16. In fact, I have argued elsewhere (Harbert 1980) that such
a principle should be included in the inventory of binding conditions
in universal grammar. The condition in (8), of course, would dupli-
cate the effects of a tensed-clause principle of this type. Therefore, a model of universal grammar containing both would be less than
optimally elegant. However, it is justified by the existence of
numerous languages in which tensed clauses remain opaque to binding
even though governing categories of other types are transparent.
     17. Other possible candidates, listed by Edmondson (1978:643)
are Gã, Japanese, and Okinawan. Examples from Icelandic, Swedish,
Latin, and Russian will be given below. Hindi examples are presented
in Harbert (1980) and the references given there.
     18. Faltz (1977:158) observes an asymmetry in Russian between
tensed and untensed clauses similar to that found in Gothic. The
latter, but not the former are transparent to reflexive binding.
     19. The question arises, of course, concerning how Gothic (and
Germanic) acquired a marked distribution of reflexives in the first

place. An interesting suggestion is advanced by Faltz (1977:250 ff.), who proposes that the Germanic reflexives and their cognates in other Indo-European languages originated as reportative subordinate reflexives, which were used in indirect discourse and which were restricted to occurring in clauses not containing their antecedents. Only subsequently did they develop into true reflexives, subject to conditions on binding. The reader is referred to Faltz' discussion. Compare also note 29.

20. The damaged and fragmentary manuscript in which the *Skeireins* has been transmitted was painstakingly edited by Bennett (1960), whose edition I cite here.

21. Once again, this is the sole example of its kind in the corpus.

22. As in Gothic, this applies only to third person pronouns. In the first and second persons, for which no distinct reflexive forms existed, the personal pronoun was used in both reflexive and nonreflexive functions. Moreover, the dative third person reflexive was lost prehistorically in German, and the corresponding personal pronoun was used in Old High German in reflexive as well as nonreflexive functions.

(a) *got$_i$ giberehot inan$_j$ in imo$_i$* (-R) *selbemo*
     God^i glorifies him^j in him^i self

    'God is glorified in him.'   (Tat 159:8)

Only later in the history of the language was a new dative reflexive introduced, formally identical with the accusative. Of course, cases like those pose an interesting problem for the theory: How is disjoint reference assignment to be constrained from applying to just those pronouns for which no corresponding reflexive exists? For an interesting discussion of this problem, see Thrainsson (1976).

23. The Old High German *Tatian* translation is preserved in a 9th century manuscript. Citations here come from the edition of Sievers (1892), whose Latin parallel text I have also consulted.

24. Corresponding to the underlined pronoun in this example, the Latin model has the reflexive *se*, in what is probably to be considered a logophoric use (cf. note 29).

25. However, elsewhere the translator failed to imitate a Latin reflexive in a comparable construction:

(a) *thiede$_i$ ni uuoltun* $_S$[*mich$_j$ rihhison ober sie$_i$* (-R: = Lat+R)
     who^i not wanted   me^j to-rule over them^i

    'Who did not want me to rule over them.'   (Tat 151:11)

26. Locative prepositional phrases in German appear to have been transparent to both DR and reflexive binding at all stages.

27. These facts were reported by Reis (1973). A reflexive in a position other than that of prepositional object can be bound across the accusative subject of the complement if that subject is the dummy neuter pronoun *es*:

        Er$_i$ lässt es$_j$ sich$_i$ nicht gefallen
        He^i lets it^j to-self^i not   please

    'He doesn't put up with it.'

28. The same facts would also argue against a hypothesis holding
that binding and historical changes in binding are governed by a
hierarchy of individual constructions ranked according to relative
accessibility, rather than by a single condition referring to a generalized configuration of which these individual constructions
are special cases. Edmondson (1978:644) has suggested the possible existence of such a hierarchy. If we assume that it does exist as
part of universal grammar, we could propose that nonsubject positions
in infinitive complements rank higher on it (and are therefore more
accessible to binding) than possessive modifiers. The cutoff point
for binding in a given language would either fall higher on the
hierarchy than either position, as in English, or lower than either
position, as in Gothic, or between the two positions. In the latter
case, represented by Old High German, binding would treat the two
constructions differently. We could account for the apparent uni-
directionality of changes in binding by stipulating that the position
of the cutoff point, if it changes at all, must move UP the hierarchy. Such an account would have an apparent advantage over the
single-condition account, in that it would predict the possibility
of situations like the one found in Old High German. This is ac-
complished, however, only at the cost of introducing considerable
apparatus, and it is not clear that it is even a desirable result,
in view of the apparent infrequency of the Old High German situation
relative to either that represented in English or that represented
in Gothic.

29. It is a well-known fact about Old Icelandic and several
other North Germanic languages that reflexives can be used in tensed
complements under certain circumstances to refer back to the subject
of the higher clause. These are traditionally referred to as indirect reflexives:

(a) Old Icelandic:
     þorbjǫrn$_i$ spyrr $_S$[ef Sámr$_j$ vildi nǫkkura lipveizlu
     Thorbjorn asks   if Samr^j wanted any   help
     veita   sér$_i$ (+R)]
     to-offer self^i

     'Thorbjorn asks if Samr wanted to offer him any help.'
                                                    (Hrafn. 66)

(b) Modern Icelandic:
     Jón$_i$ segir $_S$[að María$_j$ elski sig$_i$ (+R)]
     John says   that Mary ^{j} loves self^i

     'John says that Mary loves him.'   (Thraínsson 1976:225)

(c) Faroese:
     Gunnvør$_i$ visti $_S$[at   tey$_j$ hildu lítið um seg$_i$ (+R)]
     Gunnvor^i knew   that they^j thought little of self^i

     'Gunnvor knew that they thought little of her.'
                                                 (Lockwood 1964:118)

(d) Old Danish:
     hand gremmede   sig $_S$[*at   der   fands ingen*
     he   got   angry   that there was found none
     i   sin$_i$ (+R) ... *Hær*]
     in self's   army

     'He got angry that none was found in his army.'
                              (Ved.; Falk and Torp, 1900:137)

(e) Dano-Norwegian dialect:
     ho$_i$ *trur* $_S$[*alltid at dei tala um   seg*$_i$ (+R)]
     she believes   always that they talk about self

     'She always believes that they talk about her.'   *
                              (Falk and Torp 1900:133)

The most extensive statement of the conditions under which this can
happen is to be found in Thráinsson's discussion of Modern Icelandic
(Thráinsson 1976). He demonstrates that these conditions must be
formulated in terms of semantics or discourse, rather than in syntactic terms; in particular, reflexives of the type in question
occur predominantly (although not exclusively) in indirect discourse.
Clements (1977) notes a similar use of the reflexive in other languages and characterizes it as a discourse-level device for designating the person whose speech or thoughts are being reported. He
uses the term LOGOPHORIC for this function, and suggests that it is
accidental that the logophoric function is expressed by means of reflexive forms in these languages. In other languages, it is assumed
by personal pronouns, while some Niger-Congo languages have distinct
logophoric pronominal forms. Faltz (1977:253 ff.) also notes the
parallel between the logophoric ("reportative") forms in the Niger-
Congo languages and indirect reflexives of the type illustrated in
(a)-(e). The arguments presented by Thráinsson and Clements suggest
strongly that the linking of these logophoric reflexives to their
antecedents should be considered to be effected by processes at the
level of discourse, rather than by core grammar binding. Cf. also
Koster (1978:586 ff.).
     30. Of course, in Old Icelandic and the other languages dis-
cussed here, a reflexive in an infinitive complement can corefer with
the subject of the complement as well as the matrix subject. Examples have been omitted here due to considerations of space. The reflexive possessive could also be used in Old Icelandic, under conditions of emphasis, to refer to a nonsubject antecedent. This is true
in Modern Icelandic, Faroese, and Danish as well.
     31. Falk and Torp attribute the adoption of *deres* as the general
plural possessive to the influence of the German *ihr*. This explanation is insufficient for a few reasons. First, the introduction of
deres seems to have coincided with, and is clearly to be related to,
the spread of nonreflexive possessives to orginally reflexive contexts in the singular—a change which cannot be explained as the
result of German influence. (If anything, the model of German *sein*
would have favored the extension of the reflexive *sin* to nonreflexive contexts.) Second, a possessive adjective would constitute a
rather odd borrowing unless it had some particular system internal

motivation, such as might be provided by increased opacity on the part of NPs.

32. Or perhaps both DR and reflexive binding were blocked, and these reflexives were associated with their antecedents by the type of discourse-level linking discussed in note 29.

REFERENCES

Bartsch, K. (ed.) 1870. *Der Nibelunge Nôt*. Leipzig: Brockhaus.

Beito, Olav T. 1970. *Nynorsk Grammatik*. Oslo: Det Norske Samlaget.

Bennett, W. H. 1960. *The Gothic Commentary on the Gospel of John*. New York: Modern Language Association. [Reprinted in 1966.]

Chomsky, N. 1977. On WH-Movement. *Formal syntax*, ed. by P. Culicover, T. Wascow, and A. Akmajian, 71-132. New York: Academic Press.

——. 1981. Principles and parameters in syntactic theory. *Explanations in linguistics*, ed. by N. Hornstein and D. Lightfoot, 32-75. New York: Longman.

——. 1980. On binding. *Linguistic Inquiry* 11:1-46.

Clements, G. N. 1975. The logophoric pronoun in Ewe: Its role in discourse. *Journal of West African Linguistics* 10:141-78.

Edmondson, J. A. 1978. Ergative languages, accessibility hierarchies governing reflexives and questions of formal analysis. *Valence, semantic case and grammatical relations*, ed. by W. Abraham, 633-60. Amsterdam: John Benjamins.

——, and M. Lindau. 1974. A study of Swedish pronominalization. *UCLA Papers in Syntax* 5:18-48.

Falk, H., and A. Torp. 1900. *Dansk-Norskens Syntax*. Kristiania: H. Aschehoug.

Faltz, L. 1977. Reflexivization: A study in universal grammar. Dissertation, University of California, Berkeley.

Harbert, W. 1980. In defense of tense. *Cornell Working Papers in Linguistics* 1:66-92.

Iversen, R. 1918. *Syntaksen i Tromsø Bymaal*. Kristiania: Bymaals-Lagets Forlag.

Jónsson, Finnur (ed.) 1908. *Brennu-Njálssaga*. Halle: Max Niemeyer.

Keller, A. V. (ed.) 1957. *Konrads von Würzburg trojaner Krieg*. Publicationen des litterarischen Vereins in Stuttgart, vol. 44.

Klaeber, F. 1950. *Beowulf and the fight at Finnsburg*. 3rd ed. Lexington, MA: D. C. Heath and Co.

Koster, J. 1978. Conditions, empty nodes, and markedness. *Linguistic Inquiry* 9:551-93.

Leitzmann, A. (1963). *Wolfram von Eschenbach*. 6th ed. Tübingen: Max Niemeyer.

Lockwood, W. B. 1964. *An introduction to modern Faroese*. Copenhagen: Munksgaard.

Novum Testamentum Latine. 1971. 11th ed. Stuttgart: Württem- burgische Bibelanstalt.

Nygaard, M. 1905. *Norrøn Syntax*. Kristiania: H. Aschehoug.

Ranke, F. 1967. *Altnordisches Elementarbuch*. (3rd ed. revised by D. Hoffmann.) Berlin: Walter de Gruyter.

Reis, M. 1973. Is there a rule of Subject-To-Object Raising in German? *CLS* 9:519-29.

Robertson, A. T. 1914. *A grammar of the Greek New Testament in the light of historical research*. New York: George H. Doran.

Sievers, E. (ed.) 1892. *Tatian*. *Lateinisch und altdeutsch*. 2nd
    ed. Paderborn: F. Schöningh.
Spore, Palle. 1965. *La Langue Danoise*. Copenhagen: Akademisk
    Forlag.
Streitberg, W. (ed.) 1971. *Die gotische Bibel*. 6th ed.
    Darmstadt: Wissenschaftliche Buchgesellschaft.
Thrainsson, H. 1976a. Some arguments against the interpretive
    theory of pronouns and reflexives. *Harvard Studies in Syntax
    and Semantics* 2:573-624.
———. 1976b. Reflexives and subjunctives in Icelandic. Papers
    from the Sixth Annual Meeting, North Eastern Linguistics
    Society, 225-40.
Timberlake, A. 1980. Reference conditions on Russian reflexiviza-
    tion. *Language* 56:777-96.

ON RECONSTRUCTING A PROTO-SYNTAX

David Lightfoot

It seems to me to be profitable to view the historical evolution of languages in the context of changes in grammars. I take a grammar to be a formal system which characterizes certain structures and certain sentences as well formed, and relates phonetic form to logical form over an infinite range of sentences. Such a grammar of a particular language must accord with various restrictive principles which define grammars of natural languages and constitute a theory of grammar, or what is sometimes called Universal Grammar. I also assume that properties of Universal Grammar hold independently of linguistic experience and constitute part of the a priori knowledge which children have and which enables them to master the language to which they happen to be exposed.

Taking this view and confining our attention to syntax, one can show that grammars undergo many different kinds of changes in the course of time. A new category may be introduced; new phrase structure rules may emerge; a transformation may be lost, introduced, or re-formulated; likewise for a lexical rule; lexical exception features and strict subcategorization frames may change. And so on, together with various combinations of such changes. I have given examples of this kind of thing in Lightfoot (1979a, 1980).

In my own work on syntactic change I have paid particular attention to radical re-analyses, where a variety of simultaneous changes in permissible surface structures can be traced to a single change or a small number of closely related changes in a grammar. Such radical re-analyses often illuminate the proper description of some stage of a language and even the proper form of the theory of grammar.

Consider the story of the English modals (Lightfoot 1979a, Ch. 2). *Can, could, may, might, must, shall, should, will, would* once had no properties which distinguished them as a class from other verbs of the language. But in the course of late Old English (OE) and Middle English (ME) changes took place in various parts of the

grammar, apparently unrelated but with the effect that
these verbs became an identifiable class with distinct
properties. Then in the early sixteenth century the exceptionality of this class of verbs was "institutionalized" by a re-analysis in the grammar: a new category
(Modal) was introduced, so that there was a new phrase
structure rule (together with a concomitant and necessary
re-formulation of certain transformations involving negative and interrogative sentences). The evidence for the
re-analysis lies in some simultaneous surface changes, all
of which can be shown to be manifestations of such a uni-
tary change in the abstract grammar; so the singularity
of the change in the grammar follows from the simultaneity
of the surface changes (and, of course, certain notions
about the class of available grammars). The effect of the
change was that the earlier exceptionality was eradicated
in such a way that the new grammar was more readily attainable, i.e. required a less elaborate triggering experience on the part of the child. The nature of this
change, which I have sketched here only in the most general fashion (see Lightfoot 1979a, Ch. 2 for details),
suggested that the optimal grammar of Modern English
should contain the category Modal (as opposed to treating,
say, *can* as a verb with various exception features, cf.
Ross 1969), and that the theory of grammar should be
structured in such a way as to characterize the grammar
of fifteenth century English as highly marked, i.e. requiring an elaborate triggering experience for the child
to be able to attain it.

Consider also the change whereby a sentence such as
the king liked the pears, once construed as object-verb-
subject and with *like* meaning 'to cause pleasure for',
came to be construed as subject-verb-object and with *like*
now meaning 'to derive pleasure from'. In ME one finds
sentences like *the king like pears*, where the plural verb
form shows that it is the post-verbal noun which acts as
the subject. Such object-verb-subject sentences no longer
exist in Modern English, and in fact they became obsolete
at the end of the ME period. There is a natural explanation for this change in the framework of current versions
of the so-called trace theory of movement rules (part of
current versions of generative grammar).

It is clear that early English had an underlying
subject-object-verb order, i.e. phrase structure rules
along the lines of S → NP VP, VP → NP V. Given such
phrase structure rules, a sentence *the king like pears*
would be derived via a postposing of the subject NP, which
would leave behind a "trace" under current proposals (1).

(1) t [the king like]$_{VP}$ [pears]$_{NP}$

In the course of ME, these phrase structure rules were
replaced by ones which generated an underlying subject-
verb-object order (for details of this change, see Canale

1978). Under the new phrase structure rules, the subject
would be postposed, as in the earlier grammar, and the
object would have to be preposed into the position vacated
by the subject NP, obliterating the trace (2).

(2)   t [like the king]$_{VP}$ [pears]$_{NP}$

But such a derivation is impossible under the plausible
assumption that traces can be erased only by a designated
morpheme and not by a random NP. This assumption was motivated by Dresher and Hornstein (1979) and exploited by
Freidin (1978), who labels it the Trace Erasure Principle.
Dresher and Hornstein argue that sentences with the ex-
pletive *there* or *it* involve rightward movement, as indicated in (3) and (4), and that the trace is covered by a
designated morpheme, *there* in (3) and *it* in (4).

(3)   t [was [a student]$_{NP}$ arrested]$_{VP}$

(4)   t is obvious [that Harry left]$_S$

These are legitimate derivations, but passive sentences
cannot be derived by successive postposing of the agent
NP and preposing of the agent NP and preposing of the object, as is often supposed (5), because again a trace
would be erased by a random NP (here *a student*).

(5)   t was arrested [a student]$_{NP}$ by [the police]$_{NP}$

The Trace Erasure Principle is a plausible proposal because it guarantees that precisely one lexical item will
be associated with each deep structure NP position, and
that no second NP can be moved through a position vacated
by another NP. If it is correct, it also guarantees that
with the new subject-verb-object PS rules, *the king like
pears* will no longer be generated, and that *the king liked
the pears* will no longer be construed as object-verb-
subject. Such a sentence would no longer exist in its
original meaning ... unless, of course, there were a further change in the grammar, such as that case markings
were reintroduced to distinguish subject and object NPs.
A child, having abduced subject-verb-object PS rules and
hearing a sentence *the king liked the pears* would assign
it the only possible structural analysis, i.e. subject-
verb-object. If the child also realized the intended
meaning of the sentence, namely that the pears pleased
the king, he would abduce that *like* meant 'to derive
pleasure from'; somebody of an earlier generation, ab-
ducing subject-object-verb PS rules, would have a different meaning for *like*, 'to cause pleasure for'. So the
change in the form of the grammar here is that *like* has

a different meaning, i.e. it is a change in the lexicon.
There is also a change in the functioning of the grammar,
in that the derivation of *the king liked the pears* no
longer involves a postposing rule. This change is fully
explained on the assumption that English developed new PS
rules and that the theory of grammar is structured in such
a way as to preclude the erasure of traces by random NPs.
So the nature of this change suggests that there is something correct about a theory of grammar along these lines.

Under this approach to syntactic change, the point at
which such re-analyses occur in the history of a language
can illuminate the proper shape of a theory of grammar.
One will seek explanations along the lines just illustrated, perhaps suggesting revisions and refinements to
the existing theory of grammar in order to improve the
available explanations. It is, of course, not the case
that all historical changes will have this kind of explanation, because the history of languages is not fully determined. Languages can diverge and undergo individual
changes. The fact Latin developed into a variety of different languages suggests that one should not demand of a
theory of grammar that it be able to explain every change
in the way that we have just explained the obsolescence
of *the king like pears*; some changes will arise for idio-
syncratic reasons, and so help to distinguish, say, French
and Spanish. The history of a language evolves by an interaction of factors of chance and necessity. It may be
a matter of chance, or at least a function of something
other than grammatical concerns, that a language develops
a certain rule or property; it may be a matter of necessity that a language develops another property. A theory
of grammar, defining the class of available grammars, will
play a crucial role in the account of necessity factors,
as we have just seen, and therefore will play an equally
crucial role in our account of historical changes. Conversely, facts about historical changes may cast light on
the correct form of the theory of grammar, such that some
particular historical change might be explained, i.e. be
shown to result from some factor of necessity.

So I take a realist stance about grammars. There exists a theory of grammar, which constitutes part of our
mental capacity, defining the human species, and I assume
that its properties can be discovered. Evidence about its
properties will come from a variety of domains, such as
the distribution of morphemes, the scope of quantifiers,
perhaps even from the way in which linguistic capacities
are lost in the event of brain damage, and from historical
change. The evidence from historical change will be a
function of the ability of the theory to shed light on and
explain re-analyses, as with the change in the meaning of
like. In this way, data from historical change will play
a role alongside data from other domains, and the study of
linguistic change will be integrated with other aspects of
the study of grammar.

This is a very brief sketch of an approach to syntactic

change that I have pursued in recent years. The fact that
grammatical re-analyses occur is central to this approach
and the source for the insight on grammatical theory.
These re-analyses are like catastrophes in the sense of
René Thom (1972, 1973, etc.). Changes may occur in fairly
piecemeal fashion as people introduce new constructions
and phrase-types, but there may come a point where something more radical happens, involving a change in the abstract grammar with various surface manifestations, as
with the English modals. One might visualize the build-up
to such changes rather like a body of water which drops
steadily in temperature with no overt change until a point
where it changes to ice rather suddenly—a Thomian catas-
trophe.

The existence of such re-analyses suggests that there
can be no formal theory of change in the sense that one
might try to define formal constraints on a mapping of
one grammar on to another. Grammars emerge in children
on exposure to some linguistic environment. If the environment is slightly different, perhaps after one generation, the grammar triggered may be very different, perhaps involving a new category and associated transformational rules. Conversely, it is possible that one might
have quite different environments which would trigger
grammars differing in only one parameter. There is no
one-to-one relation between the difference in triggering
environments and the difference in the resulting grammars.
While environment$_i$ may trigger grammar$_i$ and, one generation later, environment$_j$ (slightly different from environ-
ment$_i$) may trigger grammar$_j$, there is no reason to seek
rules relating grammar$_i$ and grammar$_j$ (6). Both grammars
must conform to the theory of grammar, but, within those
limits, may have quite different properties, even though
triggered by a fairly similar experience.

$$(6) \quad Env_i \longrightarrow G_i$$
$$\vdots$$
$$Env_j \longrightarrow G_j$$

Since the grammars are formal objects, for any given pair
one can, of course, write rules mapping one into the
other, but there is no reason to suppose that those rules
will have any interesting properties or meet any interesting formal constraints. Attempts to provide such a
typology of changes have always been highly permissive;
witness Kiparsky (1968), who identified loss, addition,
re-ordering and re-formulation of rules, and changes in
underlying representations—all the logical possibilities
of the theory of phonology which he was presupposing. If
no such formal theory of change is forthcoming, one will
not be able to examine the grammars of three related languages and, on the basis of the formal properties of those
grammars, infer something about the necessary properties

of the grammar of the unattested proto-language from which
the three daughter languages have descended (7).

(7)   Proto-G

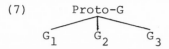

The problem is that the kinds of re-analyses that I
have mentioned constitute cut-offs to historical recapit-
ulation. When exposed to a particular linguistic environment, a child develops the most readily attainable grammar. If that grammar involves PS rules generating verb-
object order, the earlier history of the language is irrelevant and the child has no access to whether the language had object-verb order at some earlier stage.
With this perspective on syntactic change in mind,
let us now turn to the issue of reconstruction. I do not
suggest that this is the only approach that one can take
to the study of syntactic change, but it will provide a
useful point of reference and a basis for evaluating some
of the assumptions on which reconstruction work sometimes
proceeds.
A traditional view holds that reconstructed systems
play a role in comparative work in that they express relationships precisely. If Greek and Latin are "related,"
that relationship is expressed by the properties of the
parent language from which they descend and the specification of the changes which led to the two daughter languages. Meillet (1937) expresses this view forcefully
(the emphasis is Meillet's):

> *la seule réalité à laquelle elle ait affaire, ce*
> *sont les correspondances entre les langues attestées.*
> Les correspondances supposent une réalité commune,
> mais cette réalité reste inconnue, et l'on peut s'en
> faire une idée que par des hypothèses, et par des
> hypothèses invérifiables: la correspondance seule
> est donc objet de science. On ne peut restituer par
> la comparaison une langue disparue: la comparaison
> des langues romanes ne donnerait du Latin vulgaire
> ni une idée exacte, ni une idée complète ... ce qui
> fournit la méthode de la grammaire comparée n'est
> jamais une restitution de l'indo-européen, tel qu'il
> a été parlé: *c'est rien autre chose qu'un système*
> *défini de correspondances entre les langues his-*
> *toriquement attestées.*

More recently, a different view has emerged: that one
can use changes between a reconstructed system and the
daughter languages as a "data-base" for investigating the
nature of change, for learning something new about historical change. I wish to show here that this view, while
currently fashionable, has no merit.
Over recent years there has been a considerable increase in work on syntactic change, and most of this work

has been based on changes affecting unattested proto-
languages; witness almost all of the papers in anthologies
like Li (1975, 1977) and Steever, Walker, and Mufwene
(1976).[1] It is remarkable that there has been virtually
no serious discussion of an appropriate methodology for
syntactic reconstruction, despite the self-evident lack
of parallelism with phonological work ... and despite the
fact that Friedrich (1975), Jacobs (1975), and Lehmann
(1974) have offered book-length studies on particular reconstructed systems. Sometimes one sees hints of nagging
doubts in the minds of these authors: Friedrich (1975:6)
makes a remarkable reference to "the problems, some of
them insuperable, of reconstructing proto-syntax at all,"
but the insuperable problems are not specified and, whatever they are, are ignored in the remainder of the book—
which deals with a reconstructed syntax! Other writers
are more subtle, like Dixon (1973:393), who introduces his
account of Proto-Australian with the observation that "the
methodology and data on which these reconstructions are
based have not yet been published; only the conclusions
are summarized here"; this seems to be usual practice, and
three years later the relevant publication, as far as I
know, has still not appeared. In general, there seems to
be a tacit assumption that syntactic reconstruction can
be done in more or less the same fashion as reconstruction
of phonological systems—and that if there are methodological differences, their validity is not worth discussing
explicitly. All this ignores the questions raised repeatedly about the validity of syntactic reconstruction by
Allen (1953), Anttila (1972:355 ff.), Collinge (1960),
Dressler (1971), Hoenigswald (1960:137), King (1969:140),
and others.

     In many cases it is even unclear what the authors
claim to be reconstructing, whether sentences or (fragments of) grammars of the proto-language. Thus a claim
that Proto-Indo-European was SOV might be a claim about
the underlying order of initial (deep) structures, or a
claim about statistical probabilities of surface structures or of sentences. These are quite different things;
German has subject-verb-object as its most common word
order pattern, but this says nothing about the underlying
order, generated by the PS rules, and a good case can be
made that the underlying order is subject-object-verb.

     Reconstruction depends crucially on a concept of pos-
sible/impossible changes, and this keeps hypotheses within
the bounds of plausibility. So the neo-grammarians developed notions about natural changes based on their study
of changes involving two or more attested stages of some
historical development, and they postulated only those
kinds of changes when relating their reconstructed proto-
systems to the attested daughter languages. In syntax,
many authors base such a concept on Greenberg's (1966)
work on implicational universals, and "typological" concepts turn out to play a crucial role. It is assumed that
the proto-language is of a "consistent" type, and that it

is progressing along definable lines to another consistent
type. Thus a distinction is drawn between "consistent"
and "transitional" languages, as if all languages are not
in transition from one stage to another. The "definable
lines" by which a language of some consistent type pro-
gresses to another consistent type constitute the theory
of change distinguishing possible/impossible changes.

A theory of change is assumed to prescribe a universal
"slope," down which languages slide at varying rates. It
specifies the order in which a language of type a will
lose the properties of that type and acquire, again in a
prescribed order, the properties of type b. So if one
spots a mixed language, with some properties of type a and
some of type b, one can tell whether it is an example of
a type a language changing to type b or vice versa; one
can therefore deduce what the parent language must have
looked like, where it is no longer attested, simply by
listing the properties of the relevant type.

This methodology, used most notably by Lehmann, and
referred to several times by him as an EXPLANATORY historical syntax (what is being explained?), has been correctly criticized by Friedrich as a "misuse of typology";
and Watkins (1976:306) notes, in a powerful critique, that
Lehmann's theory "elevates some of Greenberg's extremely
interesting quasi-universals to the dubious status of intellectual straitjacket, into which the facts of various
Indo-European languages must be fitted willy-nilly, rightly or wrongly." This sometimes manifests itself in a cav-
alier treatment of facts. For example, almost all Indo-
Europeanists agree on the presence and the precise shape
of a relative pronoun (*yo) and a comparative morpheme
(*-$tero$-) in the parent language. But Lehmann assumes
that PIE was of an "SOV-type" and such languages are alleged to usually lack relative pronouns and comparative
morphemes; therefore he does not postulate these items in
his reconstruction. For detailed criticisms of this Procrustean methodology, see Jeffers (1976), Lightfoot
(1979a:Ch. 3), and Watkins (1976).

One fundamental problem for the whole enterprise is
that there is no real data-base for the theory of change
as defined, i.e. for establishing the order in which a
language of type a will develop the properties of a type b
language. Since the logic is one of induction, the data-
base would have to consist of a fairly large set of languages which have shifted from one type to another and
where one has documents illustrating the various stages
by which that shift took place. Such a data-base does not
exist. Latin is a moderately good SOV language by
Lehmann's criteria and French is a reasonably well-behaved
SVO language and the attestation for the intervening
stages is about as good as one is ever going to find. This
represents one of our best histories, while for the vast
majority of the world's languages we have data for no more
than 200 years. In the absence of a good number of comparable histories, it would be foolish to assume that the

manner in which the Romance languages developed their SVO
properties represents what must always happen. Unfortunately such an assumption is rather common.
    We know that French has developed from a SOV language
and that it now has SVO order. But if the direct object
is pronominal, one finds SOV order; compare (8) and (9).

    (8) *j'aime les danseuses*   'I like the dancers'

    (9) *je les aime*   'I like them'

Some writers assume that this represents a necessary state
of affairs and that whenever a language changes its word
order type, full lexical NPs will manifest the new order
before pronominal NPs; such a statement is incorporated
into their theory of change and is used as a basis for reconstructing proto-languages; whenever one spots a language with different word order patterns for lexical and
pronominal NPs, one knows that the order of the pronoun
represents the earlier state of affairs. Such a data-base
is pathetically thin for such a general principle; it also
happens to be disconfirmed by another language whose history is attested. Modern Greek has patterns like French,
with different orders for lexical and pronominal NPs (10a,
b), but here we know that the pronominal order (10b) is a
fairly recent innovation.

    (10)   a. *o kinigòs skótose tòn líko*
           'the hunter killed the wolf'
        b. *o kinigòs tòn skótose*
           'the hunter killed it'

    Consequently, it seems fair to say that a theory of
change along the lines adopted by Lehmann has no factual
base and therefore one is not surprised to find such wild-
ly conflicting claims about the nature of PIE on the part
of workers presupposing such a theory; Friedrich (1975)
claims it to be SVO, Lehmann (1974) SOV, and Miller (1975)
VSO. If this is the state of affairs in the reconstruction of PIE, where at least there is a long tradition of
scholarship, a large number of well-described daughter
languages (some of which long antedate others), one can
imagine the reliability of reconstructed ancestors of
American Indian Languages (see Li 1977 for several papers
pursuing this goal).[2]
    I have suggested that grammars can undergo radical re-
structuring from one generation to the next, and that
there appear to be no formal constraints on the ways in
which a grammar may differ from that of the preceding generation, beyond constraints imposed by the theory of grammar; i.e., both grammars must satisfy the limits on a possible grammar of natural language. The grammars must also
be triggered by linguistic environments which would normally be fairly similar. The absence of further formal
constraints should not be surprising.

Grammars are not transmitted historically, but must be created afresh by each new language learner. Each child hypothesizes or "abduces" a grammar; this enterprise is quite independent of what his parents hypothesized when they were hypothesizing their grammars one generation earlier. Two slightly different linguistic environments may trigger quite different grammars; conversely, slightly different grammars may generate mutually unintelligible outputs. If two dialects are similar in the class of sentences, it does not follow that their grammars are equally similar; there is no one-to-one correspondence in similarity of grammars and outputs. Therefore, when one considers how languages are learned, one would not expect a child's grammar necessarily to bear any closer formal relationship to that of his parents than what is required by their both falling within the class of possible grammars.

If this is correct, one can deduce very little about the form of a proto-grammar merely through an examination of the formal properties of the daughter grammars. Therefore it is also fallacious to claim (cf. Anttila 1972:358) that, when three or even all the daughter languages show a particular rule, that rule can be assigned to the proto-grammar. The grammar of a proto-language, like that of any other language, can be constructed ONLY on the basis of an interaction between a theory of grammar and the structure and meaning of sentences of the language. Thus claims about a proto-grammar can be made only if a sufficient body of proto-sentences is first established. But we shall see that successful reconstruction of proto-sentences must be very limited, given the nature of syntactic change, and it is most unlikely that there could ever be a sufficient data-base to make interesting claims about the proto-grammar.

The traditional tools of reconstruction are the comparative method—by far the more important—and internal reconstruction; these may be supplemented by various philological techniques and principles of dialect geography, to establish which forms and constructions are innovations and which are relics. Internal reconstruction can do a certain amount of work and assist inferences about an earlier syntax of a given language, if one admits certain assumptions. Lehmann (1974) (and many others) work on the assumption that there are universal diachronic principles such that certain changes will take place before others, as discussed above. Other workers assume that morphological patterns will partially recapitulate the syntax of an earlier stage of the language in a consistent way.

Givón (1971) translates the latter assumption into a slogan: "yesterday's syntax is today's morphology." The problem with the assumption as a probe into prehistory, is that morphology is notoriously slow to adapt to changing syntax, and may reflect syntactic patterns of such antiquity that the assumption becomes vacuous and untestable. Consider French verb morphology, which forms most

tenses with post-stem suffixes: *nous aimons, aimions,*
and the future *aimerons.* Classical Latin also had suffixes in all tenses: *amamus, amabamus, amabimus, amavi-
mus.* However, the French perfect tense has a pre-verbal
auxiliary: *nous avons aimé,* which can be accounted for
as preserving the innovative Late Latin pattern *habemus
amatum.* The problem is that the Late Latin future was
also formed with a pre-verbal auxiliary, *habemus amare;*
but this is not preserved in modern French verb morphology. Not only is morphology very slow to adapt to syntactic changes, but it also mirrors earlier patterns only
in a selective way. Therefore it is a most unreliable way
of reconstructing earlier syntax: each of the individual
forms reconstructed may be accurate, but there is no reason to suppose that they all reflect the same earlier
stage—they may each reflect the syntax of 500, 1000, or
2000 years ago (for another illustration, see the discussion of English compound names in Lightfoot 1979a:160).

     Internal reconstruction cannot be ruled out a priori,
even if the principles actually used as a basis for it are
highly questionable. But one must always bear in mind
that in any case (as often noted), internal reconstruction
is not a genuinely historical method. As Anttila (1972:
273) puts it, "whatever can be captured on the basis of
one language is synchronically present in that language.
All we get is a higher level of abstraction ..." Therefore, as a matter of practice, scholars usually apply internal reconstruction simply as a prelude to the comparative method, eliminating the effects of recent changes
before the real work begins.[3]

     Turning now to the comparative method, we can begin
by emphasizing an obvious but often forgotten point: the
items compared should be similar kinds of animals. Watkins
(1976) has compared relative sentences dealing with ath-
letic contests in Hittite, Vedic Sanskrit, and early
Greek, and he concludes that "the syntactic agreements are
so striking and so precise, that we have little choice but
to assume that the way you said that sort of thing in
Indo-European could not have been very different." One
may factor out the effects of more recent changes by distinguishing archaic from innovative structures and by applying, where possible, the method of internal reconstruction; one may thus arrive at identical structures in the
daughter languages, and then apply the comparative method
with some confidence.

     However, problems arise when the most archaic patterns
are not alike in the daughter languages. The success of
the comparative method in phonology is a function of the
putative regularity of sound change. In genetically related languages, a finite set of phonological segments has
regular correspondences, occurring in parallel positions
in a finite set of cognate words which are transmitted historically. The alleged regularity of the correspondences
permits application of the comparative method; but the meth
od breaks down, as often noted, with analogical changes.

There is no equivalent basis in syntax for the comparative method; there is no finite set of sentences occurring in parallel positions across languages in a finite
set of cognate (presumably discourse) contexts. The sentences of a language are not listable in the way that the
inventory of sounds is, and they are not transmitted historically in the same way.[4] The problem in syntax is that
there seem to be no principles (independent of a theory of
grammar) which formally define possible changes; syntactic
change is in large measure analogical, based on a reanalysis or "regrammatization" of old surface structure
patterns, levelling former distinctions or creating new
ones. Such analogical processes will cause as much interference for the usual methods of reconstruction as they do
in phonology and other areas of grammar; but in syntax
such changes are the normal type, and therefore the methods will be particularly limited. Jeffers (1976) points
to some desperate problems for reconstruction: what does
one do when related languages show parallel syntactic patterns with different meanings, or patterns which defy correspondence, or corresponding syntactic patterns without
cognate lexical material? For example, what could a com-
parativist conclude from a demonstration that Hittite had
underlying SOV order, Germanic SVO, and Celtic VSO? In
phonology Hitt. p, Gmc. f, and Celtic $\emptyset$ allow him to deduce a proto-phoneme; but SOV, SVO, and VSO allow no de-
ductions. Again, the IE passive has almost as many formal
expressions as there are languages. But even if one cannot reconstruct a morphological realization for the PIE
passive, Jeffers asks whether one can fail to recognize a
grammatical category which occurs in almost all the daughter languages.
    Given the lack of an independent and constrained defi-
nition of possible syntactic change, and the consequently
limited applicability of internal reconstruction and the
comparative method, it will be possible to reconstruct
very few proto-sentences. Reconstruction will be possible
via the comparative method only where the daughter languages show identical constructions, either in attested
forms or in internally reconstructed abstractions. Consequently it is most unlikely that there will ever be a
sufficient data-base of proto-sentences to make responsible claims about the proto-grammar.
    If there are no formal constraints on possible re-
analyses, imposed by a theory of change, then we cannot
use such things as a basis for claiming historical reality
for our reconstructions; nor is the mapping of one grammar into another of any interest in itself as a method of
illuminating possible changes. Reconstruction is not,
pace Jeffers (1976:1) "an important TOOL in the investigation of language change" (emphasis supplied): it is the
exploitation of acquired knowledge to express genetic relations. The knowledge is acquired from a study of actual
changes, where both the earlier and later grammars can be
deduced in the usual way from a stock of sentences attested

for both stages. We can exploit our knowledge of diachronic syntax or phonology, by applying it to the comparative work of expressing the precise relationship between languages; but we can never discover anything new
about the nature of change by examining the relationship
between attested languages and our reconstructed abstraction—which we arrive at by internal reconstruction and
the comparative method, with all their limitations, well
known in phonology and extensive in syntax. Therefore th
mapping between a reconstructed language and its attested
daughters is not an appropriate basis for illustrating
types of change, much less for acquiring insight into the
nature of change. For this one must look to analyses
where one has two attested stages of a language, where on
has sufficient recorded sentences to make responsible
claims about a plausible grammar or fragment of a grammar
     In the light of this, it is not an appropriate goal
for work on syntactic change to try to formulate "possibl
diachronic processes" or to reconstruct a proto-syntax.
Rather, it is productive to examine historical re-analyse
and to show how the point at which they occur might follo
from a reasonable theory of grammar. In this way we gain
some insight into the nature of change and work on historical change can illuminate the proper form of the
theory of grammar and thereby be integrated with work on
grammar from other points of view.

NOTES

     1. Much of what follows appeared in different form in Lightfoot
(1979a or b).
     2. Not only does a theory of change along these lines have no
factual base, but it is also irrelevant for many kinds of changes
since it deals only with word order harmonies. There is much that
can change in a grammar other than word order harmonies, as illustrated by the sketch of changes affecting the English modals and the
meaning of *like*.
     3. The limitations of internal reconstruction are often illus-
trated by the phenomena of Lachmann's Law in Latin. In Classical
Latin, the stem vowel of the participle of *ago* was long (*aktus*), although it was short in the non-participial forms; this was not true
for the participle of *fakio*, where the stem vowel was short for both
kinds of forms. By internal reconstruction one might infer that *ag*
+ *tus* underwent vowel lengthening in front of the voiced consonant
and then assimilation of voicing to give the surface *aktus*. However,
we know by the comparative method that voicing assimilation was an
old rule, presumably of PIE (since it affects all the daughter languages), whereas vowel lengthening was a later rule specific to
Latin. In such cases of conflict between the results of internal
reconstruction and the comparative method, the latter wins out as a
matter of general course.
     4. That is, it is reasonable to suppose that a child calls a
dog a dog because that is what his parents call a dog. But children
do not express a given idea in the way they do simply because their
parents expressed that idea in that way; they may never have heard

anybody express that idea before. Here the relationship between
their experience and the knowledge they eventually attain is more
indirect, being mediated and enriched by the principles of grammar
with which the child is endowed a priori. Put differently, it is
reasonable to suppose that ME *chapiter* is, in some sense, the same
word as NE *chapter*; but it would be bizarre to say that ME *the king
like pears* is the same sentence as NE *the king likes pears* or *pears
please the king*.

This relates to neo-grammarian approaches to language change.
The neo-grammarians held that sound change was PHONETICALLY conditioned and therefore they wrote rules which mapped the surface phonetic forms of one stage of a language into those of another, later
stage. Not all changes can be described in this manner (e.g. the
Lachmann's Law phenomena of Note 3) and some require reference to a
more abstract "morphophonemic" level of analysis. Nonetheless it
was a natural approach and allowed scope for a vast amount of useful
work cataloguing regular correspondences. But an analogous view of
syntax made no sense and the neo-grammarians did not write rules
mapping the sentences of one stage of a language into those of a
later stage. The lack of a syntactic legacy in any way comparable
to what the neo-grammarians left to the phonologists can be viewed
as a consequence of the theory of language which they presupposed.
See Lightfoot (1979a) for discussion.

REFERENCES

Allen, W. S. 1953. Relationship in comparative linguistics. *Trans-
    actions of the Philological Society* 52-108.
Anttila, R. 1972. *An introduction to historical and comparative
    linguistics*. New York: Macmillan.
Canale, M. 1978. Word order change in OE: Base re-analysis in
    generative grammar. Dissertation, McGill University, Montreal.
Collinge, N. 1960. Some reflections on comparative historical
    syntax. *Archivum Linguisticum* 12:79-101.
Dixon, R. 1977. The syntactic development of Australian languages.
    Mechanisms of syntactic change, ed. by C. N. Li, 365-415.
    Austin: University of Texas Press.
Dresher, B. E., and N. Hornstein. 1979. Trace theory and NP move-
    ment rules. *Linguistic Inquiry* 10:65-82.
Dressler, W. 1971. Über die Rekonstruktion der indogermanischen
    Syntax. *Zeitschrift für vergleichende Sprachforschung* 83:1-25.
Freidin, R. 1978. Cyclicity and the theory of grammar. *Linguistic
    Inquiry* 9:519-49.
Friedrich, P. 1975. *Proto-Indo-European syntax*. Journal of Indo-
    European Studies, monograph no. 1. Hattiesburg, MS.
Givón, T. 1971. Historical syntax and synchronic morphology: An
    archaeologist's field trip. Papers from the Seventh Regional
    Meeting of the Chicago Linguistic Society. Chicago: Chicago
    Linguistic Society.
Greenberg, J. H. 1966. Some universals of grammar with particular
    reference to the order of meaningful elements. *Universals of
    language*, ed. by J. H. Greenberg, 58-90. Cambridge, MA: The
    MIT Press.
Hoenigswald, H. M. 1960. *Language change and linguistic recon-
    struction*. Chicago: University of Chicago Press.

Jacobs, R. A.   1975. *Syntactic change: A Cupan (Uto-Aztecan) case-study*. University of California Publications in Linguistics.
    Berkeley: University of California Press.
Jeffers, R.   1976.   Syntactic change and syntactic reconstruction.
    Current progress in historical linguistics, ed. by W. Christie,
    1-10. Amsterdam: North Holland.
King, R. D.   1969. *Historical linguistics and generative grammar*.
    Englewood Cliffs, NJ: Prentice Hall.
Kiparsky, P.   1968.   Linguistic universals and linguistic change.
    Universals in linguistic theory, ed. by E. Bach and R. Harms,
    171-210. New York: Holt, Rinehart and Winston.
Lehmann, W. P.   1974. *Proto-Indo-European syntax*. Austin: University of Texas Press.
Li, C. N. (ed.)   1975. *Word order and word order change*. Austin:
    University of Texas Press.
———. (ed.)   1977. *Mechanisms of syntactic change*. Austin: University of Texas Press.
Lightfoot, D. W.   1979a. *Principles of diachronic syntax*.
    Cambridge: Cambridge University Press.
———. 1979b.   Review article on *Mechanisms of syntactic change*, by
    C. N. Li. *Language* 55:381-95.
———. 1980.   Explaining syntactic change. *Explanation in linguistics*, ed. by N. Hornstein and D. W. Lightfoot, 209-40.
    London: Longman.
Meillet, A.   1937. *Introduction à l'étude des langues indo-européennes*. Paris: Hachette.
Miller, D. G.   1975.   Indo-European: VSO, SOV, SVO or all three?
    Lingua 37:31-52.
Ross, J. R.   1969.   Auxiliaries as main verbs. *Studies in philosophical linguistics*, Series I, ed. by W. Todd, 77-102.
    Evanston: Great Expectations.
Steever, S.; C. Walker; and S. Mufwene (eds.)   1976.   *Diachronic syntax*. Chicago: Chicago Linguistic Society.
Thom, R.   1972. *Stabilité structurelle et morphogenèse*. New York:
    Benjamin.
———. 1973.   Sur la typologie des langues naturelles: essai
    d'interprétation psycholinguistique. *The formal analysis of
    natural languages*, ed. by M. Gross, M. Halle, and M. P.
    Schützenberger, 233-48. The Hague: Mouton.
Watkins, C.   1976.   Toward Proto-Indo-European syntax: Problems
    and pseudoproblems. *Diachronic syntax*, ed. by S. Steever,
    C. Walker, and S. Mufwene, 305-26. Chicago: Chicago Linguistic
    Society.

[This is a slightly revised version of a paper which appeared
in *Linguistic reconstruction and Indo-European syntax*, ed. by
P. Ramat et al. Amsterdam: John Benjamins. A French version
appeared in *Langages* 60 (Syntaxe générative et syntaxe comparée)
ed. by Alain Rouveret. Paris: Didier Erudition.]

Part III

LINGUISTS ON LANGUAGE CHANGE

HISTORY OF LANGUAGE CHANGE AS IT AFFECTS SYNTAX

Winfred P. Lehmann

Syntactic change was not examined in the first half century of modern linguistics, which is generally dated from the publication of Bopp's Conjugationslehre in 1816. During the next fifty years historical linguists dealt primarily with sounds, forms, and the lexicon, as have many linguists since. Bopp himself in the several editions of his comparative grammar never treated syntax. Only in 1869 did the first important study of syntactic change appear, Ernst Windisch's investigations on the origin of the relative pronoun in the Indo-European languages. Windisch's important and imaginative study, the content of which I touch on below, was followed by a steady flow of syntactic treatments of the early Indo-European dialects, as may be noted in Delbrück's repeatedly revised introduction to the study of the Indo-European languages (1919:133-45, 251).

When we examine the syntactic studies cited by Delbrück, and those which have appeared since, we find that many treatments of historical syntax do not deal with change. Rather, they set out to describe the syntactic patterns in a given historical or prehistorical period. The same procedures are followed in discussions of other language families, as in Brockelmann's on Semitic (1913). Delbrück's own monographs, and even his important comparative Indo-European syntax of 1893-1900, largely have descriptive aims. For example, he investigated the early dialects, primarily Vedic and Greek, to determine such syntactic characteristics as arrangement, use of specific forms, expressions for negation. While he sought to determine the basic meaning of these in the proto-language (*Grundbedeutung*) and of formal categories, his primary concern did not lie in syntactic change. He set out to determine the syntactic patterns of the early dialects, and through them the syntax of the parent language.

Other important studies of the time also limit themselves to such description. Among these are Behaghel's treatment of Old Saxon syntax, Speyer's two books on Vedic and Sanskrit syntax, and many handbooks on the other

143

dialects or on selected authors. It was only natural that historical linguists felt the need to determine the facts of Germanic, Latin, Greek, and Indic syntax, and even the syntax of the reconstructed parent language before they dealt with syntactic change. The course of historical phonology had been similar; only after many descriptions of the data in individual dialects was consistent treatment of phonological change undertaken. As did the historical phonologists, we must now direct our attention to the study of syntactic change as well as to descriptions of older stages of languages. This brief paper sketches steps to be carried out.

As we proceed to investigation of syntactic change, we make use of earlier studies, such as Jacob Grimm's treatment of the simple sentence in Germanic. Published as the fourth volume of his Germanic grammar, this is often characterized as still the best and most comprehensive work on the topic. What Grimm does here is present a massive number of examples of syntactic patterns in the various Germanic dialects. Further, he associates and compares the patterns of one dialect with those of others, Old High German with Old English, Old Saxon, Old Norse, Gothic and so on—also with Middle High German and New High German, as well as other modern dialects. While he discusses differences among these, even diachronically, he is not concerned with syntactic change as such. A similar approach is found in the two massive and exemplary treatments of Greek and Latin syntax in the *Handbuch der klassischen Altertumswissenschaft*. Schwyzer's syntax of Greek and Szantyr's of Latin are not in the first instance concerned with syntactic change. They of course present examples from Homer as well as Plato, from Plautus as well as Cicero. But like Grimm and many others, they do not treat syntactic change in a principled way, as I now illustrate.

As an example from the Greek grammar, we may examine Schwyzer's examination of the comparative. He discusses the meaning and use of comparative forms of adjectives at some length (2:98-101, 183-5). In these discussions he cites examples in which the standard is expressed by the genitive, which he of course treats as reflex of the earlier ablative. And he is aware of the absence of special adjectival forms for comparison in Hittite, Tocharian, and Armenian, ascribing it to foreign influence without linking it to the several means used for expressing comparison in other Indo-European dialects, such as *-yes-*, *-is-en-*, *-ero-*, *-tero-*. These alone, as well as the suppletive forms for common adjectives like *good, bad, little, great*, should lead us to suspect that the situation in Hittite, Tocharian, and Armenian was also that of Proto-Indo-European.

Moreover, Schwyzer does not bring up the possibility of syntactic change, of an earlier construction for comparison of inequality with standard preceding the adjective, as often in Homer, and a later pattern with standard

following the adjective. Such a change apparently did
not occur to him, even though he cites examples of particles other than η after the adjective which might well
have served as indication of an innovation. Linguists
are now aware of the pattern with standard preceding the
adjective as characteristic of OV languages, with standard
following the adjective as characteristic of VO languages.
It is also clear that the earliest Indo-European dialects,
such as Hittite and Vedic Sanskrit, as well as Tocharian,
Armenian, and even others were OV in structure. It is
difficult to avoid the conclusion that the comparison of
inequality construction underwent a syntactic change between Proto-Indo-European and Classical Greek, Proto-Indo-
European and Classical Latin, as well as the other dialects with VO structure. The treatment of the comparison
of inequality construction is then one example of language
change as it affects syntax.

Greek as well as the other Indo-European dialects include other examples: the development of complementation,
of adverbial clauses, of prepositional phrases, and so on.
Syntactic changes affecting these constructions are in
accordance with expectations as a language shifts from OV
to VO structure.

The changes cited have to do with verbal constructions. There are also changes in nominal constructions,
as illustrated by the changing pattern in Latin for relative clauses. Here again the treatment in the standard
grammars is illuminating. As we would expect, Szantyr is
in command of the facts (1965:554-72). He states that
relative clauses in sentences which include the antecedent
in both principal and subordinate clauses stand before the
principal clause especially in Old Latin (563-4). Moreover, providing numerous examples of sentences with repeated antecedents (563), he points out that these become
less frequent in individual authors such as Caesar and
Cicero as they develop their styles. Such patterns are
also less frequent in standard Classical Latin (*Hoch-
sprache*), the presumable ideal of authors as they develop
their style. But from these differences he draws no conclusions on syntactic change. Instead, he states flatly
that initial placement of the relative clause accompanied
by repetition of the antecedent provides no clues on the
development of the relative marker, whether from the indefinite or the interrogative (564). As far as its source
is concerned, he simply identifies the Italic relative
marker as a replacement of the old relative *$\nu\!o$- (565).
This example from the sphere of nominal syntax, which
might be multiplied, illustrates the widely evident position that the important events of syntax have to do with
lexical elements, like the *yo-* or *$q^u o$-* marker, not with
syntax itself.

Szantyr's treatment of the relative in Latin is all
the more regrettable because almost seventy years before
its publication, Jacobi had given numerous examples of OV
relative constructions which precede their antecedent.

And fifty years earlier still, Weil had pointed out the
similarity of early Latin relative constructions with
those of Turkish, citing the very example from the *Lex
agraria* which Szantyr refers to as his first in his treat
ment of repeated antecedents (1965:563). Still Szantyr
does not discuss syntactic change, let alone suggest that
the Latin examples are readily explained if we treat them
as phenomena expected when an earlier OV pattern changes
to a VO pattern.

Sadly for Indo-European and historical syntactic stud
ies, inadequate attention was given to Windisch, who al
most a century earlier had been more acute. In his essay
of 1871 he proposed, following an assumption of Apollonio
in the second century A.D. that all third person pronouns
are originally deictic, that some of these develop ana
phoric uses, and further that relative pronouns may arise
from them. Moreover, Windisch held that *yo-* did not yet
have relative force in the proto-language, but was merely
anaphoric there. Instead of applying these observations
to syntactic developments in early Indo-European, Delbrücl
unfortunately rejected Windisch's conclusions on the ori
gin of the relative marker, though he approved of those
on the general development of third person pronouns. If
Indo-European syntactic studies had pursued Windisch's in
sights, the principles of syntactic change and the devel
opment of the Indo-European languages from OV to VO struc
ture would have been generally accepted long ago. As
things stand, it is only Justus's masterly treatment of
the Hittite data which has demonstrated without question
the shift of an Indo-European anaphoric marker to a rela
tive pronoun in Hittite, clarifying in this way the Latin
relative as well as syntactic change in the Indo-European
languages.

In urging concern with syntactic change we must also
account for the failure of scholars after Windisch to
contribute to its understanding. I attribute this unfor
tunate situation to two causes: (1) the attention to
surface forms as scholars supposedly dealt with syntax,
(2) the primary concern with selection classes and their
meanings when approaching the study of syntax, that is,
with morphology rather than syntax itself.

The focus on surface forms may be illustrated with
Behaghel's *Syntax des Heliand* (1897). In this detailed
analysis devoted to Old Saxon syntax Behaghel treats syn
tactic constructions by means of the number of lexical
elements they contain. His "third book" examines *Die
syntaktischen Gebilde*, first "word groups" (109-224),
thereupon sentences, and phrases (*Satzgruppen*) (241-368).
Of two-member word groups, Behaghel finds the following
patterns, those consisting of two personal names such as
Simon Petrus, those consisting of a personal name plus
an appellative, such as *cuning Herodes* (111). Three-
member word groups which have a substantive as head, e.g.
allan langan dag 'whole long day', are sub-classified in
eleven such sub-classes (120-2), and so on. To be fair

to Behaghel, the count is not purely by lexical elements;
an adverbial modification in a three-member group may consist of preposition + noun, yielding four lexical items
as in *neriendon Crist fan Nazarethburg* 'the Savior Christ
from Nazareth'. But in general the number of members of
syntactic constructions is measured by the number of
words; the guiding principle in this way leads to syntactic classification by surface forms. Delbrück (1919:143)
comments wryly that Behaghel's *Syntax des Heliand* follows
an arrangement encouraging reflection, but not imitation.
While pursued to an extreme, Behaghel's procedure reflects
the predominant view that in syntactic study one examines
lexical elements rather than syntactic categories and the
features they express.

The influential treatise directing primary attention
to morphology was Ries's *Was ist Syntax?* of 1894. For
Ries, syntax itself was to deal only with synthesis.
Treatment of meanings of word classes and word forms was
assigned to morphology. This point of view may be sharply
illustrated by the shift from the first to the second edition of Brugmann's *Grundriss*. As is well known, Delbrück,
who produced the three volumes in the first edition, did
not participate in the second. In the second edition the
treatment of morphology swelled to three volumes of 2,737
pages. Syntax proper was reserved for a later volume.
One on the simple sentence appeared posthumously, a short
book of 229 pages (1925). Here, with reference to
Behaghel, Brugmann states that syntax (*Satzlehre*) takes
as its starting point the formal and logical relationship
of the parts of what is spoken, in seeking to show the
parts of speech at work (187). Even when in the final
chapter he treats the formation of the sentence corresponding to basic psychological functions such as excla-
mation, wish, demand, concession, threat (187-229), he
again directs his attention at specific forms and their
uses.

In this concentration on lexical and morphological
characteristics, we find no treatment of historical development, not to mention syntactic change. Moreover, for
Brugmann the treatment of syntax is descriptive. Also
subsequently, as in Bloomfield's *Language* (1933) and the
structural sketches produced by Bloomfield's followers,
syntax is largely concerned with forms and their classes.
For Bloomfield, "SYNTACTIC CONSTRUCTIONS ... are constructions in which none of the immediate constituents is a
bound form" (184). And "syntax consists largely ... in
stating ... under what circumstances ... various form-
classes ... appear in syntactic constructions" (190).
This view of syntax virtually eliminates any regard for
syntactic change; free forms and form-classes may change,
as well as when they appear in syntactic constructions,
but there is no attention to change of those constructions. In Bloomfield's influential book there is no
chapter on syntactic change.

Some time earlier Walter Porzig commented on problems

of historical syntax in his essay in the *Streitberg Fest-schrift*. While I lack the space to discuss the essay, I would like to point out his statement that "the most important task of historical syntax, with greatest significance for all humanistic study consists in the exact observation of the development of new categories" (1924: 147). As example he cites the development of the categor of tense from those of mood and aspect. His point of vie is evident also in his treatment of the clauses and syntactic groups characterized by *ya* in the older books of the *Rigveda* (Porzig 1932). His observations in this work lead him to conclude that originally relative clauses preceded principal clauses, by our interpretation that earlier they reflected OV structure. Porzig then was moving towards appropriate treatment of syntactic change.

Among his aims, like Bloomfield's, Porzig proposed to free linguistic study from direction by psychology. Linguists who do not read earlier scholarship have little idea of the confusions introduced into the study of many problems by calling on one or another psychological approach; knowledge of such confusion led to Bloomfield's adamant exclusion of psychological considerations from linguistic study. Instead of a psychological approach, Porzig advocated a phenomenological. I take this variously interpreted term to refer in linguistic study to concentration on data, by no means purely surface, and on their interpretation by means of a framework, through which their change may be perceived and described. Such change may involve arrangement. To recognize that change we need to know what the characteristic patterns are. These we state in terms of OV or VO structure.

We also need to know the syntactic features involved in the basic syntactic patterns so that we may understand how their means of expression may change. Among the features are interrogation, negation, volition, middle, and so on. These are expressed differently in OV and VO languages, whether through differing arrangement or through differing categories. A morphological category like the subjunctive may be used to express volition. A lexical element like -*self*, or Greek φιλος or Sanskrit *priyas* or Old Norse *suás*, may be used to express the middle. An intonation pattern may be used to express the interrogative feature. We can determine syntactic change by recognizing these categories and elements, and observing how they are applied in the history of languages. It is intriguing to observe how the morphological middle marker inherited by Homer is often replaced by φιλος, and this in turn by pronominal forms as Classical Greek becomes more consistently VO. Change involving other syntactic features is an equally fascinating pursuit. Our understanding of language will be deepened as such studies become more numerous.

Since language consists of a system, syntactic change correlates with phonetic, morphological, and lexical

changes.   But study of these three kinds of change cannot
obviate attention to change in syntax.   Disregard of syntactic features in change has taken its toll, as among the
successive generations of Homeric translators, for whom
the heroes have 'dear fathers' (*Iliad* 1.441), 'dear children' (1.447), 'dear mothers' (1.572), 'dear native lands'
(2.140) and so on.   It is difficult to evaluate such .
translations more highly than we do those of students who
translate German expressions like *ich fürchte mich vor dem
Feuer* as 'I am afraid of myself in front of the fire'.
Neither has a proper understanding of the changing categories used for the expression of the syntactic feature I
have called middle.   Such understanding must be provided
by linguists, among whose responsibilities is the treatment of syntactic change.

     To do so, they must know what syntax is.   They must
also deal with syntax by means of a framework, just as
phonologists have dealt with phonology in terms of a
framework for at least a century and a half.   It will not
do to dismiss such a framework, to remain encrusted in
views more characteristic of Ned Ludd than of his contemporaries Franz Bopp and Jacob Grimm.   Just as sound change
is not carried out with no reference to the phonological
system recognized throughout the flourishing of historical
phonology, so syntactic change takes place in accordance
with the patterns of a given type of language, in accordance with a system that limits the possibilities of that
change.   Since I have discussed elsewhere recent work of
promise in historical syntax (1978:37-42, 400-17; 1981,
to appear), I will not comment on it further here.   But I
cite one further example, from Old English and the other
Germanic languages, the changing pattern for the comparison of inequality construction.   Small presents the data
for the Germanic languages, especially for Old English,
patterns like the following from the Old English Riddles
(1929:45):

                    Swift was on fore
          fuglum framra fleotgan lyfte.

                         'It was swift in its course,
          stronger than the birds, to fly in the air.'

Here the dative is used to indicate the standard.   Small
provides ready access to the fifty examples in Old English
poetry and the sixty-two in Old English prose, so that
only two further instances are cited here.   The first is
from *Elene* (Small 1929:40):

     Heo wæron stærce,   stane heardran

     'They were immovable, harder than stone.'

The second is from the prose *Salomon and Saturn* (Small
1929:68):

> *And hleoðra gehwilc sy heofone hearre and helle*
> *   deopre*
> 'and if every one of the sounds was higher than
> heaven and deeper than hell'

When the standard precedes the adjective, as in these
examples, the arrangement is that of OV languages. In an
earlier study Small examined the comparative with particles, among other things their diversity, as exemplified
by English *nor*, *but*, *than*, dialectal *as*, and also by the
diversity of particles in older stages of English and
other Indo-European languages. Although he recognizes
the gradual fixing of the modern pattern, he does not discuss historical development. For example, he cites no OV
comparative as did Jacobi. Nor does he treat the comparative in conjunction with syntactic patterning as a whole;
in this effort he might have drawn on Delbrück's charac-
terization of Indo-European as an OV language. Using such
information we account for the development of the English
comparative as a shift from the inherited OV pattern
through a preliminary VO stage when the standard was
placed after the adjective and various particles were
introduced. Finally one of the particles was selected
for general use, such as NE *than*, NHG *als*.
     However careful we find Small's studies, they are dis-
appointing because they provide no understanding of the
development of the comparative construction. Like many
students of syntax, Small concentrated on selection. For-
tunately there now is attention to arrangement, as I have
noted elsewhere (1978:37-42, 400-17; 1981, to appear).
Examination of arrangement patterns has clarified many
problems in syntax and in syntactic change. Where adequate information is available, the further devices of
modulation and sandhi must also be studied for their part
in syntactic change.
     In such study we must be clear about our possibili-
ties. Viewing syntactic change in terms of a system no
more explains such change than the use of a phonological
framework explains sound change. The causes are social,
and can only be accounted for when we have adequate information about the uses of language in the society that
maintains it. Though successive linguists attempt to
explain specific linguistic patterns through proposed
psychological constructs in spite of the failure of their
predecessors, we cannot be deterred by such nonlinguistic
ventures from identifying syntactic change. A framework
assists us in that identification. When we apply the
framework appropriately, we can account for some changes.
For others we may have inadequate information, whether
about the language at the time or the society maintaining
that language. Whatever the extent of our information,
we have reached a point in the brief history of our

discipline when we must clarify syntactic change in languages with adequate data as our predecessors did phonological change.

REFERENCES

Behaghel, Otto. 1897. *Die Syntax des Heliand*. Leipzig: Tempsky.

Bloomfield, Leonard. 1933. *Language*. New York: Holt.

Bopp, Franz. 1816. *Über das Conjugationssystem der Sanskritsprache in Fergleichung mit jenem der griechischen, lateinischen, persischen und germanischen Sprache*. Frankfurt a.M.

————. 1869-71. *Vergleichende Grammatik des Sanskrit, Send, Armenischen, Griechischen, Latinischen, Litauischen, Altslavischen, Gotischen und Deutschen*, vols. 1-3. 3rd ed. Berlin.

Brockelmann, Carl. 1913, 1961. *Grundriss der vergleichenden Grammatik der semitischen Sprachen. II. Syntax*. Hildesheim: Olm.

Brugmann, Karl. 1897-1916. *Vergleichende Laut-, Stammbildungsund Flexionslehre der indogermanischen Sprachen*. 2 vols. 2nd ed. Strassburg: Trübner.

————. 1925. *Die Syntax des einfachen Satzes im Indogermanischen*. Berlin and Leipzig: de Gruyter.

Delbrück, Berthold. 1893-1900. *Vergleichende Syntax der indogermanischen Sprachen. I-III*. Strassburg: Trübner.

————. 1919. *Einleitung in das Studium der indogermanischen Sprachen*. 6th ed. Leipzig: Breitkopf & Härtel.

Grimm, Jacob. 1870-98. *Deutsche Grammatik*, vols. 1-4. 2nd ed. [Reprinted under direction of W. Scherer.] Gütersloh.

Havers, Wilhelm. 1931. *Handbuch der erklärenden Syntax*. Heidelberg: Winter.

Jacobi, Hermann. 1897. *Compositum und Nebensatz*. Bonn: Cohen.

Justus, Carol. 1976. Relativization and topicalization in Hittite. *Subject and topic*, ed. by Charles N. Li, 215-45. New York: Academic.

Lehmann, Winfred P. (ed.) 1978. *Syntactic typology*. Austin: University of Texas Press.

Porzig, Walter. 1924. Aufgaben der indogermanischen Syntax. *Stand und Aufgaben der Sprachwissenschaft*. Festschrift für Wilhelm Streitberg, (no ed.) 126-51. Heidelberg: Winter.

————. 1932. Die Hypotaxe im Rigveda. 1. Die durch das Pronomen *ya* charakterisierten Sätze und syntaktischen Gruppen in den älteren Büchern der Rigveda. *IF* 41:210-303.

Ries, John. 1927. *Was ist Syntax*. 2nd ed. Prag. [Reprinted Darmstadt: Wissenschaftliche Buchgesellschaft, 1967.]

Schwyzer, Ed. 1939-1953. *Griechische Grammatik*. 3 vols. München: Beck.

Small, George William. 1924. *The comparison of inequality. The semantics and syntax of the comparative particle in English*. Baltimore: The Johns Hopkins University.

————. 1929. *The Germanic case of comparison with a special study of English*. Language Monographs 4. Philadelphia: Linguistic Society of America.

Speyer, J. S. 1886. *Sanskrit Syntax*. Leiden: Brill.

————. 1896. *Vedische und Sanskrit-Syntax*. Strassburg: Trübner.

Szantyr, Anton. 1965. *Lateinische Syntax und Stylistik*, vol. 2 of *Lateinische Grammatik*, by Manu Leumann and J. B. Hofmann. München: Beck.

Weil, Henri. (1944) 1978. *The order of words in the ancient lan-
    guages compared with that of the modern languages.* Trans. by
    Charles W. Super. New ed. by Aldo Scaglione. Amsterdam
    Classics in Linguistics, 1800-1925 #14. Amsterdam: Benjamins.
Windisch, Ernst. 1869. Untersuchungen uber den Ursprung des
    Relativ-pronomens in den indogermanischen Sprachen. *Curtius
    Studien* 2:201-419.

LOW-BACK VOWELS IN PROVIDENCE:
A NOTE IN STRUCTURAL DIALECTOLOGY

Raven I. McDavid, Jr.

The interesting developments in linguistic theory over the past two generations have not closed the profession to those whose primary interest is in the data on which the theories are based. For such scholars, linguistic geography has a particular appeal. The evidence in field records is set forth for others to examine, and interpret as they will. The linguistic geographer is less concerned with the kinds of conclusions that can be derived from the data than that the data is scrupulously examined. For instance, it is the evidence of linguistic geography that enables us to conclude that Gullah is a creolized form of English (Turner 1949, Kurath 1972:118-21). When a linguistic geographer is informed that he has drawn incomplete or erroneous conclusions from his data, he reexamines it; if the criticism is just, he tries to see that the record is set aright.[1] It is in this spirit that this paper reexamines the evidence from the *Linguistic Atlas of New England* (LANE) on the low-back vowels in Providence, Rhode Island, in the light of the questions raised by Moulton (1968).

Moulton's criticism deserves serious consideration on any matter related to linguistic geography, especially where Providence is concerned. A native of Providence, he grew up aware that Providence has a kind of speech that does not take off its hat to any other community. At Princeton he sharpened his perceptions in dialogue with Bill Austin, Bob Hall, and Haxie Smith; at Yale he received incomparable training from Bloomfield; since gaining his doctorate he has worked with such linguistic geographers as Kloeke in the Netherlands and Hotzenköcherle in Switzerland. Furthermore, he is one of the kindest and most gentlemanly linguists who ever analyzed a phonemic system.

Moulton (1968:464) reminds us of the difficulties which the field workers for LANE encountered in transcribing the vowels in the low-central and the low-back range. He goes on to point out that in Providence he grew up distinguishing a long, low unrounded vowel [ɑ:]

153

in *cart*, a short, low unrounded vowel [ɑ] in *cot*, and a
rounded low-back vowel [ɔ] in *caught*.[2] This is at variance with the judgment of Harris (1937) that in Rhode
Island speech there is no contrast between vowels of the
types in *cot* and *caught*. It is also at variance with the
rough summary in Kurath-R. McDavid (1961:39) of the vowels
of a cultivated Providence woman interviewed in 1931 by
Harris. The summary assigns only one vowel phoneme to the
low-central and low-back range, but this phoneme covers
considerable phonic territory, ranging from advanced low-
back, lightly rounded [ɒ<] in *borrow*, to lower mid-back
with centering offglide [ɔ] in *dog*. To Kurath and
McDavid's phoneme /ɒ/ (phonetically [a·]) are assigned
words of several historical classes: *aunt, half* (but not
glass, which has /æ/) *father, palm, barn, garden*. This
group may be equated with Moulton's /ɑ:/; the difference
in symbols need not trouble us. But how do we reconcile
Moulton's clear-cut *cot/caught* contrast with Kurath and
R. McDavid's postulating of a single phoneme /ɒ/, with a
wide phonic range, in Harris's record? (1) Possibly there
was something that set off Moulton's speech from that of
the informant analyzed, perhaps a difference in age or
assurance. All of Harris's informants from the Providence
area were women, and women might be inclined to follow the
social fashion of Boston, where *cot* and *caught* are homonyms. (2) Possibly the phonetic notation employed might
have obscured contrasts in the low-back range. (3) Possibly there was something in the field worker's own dialect that interfered with her phonetic perception. As
Kurath et al. (1939:52-3) points out, no observer ever
gets completely free from the chains of his own phonemic
system.
   Let us examine these possibilities:
   1. The informant, a woman, was 63 when interviewed
by Harris; that same year Moulton was 17. Women—and all
of the informants from Providence were women—are more
likely than men to accept external models. Cultivated
women informants in the Genesee Valley in western New York
state sometimes offered Eastern New England words and pronunciations during 1949 interviews for the Linguistic
Atlas of the Middle and South Atlantic States. More recently a similar emulation of Eastern New England models
has been found in the Chicago area (Uskup 1974).
   On the other hand, the informant is described as sure
of her own speech. The feature involved is not a matter
of phonemic incidence, like adopting the /ɒ/ in *dance*
while leaving unmodified the /æ/ in *glass* and *half past*,
but the suppression of a functional contrast. Furthermore, someone who can observe structural differences in
speech within his own family—as Moulton remarks noticing
that his Boston cousins lacked the *cot/caught* difference
that his immediate family maintained in Providence—is
unlikely to overlook such differences if they separate the
speech of the younger generation from that of the older
in his own community. Finally, where a drift is taking

place in the low-back range, it seems to be from a *cot/ caught* contrast to a lack of contrast, not from homonymy to contrast: the loss of contrast has been observed and reported from various communities, ranging from Cleveland to Southern California; the converse is so far unreported.

2. Among the New England field workers, there was great diversity in recording the low-back vowels—a diversity which may have been accentuated by the choice of symbols for the LANE alphabet. Following IPA, LANE provided for only one low-back symbol, [ɒ], canonically supposed to represent a lightly rounded low-back vowel, with [ɑ] to represent a lower low-central unrounded one. Furthermore, among the phonetic symbols for LANE there was no diacritic provided for lip spreading, to complement [ɒ] for lip rounding. Thus the symbols used might encourage over-transcription.[3] During the preliminary investigations in the South Atlantic States, Lowman found it necessary to improvise a means of representing a fully unrounded low-back vowel; Kurath then introduced a new symbol [ɑ] for such vowels, restricting [ɒ] to fully rounded vowels, so as to parallel such contrasts as [i/y, e/ø], and also a diacritic for lip-spreading [ɒ̠], so that six degrees of rounding could be represented.

It is true that transcription practices may be influenced by the kind of notation available. The difficulty of representing the sounds of an alien tongue is shown in English in such doublet spellings for proper names from Celtic dialects as *Lloyd* and *Floyd*, or *Dinwiddie* and *Dunwoodie*. Significant differences may be obscured if the transcription system ignores sounds in the informant's speech, as the phonetic alphabet for the Detroit sociolinguistic study (Shuy, Wolfram, and Riley 1968:33) makes no provision for the high-central rounded vowels [ʉ,ᵿ], common in the Midland and Southern dialect areas of the United States. Till now, however, there seems to have been no revisiting of Rhode Island speech that would demand the additional symbol in the low-back range, though the practices of Kurath and Hanley in Central and Western Connecticut suggest that the additional [ɑ] would have been helpful.[4] By itself, the addition of [ɑ] to the LANE alphabet would not have helped a field worker to perceive a phonemic contrast.

3. Among the New England field workers, Harris had the least training in phonetics before becoming affiliated with the project. She became an industrious and able investigator; she enjoyed excellent rapport with informants.[5] But in the ranking of the field workers (Kurath et al. 1939:52-3) she scored rather low: in the lowest group on five of nine scales, in the top group on only four. Three of the scales where she scored high involved matters of the vocabulary: observation of lexical variants, definition of the meanings of words, fullness of notes taken from free conversation. Only one involved phonetics: avoidance of over-transcription. She ranked low in minuteness of recording, in freedom from systematization

according to her own phonemic system, in freedom from
systematization according to the phonemic system of the
informant, and in recording quantity and stress. A part
of the problem in interpreting her Providence records
could be the difference between her phonemic system and
that of her informants. The need is to examine her system.

     There are two kinds of evidence bearing on this exam-
ination. The first is within the Atlas materials themselves: the phonemic system of Harris's own dialect, of
Haverhill, Massachusetts, north of Boston. No summary
from Haverhill is included in Kurath-R. McDavid (1961),
because no cultivated speaker was among the four informants interviewed there; but the informant from Billerica,
Massachusetts (Kurath-R. McDavid 1961:33), a little further south, may throw light on Harris's speech. There is
no *cot/caught* contrast in the Billerica summary; in fact,
the speaker's low vowel ranges remind one of those of the
Providence informant (Kurath-R. McDavid 1961:52), and of
the interpretation of Harris's transcription practices
(Kurath et al. 1939:126-7). This evidence suggests that
she lacked a *cot/caught* contrast, alone among the LANE
field workers, and would have needed considerable training
if she were to perceive it.[6]

     There is other contemporary evidence. In 1931 most
of the LANE field workers made phonographic recordings of
their own speech, which were later transferred to tape by
the University of Wisconsin. Harris's sample shows no
cot/caught type of contrast, though a somewhat wider range
of phonic variants than Lowman set down for Billerica
(Lowman tended to systematize according to the phonemic
system of the informant; see Kurath et al. 1939:52-3,
Avis 1955).

     Had there been funds to make phonetic transcriptions
of the Hanley recordings of the 1930s, Kurath and R.
McDavid might have reached a different conclusion about
Providence, for both the informant analyzed for Kurath-
R. McDavid (1961) and the other cultivated informant from
Providence show the contrast on these recordings. But the
Hanley recordings have been little used until recently,
when they were dubbed onto tape for Cassidy's *Dictionary
of American Regional English*, and they are yet to be sys-
tematically calibrated against the field transcriptions.[7]

     The final step is to return to LANE and catalog all
responses with low-back vowels for the Providence speaker
summarized in Kurath-R. McDavid (1961), and classify the
phonic types in the low-central and low-back range.
Harris's transcriptions are not ideal for this purpose,
since she was inconsistent in recording vowel quantity,
and for some varieties of English—notably the Received
Pronunciation of Southern England—the distinction between
cot and *caught*, both with rounded vowels, involves not
only tongue height but length.[8]

     The informant in question was interviewed with the
short work sheets for New England, so that only about

60 percent of the LANE items were investigated. Omitted
were such forms as *crop*, *oxen*, and *want to get off*. However, the number of responses involving vowels in the low-
central and low-back range is nearly 150. These responses
fall into 21 phonic types, as follows:

[ɑ]:   Boston, hospital, can't, .laundry, hob (goblins);
           office, Martha.
[ɑ>]:   Boston, rods, hospital, oxfords, log; stocky,
           papa, mamma; borrow.
[ɑ⩾]:   wasp.
[ɒ<]:   Bostonians, Sekonk, frog, hospital, goblins, not;
           shopping, Providence, trolley, toboggan, coffee,
           cottage (cheese), Johnny.
[ɒ̆<]:   not.
[ɒ<·]:   not.
[ɒ]:   across, because, salt, frost, cloth, brought,
           drop, wash, jaundice, gone, (qua)hog; daughter,
           automobile, closet, stopper, talking, college,
           office; orchard, order, storm, morning, corn,
           horse.
[ɒ̆]:   on (purpose), Johnny.
[ɒ·]:   seesaw, trough [-θ], order, cost.
[ɒ]:   order.
[ɒ̆^]:   all, alter; dropping, strawberries, often, faucet,
           vomit; quarter, York, hornet, California.
[ɔˇ]:   watch, brought, caught, trough [-θ], cough,
           laundry, mongrel, Chicago, sausage, swallow;
           tommorrow; war, north, horse.
[ɔˇ·]:   somersault.
[ɔˇə]:   drawers.
[ɔ⩽]:   pot, God, cog, dog, hogs, fog, log, wasps.
[ɔ̆⩽]:   haunted.
[ɔ]:   God, caught, taught, ought, brought, moths, watch,
           wasp, dog, always; boughten, qua(hog), law, saw,
           often, awfully, walnut, water; Florida, orange;
           forty, morning, order.
[ɔə]:   poached.
[ɔ·]:   taught, strong, moth, cough; cork, torn, worn.
[ɔᵊ]:   dog, sauce; horse.
[ɔ<]:   strop, Sekonk; coffin, college; oranges.

    The full record displays an even wider range of phonic
types than included in the summary; it suggests that
Harris's phonetics, if not so detailed as Block and Lowman
sometimes were, were tolerably minute. It also suggests
that if there is only a single phoneme in this range, it
has an extraordinarily wide variety on the phonic level,
if we compare it with the phonemes of various other dialects of American English.
    As an alternative, we may explore the possibility
that Harris was attempting to set down a phonemic contrast
for Providence in a range where Haverhill lacked the contrast. An analysis of the responses shows clustering of
the phonic types. Responses with [ɑ, ɑ>, ɑ⩾, ɒ<, ɒ̆<, ɒ<·]

seem to fall together in one group, other phonic types in
another. Phonic variation seems to take place generally
within groups, not between groups; there are only five
exceptions. The variations between the responses for
laundry, *office*, *wasp*—involving relatively distant phonic
types—could be classed as differences in phonemic incidence, between /ɑ/ and /ɔ/, such as one finds in other
areas—say the South Carolina Piedmont (R. McDavid 1940).[9]
This leaves only two forms, *Johnny* and *Sekonk*, where there
is variation between adjacent phonic types across the
arbitrary boundary of the two groups—a very slight amount
of fuzziness.

     Thus, despite the problem in the field worker's trans-
criptions, it is possible to suggest a *cot/caught* contrast
in Providence on the basis of the evidence from LANE.
True, the low-central /ɑ/ is far less common than the low-
back /ɔ/, accounting for less than a quarter of the forms
in question; but this is a considerably larger proportion
than one finds for establishing the contrast between /ž/
and its voiceless counterpart /š/ (Bloomfield 1933:137).
There is a plausible case.

     And if a little fuzziness remains, we can return to
Moulton (1968:458). In real life, phonemic systems are
not likely to change overnight, in quantum leaps. Pace
Lees (1957), tightly closed systems, whether synchronic
like Trager-Smith (1951) or diachronic like Chomsky-Halle
(1968), take a battering on the reefs of irrefragable
data. Field workers who record alternative pronunciations,
make neat analyses difficult (see Avis 1955), not the
least for themselves. But we are better off for what they
do. The overall pattern of Trager-Smith (1951) underwent
considerable stretching to accommodate the phonetic variety found in Greenville and Charleston, South Carolina
(R. McDavid 1961). For other areas, the rigid trageremic
system would sometimes establish a phonemic contrast that
did not exist, like that between trageremic /əw/ and /aw/
in Canada or eastern Virginia or Charleston—a distinction
better explained as predictable allophonic alternation of
the /au/ phoneme (as analyzed in Kurath-R. McDavid 1961),
between [əʊ] in *out* and [aʊ, ɑʊ] in *loud*. It also ignores
minimal contrasts that exist in many varieties of Southern
speech, between [æ·] in *sad*, [a·] in *side*, [ɑ·] in *sod*,
between [æ] in *rat*, [a·] in *right*, [ɑ] in *rot*.

     And on the practical level, other evidence exists that
able and energetic field workers may not record contrasts
lacking in their own speech. In the field records for
the Atlas of the North-Central States the original transcriptions from taped interviews frequently do not indicate
a contrast between /ɔr/ and /or/, as between *horse* and
hoarse, but the later retranscriptions by R. McDavid reveal it. The difference between the transcriptions is due
less to the difference in experience of the two trans-
scribers than to the fact that the retranscriber has a
contrast that the original field worker lacked.[10] Judged

by this experience, Harris's LANE transcriptions come off
very well.

But why should Providence retain a phonemic contrast
that has been lost in Boston? The explanation seems to
lie in history. Roger Williams and his associates were
energetic dissenters from the dominant theocracy of Massachusetts. The Rhode Island colony had a population of
diverse origins, remained estranged from the rest of New
England, was not invited to participate in the short-
lived New England Confederation, and was the last of the
original colonies to ratify the Federal Constitution, over
a year after George Washington took office. Providence
early became a seaport, then a textile center; till the
middle of the nineteenth century it was an entrepot for
the so-called triangular trade in molasses, rum, and
slaves, its entrepreneurs prospering from stocking the
plantations of Brazil and Cuba. Its ethnic diversity was
increased by various waves of French (Huguenot, West
Indian, Canadian), Irish, Sephardic Jews, English, Ital-
ians, Portuguese, and Scandinavians; Rhode Island has long
been one of the most highly industrialized and densely
populated states. But it prizes its origins in individ-
ualism and dissent, and this local pride has undoubtedly
contributed to the preservation of speechways distinct
from those of Boston.

If we look at the phonemic systems of Southern British
Received Pronunciation, of Boston (and in general, of
Northeastern New England), and of Providence, we have this
picture: Boston, with the coalescence of the vowels of
cot and *caught*, represents a striking innovation. Euro-
peans who know only RP and British local dialects often
express incredulity toward this coalescence, which has
appeared in several varieties of New World English—in
Northeastern New England, in Western Pennsylvania, in most
of Canada, and in indeterminate areas of the Western
United States. Providence has been a transition area pre-
cariously balanced between Boston and the contrast-
preserving areas of Western New England and New York City
and the Hudson Valley; the older contrast has apparently
not been lost, and Moulton and younger speakers suggest
that it is likely to remain. It may be surprising that a
difference in the structure of phonemic systems should set
off two communities less than fifty miles apart, in a
heavily industrialized region; but the difference is supported by various kinds of evidence, and is explicable in
the light of cultural history.

The solution of the phonemic problem in Providence
speech posed by Moulton (1968) might have been easier had
Kurath anticipated it by providing minimal pairs of the
type *cot/caught*, *collar/caller* in the LANE work sheets.
It might not have been a problem if the study of Rhode
Island had been conducted by investigators who had the
cot/caught contrast in their own speech, or if the investigator had asked about homonyms or rhymes. But it

must be remembered that a field worker who lacks a specific contrast is not always alert to the best means of
probing for it in the speech of others. It is fortunate
that there is additional evidence in the phonographic recordings of the 1930s and the tapes of the 1960s. But it
is most fortunate that an observant native of Providence
could raise the question about the status of the evidence.
It is equally fortunate that LANE had an editor who ruth-
lessly published the original data set down by the field
workers, and who analyzed with equal ruthlessness their
transcription practices.[11] With this evidence, later
students can reexamine the earlier analysis and approach
the problem afresh. If the conclusions are still tentative, and the assignment of forms not always clear, we
have a little better basis for the next analysis of the
speech of the community with which Bill Moulton is always identified.

[The conclusions in this paper were verified by
J. Richie VanVliet, of the State University of New York
at Geneseo and a native Rhode Islander, during my 1980
NEH summer seminar in American dialects.]

NOTES

1. Kurath (1949:80) described *carry you home* as a characteristic Southern form; when reminded that the form existed in New England
and was amply attested in LANE (Map 402), he urged that a revised
statement be published. (See R. McDavid 1972.)

2. Moulton's transcription, slightly different from that in
the LANE records, is left unaltered.

3. Ironically, the unsigned staff review of the LANE Handbook
for *American Speech* (Anonymous 1940) deplored the excessive refinement of the transcription and wished for more normalization.

4. Low-back [ɒ] is not uncommon in Lowman's records from the
New York metropolitan area.

5. It says much about the field worker when an investigator
who participated in field work in both the Middle West and California
estimated that not more than 10 percent of his informants seemed to
enjoy the interviews.

6. Educated speakers from Boston and further northeast seem to
have difficulty comprehending the fact that there is a *cot/caught*
contrast in other areas. This contrast was not recognized in the
manuscript of a series of reading texts prepared by Bostonians for
publication by a distinguished Boston house; the publisher's editor
was astounded by the reader's insistence that the contrast be
recognized. For other regions, several of the ablest field workers
needed special training to perceive the *cot/caught* contrast which
was lacking in their own speech.

7. Five tapes from the Providence area, made by 1969 field
workers for Cassidy's *Dictionary of American Regional English*, show
that the contrast was still flourishing.

8. Jones (1936:75-9 and 1937) indicates a transcription of
[kɔt] and [kɔːt] respectively, with the latter vowel slightly higher
than the former.

9. I have a clear-cut distinction between *cot* and *caught*; the

former has the low-back unrounded vowel, sometimes with a trace of
rounding, the latter an upgliding diphthong with increasing rounding.
But I often vary in the incidence of the phoneme for a particular
word. *Cog* always has the vowel of *cot*, *dog* that of *caught*; *fog*,
frog, *hog*, *log* vary, as do *office*, *warrior*, and others. But as be-
fits a transition area, variation in incidence is not restricted to
the low-back range: *room*, *broom*, *hoof* alternate between the vowel
of *pool* and that of *pull*; *budget*, *bulge*, *bulk*, and *soot* alternate
between the vowel of *pull* and that of *hull*.

    10. Among the laity, Southerners are more likely than inhabi-
tants of other regions, not only to be aware of variety in pronunciations, but to accept them as desirable in a multivalent society.
Where Middle Westerners proclaim that Southerners (usually but not
always black) have reading problems because—to Middle Western ears—
they cannot distinguish *right* from *rat*, Southerners are amused that
Middle Westerners cannot hear the contrast in Southern speech.
Southerners make the contrast in a different way, by difference, by
tongue height rather than by diphthongization of the syllabic of
right.

    11. Many of the statements in Keyser's (1962) review of Kurath-
R. McDavid (1961) might have been different had he not decided to
ignore the shift signs and the distinction between on-line and
superior offglides. Field workers in New England and the rest of
the Atlantic Seaboard were taught that the difference between [ɒˇ]
and [ɑˆ] is not a quantum leap, but the same as that between [ɑˆ]
and [ɑ]. Similarly, the difference between [o·ᵊ] and [o·ə] can
have important structural implications.

                              REFERENCES

Anonymous. 1940. The atlas handbook. Review of Kurath et al.
    1939. *American Speech* 15:185-9.
Avis, Walter S. 1955. *The mid-back vowels in the English of the
    eastern United States*. Dissertation, University of Michigan.
Bloomfield, Leonard. 1933. *Language*. New York: Henry Holt and
    Company.
Chomsky, Noam, and Morris Halle. 1968. *The sound pattern of
    English*. New York: Harper & Row.
Harris, Rachel S. 1937. *The speech of Rhode Island*. Dissertation
    typescript, Brown University.
Jones, Daniel. 1936. *An outline of English phonetics*. 3rd ed.
    New York: E. P. Dutton and Company.
——. 1937. *An English pronouncing dictionary*. New York: E. P.
    Dutton and Company.
Keyser, Samuel Jay. 1962. Review of Kurath-R. McDavid 1961.
    Language 38:303-16.
Kurath, Hans. 1949. *A word geography of the eastern United States*.
    Ann Arbor: University of Michigan Press.
——. 1972. *Studies in area linguistics*. Bloomington: Indiana
    University Press.
——, and Raven I. McDavid, Jr. 1961. *The pronunciation of English
    in the Atlantic States*. Ann Arbor: University of Michigan
    Press.

———, et al. 1939. *Handbook of the linguistic geography of New England*. Providence, RI: Brown University and the American Council of Learned Societies. [2nd ed. 1973, with a map inventory and word index by Audrey R. Duckert. New York: AMS Press.]

———. 1939-43. *Linguistic atlas of New England*. 3 vols., each in 2 parts. Providence, RI: Brown University and the American Council of Learned Societies. [Reprinted 1972. 3 vols. New York: AMS Press.]

Lees, Robert B. 1957. Review of Noam Chomsky, *Syntactic structures*. *Language* 33:375-408.

McDavid, Raven I., Jr. 1940. Low-back vowels in the South Carolina Piedmont. *American Speech* 15:144-8.

———. 1961. Confederate overalls; or, a little Southern sweetening. Chicago: Department of Anthropology, University of Chicago.

———. 1972. *Carry you home* once more. *Studies presented to Tauno Mustanoja. Neophilologische Mitteilungen* 72:192-4.

Moulton, William G. 1968. Structural dialectology. *Language* 44: 451-66.

Shuy, Roger W.; Walter A. Wolfram; and William K. Riley. 1968. *Field techniques in an urban language study*. Washington: Center for Applied Linguistics.

Turner, Lorenzo D. 1949. *Africanisms in the Gullah dialect*. Chicago: University of Chicago Press.

Trager, George L., and Henry Lee Smith, Jr. 1951. *An outline of English structure. Studies in Linguistics*: Occasional Paper 3. Norman, OK: The Battenberg Press.

Uskup, Frances L. 1974. *Social markers in urban speech: A study of elites in Chicago*. Dissertation, Illinois Institute of Technology.

NETHERLANDIC CONTRIBUTIONS TO THE DEBATE ON LANGUAGE CHANGE: FROM LAMBERT TEN KATE TO JOSEF VERCOULLIE

Edgar C. Polomé

Interest in language change is based on a long tradition in the Low Countries, going back to Goropius Becanus' very influential though erroneous views on the historico-comparative position of Gothic (1569).[1] Kiliaan, the learned corrector in Plantijn's printing shop in Antwerp (1558-1607), renovated lexicography by providing accurate dialectal references and introduced a time perspective into these by designating, for example, as *vetus sax(oni-cum)*, an obsolete Low Saxon term.[2] In the 17th century, Franciscus Junius laid the foundations of comparative Germanic philology with his first edition of the *Codex Argenteus* (1665) and his posthumously published *Etymologi-cum Anglicum* (Van de Velde 1966:130-205). The field was then fully developed by Lambert ten Kate in his *Gemeenschap tussen de Gottische Spraeke en de Nederduytsche* (Amsterdam, 1710) and in his monumental *Aenleiding tot de Kennisse van het verhevene Deel der Nederduitse Sprake* (2 volumes; 1500 pages, in 4°; Amsterdam, 1723).[3]

Though ten Kate is, in many respects, a man of his time, he differs from his fellow grammarians (Moonen, Séwel, and others) in that he stresses the importance of phonology and carefully examines the degree of aperture of Dutch vowels and the point of articulation of the consonants. He also applies his insights on articulatory features to his study of language change and thus anticipates the work of 19th century linguists. He even devises a special phonetic script using both letters and figures as Lepsius or Bremer would do later.[4]

Reacting against the dogmatism of the "grammaire raisonnée" of Port Royal, he adopts an historical orientation in the study of language: Looking for the "lofty" forms, he explores the material diachronically, trying to identify the older stages of the language and to trace the origin of the words. This first work, therefore, contains mainly a list of Gothic terms which he correlates with their assumed Dutch cognates, and a survey of the nominal and verbal inflectional system of Gothic. The latter, perhaps, constitutes his most original contribution,

163

though his description of nominal stems is incomplete,
omitting, e.g. the masculine short *ja*-stems, and failing
to consider the masculine *i*-stems as a separate group,
distinct from the masculine *a*-stems in the singular and
from the feminine *i*-stems in the plural, though they are
formally similar.[5] It is indeed in the verbal conjugation
system that he recognized the regularity of vowel alternations, discovering what Jacob Grimm would later call Ablaut.[6] His classification of the verbs was not yet fully
elaborated in his first work, but he developed it into a
full-fledged system in his magnum opus, in which he distinguished six classes, each with subclasses, based on
Dutch. Sometimes they reflect the Germanic *Ablautsreihen*
or basic subdivisions fairly well, as, for example:

>   Class (1) *blaffen - blafte - geblaft*
>   *krabben - krabde - gekrabd*

—obviously the "weak" verbs—or

>   Class (2) *blijven - bleef - gebleven*
>   *sluiten - sloot - gesloten*
>   *schieten - schoot - geschoten*
>   *bewegen - bewoog - bewogen*
>   *vinden   - vond   - gevonden*
>   *bérsten - borst - geborsten*

—in which the first subclass reflects the Germanic first
class of "strong" verbs; the second and third subclasses,
the Germanic second class of "strong" verbs; and the fifth
and sixth subclasses, partly at least, the Germanic third
class of "strong" verbs. The fourth subclass is a problem, since the verb involved should actually belong to the
Germanic fifth class of "strong" verbs, but has apparently
shifted to the sixth class in post-medieval Dutch as it
did in late Middle High German. Some classes are nothing
but a mixture of verbs of various classes, e.g.

>   Class (4) *breken - brak - gebroken* (= Germanic fourth class of
>   "strong" verbs);
>
>   *bidden - bed - gebeden* (= Germanic fifth class of
>   "strong" verbs; subgroup of the *j*-presents: Goth.
>   *bidjan*);
>
>   *helpen - hielp - geholpen* (originally belonging to
>   the third class of Germanic "strong" verbs, but
>   shifted to the seventh class, corresponding to the
>   Gothic reduplicated preterites, in late Middle Dutch);
>
>   *zweeren - zwoer - gezworen* (originally belonging to
>   the sixth class of Germanic "strong" verbs: Goth.
>   *swaran*, but partly shifted to the fourth on account
>   of the umlaut in the *j*-present: OS *swerian*).

Others contain such anomalous verbs as *brengen - bracht - gebracht* (Class 5), or the verbs with "weak" preterites and "strong" past participles, such as *bakken - bakte - gebakken; weven - weefde - geweven* (Class 6). Ten Kate has an extra class of "irregular" verbs which he cannot fit into his system: they çorrespond to the so-called "praeterito-praesentia."[7]

In his analysis of the conjugation he recognizes the important distinction between Gothic and the western Germanic dialects in the second person singular of the preterite of the strong verbs (*Aenleiding* I, 635, 664; cf. Van de Velde 1966:267). He also neatly subdivides his "first" class (= the "weak" verbs) into three subgroups according to their conjugation in Gothic: (1) *dailjan*, (2) *fastan*, (3) *salbon*, but apparently does not know how to deal properly with the -*nan*- verbs, which he considers as a passive formation (*Gemeenschap* 63-5; *Aenleiding* I, 595-7; cf. Van de Velde 1966:261-2, 287).

In spite of all its shortcomings, the work of ten Kate rather stands out in the 18th century as a unique contribution to the study of "comparative philology" and his classification of Germanic verbs is far ahead of the linguistic methodology of the day: Only the discovery of Sanskrit and the reconstruction of Indo-European will provide a better background to revise and improve ten Kate's insights into Germanic morphology.

In the 19th century, the Low Countries fully participate in the development of linguistic science that is triggered by the works of several generations of German scholars from Grimm and Bopp to the Neogrammarians, but there is also a continuity in the tradition that ties in with ten Kate's work. Thus, when J. te Winkel discusses "phonetic laws" in his *Inleiding tot de Geschiedenis der Nederlandsche Taal* (Culemborg: Blom and Olivierse 1904: 156 ff.), he refers to ten Kate's basic position that "in the treatment of the science of language the laws have to be found in usage" (*Aenleiding*, Preface, *3v°)—a statement ten Kate further specifies by indicating that "tradition and respectable usage, which form the foundation of the laws, have their roots in many centuries in the past," (*Aenleiding* I, 13), but the guide for this usage must be the "Gemeenlandsche Dialect"—not a local dialect, but the recognized educated *Gemeinsprache* of the country, as it can also be found (be it with slight dialectal divergencies) in the admired authors of the "Golden Age" (17th century).[8]

J. te Winkel, who first wrote his book for the 1889 edition of Paul's *Grundriss der germanischen Philologie*, epitomizes the views of his time on language change: Besides the typical Neogrammarian statements on the "logical necessity" of admitting that purely physiological sound changes cannot show any exceptions, and the numerous illustrations of the role of analogy in language change, there are interesting discussions on "economy" and

"aesthetics" as motivating factors of sound change. Quot
ing Georg Curtius and William Dwight Whitney,[9] te Winkel
contemplates the possibility that certain drastic sound
changes like those that differentiate Pali from Sanskrit
might be ascribable to an economy of effort in articulation, but he finds such an explanation plausible only if
it is paralleled by a psychological attitude. This brings
him to the recognition of the aesthetic factor: Alveolar
r is replaced by velar *R* in Groningen because it is the
prestige form in Holland and therefore thought to be
"nicer" (192). Economy seems to be responsible for a
number of prothetic and epenthetic vowels, as they reduce
the effort necessary to pronounce definite consonant clusters, but "euphony" accounts for hiatus-fillers, elisions
dissimilations, and such. Rather unexpected is the author's theory of sound symbolism, which he calls *klankty-*
pering (137-46): He ascribes the prevalence of *â* or *ô* or
î in terms like *mân:môn:mîn* as to "choice" or "differentiation." In the case of "choice," the motivation is either
conscious or unconscious, due to physiological, psychological, or social factors, e.g., *ô* may sound nicer or remind
one of synonyms containing an *ô* or seem to "fit the meaning better." Te Winkel clearly indicates that he is aware
of the speculative nature of this argument, but also
points out that it provides an adequate explanation for
such exceptions to the diphthongization of *u* to *ui* as *du-*
velsch (: *duivel* 'devil') or for such alternations as
Gothic *þlaihan* 'hug' versus Du. *vleien* 'flatter' (143-4).
As for differentiation, the qualitative ablaut provides a
good example of its function in the inflectional and derivational system. In resorting to sound symbolism as an
explanatory device, te Winkel parallels the literary efforts of Multatuli in Holland and of the Symbolists in
France. His motivation is, however, based on the difficulty in accounting for dialectal differences to which he
constantly refers in this context and of which he was
keenly aware as the founder and leader of one of the major
centers of dialectal studies in the Netherlands.[10]

In the south, at the University of Ghent, Josef
Vercoullie, another pioneer of the historico-comparative
method was at work, promoting the development of linguistics in Belgium. His contributions were characterized by
their terse matter-of-factness: All the essential data
were there, but none too much, and in his trenchant brevity he managed to break new ground for Dutch historical
grammar and etymology. His *Schets eener historische Gram-*
matica der Nederlandse Taal (1892) contains a number of
valuable theoretical comments on the nature and function
of accentuation, on inflections, and other topics, tying
in with his more elaborate *Algemeene Inleiding tot de*
Taalkunde (1892). In the third edition (1907), Vercoullie
added two chapters on syntax and word function, using Old
Saxon, Middle Dutch, and other material, such as the Old
Low Franconian psalms and glosses, to illustrate historical developments. There were new explanations of the

diminutive suffix, of the vowel in the preterite of the
originally reduplicated forms, of the difference between
the Dutch tense and lax vowels, of the progressive prevalence of the accusative in the Netherlandic dialects,
and several more items in phonology, morphology, and syntax. With this work, Vercoullie actually provided the
first coherent synthesis of the diachronic development of
Dutch as well as a sound foundation for any further work
on Netherlandic historical grammar.[11] His etymological
dictionary (1890) performed a similar function for the
lexicon: It situated the Dutch vocabulary in its Germanic
and Indo-European background by supplying valuable lists
of correspondences within each relevant area of prehistoric contact and within each original wider speech community,
contrasting again with Franck's parallel work, which was
much less laconic, but at the same time somewhat less in-
formative as it focused on Standard Dutch (*Algemeen Beschaafd Nederlands*), whereas Vercoullie would include a
number of typically southern terms as well as some archaisms.[12]

The *Introduction to Linguistics*, which was reprinted
and revised three times from the late 19th century till
the early twenties, is the work of a disciple of the Neo-
grammarians, who flatly states almost half a century after
the decisive year 1876 that "no new materials have been
brought forward, nor new basic principles established, for
even the discovery of Tocharian ... has not modified the
prevailing linguistic views"—a statement that entails the
pessimistic conclusion: "Henceforth we shall have to be
satisfied with a more attentive study of details and with
the drawing of conclusions from the recognized principles"
(*Inleiding*, 3rd ed. Ghent: Vanderpoorten 1922:163). As
regards language change, he distinguishes, like te Winkel,
a number of internal causes such as the principle of economy, which he calls *gemakzucht* (literally: 'longing for
easiness'), and the 'trend towards uniformity' (*streven
naar eenvormigheid*). To the former he ascribes the change
of dental before *t* to *s* in Germanic, e.g. in *wist* 'knew,'
moest 'must,' as well as the elimination of *s* in various
environments in several languages, e.g. by change into
initial aspiration in Greek; through rhotacism intervo-
calically in Latin and most Germanic dialects; by loss
with compensatory lengthening of the preceding vowel in
Latin before -*d*- (as in *nīdus* 'nest'), etc. (*Inleiding*,
9). Assimilation, dissimilation, and such processes are
also assigned to the same motivation, whereas the leveling
trend accounts for analogy as well as folk-etymology (as
in *sparrow-grass* for *asparagus*). Among the external
causes of sound change he lists: (1) prestige forms used
by educated people who make the spoken forms correspond
to the written standard or preserve inherited terms and
phrases "artificially," (2) renewal through the dialects,
(3) influence of foreign languages (*Inleiding*, 18).

It would be rather tedious to survey the details of
his view on the origin and nature of language (*Inleiding*,

96-8): The picture that emerges from his discussion of the problem is an evolutive conception of language as a living organism in keeping with the Neogrammarian views, but Vercoullie also stresses the communicative function of language as a social institution. Though he brought little that was new, his standing merit remains to have paved the way for the development of linguistics in Belgium, just as te Winkel did in the Netherlands.[13]

NOTES

1. Becanus doubted whether the limited Gothic materials he had at his disposal actually reflected the language of the Goths: he considered Gothic as a "Mischsprache" with a strong Greek and Latin component (Van de Velde 1966:24-35).

2. The significance of the work of Kiliaan has long been recognized (cf., e.g. De Vooys 1936:72-3, Bakker-Dibbets 1977:210-15). Since the basic study of A. Kluyver (*Proeve eener critiek op het woordenboek van Kiliaan*. The Hague, 1884) and the extensive survey of archaisms by J. Jacobs (*De verouderde woorden bij Kiliaan*. Ghent, 1899) numerous articles by G. de Smet, F. Claes, and others have thrown new light on Kiliaan's information and reliability. The third edition of his dictionary has been republished recently by F. Claes (*Kiliaans Etymologicum van 1599, opnieuw uitgegeven met een inleiding*. The Hague, 1972).

3. The importance of ten Kate in the development of Netherlandic linguistics has been repeatedly emphasized in the Low Countries (cf. the monographs of Van der Hoeven 1896 and Rompelman 1952; the detailed analysis of ten Kate's contribution to Gothic studies in Van de Velde 1966:211-88; the histories of Netherlandic linguistics, e.g. De Vooys 1936:130-2; Bakker and Dibbits 1977:67, 72-3, 75-6, 103-5; etc.). Recently, G. E. Booij devoted a paper to "Lambert ten Kate als voorloper [precursor] van de TG-grammatica" (*Spektator* 1 1971-2:74-8; with a rejoinder by T. van der Geester, ibid. 160-1).

4. Using A. Moonen's *Nederduitsche Spraekkunst* (2nd ed., Amsterdam, 1719), W. Séwel's *Nederduytsche spraakkonst* (Amsterdam, 1708); A. Verwer's *Linguae belgicae idea grammatica* ... (Amsterdam, 1707); and other sources such as the older works of Joos Lambrecht's *Nederlandsche spellijnghe* (Ghent, 1550) or Pontus de Heuiter's *Nederduitse orthographie* (Antwerp, 1581), Van der Hoeven (1896:56-118) provides a thorough analysis of ten Kate's first monograph on phonetics which he publishes from the Amsterdam manuscript (1699) and compares with the earlier and contemporary works of Petrus Montanus (*Spreeckonst*. Delft, 1635), John Wallis (*De loquela, sive sonorum formatione*. London, 1653), and Johannes Conradus Amman (*Dissertatio de Loquela*. Haarlem, 1692). Considerable work has been done since then on early Dutch "phonologies" and grammatical works, in particular by L.P.H. Eijkman, C.G.N. De Vooys, W.J.H. Caron, W. Hellinga, and others (cf. e.g. Van Haeringen 1954:35-6, 42-3, 47-8; Hellinga 1968 [reprint of *De Opbouw van de Algemeen Beschaafde Uitspraak van het Nederlands* (1-361)], passim; Caron 1972:118-22, 135-7, 150-3; etc.).

5. Thus, the masculine *i*-stems *hups* 'hip,' *striks* 'stroke, line,' and *staps* (written *stads*) 'place,' are listed among the

masculine nomina substantiva "ending in -*s*" (*Gemeenschap*, 51), which
represent the Germanic *a*-stems. However, *gasts* 'guest' is listed as
a feminine in -*s* on account of its plural *gasteis* [*Gemeenschap*, 53;
cf. also the entry in the glossary (ibidem, 17): "gast, vreemde-
ling"—"*gasts* F. *hospes*:"]. See also Van de Velde 1966:246-56.

   6. The *Gemeenschap tussen de Gottische Spraeke en de Nederduytsche* (1710:61-84) gives the following account of the Gothic conjugation system:

Ten Kate's system	Germanic system
Class	
1: "Weak" verbs	
1 *dailjan*	1 = Class 1
2 *fastan*	2 = Class 3
3 *salbon*	3 = Class 2
2: "Strong" verbs	
1 *speiwan spaiw spiwum spiwans*	1 = Class 1
2 *bindan band bandum bundans*	2 = Class 3
3 *niman nam nemum numans*	3 = Class 4
4 *ganiutan ganaut ganutam ganutans*	4 = Class 2
5 *gabavian gabar gaberum gabaurans*	5 = Class 4 with
6 *wairpan warp waurpum waurpans*	"breaking"
	6 = Class 3 with
	"breaking"
3: "Strong" verbs	
1 *hafjan hof hofum hafans*	Ten Kate's subgroups 1,
2 *bidhan bad bedum bidans*	4, & 6, regrouped by him
3 *lisan las lesum lisans*	(1710:73-4) correspond
4 *þwahan þweh þwohum þwahans*	to Class 6; his subgroups
5 *saihvan sah sehvum saihvans*	2, 3, & 5, also regrouped
6 *standan stoþ stoþum standans*	by him to Class 5
7 *lukan lauk lukum lukans*	7 = Subgroup of Class 2
4: "Reduplicating" verbs (Class 7)	
1 *tekan taitok taitokum tekans*	1 = With ablaut
2 *haitan haihait haihaitum haitans*	2 = Without ablaut
5: "Weak" verbs	
1 *briggan brahta brahtans*	With preterites without
(instead of **brahts*)	connective vowel
2 *þagkjan þahta þahtans*	
(instead of *þahts*)	
3 *waurkjan waurhta waurhtans*	
(instead of *waurhts*)	
6: *magan, kunnan, witan, aigan,* etc.	= the so-called
	"preterito-presentia"

The criteria for this classification are the vowel alternations as
ten Kate himself points out in his letter to A.V. (= Verwer, his
former teacher): "De VERBA vond ik onderscheyden in soorten, waerom
ik die gene, welke in de lóóp hunner veranderinge eenerley rooy

hielden, onder eene zelfde *Classis* bracht; en deze wederom elk in
zyn soorte byzonder afdééélde: aldus vind 'er Uw E. ... sesderley
van de tweede (*Classis*), sevenderley van de derde, tweederley van de
vierde ... welker elk in klank of verwisselinge iets verschilt"
(*Gemeenschap*, 4). See also Van de Velde 1966:261-74.
      7. His survey in the *Aenleiding* is, however, comparative as he
adduces parallel Gothic (I, 575-97), Old High German (Tatian and
Williram; I, 598-628), Old English (I, 629-52), as well as Contemporary German (I, 653-75), and Icelandic (I, 676-96) material; moreover, he provides a sketch of the situation in Frisian (I, 706-10).
His first class (= the "weak" verbs) is characterized by the absence
of alternation of root-vowel ("VERBA, die geen verandering van
Wortel-VOCAAL gedoogen," *Aenleiding* I, 548) and the dental preterite
and past participle. The three following classes show regular vowel
alternations:

> Class 2 verbs have the same root-vowel in the preterite and the
>   past participle.
> Class 3 verbs change their root-vowel only in the preterite.
> Class 4 verbs change their root-vowel both in the preterite and
>   in the past participle, but show different vowels in the
>   two forms.

The other three classes are similarly defined on the basis of specific formal criteria, e.g.:

> Class 5, because its preterite and past participle present forms
>   in *-cht*;
> Class 6, because of its mixed character ("een mengsel van twee-
>   derhande CLASSES"), with its "weak" preterite and
>   "strong" past participle.

Though he uses the same principle of classification for the other
languages, ten Kate does not attempt to make the matrix of their
classes correspond exactly with that of Dutch: thus, in Contemporary
German, *sterben-starb-gestorben* represent subgroup 2 of Class 3,
which corresponds to Dutch Class 4, insofar as the regular vowel
alternation ("Regelmaet van de Vocaalwisseling") produces a different
vowel in the preterite and in the past participle (*Aenleiding* I,
669). He nevertheless makes important cross-references, pointing
out, for example, that in both Old English and Old High German, the
complete paradigm of the subjunctive preterite is based on the
vocalism of the indicative preterite plural (*Aenleiding* I, 635).
Ten Kate also indicates how classes more specifically defined by
formal criteria correlate, e.g. the type OE *þencan:þohte* (= Class 4;
I, 647) ~ OHG *thenkan:thãhta* (= Class 4; I, 622) ~ Gothic *þagkjan:*
þãhta (= Class 5; I, 593) ~ Dutch *denken:dôcht/dacht* (= Class 5; I,
567). He is particularly aware of divergences in Icelandic (I, 677-
8) and is very specific for each subgroup, e.g. in Class 2, subgroup
4 (I, 684), where he lumps together *bera* 'bear, carry' *hverba* 'disappear' (i.e. *hverfa* 'turn around'), *bidia* 'pray,' etc., so that he
has to refer to up to three different classes in the cognate languages.
      8. J. Knol in Bakker and Dibbets 1977:72-8. In his *Aenleiding*
(I, 13), ten Kate insists that the "Taelwetten (i.e. the phonological

and grammatical rules) ... uit het eenstemmige of agtbare Gebruik
niet alleen van eene Stad maer een Gemeen-land behooren uitgekozen
en opgemaekt te worden." But his supra-regional "common usage" is
largely an ideal standard arrived at by historical-comparative procedure (Van den Berg 1975), and it is definitely not the "Algemeen
Beschaafd" whose focus was in Holland (Hellinga 1968:359-60).

9. W. D. Whitney's *Language and its Study* (1867), which had
been greeted in 1875 as a pioneering work in linguistics by the Dutch
Anglicist P. J. Cosijn, was translated from its third edition in two
volumes by J. Beckering Vinckes under the title: *Taal en Taalstudie.
Voorlezingen over de gronden der wetenschappelijke taalbeoefening*
(Haarlem,1877-81). The work was extremely well received in the
Netherlands and had a considerable impact on the views of Dutch lin-
guists in the last quarter of the 19th century (cf. Bakker and
Dibbets 1977:152).

10. As the main representative of the Neogrammarian approach to
dialectology, he directed several dissertations on local dialects at
the University of Amsterdam (cf. Bakker and Dibbets 1977:287) and was
involved in an extensive survey of the Dutch dialects (*De Noordneder-
landsche tongvallen. Atlas van taalkaarten met tekst*. Leyden, 1899-
1901—left incomplete; cf. criticism by C. G. Kloeke in Grootaers and
Kloeke 1926:16-7; further comments by A. Weijnen 1958:6).

11. J. te Winkel's *Inleiding tot de Geschiedenis van de Nederlandsche taal* was not a historical grammar of Dutch, but rather an
introduction to linguistics and the diachronic development from Indo-
European to Dutch within its Germanic context. As a substitute for
te Winkel's *Geschichte der niederländischen Sprache*, whose second and
last edition appeared in Strasbourg in 1901, M. J. Van der Meer produced his *Historische Grammatik der niederländischen Sprache*. Vol.
I. *Einleitung und Lautlehre* (Heidelberg: Carl Winter, 1927), which
focuses on the external history of Dutch and the diachronic development of its phonology. The first comprehensive historical phonology
and morphology was M. Schönfeld's *Historische Grammatica van het Nederlands* (Zupphen: Thieme, 1921), to which a section on word-
formation was added in the third edition (1932), and which has been
kept up-to-date by constant revisions since the fifth edition (1954)
by A. van Loey. It completely superseded Vercouillie's concise introduction, whose fourth and last edition (Ghent: Vanderpoorten,
1922), was a mere reprint of the third (1907). Cf. also Van
Haeringen 1954:12-3.

12. A comparison between the third and last edition of
Vercoullie's dictionary (Ghent: Van Rysselberghe and Rombaut, 1925)
and the other two Dutch etymological dictionaries (Franck 1912, 1929,
with the 1936 *Supplement* of Van Haeringen and De Vries 1971) shows
the important differences in method and approach among the three
works (cf. Polomé 1975), as well as the extent of the divergence in
their coverage of the vocabulary. Thus, *deutel* 'small wedge,' described by Vercoullie (64) as a derivation, with *umlaut* (eu = [∅]),
from the stem of *dodde* (= *lisdodde* 'typha latifolia), a term occurring in Kiliaan with the meaning 'stalk, peg,' is not listed either
by Franck or by De Vries, who both have entries for *dodde*. The term
appears, however, currently in the standard dictionaries of Modern
Dutch, e.g. in Van Dale's *Nieuw Groot Woordenboek der Nederlandse
Taal* (The Hague: Martinus Nijhoff, 1950:386). Different is the case
of *sudde* 'marsh, swamp' (Vercouillie, 341), which is not mentioned

in Van Dale, nor in Verschueren's *Modern Woordenboek* (Turnhout:
Brepols, 1956). It already appears in Killiaan with the label *vetus*
and is accordingly omitted by both Franck and De Vries. Similarly,
Vercoullie (191), lists a verb *kwelen* 'suffer pain,' which Van Dale
(975) refers to as "regional" and illustrates with a quote from Cats
giving evidence of the meaning 'pine away'. Both Franck (359) and
De Vries (372) refer only to Middle Dutch *quēlen* 'be in bad shape,
pine away' s.v. *kwaal* 'disease, plague, agony'.

13. This paper was read in absentia by Professor Irmengard Rauch
at the Houston meeting of the Modern Language Association of America
in December 1980. It could not have been written without the most
gracious help of Professor Marcel Van Spaandonck of the University of
Ghent (Belgium), who provided access to sources unavailable in the
U.S. I wish to express my deepest gratitude to both of them for
their support and assistance.

REFERENCES

Bakker, D. M., and G.R.W. Dibbets. 1977. *Geschiedenis van de Ne-
    derlandse Taalkunde*. Malmberg: Den Bosch.
Caron, W.J.H. 1972. *Klank en Teken. Verzamelde taalkundige
    studies*. Groningen: Wolters-Noordhoff.
De Vooys, C.G.N. 1936. *Geschiedenis van de Nederlandsche Taal in
    Hoofdtreken geschetst*. 2nd ed. Antwerp: De Sikkel.
De Vries, Jan. 1971. *Nederlands Etymologisch Woordenboek*. Leyden:
    E. J. Brill.
Franck, Johannes. 1912. *Etymologisch Woordenboek der Nederlandsche
    Taal*. 2nd ed. by N. Van Wijk. [Reprinted in 1929 with *Supple-
    ment* by C. B. Van Haeringen 1936. The Hague: Martinus Nijhoff.]
Grootaers, L., and C. G. Kloeke. 1926. *Handleidung bij het Noord-
    en Zuid- Nederlandsch Dialectonderzoek*. Noord- en Zuid- Neder-
    landsche Dialectbibliotheek, vol. 1. The Hague: Martinus
    Nijhoff.
Hellinga, W. 1968. *Bijdragen tot de geschiedenis van de Nederlandse
    taalcultuur*. Arnhem: Gysbers and Van Loon.
Polomé, Edgar C. 1975. Iets over etymologische woordenboeken. *Spel
    van Zinnen. Album A. van Loey*, ed. by R. Jansen-Sieben, S. De
    Vriendt, and R. Willemyns, 243-9. Brussels: Éditions de
    l'Université de Bruxelles.
Rompelman, T. A. 1952. *Lambert ten Kate als Germanist*. Mededel-
    ingen der Koninklijke Nederlandse Akademie van Wetenschappen.
    Afd. Letterkunde. N.R., dl. 15, No. 9. Amsterdam: Noord-
    Hollandsche Uitgevers Maatschappij.
Van den Berg, B. 1975. Lambert ten Kate's "Gemeenlandsche Dialect."
    Spel van Zinnen. Album A. van Loey, ed. by R. Jansen-Sieben,
    S. De Vriendt, and R. Willemyns, 299-304. Brussels: Éditions
    de l'Université de Bruxelles.
Van der Hoeven, Adrianus. 1896. *Lambert ten Kate*. (De "Gemeenschap
    tussen de Gottische Spraeke en de Nederduytsche" en zijne onuit-
    gegeven Geschriften over Klankkunde en Versbouw.) Gravenhage:
    Martinus Nijhoff.

Van de Velde, R. G. 1966. *De Studie van het Gotisch in de Neder-*
  landen. Bijdrage tot een status quaestionis over de studie van
  het Gotisch en het Krimgotisch. Ghent: Koninklijke Vlaamse
  Academie voor Taal- en Letterkunde.
Van Haeringen, C. B. 1954. *Netherlandic language research.*
  Leyden: E. J. Brill.
Weijnen, A. 1958. *Nederlandse Dialectkunde.* Assen: Van Gorcum
  & Co.

Part IV
STRATA AND LANGUAGE CHANGE

PAIDEIA, A LINGUISTIC SUBCODE

Henry and Renée Kahane

1. NATURALNESS AND PAIDEIA

Vittore Pisani, taking Italian as the exemplar of a literate language providing excellent material for the abstraction of diachronic principles (1977:132-3), challenges the conventional hypothesis that the evolution of that language from Latin to the modern standard represents a transformation from one monolithic stage into another. Each stage of the linguistic development reflects a complex society; thus he perceives the Latin foundation, so-called Vulgar Latin (to him, a phrase, comparable to, say, the Greek Koine), as the blending, in principle, of two interlocking forces: the language of the literary tradition of the *classi colte* as against the colloquial conglomerate of archaic or innovative features with its multilingual, non-Latin ingredients absorbed in the course of history from the many cultures that impinged upon Rome, and later Italy. The intertwining of levels had its impact on language change: in many ways the rules of a systemic development were neutralized. Pisani contrasts, e.g. two variants of the same morpheme: Ital. *più*, with its regular change of Lat. initial *PL*, as against its bookish congener, *plur(ale)*, with preservation of *PL*.

Pisani's linguistic model calls to mind the analogue of a neighboring discipline. More than sixty years ago, the influential German *Literaturwissenschaftler* Friedrich Gundolf created the model (Schmitz 1965:64-5) of *Urerlebnis* and *Bildungserlebnis*, primordial experience and cultural experience, to isolate the two forces behind Goethe's creativity (Gundolf 1920:26-7). *Urerlebnis* is the impact to which man is exposed by virtue of his inner nature [die Erschütterungen, denen der Mensch kraft seiner inneren Struktur ausgesetzt ist]; *Bildungserlebnis* is the absorption of the past, of tradition, of education, of the milieu [die geistig geschichtlichen Einflüsse und Begegnisse, schon geformte Anschauungen aus Kunst, Wissenschaft, Religion] (49). The forces, in short, are polar: the one is innate, the other derived [ursprünglich/

175

abgeleitet] (26), yet they are intertwined [verwoben] (27).

It seems tempting to transfer this binary model from artistic creation to language change in literate socie-ties. A construct based on these two roots of our exis-tence as speakers, naturalness (for *Urerlebnis*) and *paideia* (as we would like, in the humanistic tradition, to translate *Bildungserlebnis*), would sharpen our insight into the linguistic process. In their opposition both evolve as essentially diachronic concepts: naturalness represents the rules which are accepted through tradition, paideia the exceptions, often the not-yet rules, which may invade the system. The following tentative remarks cen-ter on that much neglected subcode, paideia. Particularly apt to demonstrate its force is a specific constellation recurrent in the history of language: the impact of an external influence. Greenberg (1978:3), searching for universals, underlines its often lasting effect: "there is much empirical evidence supporting the view that ex-ternal influences play an important role in initiating linguistic changes."

2. THE GREEK BEHIND THE LATIN

Pisani, in his summary outline of Vulgar Latin, hints at a superb exemplum of linguistic paideia, the impact of Greek on Latin (1977:133). Greek exerted its influence on the Latin of the upper classes, partly through multi-faceted transfer, partly through the prescriptive dogma-tism of the grammarians. The presence of "the Greek be-hind Latin" (the term is borrowed from Paul Friedlander [1943-44:270]) has, of course, been commented on for some time, and the significance of the process has been stressed in persuasive statements which open a wide field of investigation. Thus, the well-documented history of Latin by Leumann-Hofmann-Szantyr (1972:88*) characterizes the final period of the ancient world as "bilingual, dis-playing a confluence and blending of languages." On the literary-colloquial level, i.e. that of the *literarische Umgangssprache*, Dietrich (1973a:20n76) believes that the stylistic mark of the Vulgar Latin Bible translations during the first three post-Christian centuries rested, precisely, on a high degree of Hellenization. For Bonfante (1960:174, 182), Italian is thoroughly "a synthesis of Latin and Greek," and he sees in the innovations involved not so much a natural development as the reflection of a Greek influence; he thus substantiates Bartoli's metaphor (1925:44) of the blending of *spirito greco* and *materia latina*. Similarly, Coseriu (1971:135) sees in the Greek impact "the central problem of so-called Vulgar Latin, i.e. the foundation of the Romance languages"; therefore he formulates a rule of thumb (141): "if a feature ap-pears in Greek and Romance but not in classical Latin, there are solid reasons to interpret that feature as a Hellenism of late colloquial Latin." Reichenkron, the

historian of Vulgar Latin, considered the role of Greek
during the entire development of Latin into Christianity
and Romance of such significance and volume that he
planned (but death intervened) to devote a <u>besonderes
Werk</u> to the topic (1965:23).

In concrete exemplification, the following, without
our specifying here the strata of borrowing or the ways
of transmission, are a few of the Hellenistic models, on
the lexemic, morphological, or syntactical levels, that
were supposedly transferred to Vulgar Latin and Romance.
The various hypotheses were proferred by Pasquali (1927),
Bonfante (1960), Coseriu (1971), or Pisani (1974, 1977).

Greek influence, then, is to be suspected behind the
Vulgar Latin article, definite and indefinite; behind the
large periphrastic verbal subsystem in the perfect, the
future, the "progressive" form; in the strengthening of
word-order rules to balance the reduction of inflection;
in the comparative and the relative superlative formed
with *plus*; in the increase of diminutive suffixes to replace the simplex; in the great number of borrowed lexemes and of calques.

We have used here terms such as supposedly/hypothesis/
to be suspected, to indicate the still experimental stage
of forays into the field of Graeco-Latin blending. The
dilemmas are recurrent: do the similarities result from
a common heritage, from the Greek impact on Latin, from
the revitalization, with restructuring, of existing patterns, or do they represent a mere parallelism?

Recently, in a review of Dietrich (1973a), we singled
out a few of the striking similarities between Greek and
Latin as an epistemological exemplar of the pros and cons
(Kahane 1978:647-8). (a) Neither Imisch nor Bonfante can
decide whether or not to ascribe to Greek influence the
Latin replacement of case endings by prepositions. (b) The
loss of the infinitive in the Balkanic languages and in
Southern Italy is interpreted by Sandfeld-Jensen and
Rohlfs monogenetically as a calque from Greek, but by
Togeby polygenetically as an independent feature. (c) The
shift of Latin adjectives to nouns (say, *discentes* 'dis-
ciples') is seen by one as the imitation of a Greek model,
by another as influence from Latin poetry. (d) The frequent irregularity of intertonic vowels in Tuscan has been
explained traditionally as an indigenous Italian development, resulting from phonological distribution, dialect
conditions, or language levels; Malkiel, however, derives
the vocalic fluidity from the effect of colloquial Hellenisms which then drew terminal word segments into its domain. (e) Above all, the emerging article has provoked
varying explanations. Trager sees in its expansion a reflection of the democratizing spirit of expanding Christianity; Löfstedt believes it was an internal linguistic
process, caused by the weakening of the pronouns and the
collapse of the inflectional system. On the other hand,
the Greek contribution to the rise of the article is
stressed by Wartburg, who discerns in its presence or

absence a new way of differentiating concreteness or ab-
stractness; but both Rohlfs and Lausberg find the Greek
role to be no more than the reinforcement of a preexistin
Latin device of identification.

As even these sketchy remarks have indicated, the
Greek linguistic influence in Vulgar Latin was, in a certain sense, a diastratic one: it came from and enveloped
the upper and the lower levels of society and survived on
the basic levels of Romance, the inherited and the
"learned." Here, however, within the frame of this essay
Greek influence will be viewed as a contribution to Western paideia, and in the following we shall try to describe briefly five typical channels of transmission whic
mediated Greek elements to the speech of the educated
elite. In other words, we are interested here in the
sociolinguistic act of the transfer.

3. LITERATURE

Observers in antiquity were already aware of poetry
as a major channel of Grecisms. Janssen (1941:115) adduces two authoritative testimonia. Quintilian, the
rhetorician and critic (1st c.p. Chr.), characterizes the
esthetic attraction of Greek for the Latin writer of poetry (Inst. or., XII, 10.33 tr. Butler): "The Greek language is so much more agreeable in sound than the Latin
that our poets, whenever they wish their verse to be especially harmonious, adorn it with Greek words." Horace
expresses the same view essentially when he rejects linguistic Hellenomania as inappropriate for the factual jar
gon of the bar; in doing this he uses the analogue of the
sweet Greek and the dry Roman wines (Sat. I, 10.20 tr.
Fairclough): "'But that was a great feat, you say, his
[Lucilius'] mixing of Greek and Latin words ... a style,
where both tongues make a happly blend, has more charm,
as when the Falernian wine is mixed with Chian.' In your
verse-making only (I put it to yourself), or does the rul
also hold good when you have to plead the long, hard case
of the defendant Petillius?"

Kroll (1924), Janssen (1941), and Leumann (1947) (all
three now available in Italian translation, updated bibli-
ographically, in Lunelli 1974) have gathered a considerable corpus of Hellenisms in Latin poetry. Kroll (6)
stresses the function of poetry as the early channel of
transmission; Leumann (157), its special role in the
transfer of syntactical Grecisms. Janssen (108), viewing
the problem from a systemic standpoint, observes, quite
in agreement with what we quoted from Pisani, that "the
syntactic deviations which occur in Latin poetry are ofte
those resulting from Greek influence." In the following
we shall try to sketch, within this particular frame, the
history of one morpho-syntactical feature, the adverbial
formans -*mente*, from Greek through Latin into Romance.

Shorey (1910) was the first to be struck by the similarity between the Romance adverbial -*mente* and a

formulaic Greek dative phrase frequent in classical drama
which consisted of a noun plus adjective with instrumental
function: *eudóxōi phrení* (Aeschylus) prefigured a Latino-
Romance *gloriosa mente*; *aphóbōi phrení* (Aristophanes) an
intrepida mente. Grk. *phrení* 'with the mind' was easily
replaced by quasi-synonyms, all in the dative: *thymôi/
nôōi/gnōmāi/kardíāi/psýchāi*. The range widened to less
spiritual parts of the body such as *cherí* dat. 'hand' and
podí dat. 'foot'. Semantically, the nouns shared the
element of a human involvement; which nuance they represented was not relevant. As Shorey points out (88), the
noun functioned as the carrier of the adjective, and the
latter was the dominant feature of the nexus.

The Greek expression was paralleled in Latin with, of
course, a shift from dative to ablative, as in *honesta
mente* (Seneca)/*timido pectore* (Plautus). Again, the noun
functioned through its case ending as the grammatical, the
adjective as the semantic, marker of the string. McCartney
(1920) lists numerous records, excerpted for the most part
from belles-lettres. The similarities of structure, the
semantic range of the nominal element, and the literary
use suggest the Greek formula as a model of the Latin,
and indeed, various investigators have advocated this
genetic relationship: Kroll (1923:275), Bartoli (1925:
88), Vendryes (1950:197-8), Battisti (1954): s.v. mente.

The broad spectrum of ablative nouns sharing the concept of mental disposition was reduced to a single item,
mente, and by the sixth century the Romance use of adverbial -*mente* was in existence (Mihăescu ap. Spitzer
1940:189). Two aspects of this final phase have been
stressed. In grammatical terms the development is one
from an analytic to a synthetic stage: Baldinger (1965:
709) thus interprets the transition from *severa mente*
'dans un esprit sévère' to *sévèrement* 'd'une manière
sévère'; Malkiel (1978:128) terms the shift one from composition to derivation, most evident in French where the
morpheme *ment* has lost its lexical autonomy. In semantic
phrasing, Lausberg (1972:100) sees in the adverbialization
of *mente* the mechanization of a former psychological content, the disposition of the agent: in, say, *l'eau coule
doucement* human involvement is no longer present; Mihăescu
(ap. Spitzer 1940:190) and Spitzer (ibid. and 1925:287)
stress the educated, intellectual foundation and connotation of the pattern.

4. TRANSLATION

Translation not only transmits the substance of a
different culture, but it also carries some impact of the
concomitant language; in other words, the source language
remains a reality behind the target language. In the long
and multifaceted history of translation certain periods
stand out in which the glory of the source language was
even cultivated; included among these was that of the
early translation of Christian literature from Greek into

Latin. The word had a weight of its own, competing for
preeminence with the meaning of the text: we are referring here to the debate between the two principles of
verbum de verbo and *sensus de sensu* (Marti 1974:64). Lit
eralism transcended, of course, the merely lexemic, and
syntactical features were drawn into the process. The
popular character of such literature as the New Testament
involves an interplay of levels which is of the greatest
interest to the history of language: while the translatc
enjoys a certain measure of education, the public for whc
he translates includes everybody; thus, the newly coined
or reawakened or restructured forms are assured a wide ar
continued reception and retention.

Linguistic change, which is stimulated through translation, chiefly Biblical translation, is, in a schematic
description (Kahane 1978:647), a three-step process:
First, a bilingual who partakes in a *Mischkultur* (in the
present context, the Graeco-Latin) weaves into his translation such patterns of the source language as are matche
by similar forms in the target language, yet deviate in
certain ways from the norms of the latter: they may occu
less commonly, convey divergent semantic shades, represen
a different function within the system, or even be just
barely understandable. In step two, the mediator perceives the finished product with his eye and transmits it
by word of mouth to the listener's ear. Third, the listener is continuously exposed, for generations, to the
phrasing of the teachings and of the stories, and the
former deviation may turn into the accepted standard.

Dietrich (1973a and b) has extensively treated one
case in point, the aspectual periphrase, *to be* + present
participle. He evidences the structure for Greek, from
Homer to the Byzantine period, as a device of the narrative and descriptive style, e.g. Herodotus (VIII, 137.4)
ên gàr tòn oîkon eséchōn ho hḗlios 'for [just then] the
sun was shining into the house'. Synchronically, Dietric
sees in the periphrastic paradigm, as against the unauxil
iaried verb, a pattern marked for aspect; he calls it,
with Coseriu, *Winkelschau*, referring to the speaker's
ability to perceive, from his standpoint, a segment
(rather than the totality) of an act; in his German rendering of the ancient records he frequently uses an adver
of involvement, *gerade dabei sein* 'to be about to/be on
the verge of/just happen to' (thus Mk. 2:18 *erant ieiu-
nantes* 'they were keeping a fast'). We are less sure tha
Dietrich seems to be (1973a:195) that the English progressive form *am (sing)ing*, with its stress on circum-
stantiality, is not closely akin in function to his
Winkelschau. Diachronically, the periphrastic aspect was
a tradition in Greek but was alien to Latin where the
form was known, to be sure, but the function apparently
different: Plautus' *sum oboediens* 'I am obedient' represents the copula relating a predicative to the subject.
With the period of increasing Greek influence and through
the translation of Biblical literature, i.e. from about

the second post-Christian century on, the Greek pattern
superimposed itself on the existing Latin form and in the
process introduced a new function. Through Vulgar Latin
this function became a feature of the Romance verbal system (so Span. *estoy cantando*) as well as, possibly, of the
Germanic (Kahane 1978:647): Mt. 7:29 *ên didáskōn* 'was
teaching' → Lat. *erat docens* → OE *wæs lærende*.

Two of Dietrich's conclusions support the basic hypotheses of this essay: on the one hand, that the transfer of the Greek periphrastic aspect into Vulgar Latin
and beyond was realized above all within the course of
Bible translations [besonders im Zuge der Bibelüberset-
zungen] (1973a:227), i.e. on the level of paideia; on the
other hand, that the transfer introduced a deviatory syntactical feature into Vulgar Latin: it had not existed
within the norms of either the older phases or of the
written level of Latin (224).

5. SYMBIOSIS

A bicultural and bilingual symbiosis is a most favorable environment for the transfer of linguistic features.
Often, in such an environment, one of the two cultures,
with its language, is dominant, and its styles of life and
of speech are apt to filter first of all into the upper
stratum of the dominated society. In the present context
that situation is exemplified by the Byzantine Exarchate
of Ravenna, where, from the middle of the sixth to the
middle of the eighth century, Vulgar Latin came under the
influence of Hellenism (Kahane 1970-76:440-2). The influence was chiefly lexical, with Greek words flowing into
the Latin of that time and that particular region. A cir-
cumspect essay by Sylviane Lazard (1976) elucidates the
patterning of the process. She registers the Grecisms
used by a single man, the Abbot Agnello, author of the
Liber Pontificalis Ecclesiae Ravennatis (c. 827-840).
Agnello was born in 805, about two generations after
Byzantium retreated (in 751) from Ravenna, and thus was
probably a good representative of the speech of that
episode of biculturalism. He came from a family in which
knowledge of Greek was a tradition, and he liked to play
(an intellectual hobby which is indicative of his educa-
tional status) with the etymologies of Greek words. Lazard
sees in him a man of culture and a man who was, to a certain degree, bilingual. His Hellenism reflects (298)
"the usage of the educated class of Ravenna at his time."

The following samples of Agnello's Hellenisms focus
on what is typical in this kind of linguistic and thereby
cultural transfer. The lexemes selected had to be truly
Ravennate: either they can reasonably be diagnosed as
adapted during Ravenna's Byzantine phase; or, if they
were remnants of an earlier period of Latinization, they
display some specific feature which ties them to Ravenna:
a shade of meaning, a phonological peculiarity, or continued presence in the regional dialects. We shall follow

Lazard's analysis (always indicated), with certain expansions and retouches.

archiergatus 'foreman (in a crew of workers)' < *archiergátēs*, a Greek term of the period of the Exarchate (290).

ardica 'narthex of a church' < *(n)árthēka*, acc. of *nárthēx*, with loss, in Greek, of the initial in synizesis with the article; the reduced form attested from Byzantine to modern Greek; the Ravenna variant, *ardica* with *d*, surviving regionally into the Middle Ages, represents a later, voiced stage of *artica*, likewise recorded for Ravenna, with rendering of Grk. θ as *t* (268-9; MLatWb, s.v. ardica; Kahane 1970-76:367-8).

argýrion 'silver, silverplate' < *argýrion* 'silver', a sheer Hellenism in the West, even recorded in Greek characters in the 9th century; in Greece the same meaning is preserved in such marginal areas as Crete and Cappadocia (290; MLatWb, s.v. argyrion; Kriaras, s.v.; Andriotis, #1147).

bisalis 'brick' < *bésalon*; a Greek Latinism of the Koine, still in use; the *i* of the stem, rendering the iotacistic pronunciation of Grk. η, indicates the Greek provenience of Agnello's term (290-1; MLatWb, s.v. bessalis; Liddell-Scott, Suppl., s.v. bésalon; Kriaras, s.v. bésalo [n]).

cereostatus 'candelabrum' < *kērostátēs*; the ecclesiastic term, which appeared from the 6th century on, and above all in Rome, must have been popular in Ravenna as indicated by the surviving regionalism *zilostar* (269; MLatWb, s.v. cerostatum; Kahane 1970-76:359).

chartularius 'keeper of the archives of the court', then an honorific title < *chartoulários*, itself borrowed from Latin; the term is repeatedly attested with reference to the Byzantine administration of Ravenna (270: Lampe, s.v. chartoularios; Niermeyer and MLatWb, s.v. chartularius; Kahane 1970-76:512).

cherumanica 'glove, sleeve' < *cheirománikon*, attested from the 6th to the 10th century (and so listed in the Etymologicum Magnum, 209.40 Gaisford), a compound of the Latinism *manikion* (from *manica* 'sleeve') and Grk. *cheîr* 'hand' (291-2; DuCange, s.v. manikion; Sophocles, s.v. cheirománikon).

diplois, acc. *diploidem* 'kind of cloak of the clergy' < *diploís, -ídos* 'cloak affording a double wrapping'; a borrowing well-attested in Late Latin, whose regional records, as late as the 16th century, in Ravenna, Emilia, Senigallia indicate a continued regional use (272; Lampe, s.v. diploís).

docarium 'frame of roof' < *dokárion*; the Greek term recorded since 7th-8th-c. papyri and still in use (292; Kriaras, s.v. dokário(n); Niermeyer, s.v. docarium, with a 10th-c. reference).

dromo, -onis 'a fast vessel' < *drómōn*; recorded in the West by the 5th century and in particular since Theodoric, i.e. in some kind of relation to Ravenna (272; Kahane 1970-76:363).

endothis 'altarcloth' < *endytē* 'garment, altarcloth'; the term was apparently borrowed in Ravenna in its ecclesiastic use and remained alive there, in its corrupt form, as late as the 11th century (272; Lampe, s.v. endytḗ; Koukoules II:2,27).

exarchus 'the exarch of Ravenna' < *éxarchos* 'exarch, viceroy'; the term refers to a specifically Ravennate institution; later this title of a worldly dignitary was transferred to a spiritual one, the archbishop of Ravenna (273; Lampe, s.v. éxarchos; Niermeyer, s.v. exarchus).

glossocomun 'coffin' *glōssókomon*; in Greek, the meaning 'Sarcophagus', an extension of the meaning 'box, casket', survived into the Middle Ages, particularly in hagiographic texts (292; Koukoules IV, 190; Lampe, s.v. glōssókomon).

graphia 'inscription' < *graphía* 'writing, treatise'; the Greek term, recorded in Gregorius Nyssenus (4th c.), was borrowed as '(piece of) writing, description, document' and quoted as a sheer Hellenism by Işidor of Seville, Orig., 6,9,2 (7th c.) (292-3; Lampe, s.v. graphía; CGL III, 131.49/495.55/511.71; ThLL, s.v. graphia; Niermeyer, s.v. graphía).

manuale 'candlestick' < *manouálion*; the latter a Greek Latinism, from *manuale* 'thing held in the hand', which in Greek was applied to an ecclesiastic object and is still in use (293-4; Lampe, s.v. manouálion).

molchus 'bolt of a door' < *mochlós*, with metathesis; the ancient term survives in such modern Greek dialects as Chios, the Cyclades, and the Dodecanese (294; Andriotis, #4128).

Orphanumtrofium, name of a monastery dedicated to St. Peter < *orphanotropheîon* 'orphanage', a neologism of the Justinian period; with the passing of time the name of a Ravennate establishment, which in all probability was founded by Greek monks, lost its meaning and its form: by the 11th century it appears as *Offeotrofeum* (275).

platanum 'a kind of vessel' < *pláthanon* 'dish or mold for baking' recorded in anc. Greek; a Latinized fem. form, **plátana*, either derived from the neuter plural *pláthana* or from a Greek fem. *plathánē*, is the base form of numerous regional names of vessels spreading from Ravenna (294; Henricus Stephanus, s.v. pláthanon; Kahane 1970-76:391).

Hellenisms such as these exemplify the lexical impact which Byzantium's colonial government exerted on the speech of the educated citizen of Ravenna. In a semantic résumé the borrowings, many of which were neologisms, referred to objects and institutions which may have been new or at least fashionable. The ecclesiastic terminology is characteristic: the clerical cloak, altarcloth, candlestick and candelabrum, and the coffin all have Greek names. The building trade is well represented: frame of the roof, brick, bolt on the door, the architectural feature of the narthex, and the foreman of the crew. Amenities of daily life: glove (or sleeve?), silverware, and baking dish. A new type of ship: the fast dromon. And, of course, the administrative contribution of State and Church: exarch, chartulary, inscription, and orphanage. As to phonology, Agnello's spelling may echo realistically the actual pronunciation of the Byzantine model: thus, the iotacistic value of Grk. η is reflected in *bisalis* and in *ardíca*; and, again, *ardíca* reflects the loss, through syntactical phonetics, of initial *n* in its base form *(n)árthēka*. In diachronic terms, some of the words were sheer Hellenisms such as *argyrion* and *diplois*. Others, such as *cereostatus* and *platanum* had popular

appeal and survived in the regional dialects. Some, interestingly, were rückwanderer: Latin words that had been
borrowed by Greek and now returned, sometimes with semantic restructuring, as Hellenisms: *bisalis, chartularius,
manuale*, and *cherumanica*, from the hybrid *cheirománikon*
half Greek (*cheir*) half Hellenized Latin (*manikon*).

6. SPECIAL LANGUAGES

With the terminology of a particular area of knowledge
the translator faced an often difficult and sometimes even
creative task. In the Empire, several professions had a
tradition anchored in the Hellenic culture, and the jar-
gons of the various linguistic fields were transferred
into Latin in three distinct patterns: direct borrowings
or calques or transformations. Transformations concern
us here. Theology, that most technical field of all,
where terminology assumes a reality and a vitality of its
own, exemplifies the process. Studer (1971), who devotes
a fine essay to the interplay, in this event, of source
language and target language, stresses a characteristic
feature (190): "The transfer of Greek concepts always
involved an *Umdeutung*, a reinterpretation, resulting from
the fact that Greek concepts and notions were being transplanted into a new environment." The following case histories, often discussed, are reported *grosso modo* after
him. They represent three types of such transmission.
     (a) Grk. *dóxa* and Lat. *gloria* (182-4). The transla-
tions of *dóxa* illustrate a case of polyvalence, Latinization of a Greek term with a multiple semantic load. After
such early renderings as *claritas/maiestas/honor*, the term
gloria was in the ascendant, supported by its profane
background, 'glory, fame, honor', which corresponded
closely to the traditional meanings of *dóxa* in Greek. In
the religious context both *dóxa*, the model, and *gloria*,
the translation, developed in common such uses as 'divine
power' and 'praise of God'. But when *dóxa* was drawn increasingly into the semantic orbit of light and radiance,
gloria did not follow all the way. The reasons are not
entirely clear: perhaps *gloria*, with its connotation of
power, was less apt to express the notion of light; perhaps the lexemic competitors *gloria/maiestas/claritas/
honor* were differentiated and used according to the shade
of meaning which each member of the set expressed.
Claritas, in any case, continued to be used as the term
for the notion of light. Interestingly, the polysemy of
dóxa as reflected in its renderings had already motivated
debate even in antiquity; St. Jerome had to defend his use
of terms other than *gloria* (and *gloriatio*); similarly,
Augustine felt impelled to stress the equivalence of
gloria/maiestas/claritas. Both justified themselves with
an appeal to *consuetudo*, the linguistic norm of the
Church.
     (b) Grk. *prósōpon* and Lat. *persona* (184-8). In this
example, an early equivalence of the two terms was voided

through semantic bifurcation; the Latin member shifted,
in contrast to the Greek which was static. Greek Biblical theologians introduced the "prosopographic exegesis":
to demonstrate the difference between Father and Son they
identified and differentiated the 'persons' to whom the
various sayings were ascribed. This method was taken over
by the earliest Latin theologians, Tertullian and Novatian,
who used the expression *ex persona*, patterned after Grk.
ek prosōpou. Thus, the term *persona* came into the dogma
of the Trinity, and with Tertullian it became a central
concept of this dogma. Then, model and translation bi-
furcated: In the East, Grk. *prósōpon* remained restricted,
as an exegetic term, to the differentiation between the
divine hypostases, but in the West, Christian *persona* under the influence of its use in the Roman tradition, took
on the concrete meaning of 'personality', body and soul,
and thus subsumed Christ's divine and human attributes.

    (c) Grk. *mystērion* and Lat. *sacramentum* (180-1). Here,
the primary meanings of model and translation were incongruent; yet their secondary uses apparently coalesced. In
Pauline literature, *mystērion* denoted the secrets of God
now revealed in Christ, and secrets known only to the
initiated, and in a formula such as *mystērion tês písteōs*
(I Ti. 3:9) simply 'faith'. But *mystērion* still retained
something of its pagan past, the mysteries, and its immediate Latin counterpart, *mysterium*, a borrowing of long
standing from Greek, might therefore have been unattrac-
tive as the label for the new acts of faith. However, in
the early Church the term *mystērion* concretized in the
direction of the 'sacramental' (Bornkamm 1942:832;
Mohrmann 1954:149, Braun 1962:437), thus opening possibilities for Latinization. Lat. *sacramentum*, on the other
hand, had been an expression of law in the classical language; it referred to an oath of allegiance, then to a
solemn obligation, and with this connotation the term
might have become applicable to some ritual of faith.
Sacramentum turned into the standard rendering of *mystērion*. But *sacramentum*, under the impact of its etymological root, *sacr-* 'holy', took on uses which went beyond
those of *mystērion* and evoked an association with holy
things, drawing the Latin term into a new linguistic
field. Thus holiness became the dominant feature of the
sacramentum, as against the notion of the unspeakable and
the secret, which was dominant in Grk. *mystērion*.

7. METAPHOR

    The metaphor shifts the meaning of a lexeme (or a
string of lexemes) from its usual linguistic field to
another, and thus represents an act of deviation: the
rules of contextual collocation have been violated. Now,
Weinrich (1976), in a most interesting and wide-ranging
essay, views the metaphor in the Western languages as a
characteristic feature of Western civilization, and even
defines the latter as *Bildgemeinschaft*, a community

sharing the metaphorical tradition; he thereby parallels
the hypothesis of the tradition of Western literary topoi,
splendidly proferred by Ernst Robert Curtius. Somewhere,
sometime, of course, the deviatory process of a metaphorization which by now has become a commonplace in innumer-
able realizations within the Western linguistic culture,
must have had its origin. In view of the paramount role
that Greek has played in the intellectual development of
this culture, it seems tempting to probe in that direction. Greek metaphor is a broad and often investigated
area. Therefore, we shall try to trace the tradition of
metaphorization from Greek through Latin into modern times
as exemplified by English, within the specific linguistic
field of rhetoric and literary criticism, as described in
Van Hook (1905). In individual instances it may be hard
to distinguish between a monogenetic and a polygenetic
origin; but we are simply trying to present the contours
of a tradition.

The metaphorizing level (*bildspendend* to Weinrich)
is the surface; the metaphorized (*bildempfangend*), the
underlying structure. The metaphorized field, in the following sample, is always some aspect of literary judge-
ment; the metaphorizing is taken from the every-day experience of man: nature/the human body/social status/arts
and crafts. We have selected examples in which the metaphor is still reasonably alive, i.e., we have avoided
learned borrowings, either from Greek to Latin, or from
Latin and French to English. The references are to Van
Hook.

(a) Nature, with reference to water, heat and cold, light
and darkness, weight and height, and flora. Gr. *katharós* lit.
'clean, clear', met. 'clear, lucid'/L. *purus*/E. *clear* (12): Gr.
tholoûsthai lit. 'get turbid', met. 'get muddy'/L. *lutulentus*
adj./E. *muddy* adj. (12); Gr. *reîn* lit. and met. 'flow'/L. *fluere*,
E. *flow*, with the adjectival set Gr. *eúrous*/L. *pulchre fluens*/
E. *flowing* (13); Gr. *thermós* lit. 'hot', met. 'vehement'/L.
calidus/E. *hot* (14); Gr. *psychrós* lit. 'cold', met. 'without
ardor, insipid'/L.*frigidus*/E. *cold* (14); Gr. *lamprós* lit.
'bright, shining', met. 'brilliant'/L. *splendidus*/E. *shining*
(15); Gr. *skoteinós* lit. 'dark', met. 'obscure in meaning, hard
to understand'/L. *obscurus*/E. *dark* (15); Gr. *embrithês* lit. and
met. 'weighty'/L. *gravis*/E. *weighty* (16); Gr. *hypsêlós* lit.
'high', met. 'lofty'/L. *sublimis*/E. *lofty* (16); Gr. *anthêrós*
lit. and met. 'flowery'/L. *floridus*/E. *flowery* (17).

(b) The human body, with reference to physique, looks, taste
sickness. Gr. *ischnós* lit. 'thin, lean', met. 'unadorned'/ L.
gracilis, exilis/E. *meagre* (19); Gr. *hadrós* lit. 'bulky, strong',
met. 'powerful'/L. *amplus*/E. *full, powerful* (19); Gr. *kállos* lit
and met. 'beauty'/L. *pulchritudo*/E. *beauty* (20); Gr. *rômê* lit.
'bodily strength', met. 'force'/L. *vis*/E. *force* (20); Gr. *xêrós*
lit. 'dry', in reference to bodily conditions 'withered', met.
'arid, austere'/L. *aridus, siccus*/E. *dry* (21); Gr. *pikrós* lit.
and met. 'pungent, bitter'/L. *amarus*/E. *bitter* (28); Gr. *oideîn*
lit. 'swell', met. 'be inflated, bombastic'/L. *turgere*/E. *swollen*

(35); Gr. *chōlós* lit. and met. 'limping, halting'/L. *claudus*/
E. *limping, halting* (21).

   (c) Social status. Gr. *dēmṓdēs* lit. and met. 'popular'/L.
vulgaris/E. *folksy* (27); Gr. *tapeinós* lit. and met. 'low'/L.
humilis/E. *low* (27); Gr. *ptōchós* lit. 'beggarly', met. 'poor'/
L. *inops*/E. *poor* (28); Gr. *ploúsios* lit. and met. 'rich'/L.
opulentus/E. *rich* (28).

   (d) Arts and crafts, with reference to harnessmaking, weaving
and embroidery, carpentry, metalworking, masonry. Gr. *achálinos*
lit. 'unbridled', met. 'unrestrained'/L. *infrenis*/E. *unbridled*
(25); Gr. *hyphaínein* lit. 'weave', met. 'compose'/L. *texere*/
E. *weave* (35); Gr. *syneírein* lit. and met. 'string together'/
L. *connectere*/E. *string together* (37); Gr. *leîos* lit. and met.
'smooth'/L. *levis*/E. *smooth*, with the verb Gr. *leaínein* lit.
'smooth', met. 'polish'/L. *polire*/E. *smooth* (38); Gr. *trachýs*
lit. and met. 'rough'/L. *asper*/E. *rough* (38); Gr. *sphyrḗlatos*
lit. 'wrought with the hammer', met. 'put in shape with intellectual effort'/L. *malleatus*/E. *hammered* (39); Gr. *hýlē* lit.
'timber for building, the stuff of which a thing is made', met.
'subject for a writing'/L. *materia*/E. *stuff* (41); Gr. *kanṓn* lit.
'mason's rule', met. 'standard'/L. *regula*/E. *yardstick* (41).

8. CONCLUSIONS

   We have outlined the Hellenization of Latin (essentially Vulgar Latin in late antiquity) as characteristic
of linguistic paideia, a non-inherited subcode cultivated
by the intelligentsia, the upper classes, and the profes-
sionals who built it into the indigenous system of their
language. The case history of the Greek impact on Vulgar
Latin reveals the contours of the four basic facets of
linguistic paideia: the media which typically channel
such linguistic features; systemic deviations within the
target language, which are represented by these features;
the frequent naturalization of such high-level features
in the standard language; and the element of universality
inherent in the entire process.
   (a) The channels. There are customary ways in which
the educated absorb a prestige language, whether a high
level of their own tongue or a fashionable foreign one.
We have isolated here five of such channels of external
influence: the literary text, which involves the learner
on all levels of training in letters (§ 3, above); translation, the impact of which implies in Bible translation,
the case under discussion, a chain from the translator to
the mediator to the listener (§ 4); symbiosis, the optimal
condition for linguistic transmission, welcomed most ea-
gerly, of course, by the upper strata (§ 5); special languages, whose transfer presupposes a professional acquaintance with practices and concepts easily varying from the
milieu of the source to that of the target (§ 6); and
metaphors, the constant stimulus to intellectual re-
creation (§ 7).
   (b) Deviations. The many features of the high-level
subcode which we have labeled paideia are likely to clash,

at least at their inception, with the inherited, "natural"
rules of a system as generally practiced. The examples
cited in the course of the discussion illustrate varied
and typical rule-violating innovations: The adverboid
ablative phrase based on *mente* with its synonyms (§ 3) has
been interpreted convincingly, because it adds the feature
of motivation to the concomitant verbal action, as a
Greek-induced innovative category of intellectual and educated foundation and connotation.—The periphrastic pattern *to be* + pres. part. (§ 4), common in late Greek,
coalesced with a Latin expression alike in form yet differing in function; and by drawing the Latin form into the
aspectual paradigm of the Greek contributed to a restructuring of the system of Latin verbal categories and established a new stylistic device of great significance.—
The influx of lexical borrowings (§ 5) is easily the most
obvious and the most concrete reflection of contacts with
a prestige language; and the more intensive the symbiosis
the more extensive is the borrowing. In the early stages,
in particular, the foreignisms are only slightly disguised
by phonological and morphological adaptation; thus they
keep their foreignness within the general lexicon and remain fashionable precisely because of their foreignness.—
The transformation of professional terms from Greek to Latin in a discipline as specialized as early Christian theology (§ 6) throws light on the innovative facet of the
process. Typically, the lexemes of source language and
target language are incongruent in part, and both have a
life of their own; therefore in the course of blending the
ingrained connotations of a term of the target language
may break through, thus deflecting the concept of the
source language into a new track.—The metaphor (§ 7) is
deviatory by definition: in the incipient stage of the
process, lexemes shift from their ordinary collocation to
an unexpected one, usually with an inherent loss of concreteness. If the metaphors are calqued after the model
of another language, as was apparently frequent with Greek
figures in rhetoric and literary criticism transferred to
Latin, the semantic deviation evolves as a typical feature of linguistic paideia.

    (c) Naturalization. We have contrasted naturalness
and paideia within a diachronic frame of reference: we
have termed inherited linguistic features natural as distinct from acquired ones, which filter in with the flux
of linguistic paideia. Clearly, the opposition is most
valid at the early stage when features stemming from
paideia are apt to be deviatory, representing so-called
exceptions. They may, of course, disappear altogether,
or they may be incorporated as part of the regular system. Thus, the quasi-autonomous and psychologically
loaded *mente* was mechanized into the adverbial suffix
-*mente* (§ 3).—The new periphrastic pattern, *to be* + pres.
part. (§ 4), restructured the aspectual system of Latin by
adding a weighty stylistic device, the isolation of a segment of the action; this was inherited by Romance, as in

Span. *estoy (canta)ndo*.—The mass of Hellenisms flooding
into Vulgar Latin (§ 5) represented, as often in such
cases, a status symbol of the period; many were just
briefly fashionable and went out of use; yet (to stay
within our Ravennate sample, a late echo of the Justinian
era) some of the borrowings caught on, "trickled down" and
remained alive in the dialects of the region, e.g. *ardica*
'narthex', *cereostatus* 'candelabrum', *platanum* 'vessel'.—
As to the transfer of special languages (§ 6), the tie between model and calque may weaken; in such a case the
equivalent of the target language develops its own conceptual offshoot, as shown by the constituent of 'holiness' in *sacramentum*, which replaced the 'mystery' of its
Greek antecedent, *mystērion*.—The tie between the Greek
foundation and our own practice as English speakers is in
our intuition least noticeable in the linguistic field of
the metaphor (§ 7): our English metaphors seem so natural
to us that we refuse to see in them anything but our own
creativity: a style is, say, *dry* because we feel a lack
of juiciness, and as speakers we are inclined to rebel
against an unbelievable past involving the chain from
Grk. *xērós* through Lat. *aridus* to our so obvious figure
of speech.

    (d) Universality. The typology of paideia, the *Bil-
dungserlebnis*, which we abstracted from the case history
of the Greek behind Latin, describes a linguistic event
many times repeated and more significant and powerful than
ever in our times. Paideia evolves as the universal subcode of the educated, and this subcode functions, on the
one hand, as a status symbol for the speaker and, on the
other hand, as the speech community's symbol of moderni-
zation. This sociolinguistic force of paideia has its
linguistic correlate: the features of the subcode, most
obviously in the early stage of their use, are often in-
congruous with the system of the target language.

    We have viewed the relation between the two linguistic
levels from varying angles: hierarchically, as code and
subcode; structurally, as rule and exception; diachronically, as inherited and acquired; and sociolinguistically,
as naturalness and paideia. Spitzer (1925:283) couches
what we call paideia in terms of attitude: he speculates
that "the speaker simply wants to take on a second nature,
that of the educated person."

REFERENCES

Andriotis, Nikolaos. 1974. *Lexikon der Archaismen in neugriech-
    ischen Dialekten*. (Österr. Akad. d. Wissensch., phil.-hist.
    Kl.: Schriften der Balkankommission, Linguistiche Abteilung,
    22). Wien.
Baldinger, Kurt, 1965. Art. *mens*. W.v. Wartburg, *Französisches
    etymologisches Wörterbuch*, VI:1, 708-9. Basel.
Bartoli, Matteo. 1925. *Introduzione alla Neolinguistica*.
    (Biblioteca dell'Archivum Romanicum, ser. II, vol. 12).
    Genève.

Battisti, Carlo. 1954. Art. *mente*. Battisti und Alessio, *Dizion-
    ario etimologico italiano*, 1950-57, IV:2425. Firenze.
Bonfante, Guiliano. 1960. Les rapports linguistiques entre la
    Grèce et l'Italie. *Hommages à Léon Herrmann*. (Collection
    Latomus, 44:171-82.) Bruxelles-Berchem.
Bornkamm, G. 1942. Art. *mystḗrion*. G. Kittel, *Theologisches
    Wörterbuch zum Neuen Testament*, IV:810-34. Stuttgart.
Braun, René. 1962. "Deus Christianorum": Recherches sur le vocab-
    ulaire doctrinal de Tertullien. (Publications de la Faculté des
    Lettres et Sciences Humaines d'Alger, 41.) Paris.
CGL = G. Loewe and G. Goetz, *Corpus glossariorum latinorum*, Leipzig
    and Berlin, 1888-1923.
Coseriu, Eugenio. 1971. Das Problem des griechischen Einflusses
    auf das Vulgärlatein. *Sprache und Geschichte:* Festschift für
    Harri Meier, 135-47. München.
Dietrich, Wolf. 1973a. *Der periphrastische Verbalaspekt in den
    romanischen Sprachen*. (Beihefte zur Zeitschrift für romanische
    Philologie, 140.) Tübingen.
——. 1973b. Der periphrastische Verbalaspekt im Griechischen und
    Lateinischen. *Glotta* 51:188-228.
Friedlander, Paul. 1943-44. The Greek behind Latin. *Classical
    Journal* 39:270-7.
Greenberg, Joseph H. 1978. Introduction. *Universals of human
    language*, ed. by Joseph H. Greenberg, I:1-5. Stanford, CA.
Gundolf, Friedrich. 1920. *Goethe*. Berlin. [The first edition
    1916]
Janssen, Hendrikus Hubertus. 1941. De kenmerken der Romeinsche
    dichtertaal. Cited after the Italian translation, Le caratter-
    istiche della lingua poetica romana. Lunelli 1974:67-130.
Kahane, Henry and Renée. 1970-76. Abendland und Byzanz: Sprache.
    Reallexikon der Byzantinistik, ed. by P. Wirth, I:345-640.
    Amsterdam.
——. 1978. Rev. of Dietrich 1973a. *Romance Philology* 31:644-8.
Koukoules, Phaidon. 1948-57. *Byzantinôn bíos kaì politismós*.
    6 vols. Athens.
Kriaras, Emmanuel. 1968. *Lexikò tês mesaiōnikês hellēnikês
    dēmódous grammateías*: 1100-1669. Thessalonike.
Kroll, Wilhelm. 1923. Rev. of McCartney 1920. *Glotta* 12:275.
——. 1924. Die Dichtersprache. Cited after the Italian transla-
    tion, La lingua poetica romana. Lunelli 1974:1-65.
Lampe, G.W.H. 1961. *A patristic Greek lexicon*. Oxford.
Lausberg, Heinrich. 1972. *Romanische Sprachwissenschaft*, III:
    Formenlehre. Berlin.
Lazard, Sylviane. 1976. De l'origine des hellénismes d'Agnello.
    Revue de linguistique romane 40:255-98.
Leumann, Manu. 1947. Die lateinische Dichtersprache. Cited after
    the Italian translation, La lingua poetica latina. Lunelli
    1974:131-78.
——; J. B. Hofmann; and Anton Szantyr. 1972. Allgemeiner Teil der
    lateinischen Grammatik. Appendix to *Lateinische Syntax und
    Stilistik* (Handbuch der Altertumswissenschaft II:2, 2). München.
Lunelli, Aldo. (ed.) 1974. *La lingua latina*. (Testi e manuali per
    l'insegnamento universitario del latino, 12.) Bologna.
Malkiel, Yakov. 1978. Derivational categories. *Universals of hu-
    man language*, ed. by J. H. Greenberg, III:125-49. Stanford, CA.

Marti, Heinrich. 1974. *Übersetzer der Augustin-Zeit*. (Studia et testimonia antiqua, 14.) München.

McCartney, Eugene S. 1920. Forerunners of the Romance adverbial suffix. *Classical Philology* 15:213-29.

MLatWb = *Mittellateinisches Wörterbuch bis zum ausgehenden 13. Jahrhundert*, O. Prinz (ed.) München, 1967.

Mohrmann, Christine. 1954. *Sacramentum* dans les plus anciens textes chrétiens. *Harvard Theological Review* 47:141-52.

Niermeyer, J. F. 1976. *Mediae latinitatis lexicon minus*. Leiden.

Pasquali, Giorgio. 1927. Rev. of Hofmann, *Lateinische Umgangs-sprache*. *Rivista di filologia e di istruzione classica*, n.s. 5:244-50.

Pisani, Vittore. 1974. *Indogermanisch und Europa*. München.

——. 1977. Tradizione e innovazione nella dinamica della inno-vazione linguistica. *Aspetti e momenti del rapporto passato-presente nella Storia e nella Cultura*, 127-40. (Istituto Lombardo di Scienze e Lettere.) Milano.

Reichenkron, Günter. 1965. *Historische Latein-Altromanische Grammatik*, I. Wiesbaden.

Schmitz, Victor A. 1965. *Gundolf: Eine Einführung in sein Werk*. Düsseldorf and München.

Shorey, Paul. 1910. A Greek analogue of the Romance adverb. *Classical Philology* 5:83-96.

Sophocles, E. A. 1870. *Greek lexicon of the Roman and Byzantine periods*. Boston.

Spitzer, Leo. 1925. Warum frz. *énormément* und warum romanisch *-mente? Zeitschrift für romanische Philologie* 45:281-8. [Reprinted in *Stilstudien* I:70-84. München, 1961.]

——. 1940. Rev. of H. Mihăescu, Despre începuturile sufixului romanic *-mente*. *Le Français Moderne* 8:189-91.

Studer, Basilius. 1971. Spätantike lateinische Übertragungen griechischer christlicher Texte und Themen. *Hermeneutik als Weg heutiger Wissenschaft*, ed. by V. Warnach, 179-95. (Salzburger Studien zur Philosophie, 9.) Salzburg and München.

Van Hook, Larue. 1905. *The metaphorical terminology of Greek rhetoric and literary criticism*. Dissertation, University of Chigago.

Vendryes, Joseph. 1950. *Le langage*. Paris.

Weinrich, Harald. 1976. Münze und Wort: Untersuchungen an einem Bildfeld. *Sprache in Texten*, 276-90. Stuttgart.

ALTERNATIVES TO THE CLASSIC DICHOTOMY FAMILY TREE/ WAVE THEORY? THE ROMANCE EVIDENCE

Yakov Malkiel

I

As has been often observed, certain metaphors widely used in humanities and social sciences contribute to the amenity of scholarly discourse and, in a way, also serve as useful shortcuts in communications among those happy few that have been properly initiated into a given specialty. On the negative side of the ledger stands the stark fact that such metaphors, and similes as well, have, as a rule, been hastily and inadequately defined and thus easily lend themselves to ambiguity or obfuscation. Abundant examples of such usage have been, over the years, contributed by almost every discipline; certain instances or trends of figurative formulae can be illustrated with several disciplines; and there has been no dearth of loan translations, especially from one Western language serving as a research tool into another. One readily thinks of such cases as *current* vs. *stagnancy*, *congealment* as against *thawing*, *blossoming* beside *flowering*, *withering* in rivalry with *waning* and *decay*, *awakening* alongside *dormancy*, *zenith* in contradiction to *nadir*, and many more. As a matter of fact, a special inquiry into this dangerously attractive vocabulary and phraseology is overdue.[1]

In glottodiachrony, there has been going on, for several centuries now, a good deal of thinking and discussion about the most effective genetic grouping of languages in families (sometimes referred to as stocks).[2] Given the age-old tradition of genealogical trees, or family trees (Ger. *Stammbäume*), institutionalized before any curiosity about languages had jelled, today's student of historical linguistics actually has to cope with two similes superimposed on each other: first, supposedly cognate languages and/or dialects arrayed in a system of relationships borrowed from the familiar pattern of human (or, by way of exception, animal) kinship ("pedigree"): hence "ancestral (or parent) language," "daughter languages," and the like; and second, this already complicated (and, as scholars now realize, controversial)

192

arrangement projected onto the model of a plant, with
roots; a trunk or a stem; limbs, branches, and sub-
branches; and the like. I might add that pioneers of the
generation of Bopp and Pott went much farther in their
whimsical or deliberately playful handling of such labels
than even the boldest advocate of a pictorially saturated
style would care to do at present, unhesitatingly calling
certain languages "fickle paramours" or "concubines," and
so forth.

It is common knowledge that slightly over a century
ago—to be specific, in 1872—Johannes Schmidt, a Berlin
Indo-Europeanist initially influenced by August Schleicher
but later able to stand on his own feet, proposed a counter model, usually referred to as the wave theory, because
in his favorite imagery he operated with innovations orig-
inating at one given spot of a major territory, then
spreading like the waves on a lake or pond produced by the
sharp impact of some object on the surface of the water.[3]
The wave theory, essentially identical with the diffusion-
ist projection made prominent by turn-of-the-century dialect geographers in Europe and by the Boas school of cultural anthropology in this country, is nowadays almost
obligatorily pitted against the older family-tree theory
in standard textbooks of linguistics, in introductions
into historical linguistics, and in the rapidly accumulating accounts of the history of linguistics.[4] This very
dichotomy has thus gradually become part and parcel of
Establishmentarian doctrine (and, incidentally, a well-
nigh predictable examination question). The most authoritative opinion, over the last half-century, has been that
the two models, family-tree and undulatory projection,
were about equally respectable, as regards their ranking.
This conciliatory view could easily be misinterpreted as
a veiled admission of a dangerous statement, if it were
indeed true that these two leading schools of thought were
mutually incompatible.[5] Not unexpectedly, the last few
decades have witnessed sporadic attempts to demonstrate
that the alleged polar opposition between the two was
something of an exaggeration if not a downright myth;
that, with a measure of flexibility, both approaches
could be brought to bear on linguistic material, as circumstances counseled: e.g. either on divergently shaped
slices of such material, or even on essentially the same
pile of material viewed at discrepant angles or at different stages of growth.[6] Aside from such soothing, me-
diatory voices one could hear others, which argued, e.g.,
that Schmidt, for all his originality, hardly came up with
a "creatio ex nihilo" in 1872. To cite just one possible
predecessor, who, as if to make any claims of his more
valid, at one time was likewise exposed to the teaching
of Schleicher in Jena, Hugo Schuchardt, through use of
effectively drawn, contrasting diagrams in Vol. I (1866)
of his revised and expanded Bonn doctoral dissertation,
Der Vokalismus des Vulgärlateins, anticipated the appeal
to wave-like diffusion as a defensible alternative to

the model of "ramifications" symbolic of organic
growth.[7]
     But while these and similarly slanted debates have
been going on, in various quarters, and while, in narrower
groups of experts, several schemes have been successively
proposed for the spatio-temporal classification of Romance
and Germanic languages,[8] certain relevant issues either
have not been raised at all or have not been tackled with
sufficient strength and, shall we say, articulateness,
which of course need not have bordered on stridency. Because, in analytical discourse, one constantly runs the
risk of becoming a prisoner of one's own metaphors and
similes, spokesmen for the family-tree allegory might have
obligingly enlightened their readers on the sort of configuration they had in mind for their branches and roots,
to say nothing of fruits and foliage. In the majority of
graphic representations that one is apt to come across
the branches evoked appear to have grown away not only
from the respective trunks, but also from one another, an
image of dispersal that strikingly dramatizes the forces
of disruption and divergence rather than those—equally
important on balance—of convergence and coalescence in
the evolution of languages. Moreover, one is left wondering whether such—not so marginal—processes as the
intertwining of branches at their far ends (or at some
intermediate points), or even their occasional concres-
cence and eventual merger could not have been graphically
suggested, with a spark of imagerial or pictorial imagination.
     Aside from this insufficient quota of attention re-
served for the limbs of a tree, as well as for its
branches, twigs, and offshoots, there remains the even
more vexing issue whether ramification and undulation (or
radiation) really exhaust the range of possibilities in
schematizing the proliferation of languages. The noted
Leipzig and Chicago scholar Walther von Wartburg fell
prey to the, I dare say, classic vision of a Romance
family sharply split into a Western and an Eastern branch,
a pattern clearly influenced by geographic considerations
of the kind which once presided over the thinking of tone-
setting Indo-Europeanists as well. However, for all his
learning, Wartburg did not succeed in squeezing into this
Procrustean bed Sardinia, that middle-sized Mediterranean
island whose most characteristic dialect communities, he
freely granted, sided now with the West, now with the
East.[9] Wartburg, a hard-working, competent practitioner
but a fairly weak, easily vulnerable theorist, apparently
was unaware of the serious implications of his virtual
admission of defeat. An apple, for instance, cannot be
cavalierly supposed to "jump" from one branch, or limb,
of an apple tree to another; to justify such leaps (i.e.
shifts of allegiance) one must first vindicate a radically
different model, providing for the possibility of such
erratic moves. Perhaps an atoll can drift with relative
ease from one island or archipelago to another, but I am

unprepared to press this issue, on account of my limited
familiarity with coral reefs.

Among European Romanists of the next generation (i.e.
those who were at their best and most active toward the
middle of this century) Heinrich Lausberg certainly deserves a hearing before our forum. Being most adept, at
that stage of his zigzagging development, at manipulating,
as an analyst, phonological data through early exposure to
Prague School concepts, Lausberg managed to eliminate the
heavy geographical mortgage inherited from Wartburg by
distinguishing, fundamentally, between an archaic and an
innovatory category of daughter language. Geographically,
most of the former, in the case of Romance, stretched to
the East, while the majority of the latter extended to the
West; but this tendential areal split was henceforth reduced to a mere concomitant, so that the discovery of a
sub-Pyrenean zone in which the intervocalic surds remained
unvoiced, counter to these consonants' "typically Western"
record, which was one of voicing and, here and there, subsequent spirantization (or even total loss, as frequently
in French), no longer needed to cause embarrassment.[10]
Scholars were thus relieved of any need to justify an exception from a postulated norm, facing as they did a mere
peculiarity or idiosyncrasy worthy, at most, of a brief
mention or crisp comment. This constituted, unquestion-
ably, a major step forward.

Even Lausberg's novel sophistication, however, left
certain vital things unexplained. In addition to being
distinctly stronger in the phonological domain than in
morpho-syntax or in the lexico-etymological realm,[11] the
former Münster scholar also acquired a far more finely
nuanced view of the Apennine than of, say, the Iberian
Peninsula. The interplay of these two proclivities, plus
the fact that, as a relative beginner, Lausberg, to a more
exclusive degree than his mentor Gerhard Rohlfs,[12] concentrated, with excellent results, on fieldwork in Southern
Italy, tended to make his influence discernibly stronger
among Italianists, particularly those concerned with the
vicissitudes of sounds and sound systems, than among
Hispanists and Occitanists.

It is, for this very reason of imbalance, from the
slightly neglected Spanish side that I intend to reopen
the discussion, placing at its center certain facts for
the most part known but, traditionally, swept under the
rug; and groping, almost simultaneously, for some theoretical model not yet sufficiently experimented with.

II

Among the prime classifiers of Romance languages, it
is customary to include, on the side of vowels, the given
tongue's acceptance of, as against its aloofness from, the
tendency to merge Lat. $\bar{e}$ and $\tilde{\imath}$, as well as Lat. $\bar{o}$ and $\breve{u}$;
and, on the side of the consonants, its attitude toward
voicing of intervocalic surds; i.e. toward the challenge

of shifting p to b, t to d, and, as a rule, except before
front vowels, c, q /k/ to g. A superadded salient peculiarity of Romance phonology is the by no means obvious fact
that the s, a rarely found voiceless sibilant between vowels in Classical Latin, as in *casa* 'cabin', *rosa* 'rose',
tended to join /p/, /t/, /k/ wherever these became subject
to voicing. One may argue, to be sure, that certain other
features of local sound developments could yield equally
valid dialect classifiers; the range of metaphony, the
presence (and, if so, specific configuration) of diphthongs, and the comportment of lengthened "geminate" consonants, not only occlusives, would qualify as examples
in point. For the sake of argument, however, one may, by
way of initial experiment, confine oneself to the two
above-mentioned features, with heightened but not exclusive attention to the state of affairs in the Iberian
Peninsula.

     As was first established in the opening years of this
century through fieldwork professionally conducted by
Paris-trained J. Saroïhandy, and as has been since con-
firmed by a string of investigations carried out by highly
competent, reliable observers,[13] ancestral /p/, /t/, /k/
have remained unvoiced in Upper Aragon, a mountainous,
once fairly isolated region, whose speech, typically for
such terrain, abounds in conspicuous peculiarities, many
of them, but by no means all, plain archaisms. One finds
a parallel situation to the north of the Pyrenees, in
Béarn.[14] While the raw, unequivocal facts have thus been
satisfactorily established, one can lean at first blush
toward interpreting them in one of several defensible
ways. (Some of these analyses may yet turn out to be
mutually compatible or complementary.)

     There will be those inclined to blame the Roman set-
lers' contacts with speakers of related or unrelated languages (varieties of Ibero-Basque?) who preceded them as
inhabitants of the Peninsula for such regional scotching
effect on a broad tendency which elsewhere in the Peninsula led to a powerful breakthrough. A variation on this
theme is the hypothesis that within the ranks of the vet-
erans of the legions assigned estates in the Peninsula
many, perhaps the majority to begin with, had come with
the command of a regionally differentiated (e.g. Oscanized)
Latin.

     Analysts temperamentally inclined to brush off as un-
realistic any such assumption of sub-, ad-, or super-
stratal influence will, foreseeably, gravitate toward an
internal (i.e. purely Romance), perhaps structurally
flavored solution. In so doing, however, they will face
another dilemma. Either they will incline toward classing
the widespread voicing as an innovation which evolved
spontaneously over the entire Peninsula except for certain
pockets of resistance (in that event the exact focal point
remains to be determined) in undeniable harmony but only
in loose actual contact with parallel developments in adjoining territories, e.g. in Southern France (again,

except for Béarn). The implication is that those "pockets," i.e. stretches of relatively inaccessible (e.g.
mountainous) territory, universally known as being pro-
tective of residual cultural features, have, in this particular case, once more (obligingly for today's historical
linguist) preserved the original state of affairs. In
case one adopts this belief, then such characteristic
Upper Aragonese forms as *mica* 'bit, crumb', from Lat.
mīca, and *dital* 'thimble', from Lat. *digitāle*, rather than
their familiar Castilian and Portuguese counterparts,
namely *miga* and *dedal*, may well—indeed, must—at some
remote point, minor details apart, have been dominant all
over the Peninsula. If this was so, then the widely upheld classification of Hispano-Romance as, having been
from the start, part of, or as a gradually emerging
"branch" of, Western Romance would have to be immediately
abandoned as grossly misleading.

Alternatively, scholars are free to operate with the
hypothesis of a Second Wave of Latinity that struck the
Peninsula from without, the tacit implication being that
the First Wave coincided with the original occupation of
the territory by the Romans, a slow, long-drawn-out process stretching from the Second Punic War until, approximately, the reign of Emperor Augustus. The First Wave
was rather sharply delimited by ancient historians, some
of them near-contemporaries of the events chronicled; the
Second Wave involved a sort of gradual, nearly impercep-
tible percolation, devoid of memorable, attention-catching
highlights. The focal point of the First Wave, which
basically corresponded to the later Republican period in
Roman history, was the city of Rome itself, the *urbs*, with
some allowance to be made for the presumed "Oscan accent,"
we recall, of the legionaries recruited in Southern Italy.
With the decline of Rome as the standard-setting social
and cultural center under the emperors—a downward curve
or spiral that picked up momentum from the third to the
fifth century—, it was Lugdunum, i.e. present-day Lyon,
located at the strategic confluence of the Rhône and the
Saône rivers, that emerged as the prime, if not the sole,
candidate for leadership in matters of norm, taste, and
decorum throughout Late Antiquity, as it was lived out by
the Romanized portion of the Empire, not least on account
of the city's enviably celebrated schools. As a matter
of fact, the entire area between Marseille (the ancient
Massilia) and Lyon shone forth as one of the few remaining
paragons of sophisticated Graeco-Roman civilization, with
a network of military, political, demographic, economic,
and socio-cultural routes spreading from Southern France,
including Toulouse, right into Spain; not exactly across
the Pyrenees (migrants, invaders, would-be settlers, and,
at a later date, crusaders knew how to by-pass the steep,
inhospitable mountain range) but to the west or the east
of them, as was dramatized in the early fifth century by
the itinerary of the Visigoths who, under pressure from
the Franks, poured from Southwestern Gaul into Hispania.

But long before the spectacular peak of the *Völkerwande-rung*, a kind of strong, persistent cultural infiltration of Spain by Lugdunum and the Narbonensis, with all sorts of novelties and innovations raying out, in the last analysis, from Lyon, may be plausibly supposed to have been in lively operation. Consequently, when we invoke the influx of early Gallicisms into preliterary or medieval Spanish and Portuguese, we must aim to distinguish between three successive processes: the cultural pressure of Southern Gaul on Hispania here referred to, culminating in the Visigothic episode; the Carolingian expansion, responsible for the crystallization of Catalan; and the distinctly later contacts associated with the Cluny Reform, the pilgrimages to Santiago, and the Crusades. It is this last-mentioned phase which is usually taken into account by students of a thin layer of loanwords, under the conventional rubric of Gallicisms and Provençalisms.[15] However, anyone concerned with phonology and grammar must take all three stages into consideration.

The Latinity filtering into those provinces of the crumbling Empire that came under the cultural sway of Southern Gaul, along the Toulouse-Lyon axis, starting with the decline of the pagan era, must have been in many respects significantly different from the older city dialect of Rome. Among other distinctive marks, it was doubtless completely free from any residue of an Oscan streak, for geographic and historical reasons alike (Osco-Umbrian having itself by then become extinct). On circumstantial evidence, it is, to say the least, plausible to hypothesize that the "Latinitas Lugdunensis" favored the voicing of /p/, /t/, /k/, and /s/ between vowels (or, on a somewhat smaller scale, between vowel and /r/, as in *patre, mātre, frātre*)—witness the unequivocal testimony of Gallo-Romance to this effect—and that the innovative fashion, after spilling over into Spain at chosen points of entry, overran certain regions, without, however, completely dislodging the older, deeply entrenched mode of pronunciation, where it could effectively ward off the invasion—primarily to the south of the Pyrenees, in the Navarro-Aragonese zone (which, we recall, was geophysically shielded), and, by way of last redoubt, in the Alto Aragón. If this reconstruction of events is accurate, then most of Spain, to the extent that it had been weaned away from allegiance to Basque (or conjectural kindred tongues), now began to show a rapidly dwindling pattern of relationship between Latin and vernacular voiceless obstruents reminiscent of South-Central Italian and Rumanian.

Playing on Wartburg's favorite terminology, or rather imagery, but in a way basically detrimental to the cause he himself championed, one can thus declare that Hispano-Romance, after having at the outset—ironically in view of its geographic position—been anything but "Western," now, at long last, indeed began to become partially "Westernized."

This idea, heterodox as it may sound at first, is
not, strictly, new; in the mid-twenties, it was broached
by Meyer-Lübke, who, however, with his staunch advocacy
of a "Südromania," ran into stiff resistance on the part
of Menéndez Pidal, a formidable opponent indeed, the
specific point at issue having been the apparently equiv-
ocal, hence controversial, representation of the consonants under study in Arabic script, within the context of
Mozarabic texts.[16] Over the last two decades, closer
examination of poetic texts from Southern Spain, traceable, for the most part, to the late tenth, eleventh, and
early twelfth centuries, as well as of telltale toponyms
scattered over the southern, especially the southeastern,
half—not only the southern tip—of the Peninsula and
over the adjacent islands have convinced seasoned and
many-sided specialists, such as the ranking explorer of
Valencian M. Sanchis Guarner, that voiced and voiceless
pronunciations may long have coexisted, presumably with
tendential social differentiation, over a hazily delimited
South-Central territory, but that Granada, Murcia,
Valencia, and far-off Mallorca, in the Balearic archipelago, for a while remained almost completely intact from
exposure to the oozing of sonantization (1961:291-342,
especially 319-21). In this country Robert A. Hall, in
the mid-seventies, resolutely sided with this opinion on,
at least, two occasions;[17] thirty years ago a more timid
Lausberg had still made a point to echo Menéndez Pidal's
skepticism.[18]
But surely, if our conjecture of two successive and,
in the end, conflicting waves is to hold water, there must
have been other vestiges, at least stray, random vestiges,
left, aside from the solid block of present-day Upper
Aragonese and adjoining Béarnais evidence and from the
debris of Mozarabic usage strewn over medieval Muslim
Spain. What about present-day Peninsular dialects, so
much more finely nuanced and differentiated than their,
by and large, leveled overseas counterparts and spoken in
a country suffering from no dearth of mountains and waste-
lands? With a measure of perseverance, pertinent dialectal illustrations from modern or recent sources can indeed
be cited, and I shall gladly produce and discuss at length
at least one such proof.
Included among my juvenilia is a rather extended study
of the vicissitudes of the Latin verb *quatere* 'to shake'
in Hispano-Romance, with constant side-glances at dialect
usage (1946:104-59). *Quatere* itself failed to survive,
having yielded ground to its iterative-intensive companion
form *quassāre*,[19] but such satellites of *quatere* (all of
them involving the allomorph *-cutere*) as *percutere* 'to
strike, hit, beat' (witness Eng. *percussion*), *recutere*
'to strike backwards, cause to rebound', and *succutere*
'to fling aloft, toss up' were all represented through
well-shaped descendants in older Spanish: *percodir*,
recodir, *sa-* or *secodir* (with vowel dissimilation). Later
the *-codir* segment, for reasons understandable in a verb,

was replaced by -*cudir*, while prefix change accounts for
the eventual transmutation of *recudir* into *acudir*, paralleled by an appropriate semantic adjustment.

There was one complication of which I was fully aware
thirty-five years ago, but which I could not at that
point satisfactorily explain away (1946:149-54, 158). In
addition to a profusion of dialectal forms in -*cudir* and
of a whole palette of prefixal and suffixal offshoots
therefrom: Ast. *recudir* 'to dry (by exuding moisture)',
Arag. (Huesca) *despercudir* 'to wash, cleanse', Leon.
(Cespedosa de Tormes) *espercudir* 'to remain clean', E.-
And., also Mex. and Cub. *empercudir* 'to sully' (laundry),
with the grotesque by-form *epencudir* 'to do a poor job
of washing', once more observed in Southern Spain, one
discovers, again and again, rival forms ending in -*cutir*,
e.g. *empercutir* in nearby Salamanca. Moreover, one de-
tects a semantically many-faceted form *cutir*, bare of any
prefix and, importantly, lacking any such counterpart as
cudir. It has been identified in Murcia and Asturias,
and Cervantes upon occasion had recourse to it four centuries ago. In Costa Rica, semantically unstable *cutir*
has been confused with *curtir* 'to tan'; in Ecuador, *tundir*
'to beat, spank' and *cutir* coalesced into *cutundir* 'to
beat up, whip, harass'.

Transparently, *cutir* cannot go back in a straight
line to *quatiō*, -*ere*; just how ancestral *qua-* has developed under varying accentual conditions is illustrated
with *quâtt(u)or* 'four' > *cuatro* and *quàdrāgíntā* 'forty'
> OSp. *quaraénta* > Mod. *cuarenta* vs. *quatt(u)órdeci(m)*
'fourteen' > OSp. *catorze*, Mod. *catorce*. *Cutir* therefore
must have cut loose from the -*cutere* group, either at the
time of the First Wave, or later, in a secluded area where
the regime of that wave was destined to continue for a
while. But why, one may ask at this juncture, was the *t*
preserved after the speakers had switched to the norm of
the Second Wave, replacing, as scholars incline to extrapolate, **capu* by *cabo* 'end, head' (from Lat. *caput*), **totu*
by *todo* 'whole' (from *tōtu*), etc.? A clear answer can,
for once, be provided: Wholesale substitutions of this
sort were impossible, because, in countless cases hazily
familiar to untutored speakers, a surd was shared by Wave
One and Wave Two; e.g., 'to bind' may well have been *atare*
(from Lat. *aptāre* 'to fit') and a 'cat' would equally well
have been *gato* (from Late Lat. *c-/g-attu*) for followers
of both norms, because in neither instance was an underlying intervocalic surd involved in the first place. So
speakers were necessarily wary in making the change; even
those eager to execute the leap from *capu* to *cabo* presumably hesitated to switch from *cutir* to **cudir*, a form
which, through a whim of circumstances, had failed to cut
loose from *per-cudir*, etc. and which they, consequently,
could not hear from the lips of more prestigious speakers.
But once *cutir* was tolerated beside *percudir* and the latter's numerous fellow satellites, compromise forms on the
order of *percutir* were apt at any moment to come into

existence; they may, but need not, be particularly old—
they are latently ever-present, as it were.

I have examined this arresting case under a microscopic lens, on account of its symptomatic importance (and, let
me confess, to poke fun at my own helplessness thirty-five
years ago). I understand that a major study of similar
(if not exactly analogous) instances of the widespread
preservation of surds at the level of Peninsular rustic
speech is in the making (or has been completed or is in
press); what is more, it is gratifying enough, from the
pen of a talented native investigator.[20]
I do not rule out the concomitancy of other factors
in regard to the ensemble of processes here examined, but
I question their comparative weight. Thus, Lat. intervocalic -d- is known to have disappeared from Galician-
Portuguese, in the company of -l- and -n-, for reasons
not easily traceable to the Latin starting point; and
its incipient, or just imminent, loss could have produced
a vacuum and, ultimately, "pulled" t in the direction of
d, with the further possibility that p and /k/, on account of their inherent affinity, may have joined it on
its way to voicing. In this manner the contrast between
Western /b/, /d/, /g/ and Eastern (Aragonese, Old
Valencian) /p/, /t/, /k/ in characteristic cognates might
have been somewhat reinforced.[21] However, an appeal to
the subsidiary agency of this force is not, strictly,
indispensable in any effort to account for the forms on
record.

The two conclusions to be drawn from this preliminary
balance sheet are, first, that Hispano-Romance, on the
strength of one important criterion, appears as an aggregate not of "Western," but of, preponderantly, "Westernized" Romance dialects. If we agree that a gradual transfer from one group to another is, at least, a strong possibility, then the family-tree projection, which resorts
for its symbolization to branches whose course obviously
cannot be reversed at some intermediate point, ceases to
be truly helpful. But its polar opposite, the unqualified wave theory, might preclude any orderly classification, too, and even erode the usefulness of such a concept as "Western(ized)." What emerges as a realistic
alternative to the classic dichotomy, at least for certain concrete historical situations, is a neatly drawn
two- or three-wave projection. In this revised diffusion-
ist view, each successive major wave may force us to re-
draw the grouping of languages or dialects within a
family.

III

On the second major problem here selected for scrutiny
there exists, once more, a slender corpus of writings.
Disappointingly, however, its specific repercussions in
Hispano-Romance, here viewed as crucial, have not yet been
recognized as a vital issue left in abeyance, yet worthy

of a fresh frontal attack. Moreover, the close connection, implied by the structure of this paper, between the
preceding question and the one now moving into the center
of attention has not, generally, been granted. We shall
thus, in certain respects, be treading virgin ground.

The problem now on our agenda has a bearing on the
Romance vicissitudes of Latin vowels. Specifically, it
concerns the tendency, in certain (in part neatly identifiable) varieties of provincial Latin, of two symmetri-
cally distributed ancestral pairs, namely *ĭ* and *ē*, as
well as *ŭ* and *ō*, to coalesce each, rather early, into a
single phoneme, namely *ę* and *ǫ*, respectively—with con-
trastable degrees of closure of the mouth significantly
replacing previous quantitative distinctions. Those familiar with the less widely studied Romance languages and
with dialect usage are aware of the fact that the parallelism between the two pairs is incomplete: In Rumanian,
above all, *ĭ* is indeed allowed to become *e* (thus, *vĭrĭde*
'green' changes to *verde*, and *dĭgĭtu* 'finger' to *deget*)
and, as a result, to merge with the outgrowth of parental
ē (thus, *mese* 'tables' [pl.] perpetuates *mēnsae*), unless
secondary metaphonic disturbances are superimposed on this
model, a shift which may in turn entail tertiary adjustments (as in the sg. *masă* 'table', via **measă*). Conversely, *ŭ* normally follows a different, less radical course,
by preserving its articulatory height, but losing in the
process its distinctive quantity, with the consequence
that *ŭ* and *ū* locally converge. Thus, *lup* 'wolf', from
lŭpu, and *urs* 'bear', from *ŭrsu*, join not only *mult*
'much', from *mŭltu*, but also *un* 'one', from *ūnu*, and *mut*
'dumb', from *mūtu*, over against, say, *nepot* 'nephew',
from *nepōt-e*, **-u*. (There is a handful of exceptions,
notably *toamnă* 'fall, autumn', from *autumna* [*aetās*], via
*tomnă, allowing us to guess that an incipient balancing
process was brusquely interrupted.) Typologically, East
Lucanian joins Rumanian in this salient feature of asymmetry;[22] this dialect was not so long ago discovered and
surveyed in the Southern Italian province of Basilicata,
wedged in between Calabria and Apulia.

Reverting now to the focus of events, without losing
sight of goings-on in this "Eastern" side arena, we may
briefly remind ourselves of the distressing fact that the
seemingly symmetric conflation of two of the front vowels
and two of the back vowels shared by the culturally most
prestigious Romance languages—Portuguese, Spanish, and
Catalan included—has long exerted such fascination in
the minds of comparativists that, in manual upon manual
of historical grammar, surely strung over more than one
century, these two vocalic mergers ended up by being projected onto the temporal (and hierarchical) level of an
ill-defined "Vulgar Latin," a term traditionally used
very loosely indeed, as Paul M. Lloyd not long ago pointedly reminded his European and American readers (1979:
110-22). Telling examples of *ĭ* either becoming *e* or at
least passing through that stage on its way, for instance,

toward some falling diphthong and of *ŭ* similarly either
ending up as *ǫ* or, transcending that stage, headed for,
let us say, *ou*, can be counted by the scores, if not by
the hundreds. As a matter of fact, on account of the
reputed triviality of this point, authors of historical
grammars rarely bother to toss off more than just two or
three examples of the norm, concentrating thenceforth on
the alleged exceptions.

Let me, for once, control this tradition of impulsive
stinginess and provide an assortment of illustrations
from Old Spanish, confining myself to the etymologically
most transparent and grammatically least complicated
cases, with consistent attention to the stressed syllable,
protected from erosion, regardless whether that syllable
was free or checked, and irrespective of the form classes
involved:

1. *atrevo* 'I dare' < *attrib(u)ō* 'I assign [to myself the
right]', *ceja* 'bow' < *cilia* (pl.) 'eyelids', *cerca* 'close' <
circā 'around', *cesta* '(large) basket' < *cista* 'basket', *dedo*
'finger' < *digitu*, *ella* 'she' < *illa* 'that one' (f.), *ende*
'thence' < *inde*, *essa* 'that there' (f.) < *ipsa* 'same, herself',
esta 'this here' (f.) < *ista*, *maestro* 'teacher, master' <
magistru, *menos* 'less' < *minus*, *meto* 'I put, place' < *mittō* 'I
send', *mermo* 'I diminish' < **minimō*, *pera* 'pear' < *pira* 'pears',
saeta 'arrow' < *sagitta*, *seco* 'dry' < *siccu*, *selva* 'forest' <
silva.

Contrastive examples, showing that *e* could be equally
well arrived at from *ē* (including *oe* and, less consistently, *ae*) as a starting point in classical usage, include such familiar pairs as:

arena 'sand' < *(h)arēna*, *césped* 'lawn' < *caespite* 'turf, sod'
fezes (Mod. *heces*) 'dregs, lees' < *faecēs*, *peso* 'weight' <
pē(n)su, *pena* 'pair, torment' < *poena* 'punishment', and *veno*
(later *vino*) 'he came' < *vēnit*.
2. *acoso* 'I pursue' < *cursō* 'I run hither and thither, to
and fro', *(en)sosso* 'tasteless' < *insulsu*, *fondo* 'bottom' <
fundu, *gordo* 'thick, fat' < *gurdu*, *lobo* 'wolf' < *lupu*, *lodo*
'dirt, mud' < *lutu*, *lomo* 'back, ridge, loin' < *lumbu*, *mondo*
'pure' < *mundu*, *olmo* 'elm tree' < *ulmu*, *os(s)o* 'bear' < *u(r)su*,
rompo 'I break' < *rumpō*, *sordo* 'deaf' < *surdu*, *tomo* 'I take' <
(aes)tumō 'I assess',[23] *tronco* 'trunk, log' < *truncu*.

Once more, it is easy to array complementary examples
tending to demonstrate that *o*, analogously placed in other
words of the same period and environment, is as smoothly
traceable to ancestral *ō*: *calor* 'warmth, heat' < *calōre*,
color 'hue' < *colōre*, *corono* 'crown' < *corōna* 'garland,
wreath', *fermoso* (Mod. *hermoso*) 'handsome, beautiful' <
fōrmōsu 'shapely', *forma* (Mod. *horma*) 'mold, shoe-tree'
< *fōrma* 'shape', *olla* 'pot' < *ōlla* (~*aula*), *roe* 'he (she,
it) gnaws < *rōdit*, *todo* 'all, whole, every' < *tōtu*.
Discoveries of this sort, which can be effortlessly

extended to other Hispano-Romance dialects and which, via
Catalan, lead to parallel findings in Old Provençal and
beyond, have convinced several generations of Romanists
that, at least so far as the concrete case of these four
vowels is concerned, Spanish and Portuguese pertain at
present, and have at all times pertained, to the core
group of Romance languages and dialects. Lausberg, in
his innovative mid-century manual,[24] carefully circumscribed the territory occupied by the aggregate of these
tone-setting languages, crediting to it a total of eight
major, median, or minor chunks: (1) all of Central Italy
(2) the northern edge of Southern Italy, (3) all of Northern Italy, (4) Dalmatia, (5) Istria, (6) the three islets
of Raeto-Romania, (7) all of Gallo-Romania, (8) all of
Hispano-Romania (short of the Basque zone, by implication), i.e. grosso modo, almost the entire extent of the
Iberian Peninsula, of France, of Continental Italy, and
adjacent areas to the North and to the East; plus fully
three quarters of Peninsular Italy. Even in strictly
spatial terms the territory thus staked out is extraordinarily impressive; add to its sheer size the further circumstance that such cultures as blossomed in Portugal,
Spain, Catalonia, Provence, Northern France, and Central
Italy produced some of the finest art and most exquisite
literature that medieval Europe exhibited, and you will
readily understand, without of course necessarily endorsing such heresy, how the trailblazers of Romance linguistics en bloc, and an embarrassingly high number of the
most competent among their followers, down to the mid-
twentieth century, could have virtually overlooked, or
cavalierly brushed off as marginal curiosities or scattered instances of unique complication, any such traces
of alternative developments as were apt to show up in
their data collections.[25]

Yet, upon more leisurely inspection, important and
copiously represented alternatives do turn out to exist,
on such a scale, indeed, that they no longer can be written off with impunity as inconsequential exceptions.
Mention has already been made of a predominantly asym-
metric Rumanian model (see note 22) and of a closely
allied East Lucanian type;[26] there is also on record a
separate, erratic Sicilian pattern, abounding in i's and
u's[27] and conceivably generated through protracted contacts with a Greek-speaking population in that island.
For our immediate purposes, this lateral aberrancy is
irrelevant, and I think we are free to disregard it. The
fourth and last pattern, however, which has of late been
referred to as "archaic," potentially constitutes very
fertile ground for the Hispanist. It is the contention
of this paper that this "archaic" system once struck root
in the Iberian Peninsula, a conjecture that chronologically makes sense, against the background of ancient histor-
iographic records; was later, to an appreciable extent,
dislodged from that territory by the very same invader
we already encountered on our previous foray into the

domain of consonantism, namely the Latinity of Lugdunum
and the nearby Narbonensis; but nevertheless has left a
wealth of relics in Standard Spanish and Portuguese, as
well as in the dialects—vestiges which, inexplicably,
have either been consistently neglected or, equally dangerous, been noticed, yet hastily moved out of the way,
through misinterpretation. But before thus plunging into
the state of affairs in ancient Spain, we shall be well
advised to examine, at least cursorily, what has already
been securely established about the manifestations of the
"archaic" vowel system in other corners of ROMANIA, where
discoveries to this effect have fallen short of triggering
heated controversy.

What encourages us to bracket together, under a single
formulaic label, developments observed at widely scattered
points of the far-flung Republic and, ultimately, Empire,
is the local speakers' recurrent disinclination to allow
$\breve{\imath}$ and $\bar{e}$, $\breve{u}$ and $\bar{o}$ to coalesce into a single unit-phoneme.
To be sure, mergers did occur in the "archaic" zones, in
step with the abolishment of distinctive vowel quantity;
but the partners on these occasions were $\bar{\imath}$ and $\bar{\imath}$, also $\bar{u}$
and $\breve{u}$, which converged through neutralization of vowel
length into phonemically indifferent i and u, respectively,
to the strict exclusion of e's and o's from this process
of regrouping.

Toward the end of the last century it was already
known that the evolution of Latin sounds had taken this
sharply profiled course in the better specimens of Sardinian dialect speech and within the thick Latin layer of
the Albanian lexicon; the latter feat we owe mainly to
the efforts of Gustav Meyer—witness that pioneering
Balkanologist's contribution to the original opening
volume of Gröber's *Grundriss* (1888:§19, as against §14).

The patterns of those earliest identifications prepared scholars to expect additional discoveries at geographically distant, rather than adjoining points; in
smaller, residual Romance language-and-culture areas
(typical "Rückzugsgebiete"); plus, not one whit less noteworthy, in lexical residues of Latin absorbed—via bilingual contexts—by other, sometimes distantly (if at
all) related languages which ultimately became dominant
as "superstrata" in territories once held by the Romans
and militarily, socially, or economically controlled by
them to astonishingly varying degrees.

As a rule, such prognosis has turned out to be essentially correct. The generally up-to-date handbooks by
Vidos and Lausberg, without fully coinciding in the bits
of information they convey, provide, in capsulized form,
the necessary briefing on what has been ascertained on
African Latinity, through intensive sifting of the Berber
vocabulary, and what, independently, has been established
about the Latin elements of Basque, as distinct from its
Spanish (i.e. Navarrese and Old Castilian) components,
which slowly percolated at discernibly later dates. But
this is not all. Lausberg is particularly authoritative

on a long badly neglected zone in Southern Italy, an old
"Sprachlandschaft" which straddles two modern provinces,
comprising portions of Southern Lucania (Basilicata) and
the adjacent northern rim of Calabria.[28] Vidos is, in-
evitably, less original on this score but, as if by com-
pensation, refers his readers to the debris of Latin in
the Serbocroat speech of the Adriatic island of Kres (It.
Cherso) and to the Latin inscriptions of Pannonia, neithe
source adduced by Lausberg. Both treat in approximately
equal detail—possibly because either depends on the pioneering research of M. L. Wagner—the evidence culled
from South Corsican as well as from three core dialects
of Sardinia. The two linguists happen to be in sharp
disagreement on the relevant finer nuances of the submerged circum-Adriatic Latinity of Istria and Dalmatia.[29]
Regrettably, neither makes the slightest allusion to the
highly pertinent Latin deposits in the British Isles,
obliquely observable through the prism of Cymric (Middle
Welsh), on which enlightening data have of late been assembled, and/or insightful analyses proffered, by Kenneth
Jackson and Harald Haarmann, in the Old World, as well
as—in briefer critical appraisals—by Madison S. Beeler
and Michael R. Dilts on this side of the Atlantic.[30] This
point-by-point comparison of the positions of just two
experts could, of course, be advantageously replaced by
a polyphonic chorus of voices, were fairly recent syntheses by C. Tagliavini, G. Devoto, and other Romanists
properly taken into account.[31]

Space is unavailable for a more than cursory illustration of the point here made—a sketch barely sufficien▸
to prepare us for a fairly searching inspection of the fa▸
more recalcitrant Hispanic material, which alone, in the
end, may enable us to draw any theoretical conclusions
worth pondering. To start almost simultaneously at two
ends of the line: Here is a sampling of the cross-
temporal equations established as early, I repeat, as
1888 by G. Meyer between Albanian and Latin, with special
reference to the preservation of ancestral $\ddot{u}$ as u, and
not by any chance as o (note his use of $ę$ in lieu of
presently favored $ë$):

> *bukę* 'bread' < *bucca*, lit. 'inflated cheek' [engaged in chew-
> ing], *funt* 'ground' < *fundu*, *furę* 'oven' < *furnu* (with gender
> change), *furkę* 'distaff, hay- or pitchfork' < *furca*, *gunę* 'over-
> coat' < Late Lat. *gunna* (a transparent borrowing), *gušt* 'August'
> < *(Au)gustu*, *gutę* 'gout' < *gutta* lit. 'drop', *kulm* 'ridge of a
> roof' < *culmen* ∿ *columen* (perhaps confused with *culmus* 'stalk,
> stem'), *k'un* 'wedge' < *cŭneu*, *kut* 'ell, yard' < *cubitu* lit.
> 'elbow', *l'uftę* 'struggle, fight' < *luctą*, *l'undrę* 'boat, ferry'
> < *lunter* (cf. Rum. *luntre*), *mušt* 'must, cider, juice' < *mustu*,
> *ngušt* 'narrow' < *angustu*, *pęlumbę* 'dove, pigeon' < *palumba*,
> *pl'ump* 'lead' < *plumbu*, *pus* 'well' < *puteu*, etc.[32]

Turning our attention next to recent statements on
British Latin, or Romano-Brittonic, to the extent that

its mosaic can be reconstructed from older and more modern Welsh, we find such testimonies to archaic modes of
pronunciation as *fide* 'faith' > *ffydd* [fɪð], *pice* 'pitch'
> [pʊg], [pɪg], and *plumbu* 'lead' > *plwm* [plʊm], all of
which takes us away, so far as the timbre of the stressed
back vowel is concerned, from the prototypes of Fr. *foi*,
poix, and *plomb*, even if we strive to pronounce these latter words in medieval fashion. Conversely, Welsh *plwm*
approximates with astonishing neatness Alb. *pl'ump* or
plump, obviously, again only with respect to the accented
vowel. Then, too, both languages, despite the respectable
distance between them whichever yardstick one cares to use
for measurement, are in substantial harmony as to the
separate treatment they mete out to ancestral *ō*: They
concur in dragging it away from *ŭ*. Thus, *corōna*, which
has already crossed our path, emerges in Welsh as *corun*
'top, crown of head' (i.e. with *u* rather than *w*), and in
Albanian, depending on the dialect chosen, as (metathe-
sized) *kunorë* or (Tosk) *kurorë* (i.e. with *o*, not *u*). Contrast this state of affairs with the tendential convergence of the two vowels in the French cognates: *plomb*
/plõ/, originally /plõ/, alongside *couronne* /kurɔn/,
originally /kurõnə/.

One·can easily obtain specimens very similar to those
just cited, in regard to the feature selected, by sifting
even small quantities of Sardinian records, or relevant
data extracted from any other of the peripheral residues
of Latin inventoried above and already investigated by
thoroughly dependable scholars.

The crucial question now, at long last, before us is:
What bearing do all these arresting discoveries, made
little by little in outlying lexical deposits of Latin,
conceivably have on research traditionally conducted in
Hispanic headquarters? The answer, couched in cautious
terms, is: The consequences for the classification of
Hispano-Romance within the confines of the larger family
may be unforeseeable, if only one is predisposed to cast
a fresh, uninhibited look at the evidence. Even if material extracted from such mines of information as Albanian
and Lucanian may seem farfetched, there surely is no ex-
cuse for neglecting the unequivocal testimony of Basque,
which coincides with those of the remote witnesses.

Consider the following fairly clear-cut instances of
vacillation between *o* and *u* as between Spanish and
Portuguese, or as between two consecutive phases of either
language, or else as between two members of the same
lexical family viewed in synchronic perspective:

OSp. *cobd-*, *cod-icia* ∿ *cudicia*, Ptg. *cobiça* 'greed', from
cupiditās, through substitution of the learned suffix *-icia*,
semilearned *-iça* < *-itia* (here cited on account of the loss of
cupidus 'longing, fond'); Sp. *corto*, Ptg. *curto* 'short' < *curtu*
(but Sp. Ptg. *cortar* 'to cut'); Sp. *corvo* beside *curvo* 'arched,
curved, bent', Ptg. *curvo* < *curvu* 'crooked'; OSp. *dubda* ∿ *dobda*
(dolda), Ptg. *dúvida* 'doubt', from *dubdar* (Mod. *dudar*), etc. <

dubitāre 'to doubt'; OSp. *duz/duce* beside *doz/doce*, Ptg. *doce* 'sweet' < *dulce*; OSp. *enxundia* (Mod. *enj-*), Ptg. *enxúndia* 'animal (e.g. pork, chicken) fat' < *axungia*; OSp. *fondo* (> Mod. *hondo*) 'deep', *fondo* (Old and Mod.) 'bottom, rear', Ptg. *fundo* 'deep' (adj.), 'bottom' (subst.) < *fundu* 'bottom, foundation' alongside *profundu* 'deep, vast'; Sp. *gola* 'gullet' beside *gula* 'gluttony' < *gula* 'throat, gullet', fig. 'gluttony' (Sp. *goloso* 'sweet-toothed', 'gourmand', cf. *golosina* 'delicacy, tidbit', contrasts with *guloso* 'gluttonous'; less frequent Ptg. *gola*, *gula* are likely to be Castilianisms, and only *guloso* is on record); Sp. *gusto*, Ptg. *gôsto* 'relish, enjoyment, pleasure' < *gustu* 'taste'; OSp. *os(s)o* (Mod. *oso*), OPtg. *usso* (Mod. *urso*) 'bear' < *ursu*; Sp. *plomo*, Ptg. *chumbo* 'lead' < *plumbu*; Sp. *punto*, Ptg. *ponto* 'point' < *punctu* 'small hole'; Sp. Ptg. *sombra* 'shade, shadow', but Sp. *umbrío* 'shady', *umbría* 'shady place', from *umbra* (+ *so-* < *sub-* 'under'? or through semantic polarization with *sol* 'sun'?); Sp. *sollozo*, Ptg. *soluço* 'I sob' < *singultiō* (via **sub-gluttiō*); Sp. *sordo*, Ptg. *surdo* 'deaf' < *surdu*; Sp. *suma*, Ptg. *so-*, *su-ma* 'sum' < *summa* (but Sp. *asomar*, Ptg. *assomar* 'to emerge, loom, begin to show', with the implication 'at the hilltop'); Sp. *tronco ~ trunco*, Ptg. *trunco* 'I cut off, lop' < *truncō*, but Sp. Ptg. *tronco* 'tree trunk, torso' < *truncu*, lit. 'maimed, mangled'.[33]

This is by no means a homogeneous group; in a few instances rival explanations are admissible, through appeal to learnèd transmission; in other cases multiple causation may be involved. (Certain exhibits of apparently similar distribution have been removed, where their irrelevance became immediately clear; thus Sp. *cost-a, -e, -o* vs. Ptg *cust-a* go back to a verb *costar/custar*, based on *cōnstāre* which is of no use in any discussion of Lat. *ŭ*, although the split illustrates one direction of subsequent spread of the wave-ring.[34]

If our broad-gauged conjecture of an overlay of native "archaic" *u* < *ŭ* by a foreign more "advanced" *o* < *ŭ* raying out from Southern France is at all tenable, then the next phase must have been one of intensive dialect mixture, a state of temporary "muddiness" of contour out of which a new order or equilibrium was bound to emerge. It is a fair assumption, the theoretical basis for which was tentatively laid in the mid-sixties,[35] that the norms presiding over such reordering of an imbroglio are very narrow, requiring at every step the analyst's close attention to fine details of each relevant word's individual biography, which may show a very zigzagging course. One can fully expect that, in such no doubt slow filtering process, small molecules of lexical units, held together by bonds of form and/or meaning, will tend to exhibit parallel directions of development; in such a context, non-phonological factors, e.g. formal polarization of semantic opposites, avoidance of bothersome homonymy, mutual attraction exercised by synonyms and near-synonyms, availability of potential substitutes, preexistence of Provençal-Hispanic cognates, are apt, in the aggregate,

to play a conspicuous role; while certain minor trends
of sound development, e.g. the suspected influence of
surrounding phonemes on the chosen feature, may indeed,
but need not, "make sense" in strictly phonological terms,
being often attributable to all sorts of associative phenomena so elusive as to appear to be bordering on chance.

Consider, by way of illustration, Sp. *cumbre* 'height,
peak, summit', which has traditionally—and, up to a certain point, cogently—been traced to ancestral *culmen*
(var. *colŭmen*) 'top, summit, ridge'.[36] This derivation
involves or implies a number of difficulties, of which
the preservation of *ŭ* as *u*, counter to what is commonly
held to be the local "law" or "rule," is merely one; the
most outstanding among the others are: (1) the loss of
medial preconsonantal *l* (in harmony with *alteru* 'the
other' > *otro* 'another', but against *altu* 'high, tall,
deep' > *alto*, which in turn is contradicted by *ot-ero*
'hillock, knoll'); and (2) the hypothesized survival of
a parental formation consisting of *-men* attached to a
consonantal root, the tendency having actually been to
eliminate such words (blurred derivatives) from living
speech (cf. the extinction of *ag-men* 'crowd, army, band',
ful-men 'lightning, thunderbolt', *seg-men* 'cutting,
shred', *tegmen* [beside *-ĭmen*, *-ŭmen*] 'cover', and of many
others).   Hardly a difficulty, but a peculiarity worth
watching, is the change of gender undergone by the supposed base: *culmen* was neuter and as such was normally
headed for the status of a masculine in any branch of
Romance, as is indeed true of its Portuguese product *cume*;
but Sp. *cumbre* has at all times been feminine.

How are these various threads to be most persuasively
connected?   To begin with, Portuguese also uses the oft-
cited word *gume* (m.) 'sharpness', which, despite the
rarity of the apheresis demanded by this genetic hypothesis, has unanimously been traced to *acūmen* 'sharpness',
i.e. to the abstract flanking the past-participial adj.
acūtus 'sharp'.   The apheresis must have postdated the
voicing of /k/.   Since 'sharpness' and 'height' do display an imagerial overlap (remember the contour of a broken cliff, a projecting rock, a mountain peak, and the
like), a gradual rapprochement between *acūmen* and *cŭlmen*
is conceivable.   It would help to explain the prevalence
of the *u* (the normal outcome almost everywhere of Lat.
ū), where speakers had a choice between the two back
vowels, and might account for the striking apheresis in
Ptg. *gume* alongside *agudo* 'sharp' (a discrepancy so far
left unexplained).   Moreover, the discovery of scattered
vestiges of *acūmen* in Gallo-Romance (inventoried in W.
von Wartburg's *FEW*) makes its extended survival in yet
other corners of Romance territory fairly plausible.
Could Sp. *cumbre* represent a blend of *acūmine* and
cŭlmine, one that has inherited its shape chiefly from
the former and its meaning from the latter?   Note the
contrast, as regards the crucial vowel and the nuclear
consonant cluster, to Sp. *colmo*, Leon. *cuelmo* 'thatch' <

cŭlmu 'stalk, stem, straw' (a reliable etymology, despite Corominas' capricious disagreement).

One can think of an alternative to this supposition of a straight lexical blend. *Cumbre* is not alone in having undergone the aforementioned gender switch: several Spanish words in *-(u)mbre* (also, secondarily and with less consistency, other items that end in *-ambre*, *-imbre*, and *-iembre*) are feminine, even though their Galician-Portuguese counterparts, less surprisingly, are masculine, while the Latin prototypes were neuter: *lumbre/lume* 'light, fire' and *legumbre/legume* 'vegetable, green' are examples in point, involving the ancestral segment *-ūmine*, *-ūmen*. The pressure of these and similar words (to whose category aforementioned *acūmen* also belongs) might have sufficed (1) to push speakers in the direction of *u* rather than *o*; (2) to prevail on them to drop the unstable *l*; and (3) to dangle before their mouths and ears the advantage of the feminine gender in this particular context.

Exiguous as the extant literature on this point of gender reshuffling happens to be,[37] enough has been established to justify the remark that the conflation on Spanish soil of the three suffixes (1) *-(t)ūdō*, *-inis*, (2) *-ūgō*, *-inis*, and (3) *-ūmen*, *-minis* (all three, significantly, lending services to derive now abstracts, now mass nouns from various classes of primitives) must have produced a real turmoil in the central section of the Peninsula, since (1) and (2) were feminine, while (3), confusingly, was neuter. The resulting blend, *-(ed)umbre*, turned out to be feminine; witness (1) *muchedumbre* 'multitude', (2) *herrumbre* 'iron rust', and (3) *legumbre*. Portuguese kept these three derivational suffixes apart (as *-idão*, orig. *-idõe*; *-ugem*; and *-ume*), assigning the masculine gender—the expected substitute—to the erstwhile neuter and leaving the other two in the original feminine gender slot.

Interestingly, there developed before long, presumably stimulated by the bold leap executed en bloc by the contingent of *-umbre* words, the broader tendency to relegate nearly all nouns in *-re* to the feminine in Spanish, whichever their specific antecedents. Hence the well-known, striking series *landre* 'small tumor' < *glāns*, *-ndis* (∿ **-inis*), *mugre* 'dirt, filth' < *mūcōre* 'mould, mustiness' (with stress shift), *podre* 'pus, corruption' (m. ∿ f.) < *pŭter*, *-tris* 'mouldering, decaying', *postre* (as in the phrase *a la postre* 'finally', which distinctly outranks *al postre*; but [m.] *postre* 'dessert') from *post* 'after(ward)', *sangre* 'blood' < *sanguine*, and *ubre* 'teat, udder' < (n.) *ūbere* 'breast that gives suck'. Here in Portuguese, assuming this language offers a pendant, that counterpart will tend to be masculine: witness *podre*, *sangue*, and *úb(e)re*. Now, some of the most sharply profiled words in this series combine the swing of the pendulum toward the feminine with a preference for the *u* vowel, as a rule traceable to *ū*. *Azufre* (originally *aç-*) 'brimstone', from Gr.-Lat. *sŭlphure*—conceivably

transmitted through Arabic—may initially have been ambigeneric, like OSp. *açúcar* 'sugar', *árvor(e)* > *árbol*
'tree', all of them ushered in by the definite article
el(l), indeterminate as to gender in words so structured
(cf. Mod. *el águila* 'the eagle', *el agua* 'the water').
Preponderantly, though far from mandatorily, the word-
final segment -*re*, in Spanish nouns, at a certain point
began to show a strong affinity with the feminine gender
and a marked compatibility with the stressed vowel *u*, so
that, even if *(a)cŭmine*, counter to probability, had been
unavailable on Spanish soil to tilt the vocalic nucleus
of *cŭlmine* toward a *u*, the combined pressure of *lumbre*,
legumbre, etc., as well as of *mugre* and *ubre*, might still
have sufficed to perform this service. (Perhaps not
coincidentally, *ŭtere* 'goatskin wine bag' was allowed to
retain its masculine gender when speakers opted in favor
of *odre*, to the exclusion of equally imaginable *ₓudre*.)

   In such a welter of confusion it was to be expected
that certain words containing *o* traceable to a source
other than *ŭ* (e.g. to *ō* or *au*), should eventually have
been dragged into the rivalry between *o* and *u* and, by way
of hypercorrection or factional overassertion, have been,
at first tentatively, and, then definitively, assigned to
the *u* camp. Thus, the familiar calendar unit *Octōbre*,
judging from the state of affairs in extra-Peninsular
languages, should have been reflected by vernacular formations containing stressed *o* rather than *u*, as was clearly not the case with OSp. *Ochubre* (> Mod. *Octubre*, partially Latinized), Ptg. *oit-*, *out-ubro*; also, the word
for 'knot', from *nōdu*, perfectly regular in Portuguese
(*nó*, contracted from earlier *noo*), might in Spanish, ideally, have been *ₓnodo* rather than *nudo*, var. *ñudo*. Cat.
uytubre and *nu* speak in unison with Spanish. Against the
voices of earlier scholars, who were willing to operate
with putative **Octobrius*, Menéndez Pidal, down to the
latest revision of his handbook of historical grammar
(1941:§2), appealed for an explanation of the aberrant
vowel to Oscan or Oscanized Latin, whose *ū* sometimes
matched Lat. *ō*, and cited even ancient epigraphic evidence
to this effect. Perhaps so; but, on balance, it appears
simpler to invoke false correction, a factor reinforced
in Proto- or Old Spanish by the affinity of -*re* with nuclear *u* in the case of *Ochubre*. As for *nudo*, it is safest
to start with the verb; *innōdāre* 'to knot' > *ₓeñ-*, *ₓañ-
odar* could easily have been influenced by *(d)esnu(d)ar*
'to bare, strip naked' despite the almost forbidding semantic distance—a factor apparently less than significant in this connection (witness the impact of *siega* 'he
mows' on *riega* 'he waters' and *pliega* 'he folds'; or that
of *acuesta* 'he lays down, puts to bed', from *accŏstat*,
on *cuesta* 'it costs', from *cō(n)stat*). It is in this
context that aforementioned Ptg. *custa* belatedly acquires
a limited measure of relevancy.

   Earlier generations of scholars were of course by no
means unaware of the wide margin of doubt attendant upon

the development of *ŭ* in Luso- and Hispano-Romance, but
insisted, or rather took it for granted, that the pattern
lŭpu > lobo represented the norm. The problem for the
spokesmen for that school of thought amounted, consequent
ly, to academic exercises in explaining away the unaccom-
modatingly numerous "exceptions," by grouping them, first
in classes and, next, wherever this was feasible, in subclasses. Since "exceptions," by definition, were embar-
rassing to historical linguists of neogrammatical persua-
sion, not a few counterexamples were simply omitted from
mention; in this respect Menéndez Pidal's *Cid* grammar,
with its goal of exhaustive treatment of all and any
aberrancies, stands in glorious isolation. Then again,
few practitioners of that approach were candid enough to
admit the self-contradictory pattern of the Peninsular
distribution of *ŭ*, now as *u* now as *o*, and the damaging
effect of this record of apparent inconsistency on the
strict doctrine unerlying their analyses; for sheer candor, Meyer-Lübke, as a comparatist, deserves recognition
(1890:§147).
     Typically, after having tacitly removed exotic words
(such as *açúcar* 'sugar' < Ar. *sukkar*) from further consideration, the authors of turn-of-the-century and even
later historical grammars would break down the residue of
rebellious cases into two categories:
     1. Learnèd (or partially learnèd) words, i.e. lexi-
cal items exhibiting *u* in lieu of *o* through deliberate
imitation of the given prototype. On this front, the
principal disadvantage has been the (continued) unavail-
ability of any theoretically underpinned study of early
"cultismos";
     2. Vernacular words influenced ("deflected") in
their growth by special, superadded phonic conditions.
These lend themselves, as a rule, to further bi- or tri-
furcation, even though opinions of experts on particulars
have not always coincided; what brackets the various consecutive pronouncements is the analysts' shared belief in
a sort of subjacent zigzag movement: Classical *ŭ* is assumed to have been, initially, transformed into /o/ in
these exceptional instances, as in all other words (bar-
ring, at most, a few isolated "cultismos" of early vintage), only to revert, with a later swing of the pendulum, to /u/, under pressure from this special—as it were
newly emergent—factor. Now, zigzag movements are known
to have indeed occurred, if only at rare intervals; thus,
the *s* of *casa* 'cabin' (a) was voiceless in Antiquity;
then (b) became voiced in Hispano-Romance and in some
other descendants of provincial Latin; and (c), more than
a millennium later, was devoiced in Spanish (though not
in Portuguese), and thus once more became /s/. While
such concatenations of events are not unparalleled, then,
their clustering on the scale visualized by most pioneers
of the *o* ∿ *u* controversy is unprecedented (and unrealis-
tic, to boot).
     One potential alternative has been lost sight of, in

the process, which acquires weight if one prefers to operate with the hypothesis of two successive and, in the
end, conflicting waves of Latinity. Assuming, as we have
done, that the first wave favored retention of *ŭ* as *u* and
the second its lowering to *o*—could it not be argued that
certain sharply silhouetted environments (hiatus, the
mediate or immediate vicinity of a palatal consonant, the
adjacency of some neatly profiled consonant cluster, and
the like) might have prevented the onrushing /o/ wave
from overrunning certain (structural) islands and islets
of resistance to innovation—a reconstruction that would,
as a result, eliminate any need for having recourse to a
zigzag movement?

     While representatives of the school of thought here
impugned have learned to distinguish sharply between the
two channels of transmission (1) and (2), most if not all
of them have overlooked the marginal possibility of interaction of forces. Thus, at first glance Sp. *dulce* 'sweet'
clashes so sharply with Ptg. *doce*, Fr. *doux* (f. *douce*),
It. *dolce*, etc., that one is tempted to declare it a form
artificially transplanted by Church Latin onto Spanish
soil. This procedure presupposes the lumping together of
all its distinctive features. Yet the example of Rum.
dulce, which in every single particular conforms to standard sound correspondences, and yet very much (except for
its assibilated *c* /č/) sounds and even looks like its
Latin model, should caution us against hasty conclusions.
The *u* of the Spanish congener could, after all, have been
imported by the first ("archaic") wave; the preservation
of *l* before consonant in a primary cluster, while avowedly
erratic, is far from unprecedented; finally, the medieval
record discloses such MS variants as *duc(e)*, *doc(e)*, e.g.
in Juan Ruiz. One could extrapolate from this array of
circumstances a more delicately nuanced biography of ancestral *dŭlce* in early Spanish. The dispersal of variants is proof that *duç(e)*, *doc(e)*, and perhaps even
dulc(e) could very well have sprung into existence without
much assistance from Church Latin. Nevertheless, the
undeniable fact that, wherever the speech community had
an option (e.g. in the choice of the stressed vowel; in
the salvaging, as against omission, of /l/ before the
sibilant; and, above all, in the restoration of the final
vowel—note the striking contrast to *hoz* 'sickle' < *falce*
and to *haz* 'sheaf' < *fasce*), the feature preexistent in
the Latin prototype was consistently preferred—makes it
highly probable that the growing influence of that model
interfered, to some extent, with the pattern of spontaneous, uninhibited growth observable elsewhere.[38]

     Let us now see, by means of quick spot checks, how
earlier authorities, over a period of slightly more than
eighty years (1888-1969), have judged the issue of learnèd
transmission of *ŭ* as *u* rather than *o*; for the sake of
fairness, appeal will be made, in chronological order,
to spokesmen for German, Austrian, German Swiss, Spanish,
and North American scholarship.

1. G. Baist (1888:§23) peremptorily declared *crudo* 'raw'
   and *ludo* 'game' learnèd, on the strength of the preservation of -*d*-; then argued that *nōdu* 'knot', after
   the loss of its central pillar (witness Ptg. *nó*), had
   the voiced dental restored through learnèd pressure,
   and in the process coincidentally adopted the vowel
   of *crudo* and *ludo*. (In crïticism it suffices to remark that the two Peninsular languages steered dissimilar courses with respect to Lat. -*d*-; that *crúo*
   and *crudo* coexisted in Old Spanish; and that, judging
   from its record, *ludo*, in lieu of *juego* 'game play',
   indeed was a "cultismo," but certainly neither *crudo*
   nor *nudo*.)
2. A still young W. Meyer-Lübke (1890:§147) decreed that
   Sp. (also Ptg.) *cruz, pulpa, surco* (Ptg. *sulco*), *yugo,*
   and *bulto* owed their deviation from the straight path
   to their status as Latinisms. Anticipating doubts as
   to how words pertaining to the humble rural vocabulary
   could possibly qualify for such a lofty status, he
   remarked parenthetically that the genuinely "popular"
   word for 'furrow' in Portuguese was not *sulco*, but
   rega (he supplied no such vernacular equivalent for
   Spanish); similarly, he felt, Ptg. *canga* 'yoke for
   oxen' represented the vernacular counterpart of *yugo*.
   (This statement contains a few glaring errors, in
   part factual; Ptg. *rega*—far more commonly *rego*—
   designates an 'irrigation ditch' rather than a 'furrow'; Ptg. *jugo* is used as a term of rural carpentry,
   in addition to denoting a 'yoke', and thus cannot be
   cavalierly written off; Sp. *pulpa* 'pulp', on record
   since 1400, is learnèd for Meyer-Lübke and semilearnèd
   for Corominas [1967:482a] but its interpretation as
   vernacular could equally well be defended; does not
   the sheer spelling of *bulto*, in preference to *vulto*,
   separate it from the contingent of straight "cultismos"? But over against such slips, note Meyer-Lübke's
   mastery in bracketing *coñusco* 'with us' with *conmigo*
   'with me', and his commendable candor in admitting
   his inability to account for Sp. *nunca* 'never' and
   junco 'reed' beside *tronco* 'trunk'; for Sp. *cumbre/*
   Ptg. *cume*—where he hesitatingly suspects the compli-
   city of the -*l*- [see above and below]; for the un-
   bridgeable gap separating Ptg. *chumbo* from Sp. *plomo*
   'lead' and from Ptg. *lombo* 'animal', 'back, loin' as
   well. Also included in this penumbra are Ptg. *curto,*
   curvo, custa, surdo, urso [as against *tordo* 'thrush',
   shared by both languages, incidentally; and as against
   Sp. *oso*]; Sp. *duda* 'doubt', if not Ptg. *dúvida*; and
   Sp. *nudo* 'knot'.)
3. R. Menéndez Pidal, in his first pronouncement on
   phonology (1904:§14.1, n.1), drew a sharp dividing
   line between (α) learnèd *púrpura* 'purple', *número*
   'number', *mundo, cruz, bul(d)a* 'bull', *lucro* 'gain,
   profit' and (β) vernacular *pórpola, nombre* 'noun',
   mondo 'clean', *bolla* 'tax on manufacture of playing

cards', and *logro* 'attainment, gain', 'usury'. (The
reader wishes he were told more about the contrasting
ambits of such authentic doublets as *púrpura* and
pórpola, *lucro* and *logro*; mention of *nombre*—unlike
the situation in French—involves a downright mistake,
since the Spanish noun is descended from *nōmine* rather
than from *numeru*.)

4. The same scholar, acting a few years later as an ex-
egete of the *Cid* epic (1908:147), reiterated his
previous comment on *cruz* and *mundo*, but added that
mondo, in Old Spanish, served not only as a qualifier
('clean') but also, intermittently, as a designation
of 'world' (in imitation, one is tempted to ask, of
an Old French model? Cf. also It. *mondo*).

5. A. Zauner, in his revised grammar of Old Spanish
(1921:§10), declared *cruz* and *mundo* Latinisms, con-
fessing his inability (despite Meyer-Lübke's helpful
hint dropped over thirty years before!) to cope with
coñusco 'with us' and *convusco* 'with you'.

6. J. Huber, another student of Meyer-Lübke's, but one
of somewhat later vintage, gratuitously complicated
matters (1933:§95, n.2) by discriminating between
"ecclesiastic terms" (including *cruz* and *culpa* 'fault,
guilt') and "book terms" (e.g. *mundo* and *segundo* 'second') in Old Portuguese. This last-mentioned remark
certainly should have entailed a brief elaboration.

7. With Edwin B. Williams (§1938:§§6, 38.1B) not only
another Lusophile, but also a representative of the
tradition of American research entered the arena. He
avowedly lumped together into a single pile all such
words as seemed to him to testify in favor of learnèd
or partially learnèd transmission: *cruz*, *culpa*,
curto, *curvo*, *fundo* (adj. and noun, one supposes),
furto'theft', *mundo*, *segundo*, *sulco*, *surdo*, plus OPtg.
usso 'bear' > Mod. *urso*. In this list only the inclusion of the progeny of *fŭrtum* is innovative; but
note that in Classical Latin *fūr* 'thief' (and its
subfamily) clashed with *fŭrtum*, the way *nīvit* 'it is
snowing' competed with *nix*, *-vis* 'snow'. Spanish
hurto, of course, followed a parallel trajectory.
More important than the enrichment of the inventory,
however, was Williams' decision to cite the minority
view of two fellow scholars who were willing to reckon
with the preservation of vestiges of parental *Ŭ* as
u, even if he, Williams, did not see fit to endorse
their opinion: the American pioneer Edwin H. Tuttle,
plus P. Fouché (a point expatiated upon below).

8. Finally, H. Lausberg (1969:§183) reverted, somewhat
anticlimactically, to a view championed long before
his time: He declared Sp. Ptg. *cruz*, Sp. *dulce*, and
Ptg. *surdo* "Buchwörter"—as if a word for 'deaf'
could have been drawn so easily from that category.
Unwittingly, by aligning *cruz* with its cognates transmitted, upon his own admission, through vernacular
channels—Sard. *rughe*, Rum. *cruce*, OProv. *crotz*, Fr.

croix, Surs. *crusch*, It. *croce*, Vegl. [i.e. N.-Dalm.]
kr̆auk—he dramatized the isolation into which his
avenue of approach, one ventures to think gratuitously, had pushed Hisp. *cruz*.

To round out this phase of the discussion: What argument forces scholars to drive a wedge between the Luso-
Hispanic and the general Romance transmission of *cr̆uce*?
In the related case of *lŭce* 'light' (Class. *lūx*, *lūcis*),
there simply are no internal criteria—phonological, morphological, or semantic—for distinguishing between word-
of-mouth and learnèd channels of transmission, as regards
Sp. Ptg. *luz* and Tusc. *luce*, even though fragments of the
external record of the word (e.g. date and place of appearance, genres of the relevant texts, bits of biographic
information on the authors involved, and the like) may
swing the pendulum of probabilistic analysis one way or
the other. With respect to *cruz*, the single internal criterion so far adduced has been, precisely, *ŭ* > *u*. But once
scholars can be persuaded, on the basis of their experience with *hurto*, *surco*, *surdo*, and the like, to accept
ŭ > *u* as a residual reflex of the archaic vowel system in
the Peninsula ("First Wave") the last barrier to joint
classification of *cruz*, *croix*, *croce*, etc. will fall.
    From these counterproposals it must not be inferred
that Hisp. *u* traceable to *ŭ* should under no circumstances
be charged to a Latinizing tendency: *diluvio* 'deluge'
and *estudio* 'study', e.g., to cite the two key formations
alleged by P. Fouché (1929:16), display sufficient independent phonic and semantic features to allow the observer
to declare them "cultismos." One simply ought to be
extra-cautious in classifying a given word as a Latinism
on the sole grounds of its exhibiting such a seemingly
erratic vowel correspondence as *u* < *ŭ*.
    On the emergence of *u* in the vernacular as a repre-
sentative of parental *u* for "non-cultural reasons," there
exists a dense network of opinions, only a few of which
can, almost randomly, be selected for our survey of earlier pronouncements. It will be remembered, from our
preliminary statement, that a strong majority of scholars
has opted, over the years, for the assumption of a zigzag
movement: *ŭ* > *ǫ* > *u*, though there has been no consensus
on certain details. The principal spokesman for this
dominant school of thought was, indisputably, for many
decades, Menéndez Pidal, whose ceaseless concern with
this problem can be followed by observing the constant
revisions made in the successive editions of the *Manuel
de gramática*. Along this meandering path, he remained
convinced that Lat. *ŭ* and *ō* had become firmly and inex-
tricably amalgamated into *ǫ* at the Vulgar Latin stage, so
that, wherever the Hispanic record showed vernacular *u*
for expected *o*, he endeavored to find a reason for the
deviation (a hypothesis which, on top of other obvious
disadvantages, also involved the given word's embarras-
sing return to its starting point in Classical Latin).

In his *Cid* grammar (1908:147-9) Menéndez Pidal saw
the problem of "*u* in lieu of *o*" dissolve into a mosaic of
individual lexical issues: an inflectional pattern explained *conuvo* 'he learned' from *conocer*; a suffix change
accounted for *rancura* instead of *rancor*; pressure of the
semantic opposite *suso* 'upward' justified the rise of *yuso*
'downward' beside etymologically more "correct," if
sparsely documented, *yoso* (a split with counterparts in
Gallo-Romance); an innovation at the level of Vulgar
Latin had transmuted *ōstium* 'exit' into **ūstium* (hence
OSp. *uço*); Portuguese and Catalan congeners with *-u-*
flank OSp. *nunquas* 'never', while Old French and Old
Provençal here opted for *-o-*. The author expressly admits
his inability to justify *dubda* 'doubt' beside infrequent
dobda, dolda, and documents the wavering *connusco* ∿
connosco 'with us', *convusco* ∿ *convosco* 'with you' leaving
it, however, unexplained. The only phonological conditioning factors that he recognized at this stage of his
growth are environmental: (1) Before a palatal consonant
traceable in part to /k/, /g/, or /l/ *u* was favored over
o, hence OSp. *conducho* 'supplied, provisions' < *conductu*,
puño 'fist' < *pugnu* [a graphy which modern Latinists, however, would tend to interpret as /pǔŋnu/], *uña* 'nail' <
ungula '(little) nail'; (2) *l* before consonants [whether
preserved or becoming submerged in the process] also favors the return to *u*, witness *azufre*, *buitre* 'vulture' <
vol-, vulture, cumbre, and *dulce* [the last item is thus
separated, by implication, from the contingent of Latin-
isms].

From these, all told, modest beginnings Menéndez Pidal
advanced very far by the time he revised his handbook for
the last time (1941:§14.2). He attributed the lion's
share of changes of **ǫ* > *u*, including those involving *ǫ*
< *ǔ* and thus, strictly, subject to the alternative inter-
pretation of retention of *u*, to metaphony (his own term
for this process was "inflexión"), whose agency, real or
reputed, had meanwhile become dramatized by M. Křepinský's
dissertation and the comments V. García de Diego had attached to its translation (1923).

Using his newly devised scheme of the "four consecutive yods," Menendez Pidal now argued that, of the consonants following upon the critical vowel (*ǫ*), (1) *ç* and
z lacked the power to raise it to *u*, hence *pozo* 'well'
< *pǔteu*; (2) *n*, to the extent that it reflected older
/nj/, did raise it, hence *cuña* [∿ *cuño*] 'wedge' < *cǔneu*,
puño [see above], and the suffix *-uño*, as against *otoño*
< *autumnu*; (3) *y* or *i*, to the extent that they perpetuated
/j/ wholly or in part, showed inconsistency, witness especially *rubio* 'blond' ∿ (dial.) *ruyo* (toponyms in Soria,
Burgos, Ávila) ∿ *royo* (toponyms in Castile, Aragon, Andalusia) < *rǔbeu* 'reddish'—there is a thin connecting line
from here to the manifestations or metaphony in conjugation (*huyo* 'I flee' < *fǔgiō*); and (4) *ch* /č/, whether
from *-ct-* or *-ult-*, on an overwhelming scale converted *ǫ*
into *u*: *aguaducho* 'aqueduct' < *aqua(e)dǔctu, lucha*

'struggle' < lŭcta, trucha 'trout' < trŭcta; escucho
[OSp. ascucho] < 'I listen' < a(u)scŭltō, mucho 'much,
very' < multu. As a sort of unaccountable residue
Menéndez Pidal listed cases like cumbre < cŭlmine, empujo
'push' < impŭlsu, azufre < sŭlphure vs. (en)soso 'tasteless' < insŭlsu; and poso 'sediment' < pŭlsu. After a
long excursus on the vicissitudes of the diphthong oi >
ue, the author briefly reverted to the ǫ > u issue at the
very end of the far too long paragraph, citing examples
of raising caused by -io < -īdu, as in dial. rucio 'dew'
< rōscidu, turbio [OSp. turvio] 'muddy, troubled, con-
fused' < tŭrbidu, all of them involving a Latin vowel
secondarily transformed into a Romance semiconsonant, as
a result of syllabic contraction.

Many Hispanists have expressed ideas similar to those
launched by Menéndez Pidal; there would be little point
in itemizing minor variations.[39] However, an assortment
of major divergences invites a short digest.

The original version of Baist's grammatical sketch
(1888:§23), which antedates Menéndez Pidal's earliest
gropings by a wide margin, may appropriately lead off this
survey. Baist assumed that ǫ changed to u in hiatus,
citing suyo 'his, hers, its, theirs' and tuyo 'thy,
thine', from suu, tuu, and charging the intercalation of
the /j/ glide to the influence of cuyo 'whose' < cūiu(s).
He distinguished carefully between the different effects
of ñ₁ (< gn, /nj/) and ñ₂ (< nn, mn), and in this framework effectively contrasted cuño 'wedge' < cŭneu with
coño 'cunt' < cŭnnu, without capitalizing on the possible
desirability, for speakers, to keep apart as neatly as
possible a neutral word and one struck by sexual taboo;
he segregated into a separate category such items as punto
'point' < pŭnctu, junto 'joint' < iŭnctu, unto 'ointed'
< ŭnctu, preguntar 'to ask' (without here giving away his
etymological credo), and nunca 'never' < numqua(m), recognizing throughout the agency of the same sound law: ǫ
> u before -nt- (nct) that is observable in Italian;
finally, he maintained that a preceding /j/ acted similarly to a following /j/, in words like yugo 'joke', junco
'reed' (from iŭgu, iŭncu)—an idea taken up, half a century later, by E. B. Williams, this time in reference to
Portuguese (1938:§38, l.B.), with special application to
chumbo 'I lead' < plumbu and justo 'just, fair' < iŭstu
(this argument, however, collapses under its own weight,
since Latinists now interpret the last-cited word as
iūstus; see Ernout and Meillet's authoritative dictionary,
s.v. iūs [1959-60:329b]).

Singularly unhelpful was A. Zauner's approach on
several occasions; where the going was difficult, he in-
vented Latin prototypes to fit them into his pigeonholes,
dreaming up *gūstus 'taste' in lieu of gŭstus (1900:47);
or expressed himself in an arcane, ambiguous way to gloss
over complications—e.g. apropos conducho (1921:§13.4).

J. D. M. Ford (1911:xvii-xix), like Baist, reckoned
with the possible effect on the vowel either of the

preceding or of the following consonant; he specifically
excluded from the range of the latter influences *cl* [i.e.
c'l-], *lĭ*, and *tĭ*—a gambit which allowed him to reconcile the word-final segment *-ucho* with the suffix *-ojo* <
-uc'lu. Ford, a staunch neogrammarian, was quite explicit
in adhering to the zigzag schema in most instances; e.g.,
his trajectory for the line *fŭgiō* 'I flee' > Mod. Sp. *huyo*
included, as the intermediate stage, V. Lat. **foyo*; similarly, he theorized that *pŭnctu*, to reach the modern form
punto, had to pass through the intermediate phase **po̧nto*
(here he correctly observed that ñ before the dental was
depalatalized); also, *tŭrbidu*, he argued, could not have
reached the present-day stage of *turbio* without first becoming **torbi̧o* (a more accurate notation might have been
*to̧rvi̧o). In a few cases, however, Ford, for some un-
stated reason, bypassed the *o* stage; thus, he allowed
buitre to have evolved from *vŭltŭre* via **vultre*; intercalated **trui̧ta*, rather than **tro̧i̧ta*, between *trŭcta* and
trucha; etc. The resulting confusion could not have been
worse, exposing the absurdity of the "zigzag theory" if
carried to an extreme.

     During the long period of ascendancy of comparative
"Romanistik" and of the Madrid School of Hispanic philology, it was a foregone conclusion that, minor variations
of opinion apart, the "zigzag theory" represented a perfectly safe reconstruction of events. What contributed
most to its solid entrenchment was the fact that, commonsensical as an (almost intuitive) opposition to it would
have been, and effective as sharp disagreement with it
might have been if persuasively presented, the few dis-
senting voices came from relative outsiders—maverick
scholars removed from the mainstream of advances and
singularly awkward, in addition to being unauthoritative,
in stating their dissent.

     The first outspoken dissenter was Edwin H. Tuttle, at
that time connected with Yale who, in a crisply worded
note on the Romanic vowel system (1914:347-53), after
laying down his principle of visualizing three "periods"
by linking them to languages and territories ("Sardic,"
"Rumanian," and a combination of Italian with Western
Romance), categorically declared: "It is commonly but
wrongly held that Italian [i.e. Tuscan] and Western Romanic represent the third-period vowel-system only. They
show many traces of earlier conditions, and their history
cannot be understood if we ignore this fact. The evidence
of Sardic and Rumanian is not isolated: in the other
Romance languages palatal influence often formed close *i*
from *ĭ*, and close *u* directly from *ŭ*." Read as a program-
matic statement, these words have a promising enough ring.
Unfortunately, the flaws in the execution of this self-
imposed program turned out to be overwhelming. Even if
one discounts numerous eccentricities of terminology and
idiosyncrasies of phonetic notation, the very model with
which Tuttle elected to operate seems bizarre in retrospect. Demographic shifts and the power of cultural

(including glottal) diffusion were wholly absent from his
schema, so that, when he assigned Ptg. *cegonha* 'stork' <
cicōnea to the "third period," but *cunha* 'wedge' < **cŭnea*
[in lieu of *cŭneu* 'corner'] and *junge* 'he joins' < *iŭngit*
to recognizably earlier strata, no independent reason for
this disparity became entirely clear at any point; as a
matter of fact, there was an element of circularity in his
reasoning.

Fifteen years later, P. Fouché came up with a real
package of studies rolled into a single monograph, titled
—hazily enough—"Études de philologie hispanique" (1929:
1-171). Essentially, he combined very extensive reviews
of the revised fifth edition (1925) of Menéndez Pidal's
Manual de gramática histórica, a classic, and of Meyer-
Lübke's highly controversial *Das Katalanische: Seine
Stellung zum Spanischen und Provenzalischen* (of that same
year) with a string of independent explorations, assigning pride of place to the relation of *ō* to *ŭ*. So far, so
good; and one is indeed encouraged to read on as one
stumbles, right at the outset, across this provocative
statement: "On confond d'ordinaire l'évolution de ces
deux voyelles, qu'il s'agisse d'ailleurs du français, du
vieux provençal ou du castillan. A tort, car les ré-
sultats, s'ils concordent souvent, peuvent ne pas être
les mêmes" (2). But in the end the reader's expectations
are not fulfilled; after briefly arousing them once more,
apropos of Sp. *puño* 'fist' < *pŭgnu*, *muñe* 'he summons' <
mŭngit 'he blows the nose', *uñe* 'he yokes' < *iŭngit*, and
ducho'skillful expert' < *dŭctu* [but others, I hasten to
add, have favored the alternative etymon *dŏctu*], Fouché
deftly polarizes the explicative possibilities ("L'*u* de
ces formes provient-il de la fermeture d'un ancien *ọ* issu
de *u* latin, ou au contraire continue-t-il un *ŭ* latin
maintenu à cause de la palatale suivante?" [12]), then
immediately lets his readers down by declaring: "A notre
avis ni l'une ni l'autre de ces deux hypothèses n'est
exacte." Throughout, Fouché refrains from assigning to
the forms he cites definite places along the coordinates
of time and space; he even chides his countryman Georges
Millardet for aiming at a chronological stratification.
Fouché's sole tool is his constant appeal to articulatory
phonetics, which he applies, like a juggler, chiefly to
undocumented intermediate stages, and there is no dearth
of "howlers," as when he apodictically declares *rubio*
'blond' [OSp. *ruvio*] a form "évidemment savante" (11).
Small wonder Menéndez Pidal had no trouble brushing off
rather cavalierly the objections raised by scholars as
poorly equipped for jousting as were Tuttle and Fouché
(also, before them, Cornu)—who otherwise might have been
formidable adversaries.

It would have been a pleasure to be able to credit a
major breakthrough to modernistically slanted linguistics.
But does the record bear out such optimism? Take the revised third edition of E. Alarcos Llorach's immensely
successful *Fonología española*, which devotes considerable

space (§§142-5) to the prehistory of Spanish vocalism
(1961:206-19). The author briefly acquaints his readers
with the Sardinian vowel system in synchronic and diachronic projection, but mainly as a foil to the alternative solution adopted by the "latín vulgar del Occidente"
—a concept he adopts from the 1949 version of the *Essai
pour une histoire structurale du phonétisme français*, by
Haudricourt and Juilland, two authors who have had no
second-hand, let alone first-hand, experience with Hispanic research. Hidden away, as inconspicuously as possible, close to the end of a footnote (213 *n*16), one finds
cursory mention of the fact that in Basque borrowings
from Latin $\bar{e}$ and $\check{i}$ were still distinguished, with a reference to J. Caro Baroja's monograph bearing on the his-
tory of Basque (1946:39-44). There is not a hint of the
parallel, at least equally relevant, discrimination, in
Basque, between $\check{u}$ and $\bar{o}$ in Latin loanwords. Above all,
a splendid opportunity has been passed up to voice the
suspicion that we might here have a priceless clue to the
vowel system presiding over the earliest Latinity of
Spain.

Conceivably, Alarcos Llorach's gaffe is atypical, as
was before Haudricourt and Juilland's hasty generalization.[40] A more sober, if less friendly, conclusion to be
drawn from these facts would be that excessive schemati-
zation, which underlies much of modernist research in
linguistics, simply does not lend itself to the fine-
tuning needed in the meticulous unravelling of historical
clues.

What makes it desirable to reopen the discussion at
this point, with entirely different chances of success,
is the unforeseen coincidence of three events: (1) the
discovery of a dozen spots scattered on the geographic
map where Lat. $\check{u}$ has been preserved as u (Albania, Basque
Provinces, North Africa, pre-Anglo-Saxon England, etc.);
(2) the gradually accumulating evidence of the protracted
preservation of intervocalic surds in Mozarabic, Valencian, Aragonese, etc. (see above), a finding which flatly
contradicts all earlier tentative classifications of
Hispano-Romance; and (3) the collection of examples, undertaken in this paper, purporting to illustrate the preservation of $\check{u}$ in contexts where neither a rash appeal to
learnèd transmission would make sense, nor the agency of
any particular phonetic environment (a preceding or a
following palatal consonant, hiatus, and the like) can be
plausibly suspected: Ptg. *curto* and *surdo*, OPtg. *usso*,
Sp. *hurto*, Ptg. *sulco* beside Sp. *surco*, to cite but a
few from among those already discussed at length. If the
history of Lat. /p/, /t/, /k/ on Peninsular soil shows an
older pattern of conservative transmission eroded through
the invasion, or contagion, of a rival trans-Pyrenean
system, more "advanced," then a similar preponderant displacement of an indigenous Latinity by a more appealing
or prestigious regional variety (probably traceable to
Lyon and Toulouse) may be chiefly responsible for the

blurring of the original, pristine diachronic contour $\ddot{u}$
> u, as familiar from Sardinian, Rumanian, etc. The the-
oretical acceptance of this possibility will force us to
take a realistic revisionist attitude toward several con-
tentions of transmission through learnèd channels and,
above all, toward the—all too frequently invoked—"zigzag movement" $\ddot{u}$ > o > u.

The dialect mixture that ensued, and may have
stretched from the third to the sixth century (or there-
abouts), led, as was to be foreseen, to the constitution
of small nuclei of words tied together by formal and/or
semantic resemblances, in which either u or o was allowed
to prevail; in some instances phonetic circumstances may
have facilitated the choice. Hence the noted affinity of
-$\tilde{n}$ and -ch radicals, perhaps also of j- and y- radicals,
for u, which has long, and deservedly, been in the focus
of discussion, on account of its transparent phonetic
implications; hence also, apparently devoid of such implications at first glance, the mutual attraction between
nuclear u and -rt, -rd, -rc and similarly structured consonant clusters, as evidenced by Ptg. $curto$ and $surdo$, by
Sp. $surco$ (Ptg. $sulco$), by OSp. Ptg. $furto$ (Mod. Sp.
$hurto$), and the like. Even here one cannot completely
exclude the factor of phonetic reverberations: given the
oft-demonstrated paradigmatic connection of l, r, and n
in Hispano-Romance,[41] one could convincingly argue that
the commonness of -nt- (as in $junto$, $punto$) and in -nd-
(as in $segundo$) could have sporadically entailed the prevalence of u before l and r followed by t, d, or some
other obstruent.

IV

The problem not yet properly broached, except for a
few anticipatory hints, is whether the vowel system of
the oldest Latinity imported into the Peninsula—and still
hazily recognizable despite subsequent overlays—in addition to keeping $\ddot{u}$ and $\bar{o}$ apart also continued to distinguish between $\check{i}$ and $\bar{e}$; that is, whether it corresponded
to the widely scattered "Archaic Type" perhaps best-known
from Sardinia's core dialects (merger of $\ddot{u}$ and $\bar{u}$, as well
as of $\check{i}$ and $\bar{\imath}$), or to the developmentally somewhat more
advanced, but territorially limited, transitional "Ruman-
ian Type" (key words lup but $verde$). In a nutshell, the
evidence so far marshalled is inconclusive, and any decision invites a much larger volume of preliminary fine-
meshed sifting.

A few exploratory appraisals of individual, almost
randomly selected case histories will highlight the degree of the difficulty involved. From the earliest texts
extant Spanish copiously used the adjective $firme$'steady,
hard, staunch', which on two scores clashes with its reputed prototype $f\breve{\imath}rmus$, -a, very neatly reflected by Fr.
$ferme$, Prov. $ferm$, It. $fermo$, etc.: Its i agrees, to be
sure, with the vowel of Sard. $firmu$ (REW_3§3320), but runs

afoul of the consensus of all other cognates, exhibiting
-*e*-; and the final vowels of the Latin base should, normally, have yielded -*o*/-*a* rather than -*e*. To explain
away the latter complication, one could with relative impunity have recourse to one of several auxiliary conjectures, none of which, however, is truly satisfactory.
Thus, one might argue, with J. Cornu (1884:289), that the
adv. *firmē*, I suppose through frequent use in notarial
texts, secondarily assumed the function of an adjective—
except that the parental -*ē* adverbs show a singularly
meager representation in the daughter languages (one such
rare instance is Ptg. *entregue* 'delivered, busy, absorbed', from *integrē*), a fact long known to scholars,
which Keith E. Karlsson's 1980 dissertation has fully
borne out. One superadded circumstance that might have
accounted for erratic -*u* > -*e* would have been an indirect
channel of transmission, namely through Gallo-Romance,
except that Old French, Old Provençal (and even Basque,
in a contiguous territory) in unison show here nuclear
-*e*-, in preference to -*i*-. The third (and, to my knowledge, last) avenue of escape from the predicament is the
assumption that colloquial Latin minted *firmis* alongside
Class. *firmus*. Such a hypothesis, indeed, has much to
recommend it; there exist precedents for the rise of such
adjectival by-forms, moving in either direction from the
standard, as when *ācer*, *ācris* 'sour' was gradually dislodged, in the vernaculars, by *ācru*, *ācra* (cf. OSp. Ptg.
agro; see *DELL₄*, 6a). Above all, the form *firmis* actually
occurs in an occasional text tinged by folk speech, e.g.
the earliest Bible translation (Itala); if so, its coinage
may have been stimulated by the preëxistence of the near-
synonym *fortis* or the antonym *infirmis* (Rönsch 1875:274),
whose leadership, in this context, has in turn been attributed to the semantic vicinity of *dēbilis* 'weak',
fragilis 'frail', lit. 'breakable', *gracilis* 'thin, slim',
and the like. In any event, the adv. *firmiter* is on
record in Classical Latin. But, once that much has been
granted, how does one justify the survival, on Spanish-
Portuguese soil, of *enfermo* 'sick' < *infirmu*, with preservation of -*nf*- (in lieu of its alternative reduction
to -*ff*-) best understood as pointing to the long survival
of a morphemic boundary (cf. D. Catalán 1968:410-35)?
Was there a time—say, ca. 500 A.D.—when adj. *firme* and
*fermu coexisted in the Peninsula? Interestingly, traces
of *fermo* have been detected in Old Portuguese (see J.
Leite de Vasconcelos 1898:422 and unsigned review in *Rom.*
28.485 [1899]).

   As one turns his attention from the ending to the
word's radical, the imbroglio tends to get worse. To be
sure, one could charge the preservation of *ĭ* as a high
front vowel to learnèd transmission and, in so doing,
place heavy emphasis on the notarial meaning of the corresponding verb (Sp. Ptg. *firmar* 'to sign', *firma* 'signa-
ture' have an isolated counterpart in Old Italian, but
the semantic development elsewhere was incomparably more

lively and, above all, more concrete, as is shown most
dramatically, but not exclusively, by Fr. *fermer* 'to shut,
close' [Meyer-Lübke 1935:§§3318, 3320]; on the Latin prelude see V. J. Fahrenschon 1938). The Latinizing trend
might have been reinforced by the "abstract" verbs *affir-
māre* and *confirmāre* handed down at this level to Hispano-
Romance (while French opposes pictorially saturated
affermir to pale *af-*, *con-firmer*, and all three to *en-*,
ren-fermer, modeled after *fermer*; Italian, as usual, opts
for *af-*, *con-fermare*). But, assuming this high degree of
learnèdness is plausible in reference to the Peninsula,
why, one is left wondering, was *firmitāte* rejected in
that territory—it could easily have been adopted as
₊firmidad, which would have formed a pendant to vernacular
OFr. *ferté*, OProv. *fermetat* 'fortress'—for the sake of
innovative *firmeza*? Similarly, why have recourse to self-
contradictory *firmedumbre* instead of *₊firmitud*, from
abundantly recorded *firmitūdō*? Clearly, the derivational
suffixes *-eza* and *-edumbre* would match *firm-* far more
snugly if only the *i* were not prejudged as a symptom of
learnèd transmission. Even these stumbling blocks, however, do not exhaust the range of legitimate doubts.
Sporadic epigraphic evidence (*CIL* 4.175, 6.1248, 5230),
which the *DÉLL*₄ (237*a*), reports without endorsing it,
shows that stone-engravers, in painstakingly recording
FIRM-, had recourse to the "*i* longa." But Ernout (1959-
60) hastens to reject this bold interpretation of the
word as *fĭrmu* solely on the basis of (admittedly conflicting) Romance reflexes, an argument which smacks of circularity. There is a slim chance, then, that *fĭrm-* and
fīrm- could have coexisted for a while, at least in certain territories, with incipient mutual semantic aliena-
tion. Alternatively, it could be maintained that *fĭrm-*
> Hisp. *firm-* represents one fairly isolated trace of the
Archaic Vowel System, which at this point in time, space,
and structure resisted the tide of the *ĭ* > *e* overlay by
reason of (1) secondary support received from learnèd
sources, and (2) special privileges accorded the following
-rm- cluster (for details see below).
      An equally intricate situation confronts the student
of a whole cluster of derivational suffixes: *-itia* and
-itiēs, appealed to for the formation of adjectival abstracts (hence functionally comparable to Eng. *-th* and
-ness), as well as *-ĭcius* beside *-īcius*, used in minting
relational adjectives, with special reference to the expanded, chain-like forms *-ātĭcius* and *-ārĭcius*. There
may be some advantage to starting out with the latter
facet of the problem.
      As has been established in searching monographs by
generations of front-line Latinists (particularly by E.
Wölfflin and Manu Leumann), speakers of the parent language had at their ready disposal the twin suffixes *-īcius*
and *-ĭcius*, marked by inchoate differentiation.[42] As
compound suffixes gained in popularity through fusion,
the interfixal element *-āt-* was paired off with *-īcius*,

while its counterpart -ār- was assigned to -icius, with
the result that Old French displays a wealth of derivatives in -eiz (originally -ediz) and another contingent
of, rather technical, qualifiers in -erez.[43] The older
stages of Italian (its dialects included) show a virtually
parallel split between (1) -aticcio, -atizzo and (2)
-areccio or -ereccio, as has been convincingly demonstrated by G. Rohlfs (1954:§§1038-9).

In Spanish and Portuguese -āriciu cast off -arigo/
-arizo (later -erizo), while -āticiu yielded -adigo/
-adizo. (To disencumber the complex problem, suffice it
to observe that the shift -arizo > -erizo is due to con-
tamination by -ero < -āriu, as when cabrarizo and cabero
both meant 'goatherd', porcarizo and porquero were interchangeably used for 'swineherd'; the local voicing of ç
to z, which drove a wedge between the two languages at
issue, constitutes a separate problem.[44]) As one inspects
such slivers of material as Ptg. achadiço 'easy to find',
Sp. antojadizo 'fickle, capricious', encontradizo 'bobbing
up all the time', tornadizo 'changeable, renegade, turn-
coat' (-izo having consistently been the medieval spelling), placing them alongside the above-mentioned slices
-ariço/-erizo (hortaliza 'vegetable', dissimilated from
-riza, may here be thrown in for good measure), one recognizes that Hispano-Romance has been steering a radically
different course, generalizing the i at the expense of
the e. From this divergent state of affairs the Hispanist
is at liberty to draw three different preliminary conclusions, for one of which he will have to opt in the end:

1. In the provincial Latinity of Spain—i.e. at the
    temporal level of Antiquity—-ícius may have over-
    powered -ĭcius (in terms of morphological "economy,"
    or tightening of resources).
2. -iço/-izo could have displaced *-eço/*-ezo at the
    Proto-Hispanic stage, much as later -illo did -iello,
    -ito did -uelo, etc.—i having been one of the three
    favorites, in the company of a and u, among those
    vowels called upon to herald, or usher in, a deri-
    vational suffix, often to the detriment of -e-, -ie-,
    and -ue-.
3. The development ĭ > i may have been "regular," repre-
    senting a remnant of the Archaic Vowel System, pro-
    tected from the tidal overlay (ĭ > e) by the vogue
    of i-dominated suffixes.

The situation is surpassed in sheer intricacy by the
development of -itia beside -itiēs in Hispano-Romance
adjectival abstracts.[45] At first glance it seems insufficient to state that -ez (as in niñez 'childhood', vejez
'old age', borrachez in rivalry with -era 'drunkenness')
reflects -ĭtie; that -eza (as in nobleza 'nobility',
pobreza 'poverty', and riqueza 'wealth') perpetuates
-ĭtia; that the replacement of -tāte (as in vetustāte,
nobilitāte, paupertāte) is a trivial matter of suffix

change; that *-icia* (as in *malicia* 'evil, trickiness',
OSp. *trist-icia* ∿ *-eza* 'sadness') testifies to learnèd
transmission, as does post-medieval *-icie* (*calvicie* 'bald-
ness', *planicie* 'plateau'). Upon closer examination,
however, things turn out to be less simple and straight-
forward. To begin with, Old Galician-Portuguese offers
two mutually competing equivalents of Sp. *-ez*, namely *-ece*
and *-ice* (*velh-ece*, *-ice* 'old age'), of which the second
won out. Then again, the counterpart of Sp. *-icia* is
Ptg. *-iça*, of distinctly less learnèd appearance, especially in lexical items like *maiça* 'malice', which visibly participated in characteristic sound changes, such
as the loss of intervocalic *-l-*. Semantically, the words
in *-ice* are at the opposite pole from any display of refinement and pretentiousness, referring as they do not
only to age levels (e.g. *meninice* 'childhood'), but also
to a profusion of patterns of comic or reprehensible behavior.

Under these circumstances, should Ptg. *-ez* be written
off as an intruder from Spanish? Should *-ice* and *-iça* be
recognized as vernacular descendants of *-ĭtie* and *-ĭtia*,
respectively—merely protected from the "overlay" by a
Latinizing tendency (whereas *-icia* and *-icie*, traceable
to modern times, could then pass off as genuine "cultismos," suggested by Latin models and precedents in neighboring Castile)? Were *-ece* and *-ice* once regionally
separated? And is *-eza* essentially a Provençalism, with
Old Spanish pressure acting as a reinforcement?[46]

Problems of this type have infrequently come up for
discussion in the past and, if so, certainly not within
the context here chosen. The Establishment has recognized
rather numerous instances of Class. $\breve{i}$ as *i* (as against
the norm, exemplified by *pĭlu* 'hair' > *pelo*, *pĭra* 'pears'
> *pera* 'pear', *ĭnter* 'between, among' > *entre*) and has
assigned them to certain categories. After subtraction
of transparently learnèd words, too trivial for their
taste to invite sustained attention (e.g. *lĭbro* 'book' <
lĭbru), spokesmen for this approach discovered a residue,
traceable to the effects of metaphony, which Menéndez
Pidal, in his revised handbook (1941:§11), subdivided as
follows:

1. If followed by /gj/ and /dj/, V. Lat. *e* (from $\breve{i}$, inter alia)
   could be raised to *i*: *fastĭdiu* 'loathing, aversion, dis-
   taste' > Sp. *hastío* 'surfeit, boredom', *nāvĭgiu* 'vessel,
   bark, boat' > *navío* 'ship' (but there were counterexamples,
   e.g. *corrĭgia* 'shoe-tie, rein for a horse' > *correa* 'leather
   strap, thong').
2. If followed by /rj/, /sj/, /pj/, whether the group was
   primary or secondary, the same vowel was almost invariably
   raised, regardless whether in the process the /j/ survived
   or perished; hence *camĭsid* 'linen shirt, night gown' > Sp.
   camisa, *vĭtreu* 'glassy' > *vidrio* 'glass', *lĭmpidu* 'transparent' > *limpio* 'clean'.
3. Final *-ĭ* raised *ę* (from $\breve{i}$) in *tibĭ* 'to thee' > *ti*, *sibĭ* 'to

himself, herself, itself, themselves' > *sí̆*, *vī̆gíntī̆* 'twenty'
> OSp. /veínte/ (Ptg. *vinte*); top. *Fonte Ĭb(e)rī̆* 'Iberian's
Spring' > *Fontíbre* (Santander).
4. The same process is observable in hiatus: *vĭ̆a* 'way' > *vĭ́a*.
5. Prefinal /w/ had the identical effect: *vĭ̆dua* 'window' >
viuda, **mĭ̆nuat*(in lieu of Class. *minuit*) 'he lessens,
diminshes, chops into small pieces' > OSp. [Ptg.] *mingua*,
lĭ̆ngua 'tongue' > Ptg. *lĭ̆ngua*, Ast. *llingua*.

Since once more, a zigzag movement is implicitly
posited here, it stands to reason that *vindēmia* 'vintage'
> Sp. *vendimia, ec(c)lēsia* 'church' (lit. 'assembly') >
OSp. *eglisa, (e)grija, vēnī̆* 'I came' > *vine*, Iber. *Garsea*
(anthrop.) > *García* should have been conjoined with the
above cases. As a matter of fact, the author threw in
for good measure, without forewarning, even a few instances of /ε/ > /e/ > /i/, as with *tĕpidu* 'lukewarm' >
Leon. *tebio* > Sp. *tibio* , or *mĕa* 'my, mine' (f. sg.) >
*/mea/ > *mĭ́a*. These are, of course, examples of a double
gambit.
Despite the ingeniousness he displayed throughout,
Menéndez Pidal ran into serious difficulties with the
method he adopted. Unable to reconcile *mĭ̆liu* 'millet' >
mijo with (pl.) *cilia* 'eyelids' > (sg.) *ceja* 'eyelid',
he reconstructed [*] *mī̆liu*, appealing to a lexical blend
with *mīl[l]e*, [pl. *mīlia*] 'a thousand'; the incompatibil-
ity of (pl.) *sĭ̆gna* 'signs' > (sg.) *seña* 'mark, token,
watchword' and *tĭ̆nea* 'gnawing worm' > *tiña* 'ringworm,
beehive spider' prompted him to toy with [*] *tĭ̆nea*. For
mancipiu 'property', 'slave, servant' (lit. 'taking by
hand'), which clashed with *sēpia* 'cuttle-fish' > *jibia*,
he substituted **mancĭ̆pu* as the alleged base of *mancebo*
'lad, youth, adolescent', oblivious of the fact that the
reconstructed form, inescapably stressed on the *a*, would
have produced an utterly different descendant. As a result, the entire paragraph gives the impression of atypical untidiness.[47] In a footnote, there is a fleeting,
evasively polite reference to E. H. Tuttle's aforementioned
1914 note, but from that hint the inexperienced reader
cannot possibly guess that the American pioneer, far from
upholding the Spanish scholar's ideas, was, as in the
case of *ŭ*, diametrically opposed to them.
Similar breakdowns can be culled from numerous textbooks and reference books, starting with G. Baist's
sketch of Spanish historical phonology (1888); as a matter
of fact, Menéndez Pidal's analysis may, on balance, emerge
as the most forceful presentation of an inherently vulnerable approach. If carried to its extreme, the "zigzag
theory" may border on the grotesque. Suppose one takes
seriously the standard formulations of post-Classical
metaphony by word-prefinal /w/; it would follow that
lĭ̆ngua 'tongue' (Stage 1) became /lengwa/ in (Common?)
Vulgar Latin (Stage 2); reverted to /lingwa/ in Proto-
Spanish through the agency /w/, except for the loss of
distinctive vowel quantity (Stage 3), judging from Ast.

llingua and Gal.-Ptg. *língua*; with the pendulum swinging
back to *lengua* (Stage 4) at an undisclosed juncture, an
assumption one is virtually forced to make to justify the
form familiar from Modern Spanish? Or is the new *lengua*
essentially identical with Stage 2 /lęngwa/, coming from
a territory that had throughout remained sheltered from
the effects of metaphony (Stage 3)? If so, how can that.
territory be geographically circumscribed, and what was
the reason for its impact, in this instance, on Standard
Spanish? Sp. *mengua* 'dearth' beside Ptg. *mingua* obviously invite a parallel scrutiny, except that in their case
no comparably reliable starting point is available to
today's analyst (the Classical verb having been, I repeat, *mĭnuere* rather than *mĭnuāre*).

But once we are compelled to operate with such assumptions as dialect cleavage and eventual dialect mixture and reconciliation within the traditional framework,
why not go one step farther and admit, at least on the
theoretical plane, that we might be facing a situation
familiar to us from earlier concern with the vicissitudes
of the *ŭ*; Colloquial Hispano-Latin may initially have
maintained the Classical distinction between *ĭ* and *ē*,
capping it with the new tendency to merge instead *ĭ* and
ī; but an overlay of dialect speech affected by the newly
prominent Lyon-Toulouse vowel system would have blurred
the picture—indeed, far more radically so than with *ŭ*,
perhaps as a result of the superadded power of metaphony.

For the time being, then, the *ĭ* - *ē* issue must remain
in abeyance. When the debate is reopened someday, it will
be useful to take into account not only syntagmatic, but
also paradigmatic conditioning, which has so far been
consistently neglected. Thus, if *-nt-* (not unlike the
situation in Tuscan) turns out to have had, somewhere
along the line, a raising effect on the preceding vowels
e and *o* (or, alternatively, if its contiguity has helped
to preserve otherwise endangered *i* and *u*), it will be
legitimate to wonder whether—given the general affinity
of *n* with *l* and *r* in Hispano-Romance, *lt* and *rt* could not
have acted similarly. For *lt* a positive answer has already been provided, by implication: *punta* 'sharp end,
tip' and *yunta* 'yoke' would simply be bracketed non-
randomly with *mucho* 'much' < *mŭltu* and *purches* 'porridge,
pap' < *pŭltēs* under a common denominator. As regards
the front vowels, Ptg. Sp. *pinga* 'it drips, leaks' <
*pĕndicat might be allied with (so far unexplained)
pírtiga 'pole, rod, staff' (OSp. *piértega*) < *pertica* and
even with Ptg. *irto* 'stiff' < **ĕrctu*, in lieu of *ērectu*
(cf. Sp. *yerto*); indeed, elusive Ptg. *irmão* 'brother' <
germānu (beside OSp. *yer-*, *er-mano*, Mod. *hermano*) might
begin to fall into place.[48]

V

In addition to the three situations here examined in
considerable detail, there possibly exist as many as half

a dozen others in Hispanic phonology that give the impression of inviting a similar analysis. These additional contexts all involve contradictions well-known to scholars but so far left unsolved or, at least, not fully resolved; the margin of doubt would, one feels, recede if one were to allow for the superimposition of one wave of Latinity (akin to, or connected with, Gallo-Romance) upon an earlier wave traceable to the late Republican (or call it Gracchan, or Punic Wars) era.

Easily the most thoroughly, if still insufficiently, investigated of these additional complications bears on the transmission of the syllable-initial (in most instances word-initial clusters) /kl/, /pl/, /fl/ of the parent-language, with some attention to /bl/ and /gl/.[49] By briefly disregarding certain crosscurrents that muddied the emerging picture, one can conveniently start from the classic opposition between the Spanish and the Portuguese outcomes, *ll* /λ/ as against *ch-* /š/ traceable to older /č/ (dialectally preserved to this day). The standard examples are *clāve* 'key' > Sp. *llave* vs. Ptg. *chave*; *flamma* 'flame' > Sp. *llama* vs. Ptg. *chama*; *plōrāre* 'to cry aloud, wail' > Sp. *llorar*, Ptg. *chorar*. The correspondences are not always that neat; *plumbu* 'lead' yielded *chumbo* in the West, but "semilearnèd" *plomo* in the Center. The vernacular development is sometimes observable only in toponymy: witness Sp. *Lloredo*, Ptg. *Choredo* < *flōre* 'flower' + *-ētu* (plantation, grove, garden, and orchard suffix), as against Sp. Ptg. *flor*, a learnèd form appropriate to a generic label (cf. *animal*, *bestia*).

The relation of /č/ to /λ/, though seemingly easy to describe in geographic terms, fails to lend itself to any smooth interpretation on other levels of analysis. The difficulty is exacerbated by certain apparently isolated word histories. Thus, Sp. *choza* 'hut, cabin, lodge'—a term of primitive pastoral culture—seems to involve the Western, rather than the expected Central, sound development if it reflects the semantically self-evident base (pl.) *plŭtea* 'sheds, parapets, penthouses', which satisfies other phonetic requirements. *Chopo* 'black poplar' can be persuasively traced to *pōpulus* via the reconstruction *plōppus*—admittedly bold, but very effectively supported by Tusc. *pioppo* [pjop:o]; the unwelcome vicinity of *pŏpulus* 'people' could have triggered the chain of events conducive to *plōppus* in the first place. OPtg. *chus* 'more' < *plūs* causes little surprise, but the emergence of that same form in far-off La Rioja, where a subdialect of Navarrese (i.e. of an Eastern Spanish dialect), on the testimony of that early thirteenth century poet, Gonzalo de Berceo, is noteworthy; apropos these bits of evidence observe that *plūs*, in the Peninsula, was a relic word doomed to extinction, as a result of the prevalence of its virtual synonym *magis* (> Sp. *más*, Ptg. *mais*). Most important of all, where *cl-*, etc. were syllable-, but not word-initial, Spanish, on a par with Old Portuguese, displays /č/ spelled *ch*. Thus, Sp. *conchabar* 'to join, unite,

hire' (surrounded by several satellites: *conchabanza*
'comfort, [coll.] ganging-up'; *conchabo* 'hiring, work',
conchabero 'pieceworker', a few of them confined to dialect speech) snugly fits *conclāvāre* 'to nail together',
marginally recorded in Graceo-Latin glosses.[50] Add to
this example such familiar illustrations as Sp. Ptg. *ancho*
'broad, wide' < *amplis* 'spacious', OSp. *finchar* (> *hinchar*),   Ptg. *inchar* 'too well' < *inflāre* and OSp.
fenchir (> *henchir*), Ptg. *encher* 'to fill, stuff' <
implēre. There exist, I repeat, a number of troublesome
side developments, as when Sp. *chubazo* 'shower' is best
understood as a "Western" word, closer to Ptg. *chuva* <
chuiva than to Sp. *lluvia* (humidity comes from the Atlantic coast!); or as when near-homonyms can be more sharply
distinguished by discriminatory treatment of the characteristic consonant group (Sp. *clavo* 'nail' < *clāvu* is
thus protected against confusion with *llave* 'nail' <
clāve, while *clavel* 'carnation' looks like an imported
Provençalism); or as when, through dissimilation of palatal consonants or consonant clusters, *playa* 'beach' was
preferred to *ₓllaya* and *flojo* < OSp. *floxo* /flošo/ 'loose,
slack' < *flŭxu* 'flow' was favored over *ₓlloxo* /λošo/.
But, if one disregards such minutiae, the general impression that one gains is that /č/ as an outcome of /kl/,
etc. represents an old, autochthonous development in Spain
and Portugal alike, faithfully preserved (gradual deaf-
frication apart) in the latter territory, whereas in
Spain, with the exception of certain noteworthy relics
like *choza, chopo*, obs. *chus*, and *conchabar, ancho,
hinchar, henchir*, and with the further exception of instances where, under learnèd or phonetic pressure, the
original consonant clusters were restored, a novel mode
of pronunciation, namely /λ/, was introduced. Philological and dialectological evidence shows that this /λ/ was
preceded by /k/, /f/, and /p/, converging dyadic clusters
from which the opening component was peeled off, at the
preliterary stage. These clusters readily lend themselves
to interpretation as palatalized trans-Pyrenean prongs of
Occ. *cl-, fl-*, and *pl-*.
     One situation of extraordinary difficulty in Spanish
—in fact, known for bristling with contradictions not
yet accounted for—is the development of word-medial *l*
before consonants. The intricacy, to be sure, has its
roots in Latin, where the preceding vowel would color the
pronunciation of the lateral; but in several Romance languages—preeminently in Florentine Tuscan—standard /l/
was before long generalized through all sorts of leveling
and tightening processes. Elsewhere ancestral *l*, in this
position, would tend to become *r*.
     Old Spanish shows the familiar split between (1) pres-
ervation of the *l* and (2) its very early (preliterary)
transmutation into /w/, with all sorts of consequences
flowing from this initial gambit (mainly, crystallization
of a falling diphthong through contact with the preceding
vowel and eventual fusion of that diphthong into a

monophthong in Spanish, if not in Portuguese). The *-ŭlt-*
segment stands apart, having yielded *-uit-* (e.g. *buytre*
'vulture', *muyt* 'much' > Mod. *muy* beside *mucho*). Except
for this minor sideline there appears to be no way of
isolating the syntagmatic factor that might have presided
over the individual choices, and certain word families
were actually torn apart by conflicting developments of
their members, not to mention the occasional rise of
doublets. The traditional explanation, transparently
lame, involves an appeal to lexical stratigraphy: It has
been argued that, aside from the consistent survival of
l in learnèd words, it was also maintained in careful,
formal discourse in the vernacular ("upper layer," "Ober-
schicht"), but was allowed to become a semivowel and
eventually to disappear in low-level parlance (highly
informal or rural). This attempt to have recourse to
stylistic or social registers as prime determinants is
visibly forced in most instances; to what layer should
one credit a "neutral" word like *olmo* < *ŭlmu* 'elm tree'?
Why does *pulvus* 'dust, powder' survive as *polvo(s)* in
Spanish, but as *pó* in Portuguese? Another dimension of
the problem is the ever-present possibility of the *l* having been secondarily reintroduced. Thus, Sp. *dulce*
'sweet' can be misleading, if inferences from it were to
be made to early evolutionary stages: Ptg. *doce*, OSp.
doc(e), *duc(e)*—which have already come up for cursory
mention in a different context—clearly show the real
sequence of events.
     If only we knew for sure how the /l/ was pronounced
in the Lyon-Toulouse area between, say, the third and
the sixth century, then it might, under certain circumstances, be permissible to appeal once more to the hypothesis of a confluence of two currents of Latinity in the
Iberian Peninsula in late Antiquity. Unfortunately, our
sole direct evidence for the provincial Latin of Southern
France is the corpus of Old Provençal texts, none of them
predating the tenth century; that is to say, we have no
reliable, immediate insight into goings-on between the
disintegration of Latin and the jelling of a newly constituted local vernacular. And that vernacular is of,
practically, no help to the Hispanist, because here he
encounters essentially the same dichotomy as in the Peninsula, especially before *t*, *d*, *n*, and *s*. To quote such
a seasoned expert as O. Schultz-Gora: "... kann es be-
stehen, es kann sich jedoch ... erweichen und tut es
häufig" (1911:§96). For fine-tuning through deliberate
appeal to an assortment of qualifying adverbs ('stets',
'fast stets', 'seltener', 'kaum je', and the like) one
can profitably consult the parallel, more circumstantial
analysis supplied by C. Appel (1918:79). The one feature
distinguishing Old Provençal from its cognates is the
abundance and diversity of falling diphthongs thus arrived
at: *au*, *ou*, *eu*, *iu*. Significantly, the sheer number of
doublets is staggering: *aut* ∿ *alt* 'high, tall', *ausar* ∿
alsar 'to raise, lift', *beutat* ∿ *beltat* 'beauty', *coutel*

∿ *coltel* 'knife', *piusela* ∿ *pulsela* 'maiden', *viutat* ∿ *viltat* 'villainy', etc.

Nothing of that sort is familiar to the Hispanist from his own corpus. He may be baffled by the cooccurrence of *alto, altear* 'to rise, stand out', on the one hand, and, on the other, *ot-ero* 'hillock, knoll', *ot-ear* 'to survey, look down upon, watch, keep an eye on' (via **out-*), but does not expect to stumble over either *∗outo* or *∗altero*. The most cogent reason for the extremely large quota of unpatterned wavering observable in tenth to twelfth century Provençal texts would be the sheer recency of the tendential vocalization of *l* before consonant; on that assumption, there simply would not have been a sufficient number of generations of speakers to segregate the scores of chaotic doublets, semantically still undifferentiated. If this tendency indeed began to operate as late as the seventh, eighth, or ninth century (i.e. during the preliterary period), one can extrapolate for the preceding centuries, i.e. for the Lyon-Toulouse Latinity at its peak, the solid preservation of *l* before consonant: *alt, beltat*, etc.

One could then argue that this original pronunciation, inferrable but undocumented, invaded, or percolated into the Iberian Peninsula toward the close of Antiquity, in alliance with *(p)ll- < pl-* (etc.), *o < ŭ*, and the other phenomena already examined. In a few ecclesiastic words, the "firming" could have been reinforced by parallel pressure culturally enforced, as was probably the case with *altar* 'altar'.

The last major point to be summarily examined, against the possibility of yield of fresh information on the two Waves of Latinity, is the compression of the structure of tri- and polysyllabic words, in regard to the loss of weakly stressed vowels. The two extremes on the scale of possibilities are (1) Sardinian, South Italian, and Rumanian which—certain narrowly circumscribed special cases apart—as a rule do not syncopate such extravulnerable vowels; and (2) Northern French, which already at its medieval stage and, a fortiori, during subsequent phases, energetically lopped off such vowels, typically to the exclusion of staunchly resistant /a/. The most characteristic positions affected by this trend were (α) the intertonic, antepenultimate vowel in tetrasyllabic words, \॑/_; and (β) the penultimate vowel in proparoxytonic words (comprising three or more syllables), /ॕ\. Closely allied situations arose in the case of unstressed and word-final vowels, in lexical units bracketing two or more syllables ("apocope"); and in word-initial vowels heralding words of virtually any length ("apheresis"). Although sporadic attempts have been made to study, say, apheresis or apocope in isolation, probings of this sort, however sophisticated their execution, have at all times been doomed to produce severely limited results, since it is precisely the interplay of such tendential compressions that promises to yield the sought-for pattern.

By way of preliminary remark, a cautionary statement
on Portuguese will prove useful: Through radical erosion
of its inherited consonant structure (loss of Lat. *d*, *l*,
and *n* between vowels) plus certain side effects of nasali-
zation, not to mention the familiar "blurring" or "skip-
ping" of weakly stressed vocalic peaks in Lisbonese, Portuguese at present gives the general impression of a
heavily eroded language, abounding in words marked by
radical syllabic contraction: Contrast Ptg. *nu* 'bare'
(< *nūdu*) with Sp. *des-nudo*, Ptg. *vir* 'to come' (< *venīre*)
with Sp. *venir*, Ptg. *rir* 'to laugh' (< *rīdēre*) with Sp.
reír, Ptg. *réis* < *rēgāles*, lit. 'royal' (as in *milreis*,
Brazilian money unit) with Sp. *reales*. But this characteristic image must not be projected onto the level of
Old Portuguese, still less on the plateau of Proto-
Portuguese, where an utterly different ensemble of conditions prevailed. Just what the pristine state of affairs
may have been in the West is best disclosed by such "un-
disturbed" vestiges as *amêndoa* 'almond' (< Gr.-Lat.
amygd-ala, *-ula*) beside Sp. *almendra*, or *táboa* 'board'
(< *tabula*) beside Sp. *tabla*, or *âncora* 'anchor' (< *ancora*)
beside Sp. *ancla*, or OPtg. *côvedo*, *-ado* 'elbow' (<
cubitu), later replaced by *cotovelo*, alongside OSp. *cobdo*
> *codo*. With respect to the word-final vowel in certain
environments one also notices the split between the West,
which has preserved *-e* on a generous scale (witness
bondade 'goodness' < *bonitāte*, *cidade* 'city, town' <
cīvitāte 'citizenry, citizenship', as against Sp. *bondad*,
ciudad, orig. *cibdad*; and *árvore* 'tree' < *arbore*, as
against Sp. *árbol*, OSp. *árvol*; also *cárcere* 'jail, prison'
< *carcere*, as against Sp. *cárcel*). Finally, from Lat.
pignerārī, **-orārī* 'to take as a pawn' there branched off
penhorar 'to pawn, pledge' in the West, but OSp. *pendrar*
> Mod. *prendar* in the Center. (True, this is contradicted
by Ptg. *honrar* 'to honor' < *honōrāre*—could it be an
adaptation of OSp. *onrrar*, *ondrar*?)

In the tenth century glosses traceable to the Navarrese area, i.e. reflecting folk speech to the northeast
of Castile, one finds such forms as *babtizare*, *bebetura*
(flanking the graphy *ueuetura*), *collitura*, *desposatos*,
duplicaot, *nafregata*, side by side with "straight" Latinisms (*benedictione*, *debiles*, *junctatione*, *manducaret*,
nominatus, *rapinaret*, *salutare*), whose evidential value
may be distinctly smaller, since they seem to involve
incrustations of bits of Church Latin. By confining oneself, then, to genuine specimens of vernacular speech,
one recognizes a degree of faithful preservation of ancestral syllabic structure reminiscent of Proto-Portuguese
and, even more so, of Sardinian, South Italian, and Rumanian. These, one begins to suspect at this juncture,
must or could all be representatives of the First Wave
of Latinity.

Over against Proto-Portuguese and Archaic Navarrese
stands Old Castilian, a dialect marked by very bold omis-
sions of weakly stressed vowels and, as a result, by the

rise of innovative dyadic and triadic consonant clusters
alien to the parent language, and, not infrequently, dis-
playing an assortment of buffer consonants: Low Lat.
carricāre, lit. 'to transport by cart', yielded *cargar* in
the Center (as against Ptg. *carregar*); *recitāre* 'to re-
cite' (prayers) led to *rezar* 'to pray' via *rezdar*; **īlic-
īna* (an elaboration on Class. *īlex, -icis* 'oak tree') gave
rise to *Ilzina*, later *Enzina*, etc.; *dēbile* 'weak' led to
deble (preserved in *en-deble*, its prefixal expansion due
to coexistence with *enfermo* 'sick').   The issue before us
is whether such syllabic contractions, coincident with
vocalic syncopes, involve a purely local process or testify to an overlay whose ultimate focus can be traced to
Southern France.
     The word-FINAL segments of Old Provençal lexical units
are, of course, not at all comparable to what one expects
to find in Old Spanish even at the height of the predomi-
nance of apocope, on account of (1) the very heavy loss
of final vowels in Provençal (except for *-a*, and for *-e*
used as a supportive minimum vowel) and (2) the simplification of consonant clusters secondarily placed in this
position (e.g. *-mentu* > *-ment* > *-men*), so that the separate Latin words for 'world' and 'mount(ain)' tend to
collide in the language of the troubadours (*mon$_1$* and
mon$_2$), whereas Medieval Spanish sharply discriminates between the two (*mundo* vs. *mon-t, -te*; *Mon-* only as an ingredient entering into orographic or toponymic compounds).
But word-MEDIALLY Old Provençal, while differing from Old
Spanish in untold details, exhibits a picture strikingly
similar to that of its congener: 'to accuse, defy, challenge', for example, was *reptar* in both languages, derived from parental *reputāre*:   the title 'count' (lit.
'[the king's] companion') was *comte* in Old Provençal and
cuende or *conde* in Old Spanish; the finite form 'he sows',
from Lat. *sēminat* (culled from the paradigm of an *-āre*
verb), would be *semna* in Old Provençal and *siemna*, eventually *siembra* in Spanish, as against Ptg. *semeia*; for
'tame' one finds *duendo* in Spanish (also, correspondingly,
dondo to the west of Castile) and *domde* to the north of
the Pyrenees; for 'elbow', OProv. *cobde* looks like a good
match for OSp. *cobdo*, from *cŭbitu*, while OPtg. *côvedo*
went off in a different direction; for 'head, leader', a
word based on *capitellu* (a diminutive, in turn, of *caput*),
one encounters OProv. *capdel*, which agrees in its treatment of the nuclear segment with OSp. *cabdiello* (> Mod.
caudillo); *membrar*, an impersonal verb for 'to remember'
in the *Cid* epic—a text which also used the epithet *mem-
brado* 'clever, judicious', lit. 'one endowed with a good
memory'—reappears, again with an impersonal construction
in Old Provençal, the common sources of the congeners
being *memorāre*. To be sure, the lexical isoglosses of
the two languages do not consistently coincide, and in
contexts where borrowings occurred they did not necessarily take place along lines inviting comparison. Thus, for
'folly, madness' Old Provençal writers used either *follia*

or *foldat* (*foudat*), and it is, through a caprice of circumstances, the former that penetrated into Spanish, much
as its Old French equivalent (*folie*) was absorbed by
English (*folly*); but had the rival form *foldat* infiltrated
into Spanish, it would not have been cacophonous in its
new environment, judging from such local abstracts as
maldat 'wickedness' and even *fealdad*, initially 'fealty,
loyalty' (later, through secondary association with *feo*,
'ugliness') and *frialdad* 'coldness, coolness'. Only under special sets of circumstances did the two languages
in question part company on this score, as when 'master'
yielded *dompne* in Provençal, yet *dueño* in Spanish, from
dŏminu as the common source.

Given this degree of affinity, which could be effortlessly documented with many more equally telling examples,
we have before us the classic dilemma of diachrony:
Should we opt for monogenesis or polygenesis? If the hypothesis of monogenesis and subsequent diffusion should
win out in the future, then the direction of the spread,
on almost crushing circumstantial evidence, could only
have been in the direction from Southern France to the
north of the Iberian Peninsula along routes that flanked
the Navarrese area, which could thus foreseeably turn into a conservative zone (witness the late tenth century
glosses), along with far-off Portugal. But the basic
dilemma, pending more thorough inquiry, for a while must
remain in abeyance.

Of the various points of diachronic phonology that
have been here in part examined under a powerful lens,
in part merely sketched out, not all have yielded equally
clear, unambiguous information. But even if it has been
established in as few as three cases—e.g. in reference
to the widespread survival of the voiceless intervocalic
occlusives, of the Latin *ŭ* preserved as *u* rather than *o*,
and of /č/ as a strongly represented alternative to the
more familiar /λ/ as product of /kl/, /pl/, and /fl/—
that we have before us, in each instance, two competing
developments of a comparable degree of regularity (or, if
you wish, legitimacy) rather than a single noun surrounded
by a suspiciously high number of "exceptions", then the
need has arisen for pausing and reflecting about the
theoretical basis underlying our analyses.

Without engaging in unwarranted, premature generali-
zations, we can simply state that the family-tree model,
whatever the wisdom of its use in other contexts, simply
does not apply to the Iberian Peninsula, where no branch-
like break-off from a common trunk has ever occurred.
Neither does it make much sense to operate with a kaleidoscopic sequence of separate areas for each successive
change, positing ever new focal points, by joining the
extreme wing of diffusionists. It suffices to posit a
single displacement of the major center of innovations,
a center which can and ideally should be determined, and
defended against possible criticism, by purely linguistic
analysis, but also one which, preferably, falls into the

broader patterns of general history, including its cultural facets. While it is true that, under certain dramatic circumstances, the forces of general history and
those propelling language change may be at loggerheads,
or totally independent of each other, it is equally true
(and not necessarily "unexciting") that philological
evidence and historical records, in the majority of cases
tend to support each other, as of course the past century
knew all along—in fact, took for granted.

It is a fact that, down to the second century A.D.,
while the Republic and the early Empire (the *principatus*)
were steadily on the upswing, Rome City acted as the in-
disputable center of an enormous, close-knit Western and
Central Mediterranean unit—administrative, military,
political, economic, cultural, and demographic—keeping
under tight control the divergent idiosyncrasies of the
individual provinces. Because of the relatively early
date of its conquest and settlement; because of its comparative distance from the metropolis; and, not least, in
harmony with a certain intrinsic conservatism observable
over a period of two millennia, the oldest layer of
Hispano-Romance ("First Wave") can very well have adopted
an archaic vowel system and, for a while, preserved intact
its intervocalic surds, to cite just two critical features. The much closer cohesion of the Iberian Peninsula
with Southern Gaul, starting with the third century and
coincident with the cultural hegemony of Lyon, was reinforced by the gradual retrenchment of communication lanes
with the Empire's rapidly aging and decaying historic
capital. This secondary rapprochement with Southern Gaul
laid Spain and Portugal open to new influences ("Second
Wave"), which, however, did not completely overlay the
older structure, leading instead to all sorts of minor
compromises, on a tactical rather than strategic scale.
The closer proximity to Gaul of Spain rather than of the
Atlantic Coast may have codetermined the survival of /č/
in Galician-Portuguese, whereas speakers of Proto-Spanish
lost no time in switching to /kλ/, etc., and eventually
to /λ/—in word-initial, but, significantly, not in media
syllable-initial position, a niche which afforded far more
effective protection of the original state of affairs.

Of course, there were at all times other forces at
work, in addition to this secondary rapprochement alluded
to; the erosion of certain intervocalic consonants in the
extreme West is just one case in point. Such concomi-
tants easily influenced the local reactions to the influx
of Lyonnais Latinity, codetermining the areas of speakers
surrender or resistance to it.

In hastening to credit Hispano-Romance to a Western
variety of provincial Latin, earlier generations of
scholars were unduly impressed, first, by gross geographic
conditions; and, second, by such a conspicuous feature as
the uniform preservation of -*s* throughout the Middle Ages
(and, for a while, also of -*t*). Viewed in the perspective
here advocated, this temporary survival of certain final

consonants, through articulatory "firming," is also attributable to the secondary sharing of certain features by
Gallo- and Hispano-Romance (under the leadership of the
former), except that this time a process of preservation,
rather than of innovation, is involved.

NOTES

*The opening sections of this paper were initially presented at
the Houston Convention (December 1980) of the Modern Language Association. Other segments were consolidated into the text of a
semiformal lecture ("Old and new ideas about the classification of
the Romance languages"), which was offered—from March through May
1981—at a variety of campuses: Texas (Austin), Illinois (Urbana-
Champaign), Northwestern, Brown, Harvard, Oxford, and Liverpool; in
most of these places it elicited a stimulating, if short, discussion.
I am grateful to the organizers of those meetings and to the dis-
cussants; also to Giulio C. Lepschy (London and Reading), who—independently—read the typescript and commented on it; and to
Nicoline Ambrose, a young linguistic scholar in her own right, who
lent the first typographic interpretation to this piece.

1. One scholar particularly concerned with this side issue
was the Italian Slavist R. Poggioli, who during his Harvard years
became an original theorist of literature.
2. For a succinct presentation of archaic family trees, in
reference to what later became known as Indo-European, or Indo-
Germanic, one may turn to George J. Metcalf's essay, "The Indo-
European hypothesis in the sixteenth and seventeenth centuries"
(in Hymes 1974:233-57). We owe a slightly more detailed, painstakingly accurate picture to Anna Morpurgo-Davies.
3. Schmidt's slender volume, of 1872 vintage, initially produced a light impact on the progress of scholarship. Approximately
a half-century later, H. Pedersen, in his incisive appraisal of that
pamphlet (see the English trans., 1931:314-8), remarked that the
discovery and decipherment of, above all, Tokharian and, secondarily,
Hittite, gave a fresh impetus to Schmidt's pioneering ideas about
"dialect waves." In examining the division of the Italo-Celtic,
Hittite, and Tokharian group of languages into a western, middle
(the one most subject to change), and eastern section, Pedersen was
reminded of the similarly patterned division, in Antiquity, of the
Southern Greek dialect group.
4. The pitting of the family-tree projection against the model
of the wave theory has gradually become a hallmark of all comprehensive handbooks of linguistics and especially of all introductions to
historical linguistics. This preoccupation was not yet clearly delineated in the classic syntheses by Sapir (1921; see 1949:205 ff.),
who took up the issue of morphological diffusion without any explicit reference to its limited compatibility with the configuration
of family trees; and by Vendryes (1921:349-66; but the writing was
actually concluded by 1914), who invoked only a single comparative
method. The picture changed radically with L. Bloomfield's thoroughly revised textbook (1933:316-8). The transition to the modern
era was marked by the appearance of W. P. Lehmann's textbook (1962:
138-42). L. Hjelmslev, as often, stood completely apart in his

Sproget (1963: written ca. 1943) in deliberately disregarding or
at least deemphasizing the wave theory.

5. Thus, Bloomfield's surprisingly evenhanded approach may
have its ultimate roots in his inability either to reconcile, in a
bold synthesis, the rigid tenets of the neogrammatical approach
with the more flexible implications of dialect geography and of
diffusionism, or resolutely to rule out the one in favor of the
other, as I have tried to demonstrate on another occasion (1967:
137-49).

6. Testifying to such a conciliatory perspective and to a
commonsensical attitude was, among other pronouncements, the short
paper by E. Pulgram (1953:67-72). For a bird's-eye view of the entire discussion see my own earlier attempt at a preliminary synthesis, with special reference to Romance (1978:467-500).

7. See (1866:1.76-103), esp. 76, 79, 82, and 94; also (1868:
3.27-57). Nevertheless, it took Schuchardt several years to yank
himself completely loose from the straitjacket of neogrammatical
doctrine; see my short comment to this effect (1980:93 ff.).

8. For the Romance side see the article identified toward the
end of note 6. One guide to the Germanic side of the issue is
W. P. Lehmann's contribution ("The grouping of the Germanic languages") to a miscellany (Ancient Indo-European dialects) relevant
in its entirety to the question here discussed (see Birnbaum and
Puhvel 1966:13-27).

9. The best known and most technical presentations of W. von
Wartburg's "theory" (to use the latter tag very loosely) are traceable to the years 1936 and 1950. There is no need here to refer to
a profusion of satellite studies from his pen. The "theory" has
provoked a deluge of criticism, including two qualifications or
disagreements of my own (1972:863-8, and 1976b:1.27-47).

10. Interestingly, although Lausberg's thinking about such
problems reached its peak in the mid-fifties, it goes back in a
straight line to his brilliant doctoral dissertation on Lucanian
dialects (1939).

11. One may go even one step farther and assert that Lausberg's
ideas on the configurations of vowel systems, as expressed in articles and other writings, left by far the strongest impact. See,
e.g. the enthusiastic reactions of A. Kuhn, characteristic of the
climate of opinion thirty years ago (1951:54, 86, 96 ff., etc.).
Even though Lausberg himself at present (i.e. in retrospect) feels
that his volume on inflection represents his single weightiest contribution within his far-flung magnum opus (personal communication,
April 1981), the fact remains that he has never mustered the strength
to attack, within the domain of morphology, the adjacent provinces
of derivation and composition, let alone the territory of syntax.

12. The appearance of Rohlfs' monograph on Gascon (1935; rev.
1970) at once placed the author in a strategically very advantageous
position: It not only afforded him instantaneous insight, as the
subtitle programmatically announced, into problems left pending of
Pyrenean linguistics, but also allowed him to counterbalance his already established expertise in South Italian with a comparable command of Gallo- and Hispano-Romance. The 1935 book was preceded by
a string of articles on Basco-Latin and Pyrenean themes.

13. Saroïhandy briefly noted the phenomenon in his original
1898 and 1901 research fellowship reports, then studied it in more

searching detail in his cartographically supported 1913 article.
Data culled from Kuhn's Habilitationsschrift (1935a:§22) can be supported or supplemented with the help of a companion article (1935b;
see 565 on the reflexes of *spatha*).
    14. See Elcock, loc. cit., and Rohlfs (1970:§§444-8), with a
digest of opinions advanced by Elcock, Gavel, Jungemann, Martinet,
Menéndez Pidal, Ronjat, and Saroïhandy. After briefly warming up
to the hypothesis of Basque influence, and after praising Elcock's
efforts directed toward data gathering on both slopes of the
Pyrenees, Rohlfs finally (§448) espouses Elcock's explicative thesis,
as elaborated upon by F. H. Jungemann (1956:243): It suffices to
assume the absence of any Celto-Latin bilingualism from the Béarn
and Upper Aragon territory, permeated as that area was by a Basque-
Aquitanian strain, to capture the factor which accounts for the
preservation of Latin intervocalic surds. For a balanced assessment
of Jungemann's approach see, in turn, Blaylock's pithy review
article (1960:414-9).
    15. For the latest panoramic view see all of T. E. Hope's chap-
ter contributed to Posner and Green (1980:241-87, and especially
253-8) with many useful bibliographic hints. For sheer precisionist
workmanship and innovative insightful analysis Anita Katz Levy's
piece and Suzanne Fleischman's slightly later book-length monograph,
both devoted to the multipronged diffusion of derivational suffixes
(-*él* and -*atge*, respectively) from the same focal area (principally
Southern France and secondarily Northern France) deserve special
commendation.
    16. Both scholars, significantly, included in their purviews
the vicissitudes of ancestral intervocalic -*f*-, as in the reflexes
of *dēfēnsa* 'protected terrain', *aedificāre* 'to build'. Meyer-Lübke
argued that in the territory seized by the Arabs, by the time of
its occupation, the surds assuredly had not yet been voiced; in all
likelihood, he added, the same holds for the North. If so, the
voicing of the surds in Spain occurred distinctly later than in
Gaul (1924:1-32). Menéndez Pidal countered that, judging from
Mozarabic and Arabic texts alike, the process of voicing had already
invaded the entire Peninsula by the year 700, but that in the South
the surds had not yet been entirely dislodged, and that in the written language (except for -*f*- > -*v*-) the more conservative variants,
deemed more refined, were favored for cultural reasons; the focal
point of sonantization was Leon, the headquarters of the Reconquest
(1926:247-65 = §45). In the revised third edition of his master-
piece (1940:240-59 = §§45-6) the author thoroughly recast his interpretation, leaning heavily on a newly published paper by A. Tovar,
slanted in the direction of epigraphy: In Roman inscriptions of the
West, where a Celtic population prevailed, the surds occurring in
the local pantheon were modified, while being kept unaltered in inscriptions traceable to the East and the South (1948:279 ff.). This
almost sounds like a prelude to the thinking of M. Sanchis Guarner
(1960).
    17. (1974:133) and (1975:530-5, at 533), where he chastises
H. Lausberg for having sided, early in 1948, with Menéndez Pidal's
rather than with Meyer-Lübke's interpretation of the state of affairs
in ancient Andalusia; see the following note.
    18. (1948a:13). What the reader would like to find out most
is Lausberg's later definitive response to the challenge of the

ambiguous Old Andalusian evidence, rather than his initial reaction. Also, Hall, in positing Gallo-Romance pressure on Hispano-Romance on such a sweeping scale, was conceivably unaware of the rival explanation proffered by Tovar in 1948 and endorsed by Menéndez Pidal two years later, to the effect that Proto-Galician-Portuguese and the adjoining dialects of Western Spain in their primitive form, reflecting a Celtic substratum long ago hypothesized, on independent grounds, could easily have exerted that pressure on Castilian first and on the fringe area of Navarro-Aragonese next. Actually, the two suppositions are not mutually exclusive: The East Central part of the Peninsula was in a sort of squeeze, with convergent waves raying out from the West and from beyond the Pyrenees, across the originally non-Celtic South of Gaul.

19. *Q(u)assāre* is rather neatly represented in French (*casser* 'to break'), but seems to have merged with Gr.-Lat. *campsāre*, originally a nautical term ('to avoid, shun, circumnavigate'), to produce *cansar* 'to wear out, tire' beside *descansar* 'to rest', whereas It. *(s)cansare* 'to escape from', refl. 'to move aside' represents a direct continuation of the Graeco-Latin base. The corresponding noun, Sp. *cansancio* (OSp. *cansacio*), Ptg. *cansaço* 'fatigue', preserved in the nominative case possibly because a medical, hence semilearnèd term was involved, still recognizably mirrors the contour of *quassātiō* 'break'. For full details see my earlier microscopic inspection of the record (1955:225-76).

20. I am referring here to the research in progress of my U.C. Davis colleague Máximo Torreblanca.

21. This tentative analysis reflects, of course, the general thinking of André Martinet and of his closest followers, as of the mid-fifties. The "chef d'école," incidentally, busied himself, at least, twice with the voicing of intermediate surds, and was fully prepared to make an allowance for the possible agency of Celtic, though not as the sole factor, and not entirely to the exclusion of alternative explanations (1952:192-217; 1954:257-96 [translated, revised, and expanded]). Here are some excerpts from his concluding remarks in the 1952 piece: "We have refrained from categorically rejecting the assumption that Celtic 'lenition' and Western Romance consonantal development, resulted from parallel evolution [i.e. A. Meillet's 'développement indépendant parallèle'] determined by structural analogy; but it must be clear that there exist potent arguments in favor of determining Western Romance development as ultimately due to Celtic influence. In such cases, it is usual to speak of a substratum—a term which would be just as good as any other if it had not been extensively abused ..." My single mild disagreement with Martinet here is his continued readiness to operate with the concept of "Western Romance" adopted from W. von Wartburg, the advice to the contrary implied in the research conducted by Tovar and Menéndez Pidal just a few years before, which recognized the long-drawn-out survival of surds in the East and the South of the Peninsula apparently had not yet seeped through. See also Chap. 6 in Jungemann (1956), who likewise gravitated toward the assumption of Celtic substratum, drawing neither Blaylock's applause nor his disapproval (1960:415). I have not yet familiarized myself with G. Hilty's presumably relevant study bearing on the Mozarabic outcomes of the Latin intervocalic voiceless obstruents (1979:145-60).

22. On this latter point see especially Lausberg (1969:160).

Characteristic examples, picked from Daco-Rumanian, are *cerc* 'circle' < *cîrcu*, *lemn* 'wood' < *lígnu*, (m. sg.) *negru* 'black' < *nígru*, *plec* 'I depart' < *plícŏ* lit. 'I fold' (the tents), *verde* 'green' < *víride*, throughout with stressed /e/, beside *cruce* 'cross' < *crúce*, *furcă* 'hay fork' < *fúrca*, *mulge* '(s)he milks' < *múlget*, *nucă* 'walnut' < *nŭx -cis* + *-a*, (m. sg.) *surd* 'deaf' < *sŭrdu*. East Lucanian chimes in, with *cruce*, *furca*, *munge*, *nuce*, *surda*, except that in the front-vowel series the *e* from *ī* tends to become /ε/, particularly in checked syllable: *lᵉnga* 'tongue' < *língua*, *verde* < *víride*. The state of affairs in Rumanian has been known for, at least, one century, but the older scholars refrained from drawing any sweeping conclusions from the essential assymmetry between the courses followed by *ī* and *ŭ*, respectively; e.g. Tiktin, in his experimental sketch: "Die rumänische Sprache" §§15, 18, 19, 23 (cf. Gröber 1888: 443-50); also, with discernibly greater assurance, in his book-length treatment (1904:§§22, 35-9). The development has been slightly obscured by the fact that, in the wake of a secondary crosscurrent, *ē* and *ō*, in certain environments (e.g. before a nasal consonant), have tended in Rumanian to be raised to *i* and *u*, respectively. In the unsatisfactory perspective chosen by C. Tagliavini for his Lautlehre (1938:1-57), an approach which stresses change but neglects preservation, the transmutation of *ī* into *e* appears blurred (45) and the survival of *ŭ* as *u* is wholly camouflaged.

23. For a vindication of this hypothesis see the excursus appended to my earlier inquiry into the lexical polarization *aestimāre* 'to assess, esteem' vs. *blasphēmāre* 'to curse' (1976:115-7).

24. (1969:156). The volume goes back to the year 1956, and could thus be put to use by Vidos (passim).

25. The following examples are cited, on purpose, almost randomly, without any serious effort to be consistent about the choice of the original or of the revised latest editions available, but with a measure of attention to the various matrixes (national cultures) involved in the gestation of the books: G. Baist, in Gröber (1888: §§20, 23), with lapidary simplicity (e.g., "*ī* und *ē* mit *oe* fallen in *ę* früh und unbedingt zusammen", "*ŭ* und *ō* fallen in *ǫ* zusammen"); B. Wiese (1904:§§19, 26); C. H. Grandgent (1905:§§33), formulaically; e.g. "Cl. L. *ō*, *ŭ* V.L. *ǫ* > Prov. *ǫ*"; A. Zauner (1908:§§9, 11), again sweepingly ("Betontes asp. *e* beruht: [a] auf vulgl. *ę* (= klass. *ē* und *ī*", etc.), although the same author previously set apart the course taken by Sardinian and Rumanian (1900:§22; 1905:§18). J.D.M. Ford (1911:xiii, xvii); F. Hanssen (1913:§47): "... *ă* y *ā*, y casi siempre también *ī* y *ē*, *ŭ* y *ō* dan un mismo resultado en todas las lengues románicas"; E. B. Williams (1938, 1962, 1968:§6), who brackets, e.g. Class. *ŭ* and *o* under V. Lat. /ǫ/; F. Brunot and C. Bruneau (1949:33), who credit /nǫké/, from *nŭce*, and /kǫrréré/, from *cŭrrere*, to "roman commun"; P. Bec (1963:26): "Pas de diphtongaison des voyelles du latin vulgaire [ę, ǫ] fermées = lat. class. *ē*, *ī*, *ō*, *ŭ*."

Only a minority of scholars have adopted an attitude of caution and restraint, as when H. Suchier (1904-06, 1912:§8), in Gröber (1929), pointedly limited his remark to Old French and Old Provençal and added the qualification that occurrence in checked stressed syllable was initially a vital constraint; or as when E. Bourciez (1930: 148) specifically excluded from further consideration Sardinian, South Corsican, and Rumanian; or, to switch attention to a much younger scholar, as when E. Alarcos Llorach (1961:206-19)—a victim,

like his constant mentor Martinet, of the fascination exuded by
Wartburg's dazzling model—operated explicitly with Western Vulgar
Latin.

Interestingly, Meyer-Lübke, at the outset, not only correctly
recognized that the merger of $\breve{\imath}$ and $\bar{e}$ may, by a significant margin,
have preceded the amalgam of $\breve{u}$ and $\bar{o}$, but, less cogently, argued
that in Rumanian, pervasively, and in Spanish, under certain conditions, there later occurred a secondary rapproachement—culminating
in conflation—of $\breve{u}$ and $\bar{u}$, $\bar{o}$ and $\bar{o}$; see Gröber (1888:360). The classic formulation of Meyer-Lübke's subsequent thinking is found in the
various editions of his *Einführung* (e.g. 1901:§85, 1909:§§97-98),
where, even though he leaned toward labeling $\breve{u} > \varrho$ and $\breve{\imath} > \varrho$ as pre-
Romance shifts, he remained noncommittal vis-à-vis the dilemma of
single sweeping change vs. parallel independent developments. This
thinking, in cruder, simplified form, became tone-setting among his
followers (e.g. Wiese 1908:§19). The total exclusion of $\breve{\imath} > \varrho$ and
$\breve{u} > \varrho$ from the approximately chronological tables of sound shifts
appended to Meyer-Lübke's historical grammar of French (1913:266 ff.)
—a table serving the needs of relative rather than absolute chronology—may testify to his growing belief in pre-Romance dates for both
processes. The entire discussion eventually rests on the immense
collection of materials laboriously assembled and tentatively sifted
by H. Schuchardt (1867-68:2.1-191, 3.163-226).

26. On the state of affairs in nearby Northern Calabria see
R. Stefanini's insightful review (1968:65-7) of Rensch's *Beiträge*
(1964). The latter's spadework is now supplemented by his own similarly tilted dialect atlas (1973).

27. According to Lausberg (1969:§162) the "Sicilian" system en-
compasses also Calabria (except for a patch of territory in the extreme north) and Southern Apulia (beyond Brindisi). The author
reckons with the agency of Greek adstratum and substratum. For a
mature reflection on the motley tapestry of dialects in Southern
Italy, with heightened attention to stressed vowels, see Devoto
(1975:146-8).

28. Cf. 1969:§§158-60. Lausberg associated this "archaic system" principally with Sardinian, Southern Lucanian, and with African
Latinity, throwing in for good measure—in the text, if not in the
subtitle—the evidence of Latin words in Basque. For Sardinian he
could fall back on the entire *oeuvre* of M. L. Wagner; the single
most relevant (also, most handy and most up-to-date) piece being the
separate volume on historical phonology, a very elaborate survey
(1941:§14), plus his subsequent attempt at a synthesis, couched in
semitechnical terms (1951:310).

29. Vidos' rather meticulous documentation, which clearly out-
weighs his slightly pedestrian discussion—how can one continue to
invoke a law or a rule in the face of so many exceptions?—(1959:
193-5), owes much to the writings of W. Meyer-Lübke, M. G. Bartoli,
E. Bourciez, G. Rohlfs, H. Lausberg, E. Gamillscheg; he is particularly beholden to C. Tagliavini's well-known textbook (1952:151, 153,
189), which, among other clues, digested for him a difficult-of-
access source on the Latinity of Pannonia (A. Luzsensky's 1933 Hun-
garian grammar of Latin inscriptions unearthed in that province of
the Empire). For Rumanian he depended on the guidance of S. Puşcariu
(1937:28). Wagner's expertise was appealed to not only for Sardinian, but, equally important, for scattered remnants of Latin

collected in North Africa (1936:29, 32). Rohlfs, who in the first
place had inspired Lausberg's dissertation, became the logical authority for the establishment of a bridge between Sardinia and South
Italy—chiefly through his 1937 piece (32 ff.), whose writing coincided rather neatly with the approaching completion of Lausberg's work
on his own dissertation.

In regard to the issue of continued distinction between, versus
merger of, $\bar{e}$ and $\bar{\imath}$, $\bar{o}$ and $\bar{u}$, in Vegliote (i.e. in Northern Dalmatia),
M. G. Bartoli's verdict was not to be trusted; see the authoritative
qualification by Ž. Muljačić (1971:405), who in turn credits the
pivotal correction to R. L. Hadlich (1965:405).

30. See Jackson (1953:86 ff., 107 ff.); Haarmann (1970:135);
Beeler (1975:629); Dilts (1977:296). The discussion started out
much earlier, with J. Loth's trail-blazing 1882 monograph, which es-
tablished not only that $\bar{\imath}$ and $\bar{e}$, $\bar{u}$ and $\bar{o}$ were differently pronounced,
judging from the reflexes of Latin words borrowed into Cymric, but
that $\bar{\imath}$ and $\bar{\imath}$, $\bar{u}$ and $\bar{u}$ (plus, even more remarkably, $\bar{a}$ and $\bar{a}$) were
separately treated. From here Meyer-Lübke took over (1901:§86;
1909:§95), combining as best he could the Celtic with the Germanic
evidence (Old High German, Old English). He drew a sharp line of
distinction between the Cymric reflexes, presupposing a Latinity with
all quantitative vowel distinctions left intact, and the Corso-
Sardinian reflexes, resting on a Latinity drifting toward certain
convergences ($\bar{\imath} = \bar{\imath}$, $\bar{u} = \bar{u}$). In E. Gamillscheg's circumstantial review of the Brunot-Bruneau manual one also finds a hint of the resid-
ual distinction between Lat. $\bar{a}$ and $\bar{a}$ in Celtic (1952:420); but he
unwisely projected this discrimination onto the level of "Vulgar
Latin" (left temporally and territorially undefined) and uncautiously
equated it, if only by implication, with the contrast Old Provençal
orthoepists would make between *a larc* and *a estreit*.

31. Much of Tagliavini's thinking has been perpetuated by Vidos.
Devoto, in his concluding summation (1974:146-8), confined himself
to epitomizing the views of Rohlfs, Lausberg, and Hall. The latter's
investigations stretch from an article-length synthesis (1950:6-27)
to a book-length panorama (1974); for a critique of the latter see
the detailed review article by Thomas J. Walsh (1980:64-77). Although Hall's successive researches contain some feeble attempts at
self-improvement, in regard to details, he has been, I believe,—unlike myself—a consistently staunch supporter of the concept of
"Western Romance" as a sub-branch of "'Italo'-Western Romance."

In the Classification of Romance Languages appended to P. Bec's
attempt, ten years or so ago, at emulating Gröber's Grundriß (2.472
ff.), one finds, unoriginally enough, Sardinian subclassed with
South-Central Italian, then assigned to Eastern Romance; while
Spanish and Portuguese, bracketed under Ibero-Romance, enter into
Western Romance.

32. In his exhaustive review of H. Haarmann's *Der lateinische
Lehnwortschatz im Romanischen* (1972)—for which he could afford to
fall back on landmark studies by E. Çabej (1962), H. Michăescu
(1966), and E. P. Hamp (1972)—Michael R. Dilts made it clear that
Romano-Albanian shared the phonemic merger of Lat. $\bar{\imath}$ and $\bar{e}$ with Continental Western Romance, but not with Romano-Brittonic; conversely,
it joined Romano-Brittonic in opposing the fashion of fusing $\bar{u}$ and $\bar{o}$
peculiar to Continental Western Romance (1977:296). All of which,
one might add, is reminiscent of the state of affairs in Rumanian.

33. Of these words, or word-families, I have in the past studied
two under a microscopic lens, namely *sombra/umbrío* (1968:268-79) and
du(l)ce/doce (1977:24-45), without, however, paying heed as much as
I should have done to the partial retention of Lat. *ŭ*. Moreover,
the paper on the adjective for 'sweet' might have gained from ex-
ploration of one sorely neglected dimension: the general decay of
such Old Spanish qualifying adjectives as tended to become monosyllabic (*duz/doz*, *vil*, and *rez* from older *rafez* > *rahez*). The one
exception from this rule is the—fairly late—Gallicism *gris* 'gray',
superimposed on native *ceniciento* lit. 'ashen', cf. Ptg. *cinzento*.
34. One nevertheless faintly recognizes a side-connection with
the intricate case of Sp. *gusto*, Ptg. *gôsto* 'taste, pleasure' < *gŭstu*
beside Sp. *gustar*, Ptg. *gostar* 'to taste, enjoy' < *gŭstāre*, except
that here it is the West that favors the *o* and the Center that has
settled for an *u*, counter to distributional pattern of the vowels
in the case of Sp. *costar*, Ptg. *custar*. The link becomes even more
elusive when one reminds himself that the forms of Old and Classical
Spanish were still *gosto* and *gostar*; and that neither *agosto* 'August'
(from *Augustu*) nor *angosto* 'narrow' (from *angustu*) display any
wavering. Note the frequency of the spelling *custume* in older
Portuguese.
35. See the excursus on primary vs. secondary causation appended
to my 1955 LSA Presidential Address (1967b:242-5).
36. There seems to be a consensus of opinion among experts, including the Royal Spanish Academy, about the descent of Sp. *cumbre*
from *culmine*, an oblique case (= ablative) form of *cŭlmen*. While
Meyer-Lübke, in his comparative phonology (1890:§147), candidly ad-
mitted that the *u* < *ŭ* was unexplained—except possibly as a vestige
of the vanished *l*—he had no qualms, in the original version of his
dictionary (1911[-20]:§2376), to class Sp. *cumbre*, Ptg. *cume* with
Rum. *culme* 'top, roof-tree', Mac.-Rum. *culmu* 'gable', It. *colmo*
'ridge of the roof', along with It. *colmare*, Cat. Sp. Ptg. *colmar*
'to fill to the brim', with the truncated past participle *colmo*
'full'—involving the past authority of Diez and Gröber as having
voiced this idea in unison. This analysis obviously left the ir-
reducible contrast between *-mbr-* and *-lm-* in Spanish accounted for
(in Italian, it was arguable that the verb had branched off the noun
colmo 'ridge, brim' rather than perpetuating ancestral *culmināre*).
Despite this transparent difficulty, and the additional embarrassment at having to separate genetically two verbs so similar in
appearance, and virtually identical in semantic load, as Sp. *colmar*
and Fr. *combler*, Prov. *comolar* < *cumulāre* 'to pile up' (Meyer-Lübke,
1911[-20]:§2389), visibly akin to *cumulus* 'pile, heap' (which Meyer-
Lübke saw reflected in Ptg. *combro* ~ *cômoro* 'elevation, steep bank'),
the support for the derivation of *cumbre* from *cŭlmine* continued un-
abated, even though J. Corominas, for example, tends to class the
verb *colmar* and the noun *colmo*, both initially recorded in the late
fifteenth century, with *cumulāre* and *cumulu*, respectively (1967:159b).
The etymological problem is further complicated by the genetic
uncertainty surrounding Sp. *colmena*, Ptg. *colmeia* 'beehive', and by
the intrusion of the family of *columna* 'column', via its diminutive
offshoot *columella* ('little column'), Late Lat. *-ellu* 'eye tooth,
canine tooth' as *colmillo* 'tusk'. It would seem, then, that *colm-*,
suggestive of 'protrusion', was fed by at least two separate sources,
cŭmŭl- and *colŭm-*, but that, despite semantic affinities and striking

formal resemblances, *cŭlmine > cumbre* steered its separate course.
As if this imbroglio were insufficient, there enters into the picture
the word biography of *cŭlmus* 'blade, stalk, straw', which, normally
developed in Portuguese (*colmo* 'straw used for the roof'), is so
troublesome, on account of its diphthong, in Asturo-Leonese (*cuelmo*
'bundle of rye straw') as to have pushed J. Corominas into a blind
alley, seducing him to posit an identical Celtic reconstructed base
both for *cuelmo* and *colmena* (1967:159b, and on earlier occasions),
without winning much support from such an expert in Peninsular dialectology as V. García de Diego (1955:707b). Add to this knot, increasingly difficult to untie, the facts that (a) *columbrar* 'to
glimpse, descry' (documented not before the mid-sixteenth century,
as a slang word) calls to mind Mod. Dial. *acumbrar* 'id.' and may
represent—so Corominas conjectures—*culmināre* (reinterpreted as
'to view from a summit') conflated with *alumbrar* lit. 'to enlighten'
< *illūmināre*, and that (b) Ptg. *gume*, as against *cume*, invites as-
sociation with *(a)cūmen*, and the lexical tangle, clamoring for a
monographic inquiry, will impress itself on one in all its com-
plexity.

37. On decades of earlier dissections of Sp. -*(ed)umbre*,
Ptg. -*(id)ão* see Martha E. Schaffer's recent paper (1981:37-62), a
thoroughly revised chapter of her 1980 Berkeley dissertation.
Hanssen unhesitatingly made the suffix -*(ed)umbre*, based on a blend
of -*(it)ūdine* (abstracts) and -*ūmine* (mass nouns), responsible for
the gender adopted by primitives and blurred compounds like *cumbre*,
legumbre, and *lumbre* (1913:§459). The same consideration would hold
for the choice of *u* in preference to *o*.

38. The problems of preference granted to Latinisms, choice of
gender, continued vitality of derivational suffixes, cohesion of
vocalic gamuts, and influence of leader words on other members of
the given series are so tightly interwoven as to invite a far more
thorough discussion than is compatible with the main thrust of this
paper. Thus it is arguable that speakers adopted the learnèd form
for *pulpa* 'pulp', *pulpo* 'octopus', and *pulpejo* 'soft flesh' from (a)
Lat. *pŭlpa* 'lean meat, flesh' and (b) the zoonym *pulpus*, traceable
to the Hellenism, *polypus*, in an effort to avert an unwelcome hom-
onymic collision with the descendants of *palpāre* 'to stroke, touch
softly', preserved in the Peninsula (cf. Ptg. *poupar*). *Bulto* 'bulk',
'bundle, package', 'form, body, shadow'—a straight Latinism except
for the trivial substitution of *b-* for *v-*—steers clear of any conflict with the (religiously significant) family of *voto* 'vow', etc.,
an advantage that would not have accrued to the "ideal" outcome
**voto* < *vŭltu*; etc. Then again, the fact that derivatives in
-*ambre*, except for *raigambre* 'intertwined roots', fig. 'deep-
rootedness', tend to be masculine (e.g. *osambre* 'skeleton, bones',
pelambre 'batch of hides to be fleshed', 'hair stripped from skins'),
whereas those in -*umbre* are mostly feminine, testifies first and
foremost to the decay of the -*āmen*/-*īmen*/-*ūmen* gamut; secondarily,
it catapults OSp. *(ell) enxambre* 'swarm', *(ell) estambre* 'worsted,
woolen yard', figuratively, 'thread, course', into a position of
prominence, since the definite article *ell*, here ambigeneric, tended
to be interpreted by the speech community as being masculine. (Note
that *mimbre* 'osier, wicker' < *vīmine* continues to be ambigeneric.)
Then again, such lexical items, invariably of rural background, as
involve a switch from preconsonantal *l* to *r* after *ŭ* (*surco* 'furrow,

wrinkle' < *sŭlcu* [more faithfully preserved in Portuguese], *urce*
'heath' [phy.]) clamor for a separate investigation.

39. Menéndez Pidal's advantage over his contemporaries consisted in his joint discussion of the entire issue, which they, conversely, tended to fragment. Thus, Hanssen discussed separately the
trajectories of (a) *cuño* 'stamp, die, mark' (cf. *cuña* 'wedge') <
cŭneu, uña 'nail' < *ŭng(u)la, punto* 'point' < *pŭnctu, puño* 'fist'
< *pŭgnu*; (b) *ducho* 'skillful, expert' < *dŭctu*; and (c) *puches* (m.)
'porridge, gruel' < *pultēs*, as if these evolutionary threads were
not closely interwoven (1913:§§55, 87, 89). In the process, to be
sure he made valuable incidental observations, e.g. on the tendential
dialectal reduction of *ui* to *u* (Old Nav. *empuyssa* beside OSp. *empuxa*
'he pushes') < *impŭlsat*); but he altogether omitted important data
for the sake of decorum (*coño* 'cunt' < *cŭnnu*); failed to mention
alternative etymological proposals (as when *ducho*, OSp. var. *duecho*
had been authoritatively traced to *dŏctu* 'learnèd'); hesitated to
draw obvious chronological conclusions from the contrast *cuño* vs.
coño (/nj/ became /ŋ/ at a distinctly earlier date than /n:/); and,
above all, accepted, if only by implication, the zigzag movement
ŭ > *ŏ* > *u* in the biographies of, say, *punto, puño, uña* (plus) *ĭ* >
e > *i* in *cinta* 'ribbon, tape, band' < *cĭncta*) without so much as
considering the possibility of selective preservation of *ŭ* as *u*
and of *ĭ* as *i*.

40. More in a spirit of self-discipline than in one of optimism
I have attempted to determine what help, if any, can be derived from
avant-garde research in phonology. James W. Harris, for one, to cite
a spokesman for the orthodox transformational approach, discusses
competently the morphophonemic alternations *u* ∿ *o*, *i* ∿ *e*, as visible
in the paradigms of *dormir* 'to sleep' and *pedir* 'to ask', viewed in
synchronic perspective; as a matter of personal preference, I suppose, he trespasses on the domain of diachrony only with respect to
certain categories of consonants. My experience with Joan B[ybee]
Hooper's *Introduction* (1976) has not been any better, despite the
wide margin of attention she pays to Spanish.

41. Aside from knowledge gained from general linguistics, the
specifically close ties among /l/, /n/, and /r/ in the development
from provincial Latin into Hispano-Romance could be demonstrated
with such facts as (1) the failure of the respective geminates to
be simply shortened—the treatment undergone by all other consonants
in medial position; (2) the evolution of word-initial *r-* (and, in a
smaller territory, of *l-* and *n-* as well) in the same direction as
word-medial *-rr-, -ll-, -nn-*; (3) the vogue of buffer consonants
intercalated between word-medial, particularly radical-final, *n*, *l*,
r and some other consonant, in words like *saldré* 'I'll leave' (lit.
'I'll hop out'), from *salir*; *tendré* 'I'll have or hold', from *tener*;
(4) the strong representation of the clusters *-lz-, -nz-*, and *-rz-*,
side by side with *-lǵ-, -nǵ-*, and *-rǵ-*, and the ability of the former series to capture the descendants of *-lǵ-, -nǵ-*, and *-rǵ-*, under
circumstances described by me on several occasions (1968b:21-64; in
greater detail: 1977:33-75; with a qualification: 1982:247-66).

42. For a critical digest of Wölfflin's and Leumann's analyses,
as well as of several other relevant contributions (by G. Cohn,
F. T. Cooper, and G. N. Olcott, among others), see my contribution
to the Kurt Baldinger testimonial (1979:361-74).

43. The key study, conducted with exemplary care, came from

A. Thomas (1904:62-110). Later E. Gamillscheg took his cue from his former teacher's monograph (1921:1-60).

44. A brief discussion of the agentives in -*arigo*, -*erizo* is included in my 1956 review article dedicated to Delmira Maçãs' dissertation, *Os animais na língua portuguesa*. On the difficult problem of the seriatim voicing of *ç* to *z* in certain Proto-Spanish derivatives, to the strict exclusion of their Portuguese counterparts, see my exposition of a new hypothesis (1971:1-52).

45. The information available on the distribution of -*ez* and -*eza* in Spanish, at different cut-off points (Medieval, Golden Age, modern literary usage) is scarcely more than an incision performed on the tip of an iceberg (1966:341-3).

46. Phonologically, the relation of -*ez* to -*ece* reminds one strongly of Sp. -*d* as the counterpart of Ptg. -*de*, as in *ciudad* (originally *cibdad*) vs. *cidade* 'city' < *cīvitāte* lit. 'citizenship' (to the exclusion of cases like Sp. *merced* vs. Ptg. *mercê* 'mercy, grace' < *mercēde*, which involve ancestral -*d*-, rather then -*t*-, in radical-final position). Morphologically and lexically, Sp. -*icia* vs. Ptg. -*iça* calls to mind other instances of derivational suffixes transmitted through a learnèd conduit in the Center, but not in the West; witness (O)Ptg. -*ença* beside Sp. -*encia* < -*entia*, except for scattered relics of older usage, such as OSp. *simiença* 'seed' < *sementia*.

47. A hypothetical base which clearly yields no satisfactory results is untenable, even if Corominas lends it his support (1967: 377a). The latter, in addition to listing the fem. *manceba* 'lass', records as suffixal derivatives only *mancebía*, the verb *amancebarse*, plus the verbal abstract *amancebamiento*. Actually, Medieval Spanish had a whole corolla of offshoots: not only *mancebía* but also *mancebez*, plus the diminutives and hypocoristics *mancebillo*, -*illa*. *Manceb-ía*, -*illa*, and -*illo* could very smoothly have branched off **mancebio* < *mancipiu*, and under their joint pressure, on the analogy of *neuvo* ∿ *novillo*, and the like, *mancebo* could secondarily have been extracted and substituted for isolated, erratically built **mancebio*. Cf. such germane cases as *limpi-o* 'clean, neat' alongside *limp-ito*; *agri-o* 'sour' alongside *agr-ete* 'sourish', *agr-illa* = *acedera* 'sorrel', *agr-ura* 'sourness, acerbity'' (even though this cluster of derivatives, strictly speaking, is based on OSp. *agro*).

48. These words are, on the whole, singularly recalcitrant to analysis; despite an ever present margin of doubt, one suspects that the pressure of certain adjacent consonant groups (*nt, rc, rm, rt*) acted, at least, as a coconditioning factor. Ptg. *irto*, Sp. *yerto* transparently continue ancestral **erctu* (in lieu of well-attested *ērēctu*), .a "strong", i.e. rhizotonic past participle accompanying the paradigm of amply documented *ērigere* 'to set oneself up, rise', 'to raise, build' on its way to **ergere*, which in turn is cogently explained as echoing: *pĕrgere* 'to go on, continue, proceed' and *pŏrgere* 'to spread or stretch out' (∿ *porrigere*), as well as *sŭrgere* 'to raise up' (∿ *surrigere*). The brevity of the nuclear vowel in *pĕrgere*, *pŏrgere*, *sŭrgere* spread to **ērgĕre*. The *ĕ* thus obtained triggered a rising diphthong in the past participle *yerto*, with collateral support from the present indicative forms *yergo*, *yergues*, ... and from subjective *yerga*, ... , preferred to *irgo*, *irga*. The latter forms, mandatory in the West, coincide with the Ptg. past participle *irto*. Dial. Sp. *erecho* (var. *arrecho*) could

then be classed as perpetuating the nonsyncopated parental form, with gradual switch from *e-* < *ē-* to *a-* < *ad-*.

OSp. *ermano*, in lieu of arch. *yermano* (preserved in anthroponymy) falls into place—except for the erratic mute *h-* —as yet another instance of enforced monophthongization of pretonic /je/ (cf. *enero* 'January' in lieu of **yenero*, from *lēn(u)āriu*, and *enzía* 'gum', instead of **yenzía*, from *gingīva*). But Ptg. *irmão*, instead of foreseeable **germão* < *germānu*, is baffling. An old intruder from the Central dialects, with *ye-*, alien to the West, reduced to *i*? The coexistence of the obsolete kinship terms Sp. *cormano*, Ptg. *cormão* may have played a minor role.

Ptg. *pírtiga*, on balance, causes less surprise than does Sp. *pértiga*, as a replacement of OSp. *piértega*, a perfect reflex·of *pĕrtĭca*. Can one posit the collateral influence of *pertig-al* (orig. *-egal*) 'rod, staff' and *pertiguero* 'verger' (*-eria* 'office of verger') as a joint agent—the way *mancebillo*, etc. has been credited with deflecting **mancebio* < *mancipiu* (see above, note 47) from its straight course? In this context note that Sp. *pérdida* 'loss' conflicts with *pierdo* 'I lose' < *perdō*; one may invoke either the growing rarity of rising diphthongs in proparoxytones (despite *tuétano* 'marrow' and the like), or the derivative's alliance, through semantic polarization, with *búsqueda* (∿ *busca*) 'search', which of course has an unchangeable monophthong in the stressed syllable. Conceivably, the latter factor, plus the pressure of *perdigal*, etc., transmuted *piérdega* into Mod. *pérdiga*. For Ptg. *pírdiga*, however, the contiguity of *-rd* remains by far the best explanation.

49.   On the difficult problem of the five Latin word-initial consonant clusters including *l* as their second component see, by way of preliminary orientation, my own attempt at a provisional balance sheet: (1963:144-73), (1964:1-33), plus, among the more elaborate reactions to it—by no means consistently friendly—, the reviews by K. Baldinger, H. Meier, J. Simon, and H. G. Tuchel.

50.   Other examples are *ancho* 'broad' < *amplu* 'wide' and *chumacera* 'pillow', for the most part figuratively: (mach.) 'pillow block, journal bearing', (naut.) 'row lock, oarlock', 'strip of wood through which tholepins are driven', from OSp. *chumazo* 'feather pillow' < *plūmāceu* 'feathery'.

I am now prepared to go one step farther than in the mid-sixties by arguing that the word-medial outcome /č/ in *-Cc(u)lu*, *-Ct(u)lu* (and their feminine counterparts), significantly shared by Spanish and Portuguese, pertains to the very same layer—the First Wave of Latinity—as the /č/ in *chopo*, *choza*, *chubasco*, and *chumacera*. Illustrations can be culled from any representative historical grammar (e.g. Menéndez Pidal 1941:§61.2):   *cercha* 'segment (of rim of wheel), rib (of center of arch)' < *circulu* (with gender change); *concha* '(tortoise) shell' < *conchula*; *macho₁* 'male' < *masculu* (beside OSp. *maslo*, reminiscent of *muslo* 'thigh' < *mūsculu*, lit. 'little mouse'); *macho₂* 'sledge hammer' < *mar-culu*, *-tulu*; *mancha* 'blot' < *macula* (with echoing of word-initial nasal); *sacho* 'weeding tool' < *sarculu*. The survival or disappearance of the opening consonant of the cluster (e.g. /r/ or /s/) is as unimportant in this context as is the sporadic insertion of a nasal echoing word-initial *m-*. The sole assumption that must be made in bracketing *cl-* with *-c(u)lu*, etc., is a conspicuously early date for the syncope of *ŭ* in the penultimate.

It would seem, then, that at a certain juncture the use of, say, *(p)ll-* and, later, of *ll-* in lieu of indigenous *ch- /č/* became fashionable, inviting speakers in the Center who until then would render Class. *plēnu* 'full' by **cheno* (cf. Ptg. *cheio*) to switch instead to *lleno*. Very unpretentious country folk, who could not have cared less about speech fashions, persisted in using *ch- /č/* in rustic speech at its humblest (hence *choza, chumazo, chubasco,* etc.). Also, speakers' alertness being at its peak in word-initial segments and at its ebb word-medially, *ancho, conchabar,* plus *cercha, concha, macho,* etc. were somehow overlooked by the fashion-conscious and left unchanged, often receiving additional protection from the solid embedment of */č/* in such sequences as *-nch-* and *-rch-*.

REFERENCES

Alcarcos Llorach, Emilio. 1961. *Fonología española.* Rev. 3rd ed. Madrid: Gredos. [A 4th ed. dates from 1968.]

Appel, Carl. 1918. *Provenzalische Lautlehre.* Leipzig: O. R. Reisland.

Baist, Gottfried. 1888. Die spanische Sprache. *Grundriß der romanischen Philologie* I, ed. by G. Gröber, 689-714. [Rev. 2nd ed., 1904-06:878-915.]

Baldinger, Kurt. 1969. Review of Malkiel (1963-64). *Zeitschrift für romanische Philologie* 85:512-6.

Bartoli, Matteo Giulio. 1906. *Das Dalmatische: Altromanische Sprachreste von Veglia bis Ragusa und ihre Stellung in der apennino-balkanischen Romania.* Schriften der Balkankommission, Linguistische Abteilung 4-5. Wien: Akademie der Wissenschaften (A. Hölder).

Bec, Pierre. 1963. *La langue occitane.* Que sais-je, No. 1059. Paris: Presses universitaires de France.

———. 1970-71. *Manuel pratique de philologie romane.* Connaissance des langues 5-6 (dir. Henri Hierche). Paris: A. & J. Picard.

Beeler, Madison S. 1975. Review of Harald Haarmann (1970). *Romance Philology* 28:4.626-30.

Birnbaum, Henrik, and Jaan Puhvel. (eds.) 1966. *Ancient Indo-European dialects. Proceedings of the Conference on Indo-European linguistics held at the University of California, Los Angeles, April 25-27, 1963.* Berkeley & Los Angeles: University of California Press.

Blaylock, Curtis. 1960. Substratum theory applied to Hispano-Romance. *Romance Philology* 13:4.414-9.

Bloomfield, Leonard. 1933. *Language.* New York: H. Holt & Co.

Bourciez, Édouard. 1930. *Éléments de linguistique romane.* Rev. 3rd ed. Paris: Klincksieck. [4th ed., 1946, is a mere reprint; 5th ed., 1967, involves revision by author's son.]

Brunot, Ferdinand, and Charles Bruneau. 1949. *Précis de grammaire historique de la langue française.* Rev. 3rd ed. Paris: Masson et Cie.

Caro Baroja, Julio. 1946. *Materiales para una historia de la lengua vasca en su relacíon con la latina.* Acta Salmanticensia, Filosofía y Letras, 1:3. Salamanca: La Universidad.

Catalán Menéndez-Pidal, Diego. 1968. La pronunciacíon [ihante] por /iffrante/ en la Rioja del siglo XIII. *Romance Philology* 21:4.410-35.

Cornu, Jules. 1884. Remarques sur les voyelles toniques. *Romania* 13:285-314.

Corominas, Juan. 1967. *Breve diccionario etimológico de la lengue castellana*. Rev. 2nd ed. Madrid: Gredos. [A revised 3rd ed. dates from 1973.]

Corpus Inscriptionum Latinarum. 1893. Berlin: Academia Litterarum regia Borussica.

Çabej, E. 1962. Zur Charakteristik der lateinischen Lehnwörter im Albanischen. *Revue linguistique* 7:161-99.

Devoto, Giacomo. 1974. *Il linguaggio d'Italia. Storia e strutture linguistiche italiane dalla preistoria ai nostri giorni*. Milano: Rizzoli.

Dilts, Michael R. 1977. Peripheral Latinity in Albanian. *Romance Philology* 31:2.283-98.

Elcock, W[illiam] D[enis]. 1938. *De quelques affinités phonétiques entre l'aragonais et le béarnais*. Paris: Droz.

Ernout, A., and † A. Meillet. 1959-60. *Dictionnaire étymologique de la langue latine. Histoire des mots*. Rev. 4th ed. Paris: C. Klincksieck.

Fahrenschon, Johann. 1938. *Firmus*, Geschichte der Bedeutungen dieses Wortes und seiner Ableitungen in den romanischen Sprachen. Dissertation, München.

Fleischman, Suzanne. 1977. *Cultural and linguistic factors in word formation: An integrated approach to the development of the suffix -AGE*. University of California Publications in Linguistics 88. Berkeley: University of California Press.

Ford, Jeremiah D. M. 1911 (and later printings). *Old Spanish readings, selected on the basis of critically edited texts*. Rev. 2nd ed. Boston: Ginn & Co.

Fouché, Pierre. 1929. Études de philologie hispanique. *Revue hispanique* 77:1-171.

Gamillscheg, Ernst. 1921. Grundzüge der galloromanischen Wortbildung. E. G. and Leo Spitzer, *Beiträge zur romanischen Wortbildungslehre* 1-60. Biblioteca dell'"Archivum Romanicum" 2:1. Genève: Leo Olschki.

———. 1952. Review of Ferdinand Brunot & Charles Bruneau, *Précis de grammaire historique de la langue française*. *Zeitschrift für romanische Philologie* 68:424-49.

García de Diego, Vicente. 1955. *Diccionario etimológico español e hispánico*. Madrid: S.A.E.T.A.

Grandgent, C. H. 1905. *An outline of the phonology and morphology of Old Provençal*. Rev. ed. Boston: Heath.

Gröber, Gustav (ed.) 1888. *Grundriß der romanischen Philologie, 1*. Straßburg: Trübner. [Rev. 2nd ed., 1904-06.]

Haarmann, Harald. 1970. *Der lateinische Lehnwortschatz im Kymrischen*. Romanische Versuche und Vorarbeiten 36. Bonn: Romanisches Seminar.

———. 1972. *Der lateinische Lehnwortschatz im Albanischen*. Hamburger Philologische Studien 19. Hamburg: Helmut Buske.

Hadlich, Roger L. 1965. *The phonological history of Vegliote*. University of North Carolina Studies in the Romance Languages and Literatures 52. Chapel Hill.

Hall, Robert A. (Jr.) 1950. The reconstruction of Proto-Romance. *Language* 26:6-27.

———. 1974. *External history of the Romance languages* (=

Comparative Romance Grammar I). New York: American Elsevier Publishing Co., Inc.

——. 1975. La non-lenizione nella Romània occidentale. *Romance Philology* 28:4.530-5.

Hamp, Eric, P. 1972. Albanian. *Current trends in linguistics*, ed. by Thomas A. Sebeok, 9.1626-92. The Hague: Mouton.

Hanssen, Federico. 1913. *Gramática histórica de la lengua castellana*. Halle: Niemeyer.

Harris, James W. 1969. *Spanish phonology*. Cambridge, MA: M.I.T. Press.

Haudricourt, A. G., and Alphonse Juilland. 1949. *Essai pour une histoire structurale du phonétisme français*. Paris: C. Klincksieck. [Rev. 2nd ed. The Hague: Mouton, 1970-71.]

Hilty, Gerold. 1979. Das Schicksal der lateinischen intervokalischen Verschlußlaute -p-, -t-, -k- im Mozarabischen. *Festschrift Kurt Baldinger zum 60. Geburtstag*, ed. by Manfred Höfler, Henric Vernay, Lothar Wolf, 145-60. Tübingen: Niemeyer.

Hjelmslev, Louis. 1963. *Sproget. En introduktion*. København: Berlingske forlag.

——. 1970. *Language. An Introduction*. Trans. by Francis J. Whitfield. Madison: The University of Wisconsin Press.

Hooper, Joan B[ybee]. 1976. *An introduction to natural generative phonology*. New York: Academic Press.

Hope, Thomas E. 1980. Inter-language influences. Posner and Green 241-87.

Huber, Joseph. 1933. *Altportugiesisches Elementarbuch*. Sammlung romanischer Elementar- und Handbücher 1-8. Heidelberg: C. Winter.

Hymes, Dell (ed.) 1974. *Studies in the history of linguistics: Traditions and paradigms*. Bloomington: Indiana University Press.

Jackson, Kenneth. 1953. *Language and history in early Britain, a chronological survey of the Brittonic languages*. Cambridge, MA: Harvard University Press.

Jungemann, Frederick H. 1956. *La teoría del sustrato y los dialectos hispano-romances y gascones*. Trans. by Emilio Alarcos Llorach. Biblioteca Románica Hispánica 1:7. Madrid: Gredos.

Karlsson, Keith E. 1981. *Syntax and affixation: The evolution of MENTE in Latin and Romance*. Suppl. 81 to *Zeitschrift für romanische Philologie*. Tübingen: May Niemeyer. [Title of original 1980 Berkeley dissertation: The adverbial suffix -MENTE; its rise in Late Latin and evolution in Romance.]

Křepinský, Maximilian, and Vicente García de Diego. 1923. *Inflexión de las vocales en español*. Suppl. 3 to *Revista de Filología Española*. Madrid: Centro de Estudios Históricas. [The Czech original dates from 1918.]

Kuhn, Alwin. 1935a. Der hocharagonesische Dialekt. *Revue de linguistique romane* 11:1-312. [Also, separately, 1936, Paris: Champion.]

——. 1935b. Studien zum Wortschatz von Hocharagon. *Zeitschrift für romanische Philologie* 55:561-634.

——. 1951. *Romanische Philologie, 1: Die romanischen Sprachen*. Wissenschaftliche Forschungsberichte, Geisteswissenschaftliche Reihe 8. Bern: A. Francke.

Lausberg, Heinrich. 1939. *Die Mundarten Südlukaniens*. Suppl. 90

to *Zeitschrift für romanische Philologie*.   Halle: M.
Niemeyer.
———. 1947. Zum romanischen Vokalismus. *Romanische Forschungen*
60:295-307.
———. 1948. Zur Stellung Italiens in der Romania. *Romanische
Forschungen* 61:320-3.
———. 1956. *Romanische Sprachwissenschaft*, vols. 1-3:1. Sammlung
Göschen 128/128a, 250, 1199. Berlin: W. de Gruyter. [The
revised 2nd ed. of Vol. I appeared in 1963; the revised 3rd ed.
in 1969.]
———. 1965. 1965. *Lingüística románica*. Biblioteca románica
hispánica 3:12. Madrid: Gredos.
Lehmann, Winfred P. 1962. *Historical linguistics: An introduction*. New York: Holt, Rinehart, and Winston. [Rev. ed., 1973.]
Leite de Vasconcelos, José. 1898. Notas filológicas, II. *Revue
hispanique* 5:417-29.
Leumann, Manu. 1917-18. Die Adjektiva auf *-ĪCIUS*. *Glotta* 9:129-68.
Levy, Anita Katz. 1965-67. Contrastive development[s] in Hispano-
Romance of borrowed Gallo-Romance suffixes. *Romance Philology*
18:399-429, 20:296-320.
Lloyd, Paul M. 1979. On the definition of "Vulgar Latin"; the
eternal return. *Neuphilologische Mitteilungen* 80:110-22.
Loth, J[oseph]. 1892. *Les mots latins dans les langues brittoniques:
gallois, armoricain, cornique; phonétique et commentaire, avec
une introduction sur la romanisation de l'Ile de Bretagne*.
Paris: E. Bouillon.
Luzensky, A. 1933. A Pannoniai latin feliratok nyelötona.
Egyetemes philologiai közlöny 57 (Budapest).
Malkiel, Yakov. 1946. The word-family of Old Spanish *recudir*.
Hispanic Review 14:104-59.
———. 1955. En torno a la etimología y evolución de *cansar, canso,
cansa(n)cio*. *Nueva Revista de Filología Hispánica* 9:225-76.
———. 1956. Studies in Spanish and Portuguese animal names.
Hispanic Review 24:115-43, 207-31.
———. 1963-64. The interlocking of narrow sound change, broad
phonological pattern, level of transmission, areal configuration, sound symbolism: Diachronic studies in the Hispano-Latin
consonant clusters *CL-, PL-, FL-*. *Archivum Linguisticum* 15:
144-73, 16:1-33.
———. 1966. Genetic analysis of word formation. *Current trends
in linguistics*, ed. by Thomas A. Sebeok, 3: Theoretical
foundations, 305-64. The Hague: Mouton.
———. 1967a. Each word has a history of its own. *Glossa* 1:137-49.
———. 1967b. Linguistics as a genetic science. *Language* 43:223-45.
———. 1968a. Identification of origin and justification of spread
in etymological analysis. *Romance Philology* 22:3.259-80.
———. 1968b. The inflectional paradigm as an occasional determinant of sound change. *Directions for historical linguistics:
A symposium*, ed. by Winfred P. Lehmann and Yakov Malkiel, 21-
64. Austin: University of Texas Press.
———. 1971. Derivational transparency as an occasional codeter-
minant of sound change: A new causal ingredient in the distribution of *-Ç-* and *-Z-* in ancient Hispano-Romance. *Romance
Philology* 25:1.1-52.
———. 1972. Comparative Romance linguistics. *Current trends in*

linguistics, ed. by Thomas A. Sebeok, 9: Linguistics in Western Europe, 835-925. The Hague: Mouton.

———. 1975[-77]. En torno al cultismo medieval. Los descendientes hispánicos de *DULCIS*. *Nueva Revista de Filología Hispánica* 24: 1.24-45 [Homenaje a Raimundo Lida].

———. 1976a. The etymology of Hispanic *tomar*. *Romance Philology* 30:1.115-17 ["Jean Frappier Memorial"].

———. 1976b. Critères pour l'étude de la fragmentation du latin. *Atti del XIV Congresso Internazionale di Linguistica e Filologia Romanza* (Napoli, 15-20 Aprile 1974; 3 vols., ed. Alberto Vàrvaro) 1:27-47. Napoli: Galtrano, Macchiaroli, and Amsterdam: John Benjamins B.V.

———. 1977. Il paradigma flessivo come fattore determinante di mutamenti fonetici. *Nuove tendenze della linguistica storica*, ed. by W. P. Lehmann and Y. Malkiel, 33-75. Trans. by Ruggero Stefanini. Bologna: il Mulino.

———. 1978. The classification of the Romance languages. *Romance Philology* 31:3.467-500.

———. 1979. The prelude to the Old French "frequentative action nouns" in *-ëiz*. *Festschrift Kurt Baldinger zum 60. Geburtstag*, 361-74. Tübingen: Max Niemeyer.

———. 1980. Was Schuchardt ever a neogrammarian? *Romance Philology* 34:1.93 ff.

———. 1982. Interplay of sounds and forms in the shaping of three Old Spanish medial consonant clusters. *Hispanic Review* 50:247-66.

Martinet, André. 1952. Celtic lenition and Western Romance consonants. *Language* 28:192-217.

———. 1954. *Économie des changements phonétiques*. Bibliotheca Romanica 1:10. Berne: A. Francke.

Meier, Harry. 1969. Review of Malkiel (1963-64). *Archiv für das Studium der neueren Sprachen* 24:385-90.

Menéndez Pidal, Ramón. 1904. Manual (elemental) de gramática histórica española. Madrid. [Also, revised 5th ed., 1925; revised 6th ed., 1941.]

———. 1908-11. Ed. *Cantar de Mío Cid*, Vol. 1: Gramática. Madrid.

———. 1926. Orígenes del español. *Estado lingüístico de la Península ibérica hasta el siglo XI*. Suppl. 1 to Revista de Filología Española. Madrid: Centro de Estudios Históricos. [Rev. 2nd ed., 1929; rev. 3rd ed., 1950.]

Meyer, Gustav. 1888. Die lateinischen Elemente im Albanesischen. G. Gröber, Grundriß 1:804-21. [Rev. 2nd ed. (1904-06): 1038-57.]

Meyer [-Lübke], Wilhelm. 1888. Die lateinische Sprache in den romanischen Ländern. In Gröber (1888:351-82).

———. 1890. *Grammatik der romanischen Sprachen, 1: Lautlehre*. Leipzig: Reisland.

———. 1901. *Einführung in das Studium der romanischen Sprachwissenschaft*. Sammlung romanischer Elementar- und Handbücher 1:1. Heidelberg: C. Winter. [Rev. 2nd ed., 1909; rev. 3rd ed., 1920.]

———. 1911[-20]. *Romanisches etymologisches Wörterbuch* [= *REW*]. Heidelberg: C. Winter.

———. 1913. *Historische Grammatik der französischen Sprache, 1: Laut- und Flexionslehre*. [Rev. 2nd and 3rd eds.] Sammlung

romanischer Elementar- und Handbücher 1:2. Heidelberg:
C. Winter.
———. 1924. La sonorización de las sordas intervocálicas latinas
en español. *Revista de Filología Española* 11:1-32.
———. 1925. *Das Katalanische. Seine Stellung zum Spanischen und
Provenzalischen.* Heidelberg: Carl Winter.
Mihăescu, H. 1966. Les éléments latins de la langue albanaise.
RESEE 4:5-33, 323-53.
Morpurgo-Davies, Anna. 1975. Language classification in the 19th
century. *Current trends in linguistics*, ed. by Thomas A.
Sebeok, 13:1.607-716. The Hague: Mouton.
Muljačić, Žarko. 1971. Dalmate. Pierre Bec, *Manuel pratique de
philologie romane* 2:393-416. Paris: A. & J. Picard.
Pedersen, Holger. 1924. *Sprogvidenskaben i det Nittende Aarhund-
rede; Metoder og Resultater.* København: Gyldendalske
Boghandel.
———. 1931. *The discovery of language. Linguistic science in
the nineteenth century.* Trans. by John Webster Spargo.
Bloomington: Indiana University Press.
Posner, Rebecca, and John N. Green (eds.) 1981. *Trends in Romance
linguistics and philology*, Vol. 1: Comparative and historical
Romance linguistics. The Hague: Mouton.
Pulgram, Ernst. 1953. Family tree, wave theory, and dialectology.
Orbis 2:67-72.
Puscariu, Sextil. 1937. *Études de linguistique roumaine, traduites
du roumain* ... Cluj-Bucureşti: Imprimerie nationala.
Rensch, Karl-Heinz. 1964. *Beiträge zur kenntnis nordkalabrischer
Mundarten.* Forschungen zur romanischen Philologie 14 (dir.
H. Lausberg).
———. 1973. *Nordkalabrischer Sprachatlas, an Hand der Parabel vom
verlorenen Sohn.* The Hague: Mouton.
Rönsch, Hermann. 1875. *Itala und Vulgata. Das Sprachidiom der
urchristlichen Itala und der katholischen Vulgata unter Berück-
sichtigung der römischen Volkssprache durch Beispiele erläutert.*
Rev. 2nd ed. Marburg: N. G. Elwert [original ed.: 1869].
Rohlfs, Gerhard. 1931. Beiträge zur Kenntnis der Pyrenäenmundar-
ten. *Revue de linguistique romane* 7:119-69.
———. 1935. *Le gascon; études de philologie pyrénéenne.* Suppl.
85 to *Zeitschrift für romanische Philologie.* Halle: M.
Niemeyer. [Rev. 2nd ed.: Tübingen: M. Niemeyer, & Pau:
Marrimpouey Jeune, 1970.]
———. 1937. Sprachliche Berührungen zwischen Sardinien und
Süditalien. *Donum natalicium K. Jaberg.* Zürich & Leipzig:
M. Niehans.
———. 1954. *Historische Grammatik der italienischen Sprache und
ihrer Mundarten.* Vol. 3 (Syntax und Wortbildung). Bern:
Francke.
Sanchis Guarner, Manuel. 1960. El mozárabe peninsular. *Enciclo-
pedia lingüística hispánica*, dir. M. Alvar et al., 1 (Antece-
dentes, onomástica) 291-342. Madrid: Consejo Superior de
Investigaciones Cientificas.
Sapir, Edward. 1921. *Language. An introduction to the study of
speech.* New York: Harcourt, Brace, & World. [The page
references here are to the 1949 paperback.]

Saroïhandy, J[ules]. 1898, 1901. Mission ... en Espagne. *Annuaire de l'École pratique des Hautes-Études* 85-94; 106-18.
———. 1913. Vestiges de phonetique ibérienne en territoire roman. *Revue internationale des études basques* 7:475-97.
Schaffer, Martha E. 1981. Portuguese *-idão*, Spanish *-(ed)umbre*, and their Romance cognates. *Romance Philology* 35:1.37-62 [Henry R. Lang Memorial/Frank M. Chambers Testimonial].
Schmidt, Johannes. 1872. *Die Verwandtschaftsverhältnisse der indogermanischen Sprachen*. Weimar: H. Böhlau.
Schuchardt, Hugo. 1866-68. *Der Vokalismus des Vulgärlateins*. 3 vols. Leipzig: B. G. Teubner.
Schultz-Gora, O[skar]. 1911. *Altprovenzalisches Elementarbuch*. Rev. 2nd ed. Sammlung romanischer Elementarbücher 1:3. Heidelberg: Carl Winter. [Rev. 4th ed.: 1924.]
Simon, J. 1969. Review of Malkiel (1963-64). *Zeitschrift für Phonetik, Sprachwissenschaft und Kommunikationsforschung* 22: 412-15.
Stefanini, Ruggero. 1968. Review of Karl-Heinz Rensch, *Beiträge zur Kenntnis nordkalabrischer Mundarten* (1964). *Romance Philology* 22:1.65-7.
Suchier, Hermann. 1904-06. *Die französische und provenzalische Sprache und ihre Mundarten, nach ihrer historischen Entwicklung dargestellt*. Gröber (1:712-840). [Reprinted in 1912.]
Tagliavini, Carlo. 1952. *Le origini delle lingue neolatine, introduzione alla filologia romanza*. Rev. 3rd ed. Bologna: Riccardo Pàtron.
Tagliavini, Karl [sic]. 1938. *Rumänische Konversations-Grammatik*. Heidelberg: Julius Groos.
Thomas, Antoine. 1904. Le suffixe *-aricius*. *Nouveaux essais de philologie française* 62-110. Paris: Librairie Émile Bouillon.
Tiktin, H. 1888. Die rumänische Sprache. In G. Gröber (1888: 438-60).
———. 1905. *Rumänisches Elementarbuch*. Sammlung romanischer Elementarbücher 1:6, dir. W. Meyer-Lübke. Heidelberg: C. Winter.
Tovar, Antonio. 1948. La sonorización y caída de las intervocálicas, y los estratos indoeuropeos en Hispania. *Boletín de la R. Academia Española* 28:265-80.
Tuchel, H. G. 1969. Review of Malkiel (1963-64). *Romanische Forschungen* 81:617-21.
Tuttle, Edwin H. 1914. The Roman vowel system. *Modern Philology* 11:347-53.
Vendryes, J[oseph]. 1921. *Le langage: Introduction linguistique à l'histoire. L'évolution de l'humanité* (dir. H. Berr). Paris: La Renaissance du Livre.
Vidos, B. E. 1959. *Manuale di linguistica romanza*. 1st ed. italiana, completamente aggiornata dall'autore. Trans. by G. Francescato. Firenze: Olschki.
Wagner, Max Leopold. 1936. *Restos de latinidad en el norte de África*. Biblioteca Geral da Universidade, Nos. 45-46 (Coimbra).
———. 1941. *Historische Lautlehre des Sardischen*. Suppl. 93 to *Zeitschrift für romanische Philologie*. Halle: Niemeyer.
———. 1951. *La lingua sarda: storia, spirito e forma*. Bern: A. Francke.

Walsh, Thomas J. 1980. Hazards in the reconstruction of Proto-
    Romance. *Romance Philology* 34:1.64-77.
Wartburg, Walther von. 1928- . *Französisches etymologisches
    Wörterbuch* [= *FEW*]. *Eine Darstellung des galloromanischen
    Sprachschatzes*. Bonn: F. Klopp.
———. 1936. Die Ausgliederung der romanischen Sprachen.
    Zeitschrift für romanische Philologie 56:1-48 [with seven maps].
———. 1950. *Die Ausgliederung der romanischen Sprachräume*.
    Bibliotheca Romanica 1:8. Bern: A. Francke.
Wiese, Berthold. 1904. *Altitalienisches Elementarbuch*. Sammlung
    romanischer Elementarbücher 1:4 (dir. W. Meyer-Lübke).
    Heidelberg: C. Winter.
Williams, Edwin B. 1963. *From Latin to Portuguese. Historical
    phonology and morphology of the Portuguese language*. Rev. 2nd.
    ed. Philadelphia: University of Pennsylvania Press. [Reprinted
    in 1968.]
Wölfflin, E.   1888. Die Adjektiva auf *-icius*. *Archiv für latein-
    ische Lexikographie und Grammatik* 5:415-37.
Zauner, Adolf. 1900. *Romanische Sprachwissenschaft*. Leipzig:
    G. J. Göschen. [Also revised 2nd ed. in 2 vols., 1905.]
———. 1908. *Altspanisches Elementarbuch*. Sammlung romanischer
    Elementar- und Handbücher (dir. W. Meyer-Lübke). Heidelberg:
    C. Winter. [Also revised 2nd ed., 1921.]

SIGLA

CIL	*Corpus Inscriptionum Latinarum*, ed. by the Berlin Academy
DÉLL$_4$	*Dictionnaire étymologique de la langue latine*, 4th ed., by A. Ernout and A. Meillet
FEW	*Französisches etymologisches Wörterbuch*, by W. von Wartburg
REW$_3$	*Romanisches etymologisches Wörterbuch*, 3rd. ed., by W. Meyer-Lübke

SYMBOLS

*foyo	form reconstructed and assumed to have existed
*udre	form reconstructed, but not assumed to have existed

SOCIOCULTURAL ASPECTS OF LANGUAGE CHANGE

Els Oksaar

I

The development of linguistics during the last two
decades has been marked by an increasing emphasis on
socio-, psycho-, pragma-, and paedolinguistics. Common
to all these areas is their contribution to a renaissance
of Empiricism, which is rooted in dissatisfaction with
the results of linguistic theories based on an idealized
speaker/listener in a homogeneous society, rather than on
the language of real speaker/listeners in a real, i.e.
heterogeneous society. This renewed emphasis on Empiricism was embodied in two major approaches to sociolinguistic research in the sixties: in the correlational
approach of Labov and Bernstein, and in the interactional
approach of Hymes and Gumperz. The significance of these
two approaches will not be discussed here, but it is important to note that both approaches have focused attention on linguistic varieties and the importance of research into language change in its social context.
The study of language change in its social context is
by no means new. As early as 1867, Whitney (1867:18) remarked that language change is to be traced to the reciprocal influence of the individual speaker and the language
community. The social aspect of language change has been
mentioned by Bréal, Meillet, and de Saussure, who emphasized the connection between the change of signs and the
change in social systems. Hermann Paul, Otto Jespersen,
Wilhelm Havers, and Hugo Moser delineated the conditions
and motives that DETERMINE language change. Havers (1931:
144 ff.) lists several: the desire for lucidity, for
emotional release, for conservation of strength, for aesthetic expression; the tendency towards order; and social
motives, e.g. politeness and consideration. Paul (1909:
34) spoke of language change as a result of the individual's spontaneous activity and the constant influence on
him of other individuals. He did not, however, treat the
relationship between the individual and his complete social environment, in which not only linguistic behavior

257

patterns, but also socioculturally determined behavior
patterns serve as norms.

Although the principle of the Prague School of structuralism—that language change must be viewed as a part
of synchronic linguistics—is well-known, no consequences
for research into the dynamic synchrony of various sec-
tors of Modern German have yet been drawn. In order to
understand the conditions and mechanisms of language
change, we have to know how language is USED. In my opinion, linguists have not sufficiently considered the possibility that the same conditions and motives that lead
to the "Umgestaltung der Sprache," as Havers (1931:144
ff.) puts it, can also direct language use. Because language use ranks above language change, the conditions of
language use must be examined first. One can hypothesize
that the conditions and motives controlling language use
also cause language shift.

For example, in the field of lexis the phenomenon of
up- and downgrading in the occupational and professional
fields can be traced throughout the history of various
languages. In contemporary German, *Dienstmädchen* has been
replaced by *Hausgehilfin* and *Hausangestellte*; in American
English *beautician* is often used instead of *hairdresser*,
and *landscape architect* replaced *gardener*, to give only
a few examples. This phenomenon can be correctly interpreted only by means of the social frames to which the
designations belong. Up- and downgrading depend largely
on connotations: *Hausangestellte* evokes socially more
favorable connotations than *Dienstmädchen*; cf. *Raumpfle-
gerin/Putzfrau* (Oksaar 1976). The strongest conditioning
factor determining the use of the new words, and the downgrading in the social motivation of the older words, is
social prestige. It must be emphasized, however, that
not all groups in society use these new words with the
same attitudinal motivation. In order to treat this aspect of language change more thoroughly, Hermann Paul's
primarily psychological theses must be combined with so-
ciological theses. The examination of human behavior
patterns, including language behavior, may be approached
from several perspectives: cultural, economic, and
social.

The aim of this paper is the analysis of several sociocultural phenomena that could influence language change
in the dynamic synchrony of the present time. I will
present examples of the interaction between social and
linguistic variation.

II

The starting point of any such analysis is the individual as a member of various social networks. His linguistic repertoire can be assigned to one or several languages, dialects, and sociolects. The crucial point is
that an individual can have mastered heterogeneous expression and content structures, the use of which is

dependent upon various sociocultural conditions. He not
only selects but also interprets the elements of communication in various ways, depending on his various roles
in society, whether he is using language as a teacher, a
father, a politician, an employer, and so on. The existence of such structures can be experimentally proved,
for example through tests where informants are asked to
determine who says a sentence to whom (Oksaar 1977b).

The ability of the subjects to identify single sentences as belonging to communicative acts in which some
variants even "break" the rules of normative grammar leads
to the following considerations: One must assume the
existence of a variable communicative competence of language users not only at the interlanguage level of bi-
and multilingual persons but also at an intralanguage
level. Although certain sequences in tests can be classi-
fied as adult speech by children or native speakers'
speech by foreigners, for example, this does not mean that
adults always speak in that manner to children or native
speakers to foreigners.

This fact clearly implies that the methods and certain
results of interlanguage language contact research ought
to be used as a realistic basis for research into intralanguage change, because the various subcodes, styles, and
variants that an individual masters are in contact with
each other. The results of such contacts can be identified as various types of alternations and interferences,
e.g. *Haben Sie Ihr Ticket schon gescheckt*? There are not
only linguistic but also situational interferences. Both
arise in performance, in direct or indirect interaction;
however, they can also become part of the language user's
competence, not only in his idiolect, but also in sociolects and at higher levels.

SITUATIONAL INTERFERENCES are deviations from the
pragmatic norms of the situation in which the languages
or codes are used. They are usually dependent upon sociocultural patterns; they can occur, for example, when
the rules governing social relations are not followed.
An example of a situational interference is when Swedish-
Germans use the German *du* as they would use the Swedish
du in communicative acts in which only the use of *Sie* is
allowed in German. The conventions of address in the
Federal Republic of Germany are changed by situational
interferences also, for example in communication between
students.

I have mentioned that interferences arise in interactions. Therefore, it is important to define the concept of INTERACTIONAL COMPETENCE. I understand interactional competence to be a person's ability to complete
and interpret verbal and non-verbal behavior in an interaction, according to the sociocultural and psychological
rules of his group. (The concept of interactional competence is more differentiated than Hymes' (1967) "Communicative competence.") Interactional competence is
realized through communicative acts. A communicative act

is the entire frame of action in which a bit of language
behavior takes place. The primary elements of a communicative act are: (1) partner/audience, (2) verbal elements, (3) paralinguistic elements, (4) kinesic elements,
and (5) all affective behavior characteristics. This concept of interaction/competence takes into consideration
both the speaker and the listener, whereas the speech act
as defined by Searle (1969) does not consider the listener.

The strategy of CODE SWITCHING, that is, the alternative use of at least two codes or subcodes with or without
interferences, becomes visible in the communicative act.
The communicative act forms one of the platforms for the
origin and spread of variations.

The SOCIAL DIMENSION OF LINGUISTIC VARIATION can best
be approached from the perspective that allows answers to
the following questions: Who chooses which expression to
whom, when, in which situation and why? (see Laswell
1948). How does the hearer react? His reaction is important for the spreading of the changed elements. Variables like age, sex, status, and role do not alone determine the choice of expression, but also the relation
of the speaker to the listener: stranger, acquaintance,
friend, relative, superior, or subordinate. The differences between native and foreign speakers' language, or
men's and women's language become clearer in this dimension, as well as the differences between various interactional models, e.g. in addressing people with "du" or
"Sie" in German, or with a title. Here also is the source
for alternation and interference as manifestations of
variable competence. By no means do they originate only
through the expressive and communicative functions of language; rather, they are caused by the fact that language
serves as an identity factor for the speaker and an identification instrument for the listener. Expressions characteristic of the language behavior of a certain group
can be used by persons outside of the group in order to
be identified as members of that group. However, both of
the language functions previously not given so much attention, i.e. the identity and identification functions,
could also lead to not just one, but to parallel alternatives. This occurs above all when the alternative and
the previously common form of expression are no longer
fully acceptable for socio-psychological reasons. For
example, if someone is addressed by "du" when he expects
"Sie," it can happen that he confronts this situational
interference with a model new or infrequent for that
situation:

Student A to student B (whom he doesn't know) in a seminar:
Was du da gerade gesagt hast ...

Student B to student A, using a passive construction instead
of the usual Sie: *Was hier soeben behauptet wurde* ...

Here we can perceive the connection to the LINGUISTIC DIMENSION OF SOCIAL VARIATION. One expression can have different specific collective and social connotations for different groups of language users, whereby in turn the social variables play a role, e.g. age and sex differences. Speaker and listener can have different interpretations at this level, leading to possible changes in meaning. An interpretation is made on the basis of one's knowledge, but at the same time from a certain point of interest. Children's utterances illustrate this point most clearly. A seven-year-old boy from Hamburg was asked what the following saying meant: *Müßiggang ist aller Laster Anfang.* His answer: *Das ist der erste Gang. Den legt der Laster ein und fängt an zu fahren* (see Oksaar 1980).

But even with adults, it is their complex experimental background, and the so-called situation consciousness, which according to Bühler also includes knowledge of the speaker's intention, that make possible the interpretation of an utterance (see Havers 1931:65). Differences can lead to a change of behavior, also in language. The confusion of both partners can be easily understood when the lady in Germany asks the train conductor: *Do I have to pay for the children?* Answer: *Not under six.* Lady: *Oh, wonderful. There are only three.*

III

The above comments are also intended to emphasize the role of the receiver of an utterance in a transmitting of changes. This role has been given little consideration in psycho- and sociolinguistic literature, in comparison to the sender's role, although as early as 1909 Hermann Paul (1909:VI) wrote in his criticism of Wundt that a complete understanding of language development could not be reached without consideration of the listener's role. Wegener (1885:182) emphasized the listener's role by claiming that the issue of language comprehension belongs in the foreground of linguistic inquiry. The listener's grammar differs from that of the speaker, as the Petersburg Linguistic School, as well as the Prague School, have told us. HOMONYMY exists only in the listener's grammar, leading to the above-mentioned misunderstandings.

The listener's deviation in interpretation can also be explained by the fact that not everything is verbalized in the communicative act. The creativity of natural language depends upon its ability to not express everything, in order to avoid superfluous elements, according to Jakobson (1974:74). This level is also important for language change research. The mother who sees her son putting on his old jeans and says, *Today is Sunday,* has not verbally expressed what can be interpreted by the hearer as a request to change his behavior. However, the utterance, used on other days, can be idiomized quickly within the family to a prohibition—'you shouldn't do that.'

The expression *auf den Steinen sitzen*, which in Thomas
Mann's *Buddenbrooks* acquired the meaning 'vereinsamt sein
und sich langweilen', shows how this idiomization process
can occur. To judge by the many editions of the novel,
one might have expected this saying to become commonly
used, as was the case with *es ist die höchste Eisenbahn*.
This, however, did not happen. ·

Such observations show that not all innovations and
changes become part of the standard language, and that
different levels in the process of language change are to
be expected. The conditions leading to these levels have
to be examined because, up to the present, almost all
studies of language shift have started with its consequences and have not taken into account regional and social differences in the acceptance and spread of language
innovations. The process of language change is to be
seen in connection with the change in an individual's
language habits. The latter is, however, not a common
object of study, because it is not retrievable in detail
for the past and is considered either too difficult or
as being only occasional in the present.

One should not speak of occasionality or marginality
if the function of a phenomenon has not yet been studied.
Such metalinguistic comments may not serve as an alibi
for excluding them from linguistic observation. Weinreich
et al. are correct in stating: "Not all variability and
heterogeneity in language structure involves change; but
all change involves variability and heterogeneity" (1968:
188). Variations in the synchrony can become norms when
seen diachronically. Research into language change must
be motivated into theoretical consideration of the socio-
psychological aspects of the communication process.

Such variables as the communicative channel, motivation, linguistic context, and relation to non-linguistic
reality, e.g. if and when social change can lead to linguistic change, must be considered in this area of research. In addition, several factors can simultaneously
affect the process. If a deviation is spread by the mass
media, for example in advertisements with the motive of
attracting attention to the advertisement, it can reach
several groups of readers and act as a language model.
The following examples illustrate how several factors
can work hand-in-hand (see Oksaar 1976:23).

Social changes in the Federal Republic of Germany,
such as shorter work weeks and longer vacations, have led
to a number of linguistic innovations, among others in
occupational names: *Freizeitplaner*, *Freizeitgestalter*,
Freizeitberater, *Freizeithelfer* and *Freizeitpädagoge*.
One can notice linguistic consequences of this development in two areas: on the one hand, the rapid increase
in the number of compounds as names for the new concepts,
and on the other hand, the change in meaning of such
words as *Freizeit*, *Arbeitswoche*, *Wochenende*, etc. Another
consequence is to be found in certain types of interaction
rituals, for example of the category "leave-taking."

Instead of *einen schönen Sonntag*, which one traditionally
said on the last workday of the week, Saturday, one now
wishes *ein schönes Wochenende*, because the last workday
is usually Friday. These examples show such changes in
content spheres to be important for research into dynamic synchrony and the process of language change.
Hermann Paul (1909:104) sees these changes as a direct
consequence of the change of cultural relations and therefore not a change in meaning. But we notice that they
can lead to the building of content variants, polysemy,
and a change in labels. They are evidence of changes in
the language behavior of speakers, changes which are determined by the adaptation of language to the sociocultural frame.

Formations in present-day German such as *Parkstudent*,
Tagesmutter or *Nur-Hausfrau* are some of the lexical innovations that mirror social changes or attitudes and simultaneously cause innerlanguage changes of meaning. The
differences between *Parkstudent* 'a student that cannot
study the subject he wants because of numerus clausus
and is "parked" in another subject waiting for his
chance', *Tagesmutter* 'a woman who takes care of a child
during the day, while the mother is working'. The differences between *Student*, *Mutter*, and *Kind* are not the
same as the differences between *Werkstudent* or *Korp-
student*. The label *Nur-Hausfrau* makes *Hausfrau* an abstraction and class label; furthermore, at least one
other label is implied, i.e. **Werkhausfrau* 'a woman who
works in and outside of the home'. *Tagesmutter* is directly related to the functional change in structure of
the working world caused by working women. The label
Tagesmutter is the only formation with *Mutter* belonging
to the set of occupational labels.

This type of research, at the micro-level, makes it
possible for us to follow the development and effects of
conflicts of content in present-day language. The above-
mentioned example categories, meaning and labelling, can
be easily expanded. Less attention has been paid to the
phenomena of change in language behavior arising from
certain differences between partners in conversation and
from their adaptability. Such a process can occur when
the partner or partners do not have full command of the
standard code of a speech community, for example. This
can lead to new subcodes. Examples of such subcodes, in
different languages known as simplified speech or simplified register, are child language and foreigners' language (Oksaar 1977a:124-32; 1977b:108-13). They are
marked by a simplified syntax and deviations from the
norms of standard grammar. However, simplified speech
is found not only in the language learning process of
children and foreign speakers. Adult, chiefly female,
speech to small children and the native speakers' subcode
with foreigners are also two independent variants belonging to this category. Because they are less well
known, but like other subcodes can influence the process

of language change by their variants, and because they
illustrate well the changes in language behavior of the
language users, we shall discuss them here. One must remember that these differences between speech partners and
their reciprocal adaptability decisively influence the
increase and differentiation of subcodes within a language
community and within the linguistic competence of its individual members, as Jakobson (1974:183) emphasizes.

The subcode of adults to small children is known as
baby talk; in German, where it is known as *Ammensprache*,
systematic studies of it have not been undertaken, as is
also the case with the subcode to foreign speakers. My
data are based on observations of five mothers and three
other caretakers in our longitudinal studies of child language in Hamburg. These data confirm sporadic observations made since the beginning of the century. The code
is marked by typical intonational and paralinguistic patterns. Furthermore, speakers use phonological and grammatical modifications: They avoid difficult consonant
combinations and use mainly bisyllabic words and a simple
syntax: *Hier Buch!* Not only is the duplication of syllables conspicuous, e.g. *wauwau*, but also of words. For
example, a mother points out a bird in a puddle and says
to her two-year old: *Da Vogel, macht schwimme, schwimme.*
The use of the third person singular in direct speech is
common when an adult refers to himself or the child:
Mutti kommt gleich or *Wie groß ist das Kind?* or *Wo ist
Hansi?*

The associative *we* is also to be found in various
situations: *Wir waschen uns nun die Händchen*, which can
have different meanings: 'Wir waschen Deine Händchen'
or 'Du wäschst Dir nun die Händchen'. In communicative
acts in this subcode, diminutives are also more frequently
used than in standard speech, e.g. *mein kleines Mäuschen*,
or in a Southern German dialect the suffix *-i*: *Buchi,
Hausi, Betti*. According to Sieberer (1950:87) not only
verb diminutives such as *trinki* and *schreibi* are common
in this subcode in Austria, but also forms like *waserl
denn?* Kruisinga (1942:9) points out that the hypocoristic
forms *-y* and *-i* are limited almost exclusively to speech
with small children. However, they can cross over into
adult speech; Von der Gabelentz (1901:227) claims that
this type of language behavior can constantly influence
adult speech. This would explain "das Überhandnehmen der
Diminutiva" in the Slavic languages and in some German
dialects, e.g. in East Prussian.

Although this subcode has a large range of idiolectal
variation and not all of its linguistic elements are used
by all adults who speak to small children, the speech
elements mentioned above have been shown to exist—even
in the speech of those adults who deny their usage. This
subcode illustrates variable interactional competence:
The speaker consciously or unconsciously adapts his speech
to what he thinks the level and the subcode of the child
are. One must not confuse this variant with the code of

the small child, as is often done. The reciprocal influence of these codes on each other leads in many languages
to pet or unique names: *Bob* or *Peppo* for Guiseppe, *Nenne*
for Sven. Systematic studies, including contrastive ones,
are very important here, because the social aspect adult#
child in the formation of the adult variant illustrates
from a different perspective the forces determining change
mentioned at the beginning of this paper: economy and
vividness for emotional reasons. It is a fact that variants of this subcode also appear in adult interactions.
As early as 1901, Von der Gabelentz (1901:278) pointed
out that "Liebende in ihrem Gekose in die Kindersprache
verfallen." One wonders if that is correct; rather it
seems to be a variant spoken both by children and adults—
an "average" of their subcodes. Von der Gabelentz (1901:
278) is certainly correct in saying that this is a type
of language-mixing. However, he attributes this to the
irrational factors that influence the history of language.
We know from present-day observations that the factors
influencing language-mixing can be highly rational
(Oksaar 1979), as we are dealing with basic factors of
human language activity, with accommodation and assimilation of behavior patterns, with the so-called "Partnerzwang." The analysis of the phenomenon "Partnerzwang" in
various communicative acts is an important task for socio-
and psycholinguistics.

     With these examples we have not considered more close-
ly the fact that a message is also transmitted by paralinguistic and kinesic means. Research into language
change has hardly taken this into account, although
Havers (1931:20 ff.) illustrated these parameters with
examples. Speech melody, accent, rhythm, tempo, and
pauses, which he calls indirect language instruments, and
the external situation, posture, gestures, and facial expressions of the speaker as non-linguistic forms of expression can be determining factors in syntactic changes.
However, one wonders if the well-known explanations of
the origin of the relative clause, mentioned by Havers
(1931:23) could not be viewed differently. It has been
claimed that the sentence *Ich sehe das:er kommt* becomes
Ich sehe, daß er kommt by shifting the pause. This is a
view of the situation from the speaker's perspective.
One could look at the matter from the listener's perspective. Why should a pause be moved to a spot in the sentence where previously there was none? One could instead
argue that in the sentence *Ich sehe, daß er kommt* a pause
has been eliminated, therefore assuming two pauses in the
first place. *Ich sehe—das* (perhaps appearing with a
kineme such as pointing)—*er kommt*. The implied content
of the demonstrative *das* melts together in the listener's
reception without a pause.

     The analysis of living language can help us to find
hypotheses for the dynamics of the past. What can be
gained by an investigation of the pre-stages of language
change in the form of social and linguistic variation?

In the first place, new possibilities for understanding
the origin and spread of variants are opened. In the
second place, one can find connections that remain hidden
when language change is seen as an end condition and not
as a process. Further investigations into the dimensions
of social and linguistic variation will be necessary for
a complete understanding of the dynamics of language
change.

REFERENCES

Ferguson, C. A. 1964. Baby talk in six languages. *American
    Anthropologist* 66:103-14.
Havers, W. 1931. *Handbuch der erklärenden Syntax*. Heidelberg:
    C. Winter.
Hymes, D. 1967. Models of the interaction of language and social
    setting. *Journal of Social Issues* 23:8-28.
Jakobson, R. 1974. *Aufsätze zur Linguistik und Poetik*, ed. by
    W. Raible
Kruisinga, E. 1942. *Diminutieve en affektieve suffixen in de
    Germaanse talen*. Amsterdam: Noord-hollandsche uitgevers
    maatschappij.
Lasswell, H. D. 1948. The structure and function of communication
    in society. *The communication of ideas*, ed. by L. Bryson, 37-
    52. New York: Cooper Square Publishers, Inc.
Moser, H. 1955. *Deutsche Sprachgeschichte*. 2nd ed. Stuttgart:
    C. E. Schwab.
Oksaar, E. 1965. *Mittelhochdeutsch: Texte, Kommentare, Sprach-
    kunde, Wörterbuch*. Stockholm: Almqvist & Wiksell.
———. 1976. *Berufszeichnungen im heutigen Deutsch. Sozioseman-
    tische Untersuchungen. Mit deutschen und schwedischen exper-
    imentellen Kontrastierungen*. Düsseldorf: Pädagogischer
    Verlag Schwann.
———. 1977a. *Spracherwerb im Vorschulalter. Einführung in die
    Pädolinguistik*. Stuttgart: Kohlhammer.
———. 1977b. Zum Prozess des Sprachwandels: Dimensionen sozialer
    und linguistischer Variation. *Sprachwandel und Sprachge-
    schichtsschreibung im Deutschen*. (Sprache der Gegenwart 41:
    98-117) Düsseldorf.
———. 1979. Models of competence in bilingual interaction. *Socio-
    linguistic studies in language contact*, ed. by. W. F. Mackey and
    J. Ornstein, 99-113. The Hague.
———. 1980. The multilingual language acquisition project. *Inter-
    national Review of Applied Psychology* 29:268-9.
Paul, H. *Prinzipien der Sprachgeschichte*. 4th ed. Halle:
    Niemeyer.
Searle, John R. 1969. *Speech acts*. Cambridge: University Press.
Sieberer, A. 1950. Das Wesen des Diminutivs. *Die Sprache* 2:85-
    121.
Von der Gabelentz, G. 1901. *Die Sprachwissenschaft*. Leipzig:
    C. H. Tauchnitz.
Wegener, Ph. 1885. *Untersuchungen über die Grundfragen des
    Sprachlebens*. Halle: Niemeyer.

Weinreich, U.; W. Labov; M. I. Herzog. 1968. Empirical foundations
for a theory of language change. *Directions for historical
linguistics: A symposium*, ed. by W. P. Lehmann and Y. Malkiel,
95-188. Austin: University of Texas Press.
Whitney, W. D. 1867. *Language and the study of language.* New
York: G. Scribner and Company.

INDEX